DOWN

DESIGNING FOR THE ENDGAME

George Brugmans

IABR
nai010 publishers

O EARTH

DOWN

DESIGNING FOR THE ENDGAME

George Brugmans

in view of the 9th edition of
the International Architecture
Biennale Rotterdam
September 2020 – August 2021

TO EARTH

You're on Earth.
There's no cure for that.

Samuel Beckett
Endgame

CONTENTS

INTRODUCTION 006

CURATOR STATEMENT 012

HOW CAN WE LAND? 018

ENERGY

The IABR and the Energy Transition 020

IABR—Atelier Rotterdam III 029

IABR—Atelier East Flanders Core Region 039

DOWN TO EARTH:
WHOSE ENERGY IS IT, ANYWAY? / RECLAIMING THE COMMONS 049

WATER

The IABR and Water 140

IABR—Atelier Drought in the Delta 159

DOWN TO EARTH:
DROUGHT IN THE DELTA 167

DOWN TO EARTH:
METEOPOLIS 239

DOWN TO EARTH:
WATERSCHOOL M4H+ 245

IABR—Atelier Dordrecht 275

DOWN TO EARTH:
THE HIGH GROUND 299

WHERE CAN WE LAND? 330
Spaceship Earth — George Brugmans
1: The Embarkment 332
2: World Game Over 350
The System's Ceiling — Dirk Sijmons 360
Designing in Times of Climate Crisis — Rotterdam Academy of Architecture and Urban Design 380
Spaceship Earth — George Brugmans
3: Turbulence 392
Epilogue 425

APPENDIX 432
Biographies 434
Credits IABR—DOWN TO EARTH 436
Mission Statement IABR 437
Overview QR codes 438
Colophon 439

INTRODUCTION

All things considered, 2030 is further away now than in 2015.

The fiasco of COP27, the climate summit where fossil lobbyists were given free rein, held in a country, Egypt, where critics are silenced, ended 2022, a year that started with the Russian invasion of Ukraine and was dominated by energy panic and inflation anxiety. To boot, COP28 will be chaired by the CEO of Abu Dhabi National Oil, which has announced that it intends to increase its production from 4 to 5 million barrels of crude oil per day. Now, in January 2023, we are halfway between 2015 and 2030, when the climate goals agreed upon by the global community are supposed to be achieved, but there is not much left of the moderate optimism unleashed by the Paris climate accords. It feels like the genie set free in Paris is back in its bottle.

Against this sobering backdrop, I am writing an introduction to a book that is the concluding project of DOWN TO EARTH, the second of a pair of biennales conceived in 2016 in the spirit of that very Paris climate agreement. In 2018, THE MISSING LINK, provoked by the maddening observation that excellent plans and sustainable implementation just would not come together, pinned down the reasons why things continue to go wrong. In 2020, DOWN TO EARTH was to focus on water issues and the energy transition to show that design and imagination could yet help deliver tangible solutions.

PANDEMIC

It didn't quite work out. In the spring of 2020, six months before DOWN TO EARTH was to open, it became clear that the new Covid-19 virus was going to throw a spanner in the works. There was little chance that the 9th edition of the International Architecture Biennale Rotterdam would be able to open as planned. An international crowd of as many people as possible wanting to get through the same door at the same time; a festive affair with lots of human traffic and packed halls? All of a sudden it was unconceivable. Cancel or come up with an alternative? It was an easy choice to make. The pandemic constituted an ideal opportunity to radically test a number of issues that had been on my mind for a long time. How to responsibly organize an international rush hour in times of climate crisis? Slow it down, deepen and unfold it, break it up, turn it on its head and inside out: it's hard to experiment with and recalibrate a clunky and complex object like a biennale. But now we could, and so we had to. *To think and act anti-typically*, that's what Covid demanded. DOWN TO EARTH could become an *anti-biennale*.

FLYING IN FOG

When the world shuts down and you cannot bring in things from afar anymore, you're left empty-handed unless you produce enough yourself or can get products nearby – it's the logistical law that was drilled into us over the past few years. Well, unlike 'regular' biennales, the IABR always has something on hand – it's a research biennale, after all. Since 2008, it has

been managing research by design projects in the IABR–Ateliers, set up together with domestic and foreign governments, and always with the explicit aim to achieve concrete results. When the pandemic broke out, the IABR had four active Ateliers up and running – in the Belgian province of East Flanders, in the cities of Rotterdam and Dordrecht, and Atelier Drought in the Delta – whose results were already scheduled to be presented during DOWN TO EARTH. This was also true of the Waterschool, a research project by our neighbors Studio Makkink & Bey, which the IABR had been supporting since 2017.
By slightly modifying their approach, these research projects were able to proceed, but the pandemic now allowed us to emphatically put the outcomes center stage. DOWN TO EARTH was conceived, not as a typical biennale – an accumulation of people, project presentations, and international submissions, a single spectacle compressed in time and space – but as a series of smaller presentations that would unfold over time, built around specific research results. And because the funding of the Ateliers was realized outside the regular cultural subsidy schemes and conditions, the success of such an approach did not depend on box office revenues. Any time an exhibition was allowed to open, free access could be given to whoever turned up.
This allowed us to wing it. We were still flying in fog, of course, because in the spring of 2020 no one knew what the following months, let alone years, would bring. No one. But in the end, this open approach led to seven exhibitions, organized from September 2020 to September 2021, in Rotterdam and Dordrecht. Four of these centered on the outcomes of IABR–Ateliers: DROUGHT IN THE DELTA, WHOSE ENERGY IS IT, ANYWAY?, RECLAIMING THE COMMONS and THE HIGH GROUND. The other three did not originate from the IABR, but came from nearby: in addition to WATERSCHOOL M4H+, they were METEOPOLIS and NOW!, partner exhibitions by Rotterdams Weerwoord and the Rotterdam Academy of Architecture, respectively. Unfortunately, the latter two were confronted with severe lockdown measures and could only be visited virtually.

STRUCTURE

The structure of this book is relatively straightforward. The Curator Statement is followed by *How Can We Land?*, made up of two parts, Energy and Water, each of which consists of three components: first, a brief retrospective of the way the IABR, as a research biennale, has dealt with the energy transition and water issues over the years; next, an account of the research in the pertinent Ateliers; and finally, a 'catalog-in-retrospect,' a representation in words and images of the exhibitions organized under the banner of DOWN TO EARTH. This first section includes QR codes that link to web videos and publications that provide further insight into the research by design and its results.
In the second section, *Where Can We Land?*, follows reflection – not on the biennale itself, but on how we are doing and what we are to do in times of climate crisis.

ENDGAME

Yet, this book moves backward and forward, is set in different times, and adopts a variety of styles. It has no continuous narrative, and little chronology. The repetitions, like the extensive footnotes, are as inevitable as,

I expect, functional. Some texts may be more topical than others. The friction between periods and their moods that swung by one after the other in rapid succession is palpable. For example, the Curator Statement I wrote in the summer of 2020 reads dated two and a half years later. I would write a more angry and dejected statement today. Whereas 1.5 degrees Celsius of warming seemed achievable at the time, we now know that we had better count on 2.5 degrees or more, a catastrophic difference in terms of consequences.

What keeps the book together is that which held the biennale itself together: the need to persistently start directly from the observation that the climate crisis is a given and that we are smack dab in the middle of it. It follows that an architecture biennale that asks how and where we can land owes it to its standing to come up with practicable clues for designing for the endgame.

HOW CAN WE LAND?

There's one important insight we can derive from the Club of Rome report that is now as topical as it was in 1972: deploy systems thinking. Still, if everything is connected with everything else, the question is where and how to start. Archimedes had an answer: 'Give me a firm place to stand and a lever and I can move the Earth.' This is why in recent years, we have unreservedly used the free space of the IABR as a place to stand, and water management and the energy transition as the key levers.

Water is an excellent lever for realizing research by design projects at any scale. Worldwide, more than 80 percent of all climate-induced emergencies and disasters are water related. Everywhere and increasingly often floods and droughts, pollution, drinking water shortages, and water conflicts in conjunction with population growth, increasing migration, rapid urbanization, and a growing demand for food and energy lead to problems and, more and more frequently, disasters. The risks have become too great, and that very fact provides excellent opportunities for a *water-as-leverage* approach.

Against the backdrop of the climate crisis, achieving the energy transition was always an urgent goal in itself. Then the war in Ukraine painfully confronted us with the political impact of our over-reliance on fossil fuels. The transition is now a geopolitical issue as well, energy panic can affect both individuals and countries. Looking for solutions, it is therefore even more important that we realize that the energy transition can be used as a tool to achieve sustainability and livability in a wider sense. If we focus on the socio-civic benefits that come with linking the energy transition and other transitions, and judge them by the other Sustainable Development Goals, we see that the energy transition can be a powerful lever.

SUSTAINABLE DEVELOPMENT GOALS

Although just about every country put its signature to the United Nations' Sustainable Development Goals, I have never believed that these goals can succeed in helping the world escape destruction. But I do believe that they can help us not escape that world. What's more, that's precisely why they are important: far from perfect – the result of political compromise – the SDGs nevertheless keep us on our toes and, I discovered, allow a targeted conversation globally about achieving climate goals locally. Gradually, helping to realize the SDGs became the IABR's main objective, because in

practice they constitute a lever a small Dutch cultural research institute can use to help make a difference anywhere in the world.
However, the question remains: How? We therefore investigated how the 17 core values propagated by the SDGs could be used concretely in city-making processes. And not merely as goals, that would be too non-committal, but as starting points for (monitoring) behavior, approaches, research, and action. This became an additional layer of research, particularly in the Ateliers in Dordrecht (Water Safety as a Lever for Sustainable Urban Development) and Rotterdam (Energy Transition as a Lever for Socially Inclusive City Making).

WHERE CAN WE LAND?
The final section of this book, *Where Can We Land?*, contains two essays and an account of a conversation with design students.
Together with his own students and students of the Royal Academy of Art The Hague, head of the Master's program in Urban Design at the Rotterdam Academy of Architecture and Urban Design and curator team member Thijs van Spaandonk created the exhibition NOW! DESIGNING IN TIMES OF CLIMATE CRISIS. Afterwards, he discussed its premise and conclusions with colleagues and students; a report is included in this book.

I asked former IABR curator Dirk Sijmons to reflect on an issue I have often discussed with both him and other curators and designers: Just what *can* we and what *may* we ask of designers? Are our expectations of what design can do actually realistic? And vice versa, how can designers join in new developments and growing activism? In fact, Sijmons writes, the question is what exactly design's system's ceiling is, and whether and how designers can break through it, now that it comes down to it.

My essay Spaceship Earth was inspired by Richard Buckminster Fuller's concept of Spaceship Earth and Bruno Latour's question, *Where can we land?* As a cultural historian, I wanted to write down again how I think we ended up in the Anthropocene, and why we now find ourselves at the controls of Spaceship Earth without an operation manual. This very much in relation to what I have always committed to as president of the IABR: to using the biennale, not as an end in itself, but as a means – to use the free creative space it can generate to try to trigger necessary, real change. In the end, more than two-thirds of the IABR's turnaround and effort was involved in results-oriented research by design to find answers to the question of how and where we can land.
This, incidentally, was never self-evident. The free space had to be fiercely defended against the neoliberal storm that in recent decades has suppressed genuinely free and creative thinking and has left behind a barren landscape in which the market rules, creativity is a sales trick, and innovation is nothing but a check-off exercise for process managers and advice-givers. As a result, barring a few exceptions, the free creative space is in a sorry state in the Netherlands. Culture is now supposed to be an 'economic sector.' Not surprisingly, it collapsed like a house of cards during the pandemic. The sector is down for the count.
This makes for a crucial moment. Art is not autonomous anymore, those days are long gone, but the creative imagination can actually serve much

better purposes than those of power and market. We have to prioritize a broad, probing, open, and fearless debate about the socio-civic role and position of art as a 'firm place to stand' in times of growing inequality and climate crisis. To this, my essay aims to give a modest impetus.

ACKNOWLEDGMENTS
It was not self-evident to organize a biennale in times of pandemic. It felt like we were all in our own cave, at a 'healthy,' that is, at a considerable distance from each other, with only a reflection of a biennale on our screens. But together we kept finding solutions to everything the virus hurled at us. As chief curator I would therefore like to thank the members of the DOWN TO EARTH curator team, Jurgen Bey, Rianne Makkink, Thijs van Spaandonk, and Robbert de Vrieze (for the latter, things have undoubtedly been frustrating; due to the pandemic what he set out to do could never gain much momentum), who were always ready to do whatever it took. As was my always cheerful curator assistant, Alexandra Sonnemans. As were the lead designers of these last four IABR–Ateliers, Joachim Declerck, Adriaan Geuze, Eva Pfannes, and Marco Vermeulen, and their outstanding teams. And as were all the design offices that did critical research, despite the difficult conditions. Their names can be found wherever this book addresses the research with which they have made such a difference. The same goes for the biennale team itself: it brought a job that was difficult because we simply did not know what it demanded to such a successful conclusion. Kudos!

Like a biennale, a book like this is not made by a single person. I am indebted to all the thinkers who have inspired me over the years, especially the philosopher Bruno Latour, who sadly passed away in 2022, whose contribution to the debate on how to relate to the climate crisis is already missed. With his book *Où atterrir?* – published in the Netherlands as *Waar kunnen we landen?* (Where can we land?) and in the English-speaking world as *Down to Earth* – he gave our enterprise a name and a direction. I have quoted all pertinent thinkers often and frequently in my essay. Not because I have a mania for quoting, but because I want to chant together, in an ever-louder choir of philosophers, economists, anthropologists, scientists, writers, artists, designers, activists, and more and more others that join the climate struggle, in the face of the tragedy unfolding under our very own noses.
I owe a lot to those curators – Asu Aksoy, Kees Christiaanse, Joachim Declerck, Adriaan Geuze, Fernando de Mello Franco, Vedran Mimica, Henk Ovink, and Dirk Sijmons – with whom I have worked so wonderfully during previous editions, because they were unreservedly willing to use the biennale as an opportunity to learn from each other and progress together. Starting in 2005, they wrote important chapters for the consequential book that the IABR strove to become.
I also thank the designers who taught me to look at the city through their eyes – Louise Low and Aaron Tan in Hongkong, José Castillo in Mexico City, Hubert Klumpner and Alfredo Brillembourg in Caracas, Orhan Ayyuce in Los Angeles, Marta Moreira, Milton Braga, and Fernando de Mello Franco in São Paulo, Asu Aksoy in Istanbul, Shian-Wen Chu in Beijing and Johannesburg, Joni Baboçi in Tirana, Rahul Mehrotra in Mumbai, Amit Prothi in

Singapore, Alexandros Washburn in New York City, Edgar Pieterse in Cape Town, Daliana Suryawinata in Jakarta, and many others. I am immensely indebted to Elisabete França, who in 2008 gave us the opportunity to develop a new methodology in and with the metropolis of São Paulo. And to Edi Rama, who said 'yes' without reservation when Freek Persyn, Johan Anrys, and I asked him to turn the country of which he had just become prime minister into a single Atelier Albania. Unconditional support also came from many others, notably Eric Hercules on Texel, Yves de Boer in Brabant, and Henk Kranendonk and Ellen Kelder in Dordrecht. Theirs was the kind of trust that is a *sine qua non* for the success of the fragile method underlying the IABR–Ateliers that is described in this book.
Marieke Francke was much more important to the IABR than I have ever been able to explain to her. Zeki Baran helped me, with my Dutch eyes, to actually see Istanbul. Han Bakker helped build crucial bridges. And Willem Ligtvoet helped me cross a threshold when he asked me to think about ways to effectively weave the Sustainable Development Goals into the city-making narrative.
Over the years, biennales have been realized thanks to the indispensable input of virtuosi such as Jolanda van Dinteren, Monica van Steen, Jet Christiaanse, Fanny Smelik, Anouk de Wit, Eva Vrouwe, Yonca Özbilge, and Bart Cuppens. I am greatly indebted to them and all the other biennale team members. The same goes for Elco Brinkman who, when it came to the crunch, showed himself to be a proper chairman, and Joost Schrijnen and the sadly deceased Saskia Stuiveling, inspiring administrators without whom I would not have been able to stand firm as easily in difficult times. Many thanks to Hans Maarten van den Brink for his unwavering support and to Peter Ingelse for his clear advice on how to persist in situations where legal power play threatens to take over the reasonable dialogue between people.
Much credit to my successor, Saskia van Stein, for giving the making of this book all the space it needed. Resourcefully as well as incisively, Loes Claessens gave it its splendid and rich design; in excellent harmony D'Laine Camp and her team provided, as always, relentless text editing and inspired translations; and Noortje Weenink and Alexandra Sonnemans fulfilled the challenging job of editorial assistant with with great precision and admirable dedication.

I dedicate this book to Inger, for her unconditional support, great patience, and willingness to always put me back on my feet – even when I would rather continue to fly. And to Zoë, Mara, Sophie, Daan and Nova, whose still uninhibited faith in the future continues to inspire me to rack my brain about where to land.

George Brugmans
president IABR (2004–2021)
chief curator DOWN TO EARTH (2020–2021)
January 2023

DOWN TO EARTH

CURATOR STATEMENT

CURATOR STATEMENT

EARTHRISE

On Christmas Eve 1968, as mankind first orbited the moon while millions of people watched it happen, astronaut Bill Anders took a special picture. To allow NASA to investigate possible locations for lunar landings, he was shooting images of the lunar surface. As Apollo 8 circled the moon for the first time, the astronauts suddenly saw the Earth 'rising'. Anders didn't hesitate and captured the view. It would turn out to be one of the most influential photographs of all time, later named *Earthrise*.

Against the pitch-black backdrop of an infinite and virtually uncharted universe, the Earth, startlingly, takes on color, depth and perspective. It's an emotional and inspirational image. So, our first view from space of our *home*, a blue planet with a biosphere that makes it exceptionally suitable for life, an assurance, it seems, of wellbeing and growth.

But it's a vulnerable home, with a biosphere that we are all responsible for, warns the Club of Rome almost immediately, in 1972. With that new perspective of our home, glowing warmly in a cold, dark and unfamiliar universe, comes the understanding that the conditions under which our habitat thrives are not self-evident and, in any case, temporary. Our planet is not inexhaustible, we know right away: there are limits to growth.

Earthrise
photo: Bill Anders, 1968
courtesy of Earth Science and Remote Sensing Unit, NASA Johnson Space Center

ANTHROPOCENE

Fast forward to 2020. We can now all zoom in from 'space', anywhere, anytime. The blue planet has become Google Earth™. But what we see is not always that inspiring anymore. Our home is not in order. Rather than instilling responsibility, *Earthrise* made us even more arrogant. Drunk from the view, we've brought down the Anthropocene upon ourselves. Blind to the consequences, we're exhausting the planet, as if we are its end users.

Tailing Ponds, the by-products of mining contain toxins and heavy metals such as lead, copper, and mercury that discolor Earth. *Bleeding Tears, Study 3, Perth, Western Australia* © Yi Sun

Since that Christmas Eve in 1968, the world population has doubled and the number of people living in cities has tripled. And in the last thirty years we have emitted more CO_2 than in all the previous centuries combined. The extractive fossil economy, which enables dizzying growth, places a huge burden on the land, on the Earth, and on the biosphere. And indeed, the planet is not inexhaustible. Climate and biodiversity are under threat, at least a million species will soon be extinct. We are the most dangerous poachers in the ecosystem on which we are completely dependent.

Exactly 50 years later, in the autumn of 2018, a second warning followed, this time from the United Nations Intergovernmental Panel on Climate Change. If we want to prevent a catastrophe, we have until 2030 to fully adapt the way we live on Earth. This lies at the heart of the UN's *2030 Agenda for Sustainable Development*, the need for change on a scale for which 'there is no documented historical precedent.'

We've taken out an irresponsibly large mortgage on our home. It's imperative that we realize that we're facing the greatest crisis humanity has ever known. And that there is no time to lose.

THERE IS NO PLANET B

In 2020, the coronavirus has put the whole world on hold. This offers a truly unique opportunity to take a look behind the backdrop of the Anthropocene.
We've virtually ruined our relationship with the planet. Like the climate and biodiversity crises, but with a much more immediate effect, the pandemic is a result of human activity. Especially of our global economic and financial systems, with their emphasis on endless compound growth and the need to exploit nature to the fullest, in an increasingly violent maelstrom of people, animals, money and goods, with no regard for the consequences. But there is no Planet B. Behind the backdrop, we realize, there is no *behind the backdrop*.

Jakarta
from: *After Us the Deluge*
© Kadir van Lohuizen/NOOR, 2018

Covid-19 uncomfortably exposes how shockingly unequal and vulnerable we have become. We can no longer fool ourselves and cling to the idea that we function in an autonomous ecosystem, independent of the rest of the biosphere. It is simply not sustainable. Things have to *change completely*. The choice is now ours. But *how* are we supposed to proceed? Can we still pay off our mortgage? And how do we find a new way to live in our home, in time?

Rewind back to 1968. *Earthrise*. Let's imagine coming from behind the moon and seeing the blue planet looming in front of us. The image is emotional and inspirational. Where can we land? Can we re-settle on Earth, as it were, in a sustainable balance with all other lifeforms? Can we, as philosopher Bruno Latour proposes, redesign our living environments as that *on which a terrestrial depends* and always ask ourselves, over and over again, and always rigorously and systematically, *what other terrestrials also depend on it*?
For this is now inevitably our *new political mission*, we have to redefine all of our actions as that which takes us back to earth. DOWN TO EARTH.

LEVERS FOR CHANGE

DOWN TO EARTH endeavors to help find an answer to the question: Where can we land? Yes, the situation in which we find ourselves is scary. We have reached the point where it is all or nothing. Yet that's precisely what sharpens our focus, puts us in survival mode. Forces us to think and act in a radically different way, insisting on real world change, on solution-focused research by design that wants to truly and sustainably *ground*.

We decided to focus the IABR research by design agenda on water and energy transition-related challenges. Highly topical subjects both in the Netherlands and around the globe. The Dutch Delta is drying out, seawater levels are rising, all Dutch homes must become natural gas-free – these are some of the very concrete challenges that we've taken as our starting point. We're well aware that everything we do eventually has an impact on the entire biosphere, so our approach is an integral one. That's the only way for us to contribute to comprehensive, truly transformative change. It's why, in the IABR–Ateliers, we design solutions for the water and energy transition challenges in such a way that we also explore how those solutions, as levers for change, can help us solve other problems at the same time. We do not think linearly, but systemically. As Donella Meadows, one of the authors of *Limits to Growth* in 1972, said: 'Making a small change in one thing can lead to a big change in everything.'

Anything we *can* do now, we *must* do now. There's no time to waste. So, let's stop kicking the can down the road, and walk the talk. And let's ask ourselves again and again, and very vigilantly, how we can adapt and do things differently, smarter and more transformatively, *while we're at it*.

George Brugmans
chief curator DOWN TO EARTH
September 2020

HOW CAN WE LAND?

ENERGY

THE IABR AND THE ENERGY TRANSITION

For some time now, the challenge of the energy transition has been one of the main themes connecting the IABR's spatial research and exhibitions. Unsurprisingly really, for if we want to realize the ambitions of the United Nations' *2030 Agenda for Sustainable Development* and achieve the Paris climate goals, we have to completely change the way we use energy and land, as scientists from all over the world are warning.[1]

[1] Important benchmarks indicating where we stand in the fight against the climate crisis are the reports of the IPCC, the Intergovernmental Panel on Climate Change, a United Nations organization that evaluates the risks of climate change. In 2018, in a special interim report, *IPCC Special Report on Global Warming of 1.5 °C*, the panel, made up of hundreds of experts from around the world, from universities, research centers, businesses, environmental organizations, and others, sounded the alarm with a bleak forecast about rapid global warming. Our energy and land use were of particular and great concern to the panel.

For those without a smartphone: an overview of all website addresses to which the QR codes in this book refer is provided on page 438.

Spatially, the energy transition primarily takes place at four scale levels that are all relevant to designers: the transnational, regional, district, and dwelling levels. In the context of DOWN TO EARTH, the IABR primarily focused on energy transitions at the district level, an important challenge in the Netherlands today. This is why the third IABR–Atelier Rotterdam has been active in and together with the Rotterdam district of Bospolder-Tussendijken since 2017.

Previously, the IABR also conducted intensive research by design at the three other levels, for example into the potential of large-scale wind energy generation in the North Sea, new energy perspectives for the regional economy of the Province of Groningen and new sustainable building types for Rotterdam.

All of the research was based on what we have been calling the 'metabolism approach' since 2013: research into ways to sustainably activate, at every scale level, the potential of the territory, conceived as a single ecosystem, together with and for the benefit of all of its inhabitants.

Material Flows and Urban Metabolism

This metabolism approach, which was explored and developed in 2013 and 2014 in the first IABR–Atelier Rotterdam, starts from the idea that the urban landscape is a complex, vast and dynamic system that works incessantly to meet the needs of its residents. We can describe this system in technical or mechanical terms, but also in organic terms: just like the human body breathes, drinks, eats, uses its senses, and relieves itself, vital material flows of air, water, food, energy, waste, people, cargo, and building materials move through the city. We can analyze, connect and direct these flows to develop more sustainable models for the city.

What are the benefits of looking at the Metropolitan Region Rotterdam The Hague in this 'organic' way? Guided by lead designer Dirk Sijmons, the research by design of James Corner Field Operations and FABRICations. and the input of, among others, the Netherlands Environmental Assessment Agency (PBL), charted which flows of materials run through

[2] See the IABR website

the city, port, and region, and how. The researchers analyzed how these flows interact with the space and how they – individually and in conjunction – influence the (environmental) performance of the city and port. This allowed them to make an inventory of the most promising design assignments. The results, translated into maps, material flow animations and four strategies to design for flows, were presented at IABR–2014–URBAN BY NATURE. [2] Subsequently, they were published in *Urban Metabolism*. [3] This laid the foundations for follow-up research, not only in collaboration with the city in Atelier Rotterdam, but also elsewhere, for instance in Antwerp and Albania.

3

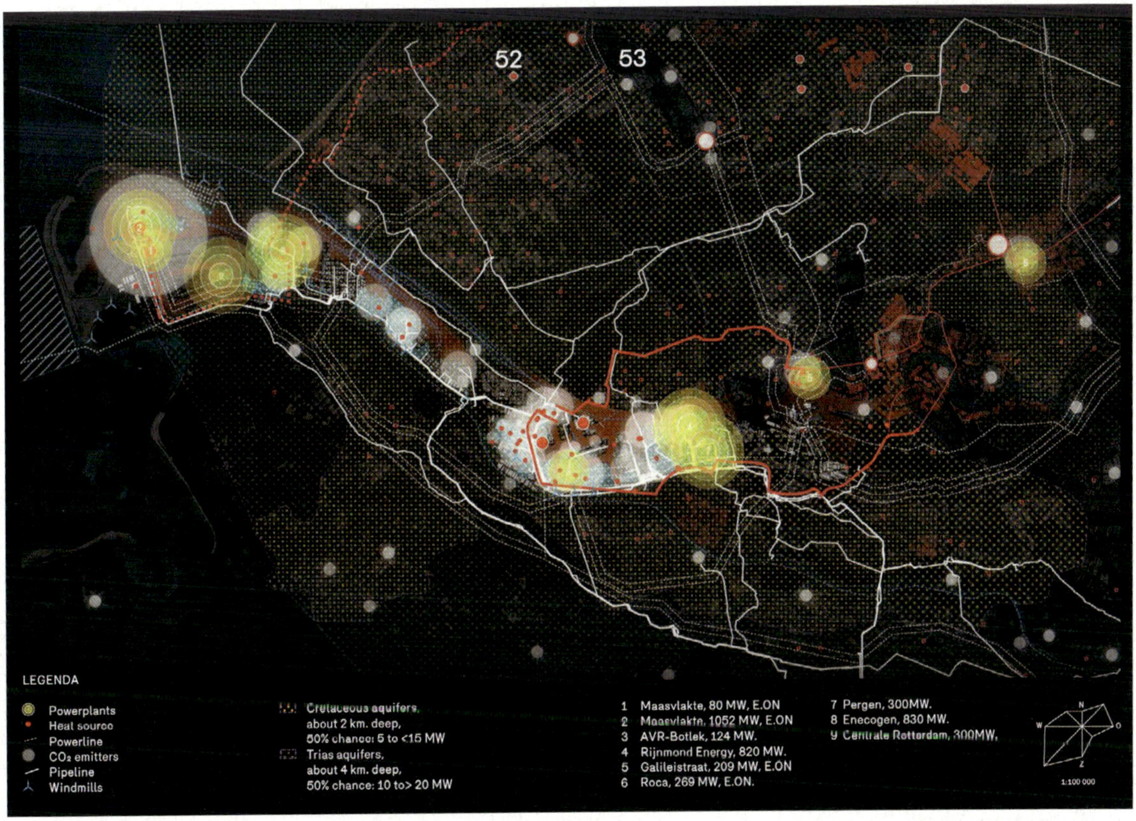

Local energy flows in the Metropolitan Region Rotterdam The Hague
from: *Urban Metabolism*
image: FABRICations. and James Corner Field Operations, IABR–Atelier Rotterdam

A Sustainable Development Model for Albania

The most important ambition of IABR–Atelier Albania, which was set up in 2015 in collaboration with the Albanian government and its National Planning Agency, was to design a sustainable economic development model for what the then newly appointed Prime Minister Edi Rama called *Next Generation Albania*. The IABR considered this an excellent opportunity to bring the metabolism approach closer to policy practice. Thanks to Rama's personal, active involvement, his new government team saw taking this approach to find out how the potential of the Albanian territory, if conceived as a single ecosystem, could be activated integrally and sustainably as a promising challenge.

Energy
URBAN METABOLISM ALBANIA
Energy production
Hydropower
large hydropower plant
hydropower concession
hydropower private
new hydropower plant
Electricity network
power plant
substation
line 400 kV
line 220 kV
line 110 kV
oh line under construction
future oh lines
Energy potential
Average daily solar radiation
Eolic system
<0.25 GJ/M3
Geothermal energy
20 - 30 GJ/M3
30- 40 GJ/ M3
temperature in depth >80°
Fossil energy
oil field
gas field
gas seep
oil field
Trans Adriatic Pipeline
TAP line
N
W
O
Z
0
5
25
50 km
FIERZE HPP
KOMAN HPP
BIOMASS 140 MW
WIND FARM 222 MW
SCAVICE HPP
KOKEL HPP
MOGLICE HPP
Durres
Divjake
Peqin
Rrasaj
Kucova
Kolonje
Bubullima
Patos - Marinza
Povelca
Frakulla
Cakran - Mollaj
Ballsh-Hekal
Gorisht - Kocul
Finiq - Krane

Under the guidance of George Brugmans and Freek Persyn, a coherent development framework materialized. *The Metabolism of Albania: Activating the Potential of the Albanian Territory* outlines the research trajectory – data and material flow research, analysis, fieldwork, presentations and lectures, reflections and concrete recommendations – carried out by the IABR and the Belgian design office 51N4E, always in close collaboration with Albanian partners and with crucial input from Delft University of Technology, the Netherlands Environmental Assessment Agency, and FABRICations.[4] The results were exhibited at IABR–2016–THE NEXT ECONOMY and the Albanian government made them part of the new spatial policy it actively promoted. After the municipal reorganization of 2017, *The Metabolism of Albania*, full of concrete project proposals, especially at the local and regional level, landed on the desk of every mayor in Albania.

4

Large-Scale Wind Energy Production on the North Sea

'If we take the 1.5 °C climate target seriously, then what are we to do?' Spurred on by this direct question, which the Ministry of Economic Affairs asked the IABR in 2016, the IABR–Atelier 2050: An Energetic Odyssey explored the possibilities of large-scale renewable energy production in the North Sea. The Atelier charted what such an ambitious systemic leap would involve, what infrastructure it would require, how all of this could be done without harming the natural system of the North Sea, what innovations and policies would be required, and what new economic dynamics this would generate, for example in the Port of Rotterdam and the offshore sector.

Presentation of IABR–Atelier 2050: An Energetic Odyssey to the participants of the *Sustainable Urban Deltas* conference during IABR–2016–THE NEXT ECONOMY
From right to left: Dutch Special Envoy for International Water Affairs Henk Ovink; Egyptian Minister of Water and Irrigation Works Mohamed Abdel Aty; Mozambique Minister of Public Works, Housing and Water Carlos Bonete Martinho; IABR-President George Brugmans; World Bank researcher Letitia Obeng; (unknown); Habitat III, UN Habitat deputy secretary-general Kumaresh Misra; (unknown)
photo: Hans Tak

With the curators of IABR–2014 and IABR–2016, Dirk Sijmons and Maarten Hajer, at the helm, a knowledge consortium was formed consisting of designers and stakeholders such as Shell, Van Oord, the Port of Rotterdam Authority, Natuur & Milieu, TenneT, and various ministries.
The result of this Atelier, a systemic leap imagined in the form of a large-

←
Energy flows in Albania
from: *The Metabolism of Albania*
image: FABRICations., IABR–Atelier Albania

scale installation with an animation that visualized the possible future of the North Sea, showed that it is possible to harvest wind energy on a very large scale, for all the surrounding countries, in the relatively shallow North Sea.[5] The centerpiece of the plan were the 25,000 10 MW wind turbines that would be able to cover about 90 percent of the electricity needs of the North Sea countries by 2050.

5

This computer animated vision of the future, which demonstrated very coherently how such an ambitious system leap could be achieved and what the final result would be, helped then Minister of Economic Affairs Henk Kamp to, in his own words, convince his EU colleagues to come to agreements that would bring the large-scale generation of wind energy in the North Sea closer.

2050: An Energetic Odyssey was a convincing example of the way in which integrated research by design can be radically translated into an engaging imagination of the future with a clear rationale to show us what we *can* want. This can help us to actually take steps towards the future we desire. Design and visualization are used as levers for policy change; the installation was one of the IABR–2016–THE NEXT ECONOMY's key pieces for good reason.

Stills from video *An Energetic Odyssey*
image: Tungsten Studio, IABR–Atelier 2050: An Energetic Odyssey

The Nordic City: The Energy Transition as a Lever in Groningen

Another key piece of that same biennale was the presentation of the results of 18 months of research by the IABR–Atelier Groningen into ways in which the Province of Groningen, together with a number of cities and businesses in Eemshaven and Delfzijl, could implement the energy transition in such a way as to generate new perspectives for the regional economy and the spatial quality of city and region. [6]

6

The Atelier, a collaboration of the IABR with the Province and the City of Groningen guided by Jandirk Hoekstra, explored how Groningen could

transition to renewable energy in the next 15 years as well as reap the economic benefits. The research – carried out by, among others, H+N+S Landscape Architects, Quintel Intelligence, MAAT, Studio MARCHA, and Van Paridon & de Groot – resulted in a number of detailed prospects for what the Atelier called *The Nordic City*. In this urban region, there would be a close relationship between a powerful and smart city with excellent amenities and an array of robust villages around it. It would be held together by a shared energy ambition and a sustainable energy and transport system, include a strong biobased economy cluster, and the Groningen-Eemshaven-Delfzijl triangle would have the potential to become one of the most important energy hubs of Northwest Europe.

Prioritizing and accelerating the energy transition – the Atelier calculated a total investment volume of approximately 7 billion euros – would also allow for decisive efforts to integrate the challenging recovery and restructuring assignments in Groningen's earthquake area by making dwellings and buildings more sustainable. This approach, welcomed by both administrators and stakeholders, offered excellent opportunities for the green next economy and would give something back to the region, after years of it contributing disproportionately to the prosperity of the Netherlands as a whole.[7]

The Nordic City. Perspective for Delfzijl: green industrial complex and center of biobased activity in the region image: MAAT ontwerpers, IABR–Atelier Groningen

7

Three Material Flows + Energy: Circular Area Development in a Rotterdam City Harbor

IABR–Test Site M4H+
from: *Wat heb je nodig?*
image: Team1010, IABR–Atelier Rotterdam

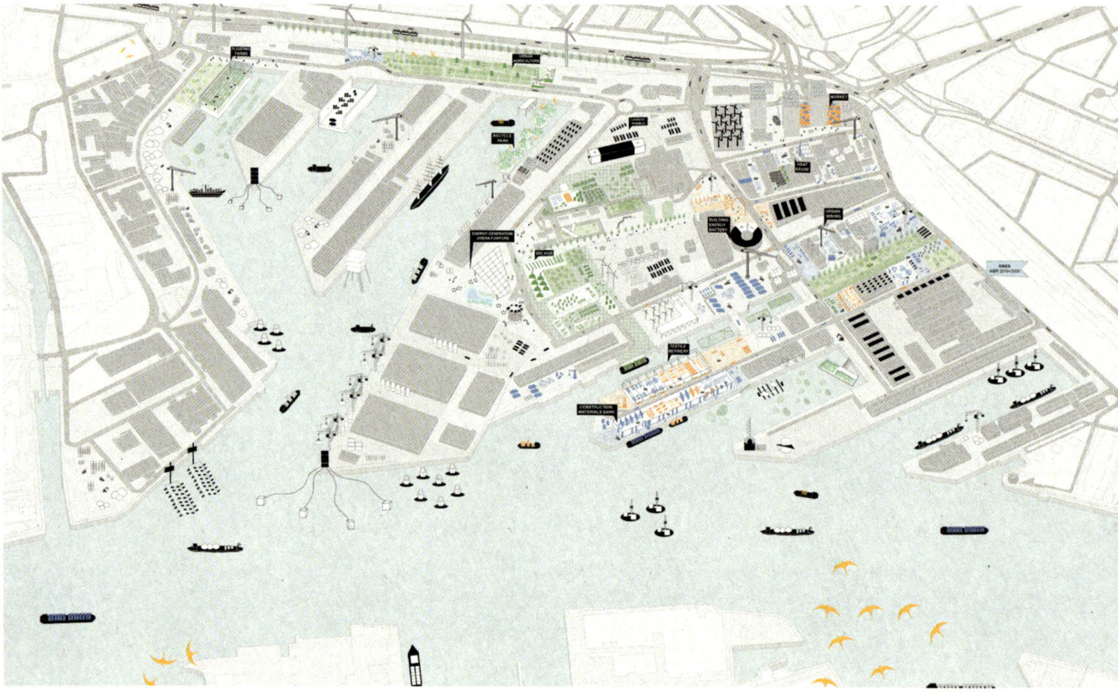

In 2018, the now third IABR–Atelier Rotterdam conducted research into the ways in which city harbor Merwe-Vierhavens (M4H), together with adjacent districts such as Oud-Mathenesse and Bospolder-Tussendijken (M4H+), could develop into a breeding ground for a circular manufacturing industry at the IABR–Test Site M4H+. Key questions were: What will this take in concrete terms? and: Who are the most important partners and players? The research by design was guided by Joachim Declerck and carried out by Team1010, a collaboration established for this occasion by 1010au, Mariska Vogel and Ronald Van Der Heijden. [8]

Globally operating port cities such as Rotterdam are places of abundance; this is where the residual flows that are the raw materials of the future urban metabolism come together. New activities and products are created at the intersection of material flows, ideas and sales markets. The question is: How can we find the missing link between the supply of residual flows present in M4H and the demand for new products and services?

After extensive research and consultation with a whole range of stakeholders in the area, Team1010, chose three regionally promising material flows for further study: agri-food, building materials and textiles. Energy was included as an intrinsic part of all three flows (embodied energy). The aim was to link local capacities and existing initiatives to dynamics that occurred on a different scale, that of the Delta region or even that of the world.

[8] In this context the Atelier could build on the results of the research that the second IABR–Atelier Rotterdam, guided by Daan Zandbelt, conducted in 2015 and 2016 into the potential of the small manufacturing industry in the Metropolitan Region of Rotterdam The Hague. The results are compiled in the publication *The Productive City: Development Perspectives for a Regional Manufacturing Economy*.

The results were presented at IABR–2018–THE MISSING LINK, published and translated into guidelines for a sustainable transition that the City of Rotterdam and the Port of Rotterdam Authority adopted in 2019 and integrated into the *Spatial Framework M4H* approved by the city council. [9]

9

Buildings for the Energy Transition in Rotterdam

There is a lot of expertise about energy-efficient building in the world, but it is fragmented. This is why the third IABR–Atelier Rotterdam commissioned CIVIC to conduct research by design into new building types for the energy transition. CIVIC brought all knowledge together in the *Lexicon Architecture & Energy*, an overview of building blocks that together lead to principles for better energy performance, better indoor climate and new architecture. [10] These principles were subsequently applied to two building types that are common in Rotterdam: the postwar housing association block and the new high-rise tower. This was a first exploration of a new architecture: one which embraces the energy transition and at the same time delivers spatial and user quality. This way the energy transition can function as a lever for the realization of better buildings in a better living environment.

The two new building types were presented at IABR–2018–THE MISSING LINK. The first type, the new high-rise tower, is meant to absorb a significant part of the demographic pressure in Rotterdam in the coming decades, especially in the city center. The Gijsing building in Bospolder-Tussendijken was the model for the second type, the postwar housing block that accounts for more than a quarter of Rotterdam's building stock and will present the biggest challenge in upcoming renovations.

10

Model by CIVIC for IABR–Atelier Rotterdam
IABR–2018–THE MISSING LINK
photo: Aad Hoogendoorn

Energy Districts in Rotterdam and East Flanders

In the context of DOWN TO EARTH, the third IABR–Atelier Rotterdam, now led by Eva Pfannes, mainly focused on the question of how energy transition at the district level can be a lever for other pressing agendas – and vice versa. In the Bospolder-Tussendijken district the Atelier made a direct connection between the need for energy transition and current social issues, such as lack of social inclusiveness and growing socioeconomic inequality. How can infrastructural and social investments sustainably reinforce each other? How can the energy transition be used as a lever for a socially inclusive urban development agenda at the district level? Meanwhile, in the Flemish town of Eeklo, the IABR–Atelier East Flanders Core Region (OVK), a collaboration between the IABR and the Province of East Flanders guided by Joachim Declerck, followed the opposite route, as it were. It examined how the ongoing urban development assignment, urgent because of strong demographic growth, can be used in Eeklo as a lever to initiate the energy transition at the district level, and how the infrastructural interventions that then become necessary can in turn be used to reflect on the morphology, on the form and structure in which this urban development can best take place.

IABR—ATELIER

ROTTERDAM III

IABR—ATELIER ROTTERDAM III

THE ENERGY TRANSITION AS A LEVER

The energy transition is one of the great challenges of the coming decades. Important issues concern the exact way in which interventions will take shape in our urban landscapes, and ways in which the benefits and burdens will be distributed among people and between the public and private sectors. The energy transition therefore amounts to more than an urgent intervention in our systems and infrastructures. We would miss an opportunity if we failed to simultaneously ask ourselves what new urban quality the energy transition will enable us to produce. This is why the starting point formulated in 2017 by George Brugmans for the third research project of the IABR–Atelier Rotterdam was that the energy transition, in addition to being a technical challenge, was also a spatial challenge that needed to be integrated in a broader sustainability and social agenda, of the city and of the world: the United Nations' *2030 Agenda for Sustainable Development*.

The Energy Transition and Sustainable Development Goals

Under its initial lead designer, Joachim Declerck, the research of Atelier Rotterdam III – again a collaboration between the IABR and the City of Rotterdam – started with the question of whether and how the energy transition, which the City and Port of Rotterdam inevitably face, can be used as a driver for inclusive urban development and as a trigger for other important sustainable development goals.

The reduction in the use of and transition to sustainable energy will affect all facets of daily life, from the way people move about to the increased energy efficiency of their dwellings and energy-producing neighborhoods. How can we implement the energy transition in such a way that other ambitions and challenges are also met at the same time, from climate adaptation, poverty alleviation and better vocational education to local employment and entrepreneurship, active participation and cooperative ownership? And is there a level playing field for everyone, will everyone be able to keep up with the changes or even benefit from them? After all, energy poverty as a consequence of the energy transition is imminent, especially in more vulnerable neighborhoods, but by empowering residents to be not only energy consumers, but also energy producers, the energy transition may be able to contribute to the development of resilient and inclusive neighborhoods. In other words: How can the energy transition very concretely help us to realize broadly supported global sustainable development goals in and from our own living environment – that is, simultaneously create ecological and social added value for the world, for the city, for the neighborhood and for each individual citizen?

The Energy Transition as a Lever for Socially Inclusive City Making

In the coming years Rotterdam will have to switch to renewable energy, district by district. The energy transition will require the largest overhaul the city has seen since the postwar reconstruction. However, many of Rotterdam's districts also have other issues to deal with, ones that residents generally consider to be much more urgent. Unemployment, school drop-outs, debts or safety on the streets: these are the pressing issues in the vulnerable neighborhoods, not the energy transition. Other neighborhoods have yet other problems to deal with, such as how to make the neighborhood climate proof, or where to make room for new housing.
On the district level, major systems affect people's immediate living environment. The energy transition will have consequences at the level of the neighborhood, the street and the dwelling. Fortunately, collective action can be organized at exactly that same level, that of the district. Can the energy transition become a driving force behind simultaneous solution-oriented work on other issues in the districts? Can Rotterdam develop a collective strategy that ensures that the large investments required for the energy transition serve other purposes as well, a strategy that generates social added value in and for the districts themselves and that can deliberately use the energy transition as a lever for a more socially inclusive form of urban development?

THE MISSING LINK

After an exploratory study in collaboration with various departments of the City of Rotterdam and a wide range of stakeholders, the Atelier decided to first explore the synergy between urban transformation and the energy transition on several fronts. It selected three different types of districts for their characteristics, to test the Energy District concept, and commissioned CIVIC to conduct research by design into new building types for the energy transition and Team1010 to explore the potential of the circular economy for the integrated area development of the Merwe-Vierhavens city harbor.
In 2018, the Atelier used the platform of the 8th edition of the biennale, THE MISSING LINK, to present the results of those initial investigations, exchange knowledge and expertise in numerous workshops and debates, and actively involve partners and actors (from the city and region, but also beyond) in the process of shared knowledge development.

New Energy for Rotterdam

In the summer of 2018, the newly elected Rotterdam City Council, having formulated its policy goals in the coalition agreement *New Energy for Rotterdam* (2018-2022), adopted the *Council Agreement Energy Transition* and thus, for all practical purposes, endorsed the Paris climate goals. The starting point was that the energy transition had to be feasible and affordable for all Rotterdammers. This is why solutions selected should cost society as little as possible. At the same time the city wanted to take advantage of the opportunities for economic development, employment and improved living environments the transition offered.

The coalition agreement designated five districts in which a 'coherent sustainable area approach' was to take shape. In these experimental energy transition areas, preparations were to be made to stop the use of natural gas in the neighborhood and to construct new energy systems and infrastructures.

Partly as a direct result of the many meetings around the presentations of the IABR–Atelier Rotterdam at the 2018 biennale, which took place during the period in which the coalition agreement was being drafted and in which a number of council members were regularly present, the city council emphasized in the agreement that it was necessary to work together with the residents of the district and to look for the social added value of the energy transition.

One of the five designated testing grounds was Bospolder-Tussendijken. In the same period, a number of local and municipal actors, including the IABR, joined the *Resilient Bospolder-Tussendijken 2028* program initiated by Mayor Ahmed Aboutaleb, which aimed to bring this vulnerable district up to the socioeconomic average level of Rotterdam in ten years. Thus it could be ensured that this program, too, approached the energy transition as a lever for realizing a social agenda: for community building, setting up training programs, creating employment and fighting poverty.

Energy District BoTu

After THE MISSING LINK, and because of her pertinent experiences in Brazil and India, Eva Pfannes took over from Declerck as lead designer. The IABR and the Rotterdam City Council decided to place the Bospolder-Tussendijken district, popularly called BoTu, at the center of the Atelier's research. The aim was to explore, step by step and with the support of as many local social initiatives as possible, how an *energy transition-as-a-lever* approach could actually be put into practice. The municipal agreements, programs, and projects formed the research trajectory's institutional context.

At that time, with the municipal intention of phasing out the use of natural gas in the neighborhood as a big stick, the Atelier was able to test possible answers to a number of important questions. How can the inevitable energy transition provide leverage for the things residents want for their districts? How can we do this in a way that contributes to social inclusiveness and sustainable improvement of the living environment and quality of life? And how can active and engaged residents effectively become co-owners of the necessary transition?

But Survival, First

Bospolder-Tussendijken is a 'vulnerable' district. Many people here are not concerned with the energy transition, but with survival. Rather than about the transition, important as it may be, they care about a good education, work, a decent income, good health and a clean and safe neighborhood in which they would want to and could continue to live, also as they get older. This marked the challenge with which the real work of the IABR–Atelier now started: Can the radical energy transition also help the people of BoTu achieve their personal goals? Can the energy transition be a lever for a safe, clean, solidarity-based neighborhood with opportunities for everyone, with residents who are able to deal with the externally induced shocks of transition?
And it should be able to. Because however vulnerable BoTu may be, there is hardly any other district in Rotterdam that shows as much initiative: new forms of local democracy, countless young entrepreneurs in maker spaces,

Social initiatives in
Bospolder-Tussendijken
photo: Frank Hanswijk

all sorts of collaborations that know how to enter into smart partnerships with more established institutions. This makes BoTu fertile ground for the development of an action perspective: the neighborhood itself can help put flesh on the energy transition and reap its benefits later. BoTu, the Atelier concluded, is both vulnerable *and* resilient.

Building Blocks for a Collaborative Approach

While the broader context of global goals created an opportunity to identify possible and desirable synergies among measures for the energy transition and for other goals, the IABR–Atelier also wanted its work to affect the daily lives of people living in the district. En route to the 2020 biennale, Brugmans therefore asked architect Robbert de Vrieze, who lives and works in BoTu, to join the DOWN TO EARTH curator team and act as a liaison to optimally integrate the ambitions of the IABR, the Atelier and the district.
Together with – and sometimes from inside – social networks, that is, in the midst of the local dynamics, the Atelier then explored how the energy transition could best be used as a lever for maximum social added value. Under the heading *Building Blocks for a Collaborative Approach*, the Atelier carried out two parallel explorations into 'local energy' in the summer of 2019. One was a study of the required spatio-energetic building blocks and the other a predominantly anthropological exploration of both the known and the as yet unidentified, one might say 'invisible,' social networks in BoTu. This was meant to create the necessary prospect for action. After all, the energy transition can only be successful in the broad sense mentioned above if technical and infrastructural solutions are linked to other physical and social changes in the district, and if this drastic transition is partly supported and realized by citizens and local networks themselves. This is why the Atelier wanted to work on a new practice and to that end combine the initiating strength, knowledge, insights and capacities of municipal departments, local networks and organizations, housing associations, anthropologists, designers, energy and organization experts, and many others. All of the outcomes of these explorations and investigations were subsequently used to design a Local Energy Action Plan: a LEAP for BoTu.

Spatio-Energetic Building Blocks

The Atelier asked PosadMaxwan and Generation. Energy to map out the potential for producing, saving, storing and exchanging energy in BoTu. For example, how much room for solar panels is there on the existing roofs and how much energy can be produced in this way? In which cases is aqua-thermy or thermal heat/cold storage an option? What are the costs and benefits, how can we create coherence and how close can we get to the goal of being carbon neutral by 2050?
The result of the study is a package of measures that can be taken, that is a set of practicable spatio-energetic building blocks that each have been assigned a 'value' based on the following questions: How does this building block perform in terms of sustainability, and on what scale? Does this building block require commitment from individuals or from the collective? Can one develop a business case for it, or is public funding required? [11]

11

IABR—ATELIER ROTTERDAM III

12

Socio-Civic Building Blocks

The study into the role that known as well as invisible social networks in the district can play in the energy transition was carried out by four closely collaborating local parties who know the district well: Transformers, Beekhuizen Bindt, Eliza Works and Steps2Inspiration. The study was actually an anthropological exploration of the self-image of BoTu, of its current problems and needs and the wishes for the future with which the residents identify. People make the district and this is why their social networks have to help support a socially inclusive energy transition: in this sense they, too, are crucial building blocks.[12]

Local Energy Action Plan

In the fall of 2019, using the results of these two explorations, Atelier Rotterdam took its next step toward the creation of a LEAP. The Local Energy Action Plan was designed especially for BoTu by Eva Pfannes's Rotterdam-based design office, OOZE architects & urbanists.
As the LEAP required an approach to the energy transition that was completely different from the usual one, the Atelier now delved even deeper into Bospolder-Tussendijken. The aim was to explore how the energy transition could serve as a lever for a broad qualitative leap on the ground, with the Sustainable Development Goals fleshed out at the district level. The Atelier meticulously examined how the spatio-energetic and socio-civic building blocks could be used, which trajectories and projects could be established from collaborations with active local networks, and how this might contribute to the design and implementation of a transition path supported by the district itself towards 2030 and beyond.
The Atelier explored four concrete cases in detail – first, the Dakpark School, later an urban block along the Schie River, the Gijsingflats and the Zelfregiehuis – with the aim of testing and portraying the joining of forces between actors and the chain reactions between the energy transition and value added to society as a whole.

Case Study 1: Dakpark School

The Board of Directors of the BOOR foundation had expressed the ambition to turn public elementary school Dakpark into the first 'Resilient School' in Bospolder-Tussendijken.[13] In the first half of 2020, this represented an excellent opportunity to the IABR–Atelier to work out an example of the way the energy transition could be concretely addressed at the district level, even before the opening of DOWN TO EARTH. OOZE saw an opportunity to improve the indoor climate in the school and designed a climate-proof schoolyard, turned the roof into a collective solar roof on which district residents could jointly produce energy and used the whole process to make pupils more climate aware and integrate resilience into the curriculum.

[13] BOOR provides public (special) primary education, secondary education and (secondary) special education in a total of some 75 Rotterdam schools, in which about 30,000 pupils are taught on a daily basis.

The research toward making the Dakpark School – including the courtyard it shares with the Centre for Culture and Participation (CCPR) and the Rijnmond Multicultural Centre Foundation (RMC) – more sustainable thus became the LEAP's first elaborate case study.[14] It is in accordance with a strategy that subsequently would be joining all the dots of 'first generation' projects to outline a coherent Energy District Bospolder-Tussendijken.[15]

14

The Sustainable Development Goals as a Toolbox

The research in BoTu took place as cohesively as possible: the social challenges and climate objectives, the global challenge and the concrete social tasks in the neighborhood, the long-term perspective and the implementation of concrete projects in the here and now. Together they were meant to amount to one of Rotterdam's first so-called 'Energy Districts' as well as provide new insights and a different approach to realizing the energy transition in other districts, in Rotterdam and beyond. It was in fact about exploring ways to use the Sustainable Development Goals as a toolbox in a socio-spatial energy transition laboratory. In other words, BoTu functioned as a test site for the energy transition at the district level, as well as for the energy transition as leverage for the realization of a much broader sustainability agenda.

Next, the results were to be presented, discussed and evaluated during the biennale, DOWN TO EARTH. But then, in the spring of 2020, Covid-19 unexpectedly caused a rift between planning and execution.

15 For all four case studies, see page 104 ff.

Work session IABR–Atelier Rotterdam III, Bospolder-Tussendijken, Summer 2019 photo: Frank Hanswijk

Launch in Slow Motion

In order to realize the ambitions of the Atelier and actually turn a Local Energy Action Plan into local energy action – for example by bringing the four cases one step closer to realization in collaboration with all of the stakeholders – a great number of work sessions, also with participants from all over the world because of the need for experience-based and expert input, would have had to take place in the months before and during DOWN TO EARTH. Each session would have seen a different group of stakeholders and experts coming together to explain the LEAP's structure and business case from different perspectives with the goal of further fleshing out the action plan, both for the individual cases and at the district level. The work sessions were meant to demonstrate what was possible, what the needs were, and what barriers still existed to further focus the LEAP. Also, interventions were to be programmed that had to connect well with ongoing initiatives and that, through the further joining of forces, were supposed to lead to (new forms of) co-ownership and energy action. These were mostly practical interventions and actions, which had to make the added value of the energy transition understandable and attractive to all residents. They were concrete projects at the intersection of energy, water, biodiversity and community that would take place in, with, for and by BoTu – because it is people that make the district.

But the pandemic prevented the Atelier from taking this final, crucial step as early as in 2020. The biennale ended up being the platform for the launch of the LEAP in slow motion. Only well after DOWN TO EARTH would end, in 2022 and beyond, can the plans begin to land in Bospolder-Tussendijken.

CREDITS

The IABR-Atelier Rotterdam, initiated by the IABR in 2013, was a collaboration between the IABR and the City of Rotterdam (Urban Development Department and the Resilient Rotterdam program). Energy Transition as Leverage (2017-2021) was, after Urban Metabolism (2013-2014) and The Productive City (2015-2016), the third and final research project of the Atelier.

STEERING GROUP
George Brugmans, president IABR
Monique van Buul, director urban development City of Rotterdam
Petra de Groene, director economic affairs and sustainability City of Rotterdam

LEAD DESIGNERS
Joachim Declerck, Eva Pfannes

RESEARCH BY DESIGN PHASE 1: BUILDING BLOCKS
Architecture Workroom Brussels
Joachim Declerck, Maxime Peeters, Jasmien Wouters

COMMISSIONS
NEW BUILDING TYPOLOGIES
Civic Architects
Jan Lebbink, Rick ten Doeschate, Gert Kwekkeboom, Ingrid van der Heijden, Leen Bogerd, Angela Solis

ENERGY DISTRICT BOTU
PosadMaxwan and Generation.Energy
Taco Kuijers, Jet ten Voorde, Froukje van de Klundert, Francesca Becchi

(UN)KNOWN NETWORKS
Willem Beekhuizen (Beekhuizen Bindt), Anne Knoop (Eliza Works), Mimi Slauerhoff (Steps2Inspiration), Robbert de Vrieze (Transformers)

RESEARCH BY DESIGN PHASE 2: LEAP
OOZE architects & urbanists
Eva Pfannes, Sylvain Hartenberg, Leanne Hoogwaerts, Nilofer Tajuddin, Hsoc Mathai George, Federica Zatta, Felipe Gonzales, Elif Soylu, Verena Balz

COMMISSIONS
COST MANAGEMENT AND THERMAL STORAGE TECHNOLOGY
Ruud Ghering (Studio Bouwhaven), Hessel Kok, Dennis Slieker (Bron Technologie)

VALUE CASE HEAT NETWORK
Jurgen van der Heijden (AT Osborne)

PROJECT MANAGEMENT
IABR
Marieke Francke, Jelte Boeijenga, Melany van Twuijver
City of Rotterdam
Helene Zeller

PROJECT TEAM
IABR
Ivo de Jeu, Nikki Mulder
City of Rotterdam
Alexander van Steenderen, Paulien Campagne, Wynand Dassen, Marjolein Rours

CURATOR IABR@BOTU
Robbert de Vrieze

PRODUCTION
IABR
Jolanda van Dinteren, Johanna Fuhler, Lisa Lambert

WE THANK THE FOLLOWING PEOPLE FOR THEIR CRITICAL REFLECTION AND/OR THEIR CONTRIBUTION
Emile Klep, director urban development City of Rotterdam
Arnoud Molenaar, chief resilience officer City of Rotterdam
Fred Akerboom, Jillian Benders, Marte van Delden, Nadia Dijkstra, Annemieke Fontein, Tom van Haaren, Danielle van den Heuvel, Karen Jakschtow, Marije ten Kate, Adrienne Lushtaku-Smedts, Astrid Madsen, Maarten Nypels, Kees van Oorschot, Roland van Rooyen, Heather Smittle, Petra van Someren, Bilal Taner, Marleen ter Vergert, Anne-Marie Verheijen (City of Rotterdam)Milja Kruijt (Delfshaven Coöperatie), Julia Hevemeyer (Delfshaven Energie Coöperatie), Nico Koedam (Stichting BOOR), Marja Damman (Dakpark School), Aboubakr Boudal, Said El Koubai (CCPR – Centrum voor Cultuur en Participatie), Ugur Arisoy, Metehan Ozdemir (RMC – Stichting Rijnmond Multicultureel Centrum), Jan-Jaap Bakker, Rob Beumer, Tim Rijkhoek (Eneco), Maria Kluijtenaar (Havensteder), Marthe van Gils, Otto Trienekens (Veldacademie), Frank Franke (Wijknetwerker), Nicole van Gils, Lenny van Klink (Rebel Group)

The IABR–Ateliers were initiated and executed nationally and internationally from 2008 to 2021 under the direction of George Brugmans. The IABR initiated and produced a number of IABR–Ateliers in the Netherlands, including the IABR–Atelier Rotterdam, as a lead partner of the Dutch National Government in the framework of the ARO, the Action Agenda for Spatial Design 2013-2016 of the Ministry of Infrastructure and the Environment and the ARO 2017-2020 of the Ministry of the Interior and Kingdom Relations.

IABR—ATELIER

EAST FLANDERS CORE REGION

IABR—ATELIER EAST FLANDERS CORE REGION

POPULATION GROWTH AS AN OPPORTUNITY FOR SUSTAINABLE SPATIAL DEVELOPMENT

The East Flanders Core Region (*Oost-Vlaams Kerngebied*, OVK) is a network of cities and municipalities around Ghent. The population in this area is expected to have grown by 15 to 25 percent by 2050. This means that an additional 100,000 to 160,000 people will settle here. To accommodate this vigorous growth, dwellings, work spaces and facilities will have to be built. This puts increasing pressure on the open space, social facilities, and infrastructure, and presents the region with several major social challenges.

Based on this observation, 23 cities and municipalities in the Ghent region endorsed the *Strategic Project East Flanders Core Region*. The province of East Flanders, which took a leading role in this initiative, wanted to investigate how it could use space in a more intelligent and multifunctional way to achieve a sustainable, climate-proof and healthy living environment before 2050.

In 2017, the Province sought and found substantive support for this research project at the IABR. Both parties endorsed the need to pass over the experimental stage and to investigate and test ways to use the population growth as a lever for sustainable spatial development of the entire East Flanders Core Region on the ground. The Province made substantial resources available for research by design and together they established the IABR–Atelier East Flanders Core Region, or IABR–Atelier OVK.

Three Ambitions, One Housing Policy

Led by Joachim Declerck, IABR–Atelier OVK investigated how the demographic growth in the region can be used to help shape necessary transitions in terms of open space, accessibility, economy and energy, in tandem with the housing policy. The Atelier set itself the task, first, of taking stock of opportunities by means of test cases and cartography and, second, of visualizing the possibilities. In practice, it functioned as an open learning environment that used research by design to develop scenarios to guide existing and new projects or initiatives in specific

locations toward desirable, concrete realization.
Initially the Atelier saw the East Flanders Core Region as a single, coherent system, a single urban metabolism, and it identified three 'ambitions' that would (eventually) be used to steer a coherent housing policy: Productive Landscape, Circular Economy and Shared Mobility.

A PRODUCTIVE LANDSCAPE AS A STRUCTURING AND RESILIENT OPEN SPACE
Not only agriculture, but also the fertile soil of the East Flanders Core Region – its rivers, canals and polders, its strong economy in city centers and port – and the various possibilities for producing renewable energy are among the key ingredients of a productive landscape. Individually, they are drivers for development and provide important ecosystem services to society. By charting the key ingredients of a productive landscape in the East Flanders Core Region and using them as starting points for the layout of different areas, the Atelier wanted to create smart links between different spatial functions and qualities.

ROOM FOR CIRCULAR ECONOMY AND LIVE-WORK DISTRICTS IN A PRODUCTIVE METROPOLIS
The creation of a circular economy is high on the agenda everywhere, but what does that actually mean? And more importantly, how can this goal actually be achieved? Today, many economic activities take place in isolation, in industrial areas. Reintroducing these productive activities into the urban environment can create new opportunities for sustainable development. This is why the Atelier went looking for ways to cleverly combine the residential fabric with various drivers, such as the economy, energy and water.

A CONNECTED FIGURE, FRAMEWORK FOR A MORE SHARED MOBILITY
In addition to mobility, also water, energy, the economy, and caring living environments can help create a 'connected figure,' a framework for shared mobility. Thinking in terms broader than those of traffic alone can lead to innovative ways of deploying alternatives to current forms of mobility, to the shared mobility that can, in turn, guide residential development. If the East Flanders Core Region plays its cards right, the Atelier argued, it can also present itself as an innovative metropolitan region (inter)nationally.

Three Demonstration Projects

In January 2018, the IABR–Atelier OVK launched a call for projects for the region, looking for ideas, initiatives, projects, and partnerships that were relevant to the entire region and could be used to establish a test trajectory. The aim of these trajectories was to develop projects that comprised feasible and replicable solutions to the spatial problems of the entire East Flanders Core Region in specific locations.
From the initiatives submitted, three demonstration projects were selected in as many locations: in Lievegem, Merelbeke/Ghent and Eeklo. Next,

design offices set to work on specific challenges in the selected municipalities.
The thematic perspectives of the projects were mobility, energy, and open space and water. The common denominator being how these challenges could serve as levers for future development, the designers had to find answers to both the local questions and to those created by the overarching regional demographic growth.

THE MISSING LINK

Globally, major long-term ambitions for meeting the challenges of the twenty-first century that have been formulated include the Paris Climate Agreement and the UN Sustainable Development Goals. At the same time, there has been and continues to be a multitude of small-scale initiatives at the regional level. Provinces, municipalities, and citizens each try to bring about change in their own way. But these experiments are still the exceptions that confirm the rule: business as usual remains the order of the day. At the same time, large-scale transformations lack depth and are far too slow to take off. The gap between real change and goals to be achieved is still too wide, in East Flanders as in the world.
This is what the IABR called 'the missing link,' and put on the agenda by making it the theme of the 2018 biennale. Finding the link between plans and realization, which is missing in regular practice, was therefore part of the task that IABR–Atelier OVK set itself. The Atelier searched for ways to allow the major goals, transitions and demographic challenges to land in concrete places and lead to real projects. It is from this perspective that the initial analyses and the proposed approach as developed in the demonstration projects were shown at IABR's 8th edition, THE MISSING LINK.

House of Dialogue and Exploration

Between the closing of THE MISSING LINK and 2021, Atelier OVK deliberately earmarked a lot of time and space for local initiatives, coalitions, and governments. The Atelier wanted to function as a house of dialogue, of new coalition exploration, and of integrated future scenario devising. It did not opt for the safest way to solutions, but for a qualitative sidestep in which new alliances, research, knowledge exchange, public dialogue, and international expertise would enrich the regional process.
The IABR–Atelier followed three trajectories simultaneously: a learning trajectory, a testing trajectory, and a policy trajectory. The learning trajectory saw the Atelier, in a collaboration with regional and local stakeholders and experts, exploring the ways the region functions, but also focusing on the question of what kind of region *we can want*. By charting the current situation and translating it into an Atlas on the one hand, and setting the course of six transitions on the other, the Atelier made the future opportunities for the region visible – and therefore accessible. Parallel to this, the testing trajectory focused on research by design at specific locations with the aim of developing reproducible solutions, explicitly grafted onto the DNA of the region. The three demonstration projects involved both testing

→
Model by Studio Paola Viganò for the presentation of IABR–Atelier OVK at IABR–2018–THE MISSING LINK
photo: Ivo Haarman

IABR—ATELIER EAST FLANDERS CORE REGION

and doing by means of participatory research by design. The Atelier made a deliberate attempt to establish links to existing projects and current developments in the region.

The demonstration project in Eeklo was linked to the Energy Landscape project of the Province of East Flanders, this with an eye to the startup and implementation of several energy districts in the region. The meeting of the water-drought challenge, especially the way it was dealt with in the demonstration project in Lievegem, was continued in a follow-up project called *Water in de weegschaal* (Water in the Balance). The insights regarding a new sociospatial mobility approach as developed in the demonstration project in Merelbeke found their way into a new regional transport strategy. The results of the Atelier's research as such were incorporated in a regional collaboration, the *North Sea Port District*, comprising the three Zeeland municipalities Terneuzen, Vlissingen and Borsele in the Netherlands, the East Flanders municipalities Evergem, Zelzate and Ghent, the Dutch Province of Zeeland and the Province of East Flanders.

This way, the IABR–Atelier OVK in collaboration with various stakeholders built on a widely supported future narrative for the region while working to translate it into concrete policy.

CREDITS

IABR–Atelier East Flanders Core Region (OVK) (2017–2021) is a collaboration of the IABR and the province of East Flanders.

STEERING GROUP
Anna-Maria Charlier, provincial executive delegate for spatial planning, Province of East Flanders
Mark Cromheecke, director of space and mobility, Province of East Flanders
George Brugmans, president IABR

LEAD DESIGNER
Joachim Declerck

RESEARCH BY DESIGN
Architecture Workroom Brussels
Joachim Declerck, Carmen Van Maercke, Marie van Loon, Nik Naudts, Chiara Cicchiani, Emma Bierens

DEMONSTRATION PROJECT EEKLO
research by design
PLUSOFFICE architects
Jitse Massant, Ward Verbakel
enprove
Sven Van Hecke

PROJECT TEAM
Province of East Flanders
Charlotte Rosseel, Jan Haegeman, Silke Lemant, Nuriël Milleville, Eline Serruys
IABR
Vivian Ammerlaan, Melany van Twuijver

WE THANK THE FOLLOWING PEOPLE AND ORGANIZATIONS FOR THEIR CRITICAL REFLECTION AND/OR THEIR CONTRIBUTION
Martine Verhoeve (Province of East Flanders), Geert Versnick (City of Ghent), Ward Deschildre (Province of East Flanders), Bob D'Haeseleer, Ben Caussyn (City of Eeklo), Marieke Francke (IABR), Maxime Peeters (Architecture Workroom Brussels) and the City of Lievegem, the City of Merelbeke, 1010 Achitecture Urbanism, Antea Group, Meneer de Leeuw, PT architecten, Transport & Mobility Leuven, Voorland

PANDEMIC

IABR–Atelier OVK did not escape the consequences of the pandemic, either. As in IABR–Atelier Rotterdam, Covid-19 affected the planned work sessions in particular. People need to talk, think and work with other people to be able to make city together. This is a prerequisite for the success of research by design, which involves integrating the aspirations of all residents and other stakeholders in the working process as best as possible. Virtual meetings, such as webinars, were only able to make up for the lack of face-to-face meetings to a very limited extent. Covid-19 not only caused significant delays in the work processes at both Ateliers, but also, over time, the adjustment of ambitions.

From the spring of 2020 onward, improvisation was necessary during the research trajectories as well as required to come up with alternative ways to show the results at the biennale in Rotterdam.

Given the Circumstances

DOWN TO EARTH materialized step by wary step. Decisions were deliberately made as ad hoc as possible and based on what was practicable and allowed for a biennale during a lockdown. To IABR–Atelier Rotterdam, this meant that the preliminary results had to be shown in two steps, in fact in two exhibitions. The first, WHOSE ENERGY IS IT, ANYWAY?, opened on 20 November 2020, but had to close exactly one month later in compliance with the lockdown measures of the Dutch government. Rather than repeat this exhibition one-on-one at a later date, the curators, George Brugmans and Thijs van Spaandonk, and the Atelier's lead designer, Eva Pfannes, decided to build on it and to include further research, which had continued in the fall and winter of 2020/2021 despite the pandemic, in a next version. Unfortunately, the second exhibition, RECLAIMING THE COMMONS, was also only open to the public for one month, from 9 June to 9 July 2021. Given these circumstances, it was only possible to use the exhibitions as arenas for public debate and international knowledge transfer, as happened at previous biennales, on very few occasions. They were primarily a demonstration of the progressing insights of the IABR–Atelier itself. The research results will only be able to really land in Bospolder-Tussendijken once DOWN TO EARTH is over, in 2022 and beyond.

It was not possible to present all of the results of IABR–Atelier OVK on the DOWN TO EARTH platform, either. In the end, only the results of the demonstration project in Eeklo, which investigated how the urbanization challenge can be used as a lever to launch the energy transition, were shown in Rotterdam. The research by design clearly showed that it is possible to formulate a project scale at which technical solutions and interventions, local social and economic dynamics, and behavioral change can be linked. Finding and developing this scale requires a substantial adjustment of the practices of the worlds of both design and policy. After all, this scale has to be much smaller and less intertwined with the techn(ocrat)ical challenges of the transition, which is often preferred in current practice.

RECLAIMING THE COMMONS
photo: Aad Hoogendoorn

But such an alternative approach is precisely what creates the opportunity to close the gap between adaptation and mitigation by means of targeted spatial transformations: small-scale adaptation projects can become levers for mitigation, for behavioral change. In this sense, the research in Eeklo was very much in line with that of IABR–Atelier Rotterdam, which was central to the exhibitions WHOSE ENERGY IS IT, ANYWAY? and RECLAIMING THE COMMONS.

DOWN TO EARTH

WHOSE ENERGY IS IT, ANYWAY? / RECLAIMING THE COMMONS

CURATORS
George Brugmans (chief curator)
Thijs van Spaandonk

WHOSE ENERGY IS IT, ANYWAY?
20 November – 20 December 2020
Keilezaal, Rotterdam

RECLAIMING THE COMMONS
9 June – 11 July 2021
Keilezaal, Rotterdam

RECLAIMING THE COMMONS

CURATOR INTRODUCTION

The transition to renewable energy is urgent, but also almost unimaginably far-reaching.
Urgent because the petroculture that characterizes modern civilization contributes greatly to global warming and climate change. More than a million life forms have already become extinct or are threatened with extinction. For humans, too, the Earth is becoming less and less habitable – although not as much for some as for billions of others. It is mainly the vulnerable and the weak who bear the consequences; petroculture contributes significantly to social inequality.
The transition is almost unimaginably far-reaching because the way we live, care and learn, consume and produce; because what we eat and how we eat, how we move around and how we interact with each other and with nature – in short, because how we organize our living environment and our *coexistence* and whether everyone has equal opportunities, is largely determined by access to and use of energy.

Our use of energy has an impact on our economy and our culture. But the era of petroculture, the extravaganza of fossil expressionism, is coming to an end. The energy transition was the elephant in the room of politics. But now, energy poverty is a clear and present danger. It is therefore crucial that we reconsider ownership of the transition to a sustainable energy supply. It is crucial to forcefully argue that the energy transition requires a transition in ownership and to ensure that the energy transition is a social transition.

Energy was once part of the commons: *that which belongs to us all and that we take care of together*. It can become that way again, we believe, because as the sun, the wind, and hydrogen belong to everyone, the transition to renewable energy should belong to everyone. But how can this be achieved? How can citizens become the co-owners of a new energy system and what will that require? How can the energy transition be used as leverage to achieve a sustainable social agenda? How can we reinvent the commons for the twenty-first century, and at what spatial level of scale can this best be explored?

THE DISTRICT: NEW PLAYERS, NEW SCENARIOS

Using the energy transition as leverage for sustainable socially inclusive urban development is advantageous at the scale level of the district. This is where all the developments and challenges come together, where old players must find new roles and new players can now actually claim their role.

Whose Energy Is It, Anyway?

The transition to the production of renewable energy requires a new organization of the energy system. Energy companies and oil- and natural gas-producing countries are the major players in the current centralized structure. The pressure put on this system by the energy transition is leading to both confusion and opportunities, to losers as well as winners. Some of the old players are finding new roles. Think, for instance, of wind farms in the North Sea – renewable energy, too, can be produced on a large scale. Some of the new, often small, players are pushing the old ones out, however, because that's how the market works at the moment. But if we continue down this road, residents and other small energy users won't necessarily gain much, if anything. They will still be consumers, their only responsibility to keep footing the bill.

Towards a New Energy Commons

However, the energy transition makes it possible for everyone to generate their own energy. If users work together, if owners' associations make good use of their roofs, or if residents' initiatives or even housing corporations become energy cooperatives, more and more energy consumers can also become energy producers. While that's all well and good, the fact remains that large-scale infrastructure will still be necessary to store and distribute the energy generated by smaller players. In the new scenario the large and small scale, the big and little players, somehow need to be connected. This will require an energy system that functions structurally as an open network in which new collaborations are given real opportunities.

The district is the level of scale at which these new collaborations can best take shape. This is where the idea of a new energy commons can be explored, a playing field in which, in addition to governments and businesses, citizens can also play a role. This is the best place for a Local Energy Action Plan that is tailored to scale and thus maximally effective to be designed and realized.

→
Work session RECLAIMING THE COMMONS
photo: Aad Hoogendoorn

5,000 DISTRICTS

There are some 5,000 districts in the Netherlands that need to become 'gas-free'. Initial experiences have made it clear that this is not that easy to achieve. There are problems with implementation and, above all, financing and governance. In fact, we just don't know how to make neighborhoods gas-free. We must investigate, work things out by trial and error.

What is immediately clear is that one district is not the other. Whether it's the buildings, the people who live there, the dynamics, the subsurface, the location, or the density, every district has its own spatio-energetic and socio-civic building blocks. If the goal is the same for all districts – to get rid of natural gas in such a way that inhabitants don't have to foot the bill and the benefits don't lead to burdens elsewhere – it is also true that the transition process slightly differs from district to district. Instead of rolling out a standard approach, making our districts gas-free requires customization. In other words: every district needs its own LEAP, its own Local Energy Action Plan.

Districts cannot copy each other's approach, but it is imperative that they learn from each other's experiences. Can Bospolder-Tussendijken's LEAP, designed by the IABR–Atelier Rotterdam, inspire other districts? And, conversely, are there other social initiatives in other places that explore the possibilities of a new energy commons, of how to deploy the energy transition as a lever? Are there other districts, in the Netherlands or abroad, where new collaborations and alternative roles are taking shape?

Visitors WHOSE ENERGY IS IT, ANYWAY?
photo: Aad Hoogendoorn

FLANDERS

The IABR also did research across the border, there too, districts and communities are finding their way through the energy transition. Unlike in the Netherlands, this doesn't always mean 'becoming gas-free' – sometimes the transition is 'to gas', because that's the next step in the local development. But the fact that business as usual is no longer the way to go is recognized in many places, and an alternative energy system, how to generate more renewable energy, solutions for storage and distribution, and new partnerships and role divisions are being investigated. For example, in the province of East Flanders, which in 2017, together with the IABR, initiated the IABR–Atelier East Flanders Core Region (OVK).

This Atelier has been investigating how the strong population growth in the region can be used as leverage for sustainable spatial development. One of the Atelier's studies is in the municipality of Eeklo. Here, the urbanization challenge is to be used as a lever to initiate the energy transition.
The energy transition is leading to a reduction in scale when it comes to the production of electricity, and this is happening more and more often locally as well as individually. But the production of heat will take place at an increasingly higher level of scale: individual boilers will be replaced by heat networks. These two energy systems intersect at the scale level of the district. Can peaks in electricity production be captured there in an underground heat system? And what role can this synergy play in the morphology of a growing Eeklo?
The Atelier's research by design explored the various techniques with which sustainable heat can be stored and distributed, at what scale level this works best, and how the synergy between the different districts in Eeklo can play an optimal role in this. The research proves as much and unmistakably shows how the densification of several districts can contribute to the realization of a sustainable heat supply for the whole of Eeklo.

EEKLO
1. Re-scaling the Heat and Electricity Landscape

As a result of the switch to renewable energy production, generating energy is becoming more and more dependent on seasonal and weather conditions. The production of energy is no longer related to its immediate consumption, so buffering and storage are necessary.
The new energy landscape also has spatial consequences. The production and consumption of both electricity and heat are changing. Electricity is produced and consumed more and more locally. Heat, on the other hand, has to be scaled up from a large group of individual systems, such as boilers, to a collective system to increase buffering capacity.
The district is at the intersection of both trends. This creates opportunities for a different (district) management of energy production, storage, and consumption. How do you entrust decentralized electricity generation to an infrastructure that was actually designed on a continental scale? How can you organize the collective heat so that it also provokes spatial benefits? What role do citizens, businesses and governments play in such a transition process?

Eeklo is the first city in Belgium to open its entire territory to the construction of a heat network, the largest in the country. The planned network is partly owned by citizens. The IABR–Atelier OVK was asked how best to organize this locally, at the district level, in the Eeklo district of Oostveld.

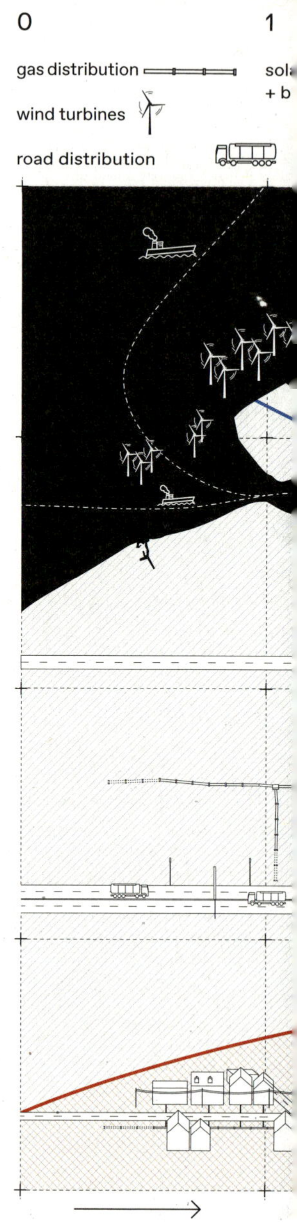

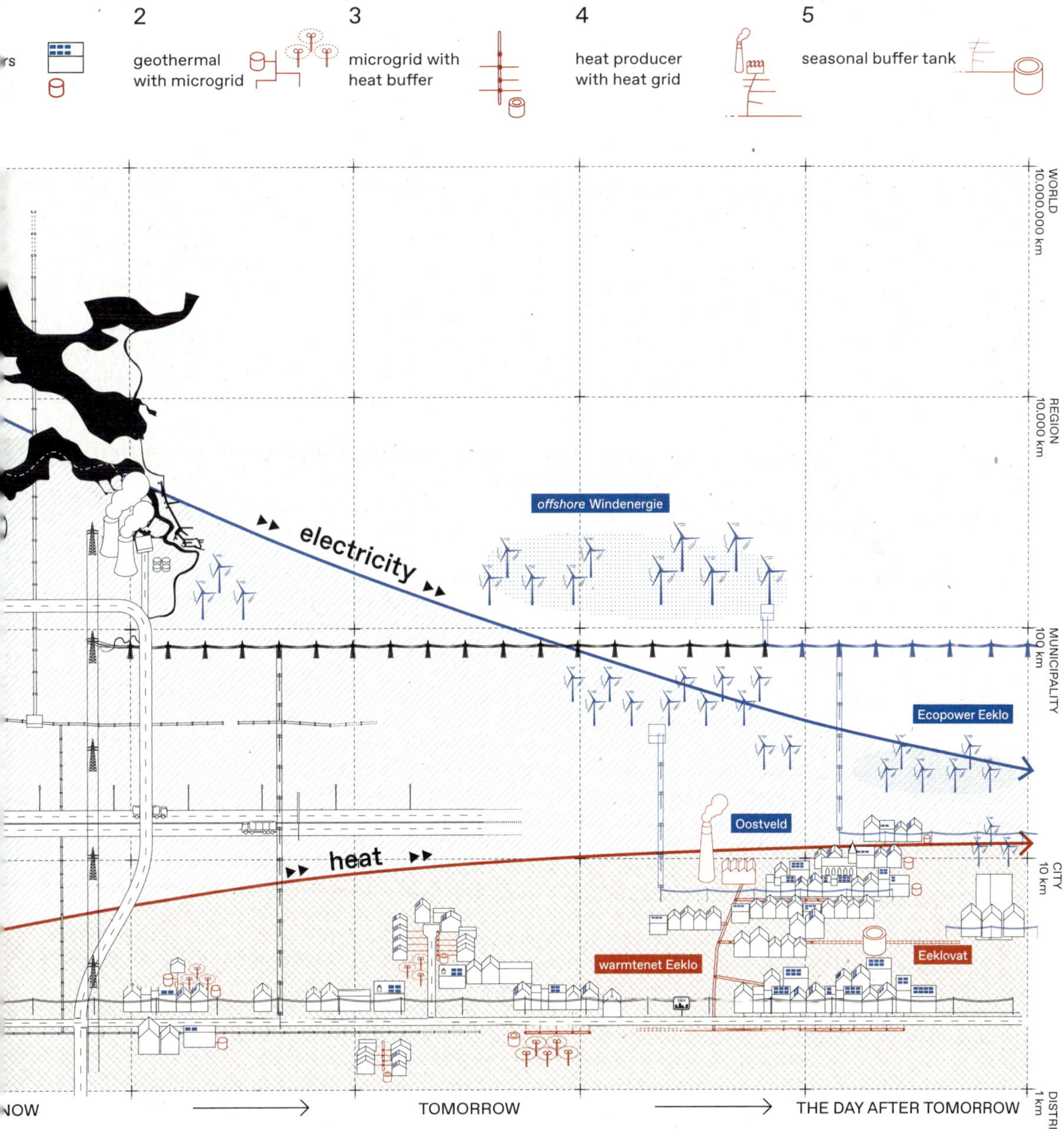

Electricity is generated on a national and European scale and distributed via the grid. This hierarchic, centralized infrastructure is a challenge: Will it be able to accommodate decentralized producers and consumers?

2a. Residential Heat Models

To study various housing types in relation to the energy transition, four spatio-energetic residential heating models were drawn up on the basis of existing housing types in Eeklo's Oostveld district. This connected the energy challenge at the district level with the question: What kind of city do we want to live in? The Atelier also examined how densification can be used both to utilize energy opportunities and to generate spatial quality. Each residential heat model relates differently to the heat network that Eeklo is planning to build.

LIVING IN ROWS

The residential heat model 'Living in Rows' is characterized by the relatively high housing density found in small Flemish cities in areas with mainly older, terraced houses. A feasibility study indicated that these homes are good candidates for being connected to the heat network in the future. In the Oostveld district this residential fabric is located close to the train station and the cycle highway, and is therefore an interesting place to densify. This not only ensures that the heat network is as profitable as possible, it is also an opportunity to prompt a qualitative improvement in the existing residential fabric and its public space, for example by realizing green crossings, activating inner areas, stimulating cycling, or building a more diverse range of housing.

THE CITY-WIDE HEAT NETWORK IS CONNECTED TO THE DISTRICT

Heat is distributed in the district via a heat network that requires a minimum of 2.5 MWh of heat demand per linear meter in order to be profitable. If simple renovation reduces the energy demand in the Oostveld district by 30 to 40 percent, 'Living in Rows' will have to be densified by 12 to 31 percent in order to keep the heat network profitable.

THE HEAT NETWORK AS A COMPLEX TRANSITION MOMENT

The pipe infrastructure of the heat network is dimensioned on the basis of the estimated heat demand. In the business model it is not easy to plan overcapacity for future expansions. Therefore, the biggest task in the construction of a heat network is to connect all existing and future private heat consumers – each with its own conversion rhythm, changing heat demand and heat generation – to the heat network at the same time.

PARK LIVING

In the residential heat model 'Park Living' the Hero Park in Oostveld is being redeveloped. The old swimming pool was recently demolished and there are relatively few buildings around it. It is one of the few places with enough open space to build an underground seasonal buffer tank for the entire district. This transforms the park into an 'energy field' that brings together heat buffering, ecological values, and district facilities. A meeting center could be built on top of the buffer tank to activate the park. Around the park, new homes overlooking it can add the necessary density. In time, the district buffer tank can function as a production hub for the heat network. This will ensure the city-wide heat network's independence of residual heat from the waste plant.

DISTRICT BUFFER TANK AS A SEASONAL BUFFER

If solar panels are installed on three quarters of the roofs in the district, there will be enough energy to cover the district's total energy demand (electricity and heat), provided that all houses also undergo a simple renovation that reduces energy consumption by 26 percent. The district buffer tank stores surplus solar energy in the form of heat. It bridges the heat demand on a seasonal basis and in the day/night rhythm.

DISTRICT BUFFER TANK AS HEAT PRODUCTION HUB

The district buffer tank can also serve as a buffer for a citywide heat network. It delivers a constant quantity of heat throughout the year – the buffer tank stores part of the heat delivered in the summer and releases it in the winter. The infrastructure can be dimensioned more efficiently, based on a constant supply and not on peak consumption.

LIVING IN ROWS

GREEN CROSSINGS
Paths to green spaces break through the monotonous streetscape, expand the pedestrian network, and reduce the street canyon effect (paved streets with low air quality where heat is retained).

- CAR-FREE LIVING
The densification allows the introduction of car-free living. Collective housing that prioritizes pedestrians and cyclists allows for safer street crossings. Small-scale neighborhood functions are located in the bases of the buildings.

PARK LIVING

ACTIVATE INNER AREAS
Possibly to be developed inner areas can give residential projects and productive functions a place that consumes energy at other times.

CONNECTED PARK
The park marks the end of a green corridor where the ecological and recreational qualities of the Meetjesland, the region in which Eeklo is located, penetrate into the residential area.

MULTI-FAMILY HOUSES AS LANDSCAPE GUARDIANS
Densification at the edge of the park with mixed housing expands the zone in which the heat network is profitable and defines the open park space.

DISTRICT SAUNA
On top of the seasonal buffer tank, a heat-demanding program, such a as a sauna, can be realized that uses surplus heat.

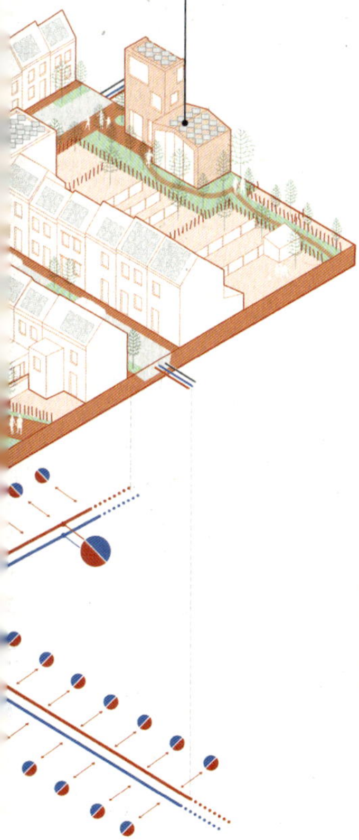

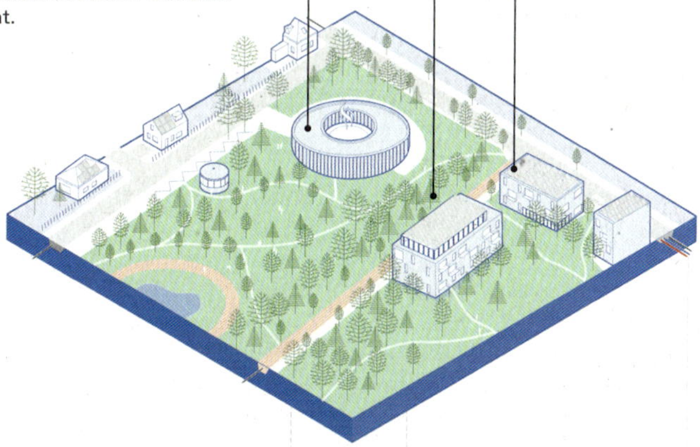

THE DISTRICT BUFFER TANK
In the district buffer tank, solar energy produced throughout the district, with production peaks in summer, is converted into heat and stored for the winter consumption peak.

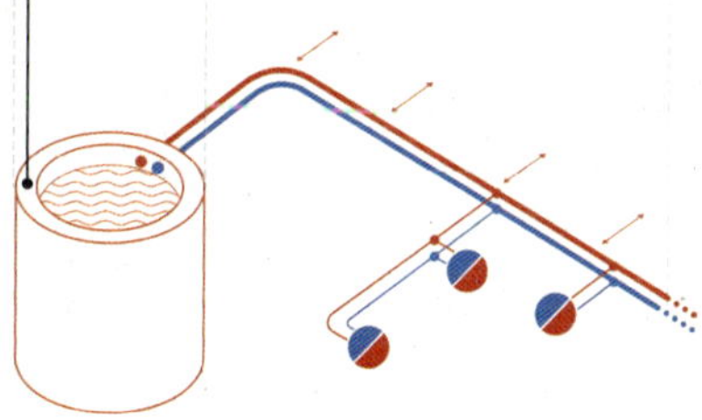

LIVING IN ROWS

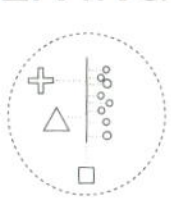

COALITION MODEL: CARING GOVERNMENT
The heat network is typically something that is rolled out by the government in cooperation with a private partner. In Eeklo, however, half of the heat network is in the hands of the civil cooperative Ecopower, resulting in a three-way coalition of public, private, and civil society resources.

PARK LIVING

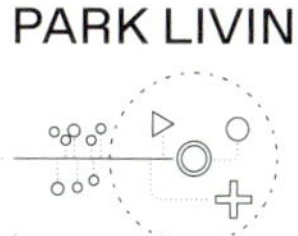

COALITION MODEL: COOPERATIVE DISTRICT ORGANIZATION
The district buffer tank functions on the scale of the district and is managed by the district energy cooperative, primarily consisting of residents of the district. In time, surplus heat could also be exported via the heat network to other districts.

2b. Residential Heat Models

LIVING ON A *WOONERF*

The residential heat model 'Living on a *Woonerf*' (home zone) is situated in streets where there is only residential traffic. The residential fabric here has a low to average density, as a result of which the heat network will not be constructed here. But there are opportunities to implement collective energy buffering of solar energy. Initially, this can be done in autonomous and small-scale clusters, which in time can be linked together to form a microgrid at the street level. The streets could be transformed into car-free, climate-adaptive residential areas where living *together* will play a central role. The right amount of small-scale densification makes this microgrid profitable and serves as an opportunity for creating a more diverse range of housing.

THE MICROGRID AS AN ALTERNATIVE TO THE HEAT GRID

Where a heat network is not profitable, microgrids are sometimes possible, especially in places with a local housing density that is isolated from the rest of the dense urban fabric. These microgrids can be constructed to connect and expand various small-scale energy buffers, for example with geothermal storage in the soil and collective day/night buffer vessels. In the Oostveld district, a densification of 14 percent around the *woonerven* is enough to make a microgrid profitable.

GREEN LIVING

The large deep plots with big green gardens have a very low housing density. Eeklo's heat network will never reach to here. The 'Green Living' residential heat model initiates a small-scale, collective connection that is self-sufficient locally. In a preselected area, owners are offered limited development rights for small-scale (kangaroo) residences in the green. Small-scale living increases density and, in combination with a main dwelling, provides solutions for energy and mobility. In exchange, the back of the plot is handed over and managed as a collective woodland garden. The new living turns inwards, towards the natural environment, creating a collective-private inner world with a richer meaning than the current street-garden logic.

OFF-GRID ENERGY SYSTEM

Seasonal and day/night buffering will be solved collectively and locally. This can be done by geothermal energy, collective heat pumps, and in the future also by phase-changing batteries (for instance on hydrogen). Heat sharing (and later also electricity sharing) is thus realized off-grid, so that this residential heat model functions completely autonomously.

LIVING ON A *WOONER*

SPATIO-ENERGETIC ADDED VALUE POLICY
Small-scale densification delivers concrete added value to the public space and is provided with a collective heat pump that connects to the microgrid.

CAR-FREE RESIDENTIAL AREAS
When the microgrid is constructed, the street will be redesigned with space for greenery, water infiltration and slow mobility. Cars are considered 'guests; parking is bundled, with priority for shared vehicles.

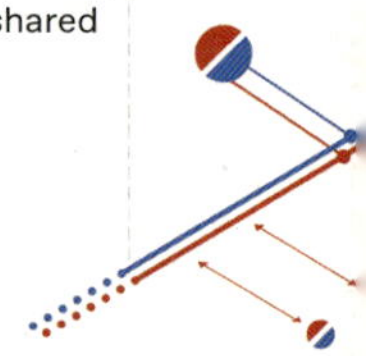

GREEN LIVING

DIVERSE TYPES OF HOUSING
The heat *woonerf* with its diversity of users not only flattens energetic peaks, it also stimulates lifelong housing in one and the same location, and thus more social cohesion.

STIMULATING INSULATION WITH SPECIAL RIGHTS
Individual expansion possibilities (such as building an extra floor) in exchange for ambitious insulation of the building shell.

COLLECTIVELY MANAGED INNER AREA
By bringing the back gardens under collective management, a wooded inner area is created that can expand the ecological value of the neigborhood.

SHARING ENERGY AND MOBILITY
The collective energy supply and associated management can be linked to the use and management of electric shared-use cars. The car batteries can buffer solar energy and, if necessary, redistribute it.

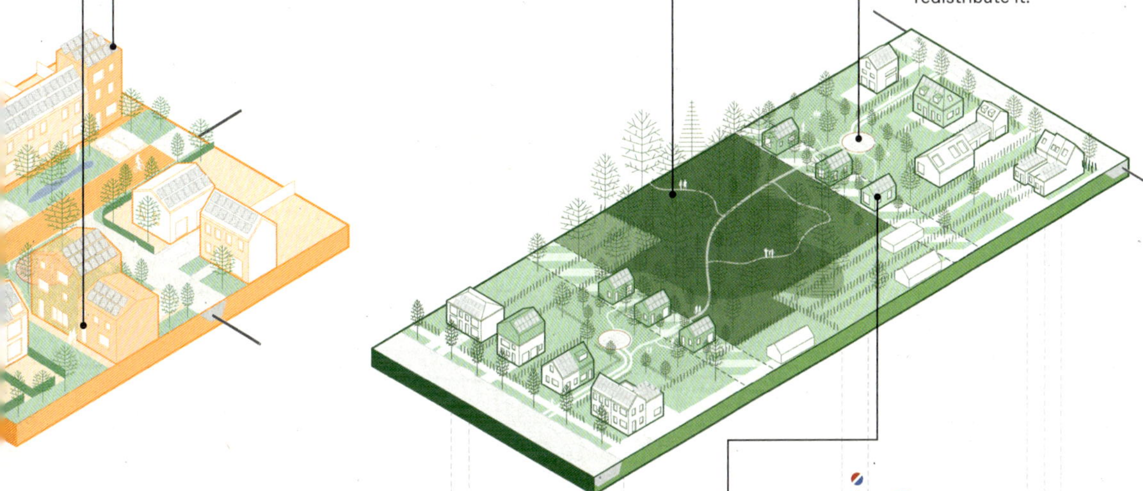

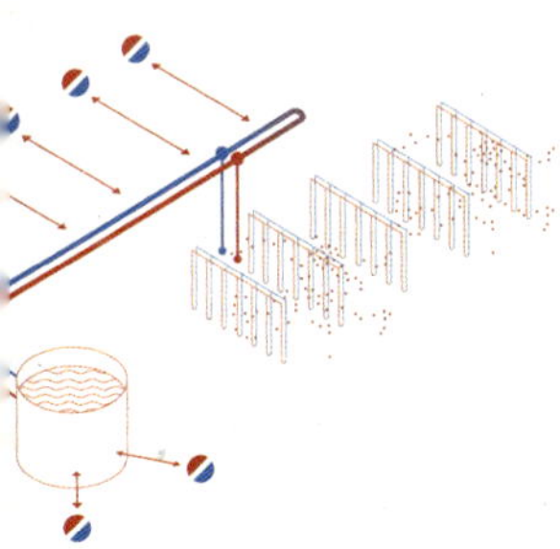

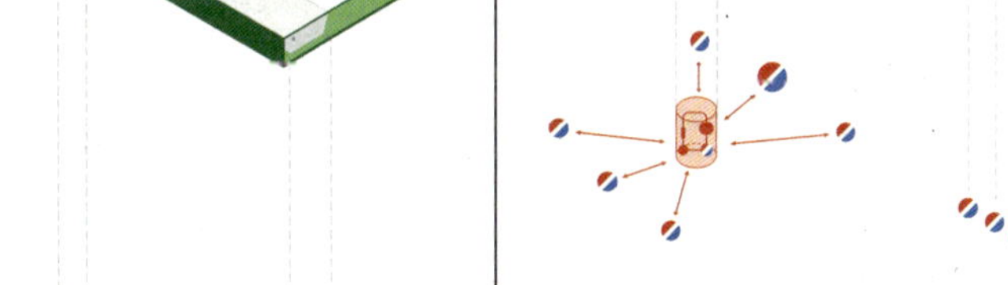

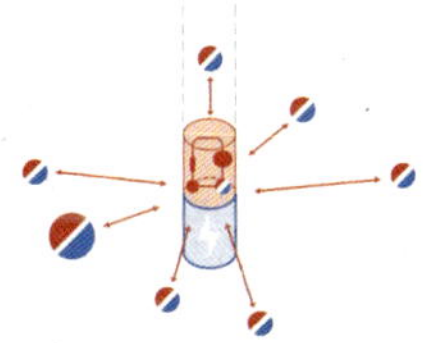

(KANGAROO) LIVING ON THE INNER AREA
Giving limited building rights to the inner area in exchange for ecological backyard management promotes a new type of care housing in which energy is shared. This form of housing creates a greater connection among residents and with the natural interior area.

LIVING ON A *WOONERF*

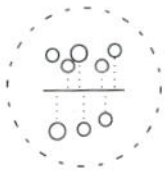

COALITION MODEL: AUTONOMOUS, OPEN COOPERATIVES
These small-scale clusters that, over time, can grow into microgrids at the street level and possibly even connect to the heat network in the long term, are created by collaborations of local residents.

GREEN LIVING

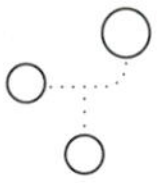

COALITION MODEL: AUTONOMOUS, CLOSED COOPERATIVES
These small-scale clusters are created by setting up local collaborations among residents. They function independently of other systems and are not meant to grow over time.

3. Dancing at the Fast Pace of Technology and the Slower Pace of Urban Development

The energy sector is in a constant state of flux, but approaching it from the perspective of urban development provides good tools to explore long-term innovations in this sector. For example, the district buffer tank may not be profitable from an energy perspective at the moment, but from an urban development perspective it will be valuable in the future. After all, it will provide added value for the city and its inhabitants, such as the

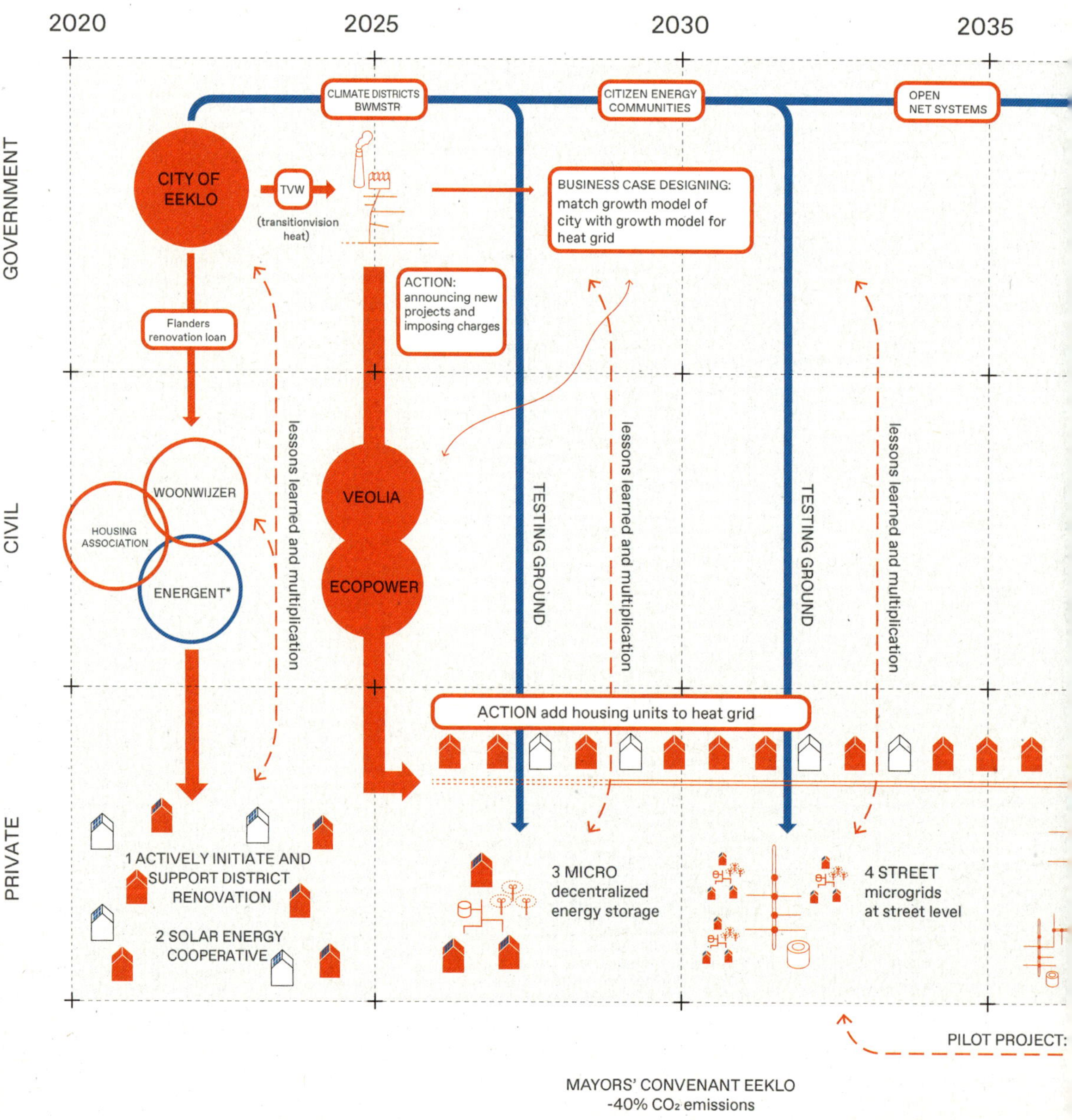

collective production of energy at the district level, diversity of housing types, and climate resilience. The spatial approach can therefore put other values than profitability and sustainability on the energy agenda.

The city of Eeklo is currently in the process of constructing a heat network. The city is doing this by making the public domain available, under well-defined conditions, to the consortium Warmtenet Eeklo, a collaboration between the local government, private developer Veolia and civic cooperative Ecopower. Thanks to the collaborative structure, residents can eventually become co-owners of the project. In the future, there will be a need for new, complementary projects that will contribute to Eeklo's progressive energy vision, in which local production of renewable energy and direct citizen participation remain crucial conditions.

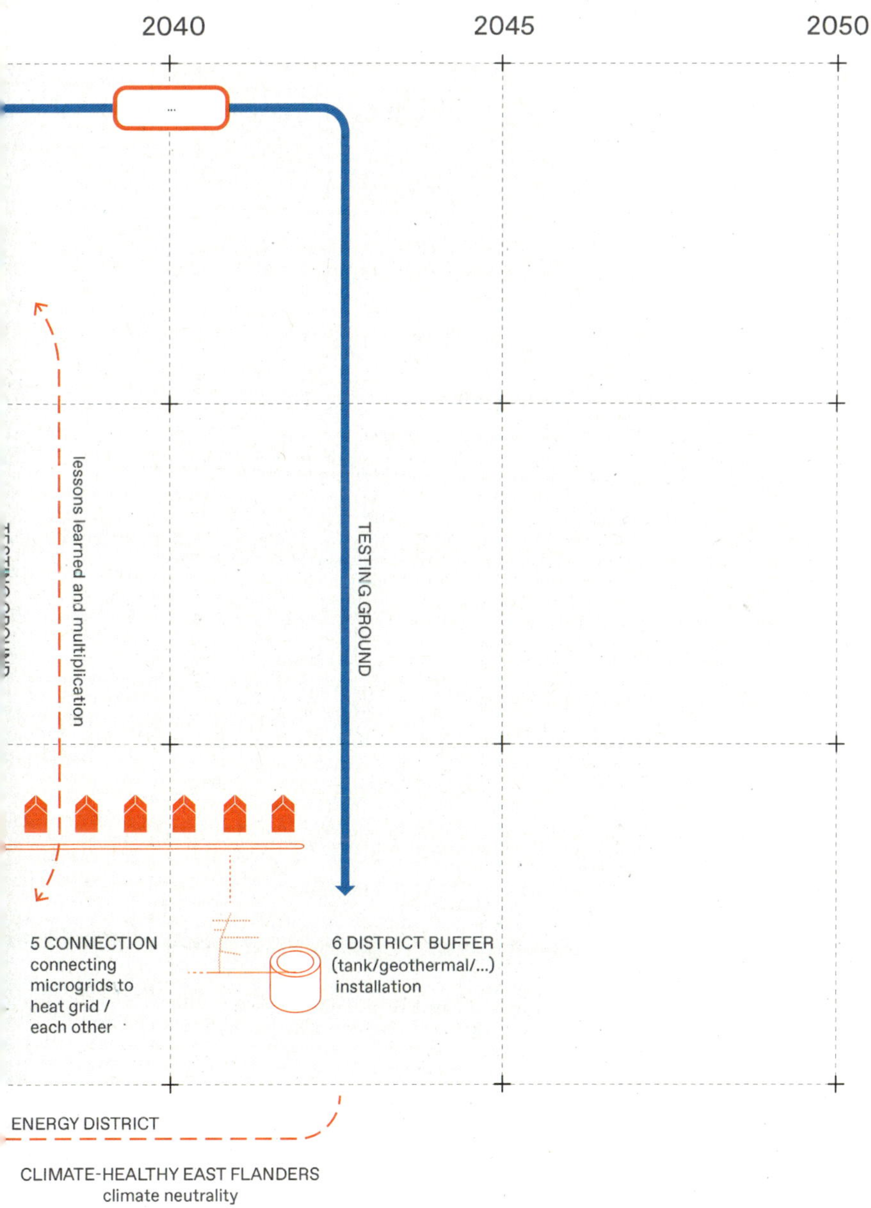

Most likely, there is not a single solution that can address all of the energy issues in the city, but there is an opportunity to test new systems and build infrastructure to which new innovations and energy systems can connect. The multiplier principle is important here: How can we design the city in such a way that both previous large-scale solutions and the many small solutions can connect to new urban patterns and energy systems? And who is to play which part? This timeline outlines a possible roadmap.

BOSPOLDER-TUSSENDIJKEN
THE DISTRICT: NEW PLAYERS, NEW SCENARIO

BOSPOLDER-TUSSENDIJKEN: VULNERABLE AND RESILIENT
KWETSBAAR EN WEERBAAR

ROTTERDAM: AMBITIONS AND AGREEMENTS

With the coalition agreement *New Energy for Rotterdam* and the *Council Agreement on Energy Transition*, the Rotterdam city council endorsed the Paris climate objectives in 2018. The city's premise was that the energy transition must be and remain feasible and affordable for all Rotterdammers. Therefore, solutions with the lowest social costs were sought. At the same time, taking advantage of the opportunities that the transition offers for economic development, employment, and improving the living environment was imperative. From a spatial perspective, the City of Rotterdam considers the development of an integral design approach that enables the energy transition and the increasing densification of the city, including the pursuit of a circular urban economy, to be its most important strategic challenge. In the *Rotterdam Climate Agreement*, for example, targets have been formulated for an integrated approach to reducing CO_2 emissions throughout the city.

In order to obtain social support for these ambitions, intensive cooperation with residents, social organizations and businesses in the city took place. At five climate tables and during more than 50 meetings, over 100 businesses and organizations and 1,000 Rotterdammers worked on the *Rotterdam Climate Agreement*. In almost 50 climate deals, concrete measures were proposed to achieve the ambition of reducing CO_2 emissions by 49 percent by 2030.

Natural Gas-Free Districts

Making the city gas-free is one of the most important tasks the city council has set itself. To realize its energy strategy, the municipality has therefore calculated the cheapest alternative to natural gas for each district. An inventory has also been made of the potential energy sources that will eventually be available to Rotterdam. Subsequently, an area-wide approach was started in five districts to disconnect them from natural gas. This approach also looked at opportunities to tackle other issues, such as climate adaptation and employment. These five districts are testing grounds for a city-wide approach. One of those five is Bospolder-Tussendijken.

Hence, the municipal programs and projects form the institutional context within which the Local Energy Action Plan (LEAP) for the Bospolder-Tussendijken district, which the IABR–Atelier Rotterdam III designed, has to be put into practice step by step in cooperation with local social initiatives.

←
Bospolder-Tussendijken:
vulnerable *and* resilient
RECLAIMING THE COMMONS
photo: Aad Hoogendoorn

BOSPOLDER-TUSSEN-DIJKEN: VULNERABLE *AND* RESILIENT

If residents of a district want to become co-owners of the energy transition, they have to bring something to the table. What does a district, in this case Bospolder-Tussendijken, have to offer?

Bospolder-Tussendijken, also known as BoTu, is one of the poorest districts in the Netherlands, a vulnerable area with a lot of poverty, inhabitants with serious debts, and high unemployment. But it's also a resilient neighborhood, self-confident and culturally diverse, with strong formal and informal networks. A place where people help each other and are already taking joint initiatives when it comes to issues such as welfare, greenery management, and the energy transition.

Using these data as a starting point, the IABR–Atelier Rotterdam III first researched the social and spatio-energetic building blocks needed for a future, truly resilient BoTu.

Research into the spatio-energetic building blocks made it clear what the specific energy challenge in BoTu actually is. How much energy is used? How much less energy will be needed after the houses are modified? How much renewable energy can be generated in the district itself? Which spatial interventions will help? How much energy will still be needed and where will it come from? An investigation into the choices that still need to be made, and the possible returns.

An anthropological exploration by the Atelier of the known and unknown, often invisible social networks in BoTu provided insight into the potential power of residents. To what extent can and do they want to be co-producers of their living environment and take responsibility for the transition? These are the socio-civic building blocks needed to link the energy transition to other, more integral local challenges, such as the sustainable improvement of quality of life and the living environment.

The first phase of the research showed that Bospolder-Tussendijken can be seen as a latent commons, an active and resilient district that has both the potential and ambition to actually take steps, as a community, towards a more sustainable future.

SOCIAL INITIATIVES IN BOTU

BOUWKEET

Bouwkeet provides free programs, especially for children between 10 and 15 years of age. The young participants learn hard skills (such as woodwork, sewing, metalwork, coding, and working with clay) to empower them and broaden their worldview. The soft skills they learn relate to creativity, collaboration, problem solving and entrepreneurship. The products the participants make are of high quality and are always practical. Bouwkeet is a place where local residents can come to make things, to meet, and to learn from each other. During the Open Workshop, local residents are allowed to use the machines and tools in exchange for a return service, for example by helping out at the workshop, as a voluntary supervisor or on other activities.

BOSPOLDER-TUSSENDIJKEN IN ROTTERDAM

14.490	RESIDENTS
6.629	DWELLINGS
2.619	JOBS

source: Wijkprofiel Rotterdam

photo: Marlissa Hilkmann

ATELIER DE KLEINE VIS

De Kleine Vis is an artist's studio that provides space for children and adults to experience art and culture, by getting to work themselves. The initiative aims to strengthen, facilitate and develop the creative and artistic capacities of children and adults. The activities of De Kleine Vis are accessible to everyone. Visitors to the studio are representative of the great cultural diversity that determines the DNA of the Delfshaven district. Children are mainly from migrant and refugee families that do not have sufficient resources to actively participate in art and culture. For adults, the emphasis is on being creative and not only discovering their own opportunities to make art, but also daring to take them further.

photo: Juan Heinsohn Huala

COOL DOWN CITY

Cool Down City encourages Rotterdammers to cool their city with trees. Cool Down City collects trees and seedlings that would otherwise be disposed of as green waste and distributes them to residents free of charge. In addition, projects and educational programs stimulate this form of green sub-economy. The ambition is to triple the number of trees in Rotterdam. Cool Down City achieves this ambition by realizing a public Rotterdam Tree Greenhouse, organizing 'Free Tree Giveaway Events' and using the 'Free Tree Exchange on Wheels' to bring tree awareness to people.

photo: Jerry Lampen

DE VERBINDINGSKAMER

De Verbindingskamer promotes social cohesion and solidarity in vulnerable neighborhoods by building up mutual trust and relationships with residents in an informal way. Its main activity is the organization of accessible meetings between residents, to which professionals are also invited. De Verbindingskamer works with residents to find an appropriate form of participation in the district, for example by linking a resident to the right party if he or she needs support or care. De Verbindingskamer does not have its own premises, but makes use of existing locations in the district, specifically the Schans-Watergeus area in Bospolder-Tussendijken. It works with partners such as the City of Rotterdam, the district police team, housing corporations, district nurses, the district team, Vraagwijzer and social work.

FASIGA BRIHANU
INITIATOR VLUCHTELINGEN VOOR VLUCHTELINGEN
Responsibility is accepting that you are the cause of and the solution to the matter.

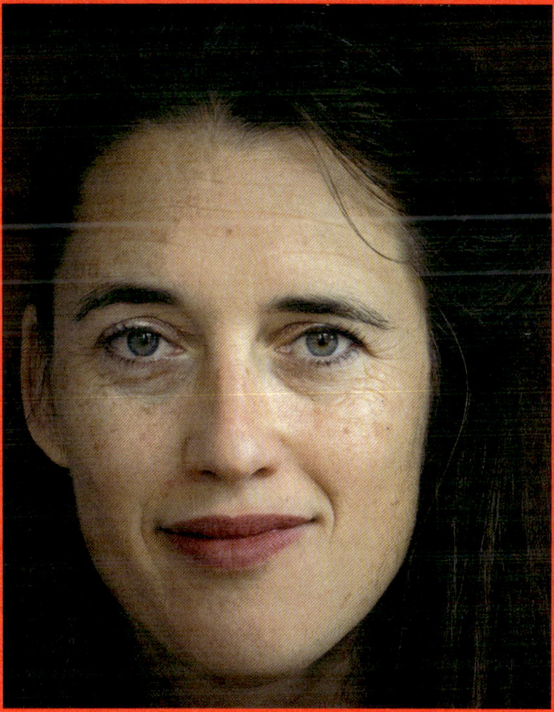

THAMAR KEMPERMAN
THEATER MAKER
As a theater maker, I enter into a conversation in the district about the energy challenges we're currently facing, because awareness is the first step towards change.

WILLEM BEEKHUIZEN
ENERGY-SOCIAL WORKER
It's more than just replacing a gas tap with a power outlet, the energy transition can also create jobs and give people energy.

HOURIA TOURICH
LANGUAGE-ENERGY COACH
As a language-energy coach, I want to make people enthusiastic about renewable energy, so that everyone can join in.

SILA SOEBDHAN
CHAIRPERSON HUURDERSRAAD WEST
I want to help make life a little easier for everyone. We can only hope to accomplish this if we join forces.

NICO VAN SPLUNTER
DISTRICT CHAPLAIN / COORDINATOR CHARITY SHOP YESS!
The greater the diversity of the group, the greater the chance of creative solutions.

ZICO LOPES
ARCHITECT
Architecture and urban design are about people. I see it as an important task of architects and policymakers to make sure that this is not overlooked during the transformation of vulnerable districts.

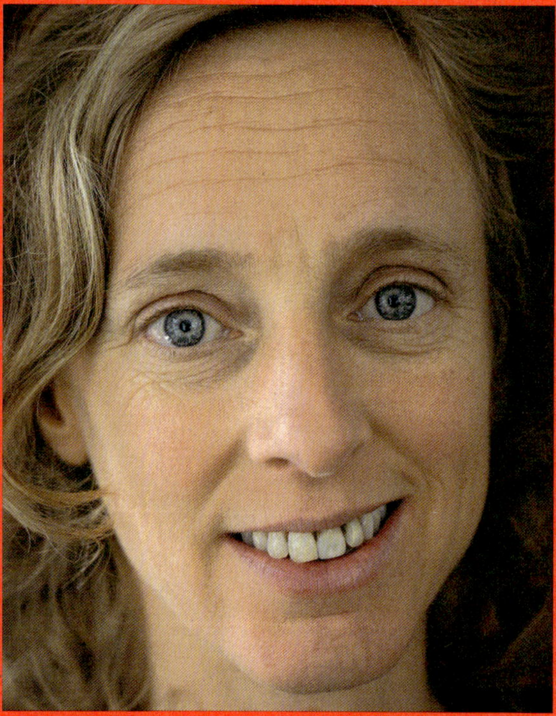

MARLIES BIELDERMAN
DESIGNER / INITIATOR BUURTMAKERS WEST
I want my child to grow up in a district that is pleasant to live in and in which people can develop. That's why I want to contribute to a living environment where people can get to know each other and can live in a healthy way.

CREATIEF BEHEER

Creatief Beheer is working on a new, integral and connecting practice in the public space, consisting of the daily execution of maintenance (clean and green) in a neighborhood, by professionals, volunteers, and residents. The focus is on ecological and social value, both in terms of urban nature and the participants. This approach, christened *urban medicine*, has been developed in practice in numerous projects in Rotterdam's working-class neighborhoods (2002–present). In addition to the development of these projects in Rotterdam, Creatief Beheer advises municipalities and businesses on how to make the outdoor space greener, healthier and cozier.

photo: Iraklis Romanopoulos–IRIX Architects

CIRKEL SOCIAAL ONDERNEMER

Cirkel Sociaal Ondernemer is a sociocultural platform that stimulates encounter at the district level in Delfshaven. Cirkel works with local residents of all ages: children, senior citizens, active residents, (young) artists, thinkers and searching souls in a crossover with isolated, lonely, silenced groups. Cirkel designs community art projects to generate awareness on a social, cultural, environmental and personal level. During the activities all kinds of art (theater, music, poetry, philosophy, visual arts) are used to promote dialogue, reflection, and encounter. Cirkel works from universal examples to meet all backgrounds, cultures or beliefs of people.

photo: Ximena Dávalos

DELFSHAVEN COÖPERATIE

Delfshaven Coöperatie is a partnership of involved residents, local initiatives, and institutional partners. Together they work on the long-term value development of the neighborhood. Delfshaven Coöperatie facilitates, initiates and combines residents' initiatives and social entrepreneurship through community building, social area development, local welfare, energy transition, and public real estate. To jointly increase the socioeconomic resilience of the district, the cooperative is actively involved in the core group of the BOTU2028 program, and with residents and district initiatives, the Rotterdam Urban Development Department, housing association Havensteder, Rabobank, 'stadsmarinier' (community support officer) of Bospolder-Tussendijken, and Era Contour.

photo: Robbert de Vrieze

DE GROENE CONNECTIE

Together with Delfshaven's green neighborhood initiatives, the team strives to strengthen the physical, social, and ecological connections in the area. To improve the quality and accessibility of urban green space and promote social cohesion, De Groene Connectie combines opportunities in urban development (such as the energy transition, new construction, or new infrastructure) by influencing urban planning processes, helping to launch new initiatives, and exchanging knowledge, experience and volunteers. De Groene Connectie emphatically establishes the relationship between wellbeing, health, and the physical environment by working together with general practitioners, welfare organizations and other social partners. The physical backbone of De Groene Connectie is an 8-km-long green ribbon, which consists of Heemraadssingel, Spoortuin, Essenburgpark, Spoordijk Spangen, Dakpark, Schie-oevers, and Coolhavenpark.

photo: Philip Kuypers

HET TAALBEDRIJF

Language is an important communication tool. Het Taalbedrijf trains women who are not native Dutch speakers to become language and energy coaches. An important goal is to promote the integration of isolated residents and contribute to their wellbeing by offering help, support and Dutch language education. The language and energy coaches contact residents of Bospolder-Tussendijken who do not have a good command of Dutch. The main aim is to provide the residents with information about energy consumption and the energy transition. Het Taalbedrijf prefers to collaborate with other parties in Bospolder-Tussendijken that are also addressing the themes of energy transition, language and social support.

photo: Klaske van Veen and Marieke Grund

HUIS VAN DE TOEKOMST

The Human Power Plant, a team of artists, community workers and local residents based in the Huis van de Toekomst, works on the imagination of the future of Bospolder-Tussendijken after the energy transition. What should this future to look like? There's one fundamental rule for this future scenario: you are your own source of energy. By working together you can save energy. Workshops with children and interviews with senior citizens, entrepreneurs, neighbors, and passers-by are the basis for a design process. Prototypes are used to test what Bospolder-Tussendijken could become with the help of manpower. The results were made accessible to the public in 2021 in collaboration with Museum Boijmans Van Beuningen.

image: Golnar Abbasi and Arvand Pourabbasi

PARK 1943

In Park 1943, various activities and events are organized by the Parkraad (for instance the opening of the sports field and water taps), or in cooperation with De Buitenboel/Het Zelfregiehuis, by local residents with financial support from the Parkraad, and by external parties (such as Besouk). The events are free, accessible and open to everyone. In recent years, the focus has mainly been on music, food, dance, theatre, and conviviality, but in the future the themes of sustainability, recycling, and energy transition will also be added to these.

HOUSEHOLDS RECEIVING WELFARE BENEFITS
percentage receiving welfare benefits (WWB)

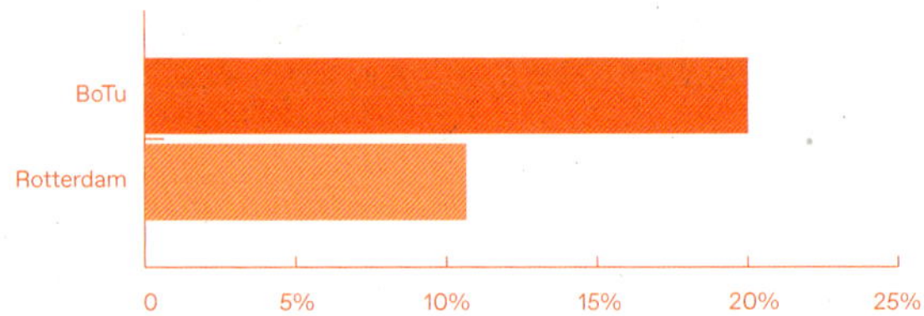

source: CBS–OBI

MENEER VAN HOUTEN, PAMEIJER

Meneer van Houten, part of the Pameijer foundation, is a sustainable furniture-making and apprenticeship workplace for people who want to (re)join the workforce and need a lot of support on a daily basis. Young people and adults are given the opportunity to gain professional experience under the guidance of apprentice coaches, with the aim of moving on to paid jobs or supported employment. Employees are taught to deal with obstacles, strengthen their own skills and talents, and are encouraged to help others. All in an imaginative way: by working together, not giving up and creating opportunities. Friends, family, neighbors, and volunteers are involved. Support is always as brief, minimal and local as possible. The goal is for people to become stronger and less dependent, step by step.

photo: Remar van Opstal

BUILDING DENSITY

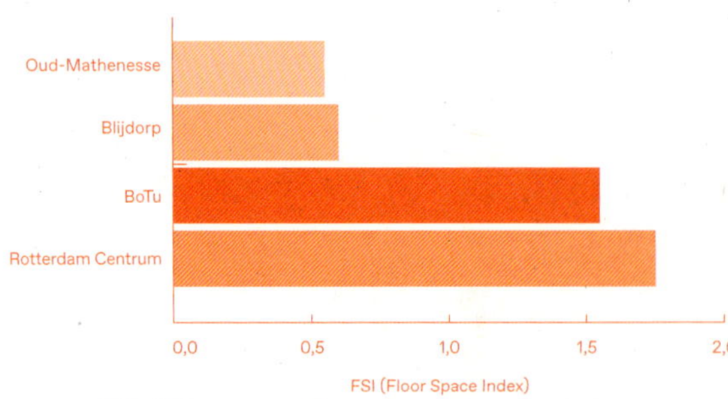

source: CBS–OBI

MAIKE DASSEN
OWNER AN-DIJVIE NATUURVOEDING
We need to pay more attention to keeping this district clean and well-maintained. If residents take the initiative more often and keep an eye on each other and their surroundings, the district will automatically become safer.

ROBBERT DE VRIEZE
CHAIRPERSON DELFSHAVEN ENERGIE COÖPERATIE
Sowing local energy initiatives reaps awareness, social innovation, ownership, and community building. That's why I make sure that profit and value stay in the district.

MALIQUE MOHAMUD
FOUNDER AND ARTISTIC LEADER THE NITESHOP
We visualize the knowledge and culture that invisibly develops in the district. This is how we give form to the maturing of this super-diverse city.

FEMKE GIELSTRA
OWNER MAAK
Good coffee and delicious cake connect people. I'm proud of that, because that's how I, as an entrepreneur, contribute to a resilient district.

WIJKCOLLECTIE BOSPOLDER-TUSSENDIJKEN, MUSEUM ROTTERDAM

Together with local residents, Museum Rotterdam collects today's heritage and the stories that go with it, resulting in an active 'Wijkcollectie' (district collection). In this way everyone who wants to devote themselves to the district can become connected to its new heritage. The collection shows that culture contributes to the development of an area. The stories about the daily life of the residents of Bospolder-Tussendijken give other people ideas, stimulate them to think and are often the starting point for something new. The stories are told in four 'Verhalencafés' (story cafés) each year and all the subjects, people, and communities that are discussed become part of the Wijkcollectie.

photo: Florian Braakman

STICHTING RIJNMOND MULTICULTUREEL CENTRUM (RMC)

The Stichting Rijnmond Multicultureel Centrum is a non-profit organization run by volunteers. It is an independent organization that offers activities such as homework tutoring, Koranic tutoring and adult literacy classes. It also hosts theme evenings in an attempt to break the isolation and loneliness of senior citizens. Information is provided about what is going on in society and there is a regular shared breakfast for local families.

photo: RMC

POPULATION BY AGE GROUPS

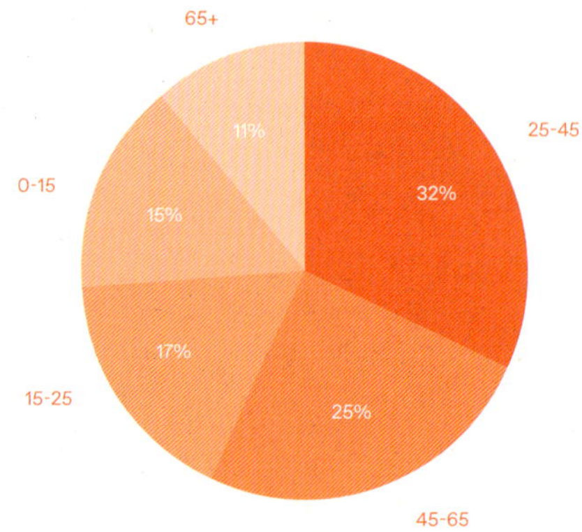

source: CBS–OBI

LSA SCHAKELWIJKEN

The LSA is a nationwide network of resident associations, independent community centers, neighborhood cooperatives, and 'BewonersBedrijven' (Community Enterprises). They share knowledge and skills, with each other and with others, to promote the position of active residents vis-à-vis the (local) government. Over the next few years, the LSA will support ten resident associations, including a group in Bospolder-Tussendijken, in their role in relation to the district's heating transition. The aim is to form a community with experience and knowledge about the position and strength of resident associations in the energy transition.

photo: Delfshaven Energie Coöperatie

EMPLOYED RESIDENTS
percentage of potential labor force (aged 15-75)

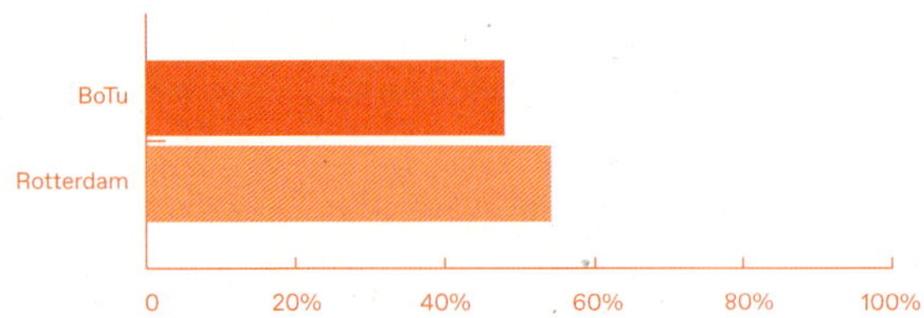

source: CBS - OBI

WILMA VAN DER WILT
INITIATOR ENVIRONMENTAL COACHING COURSE
I'm committed to the energy transition because it's necessary and to keep spirits high. And because it's fun!

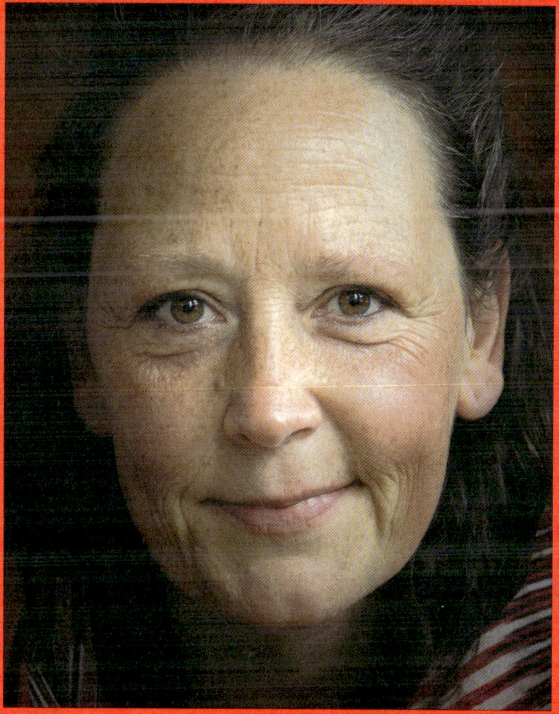

JULIA HEVEMEYER
DIRECTOR AND CO-FOUNDER OF DELFSHAVEN ENERGIE COÖPERATIE, BLIJSTROOM
Making sustainable and local energy available to and affordable for all Rotterdammers, that's my goal!

MOENNE G.S. VAN LA PARRA
SOLAR PANEL INSTALLER IN TRAINING WIJKENERGIEWERKT
Green is the future, grab it, seize it, it is yours: Go Green!

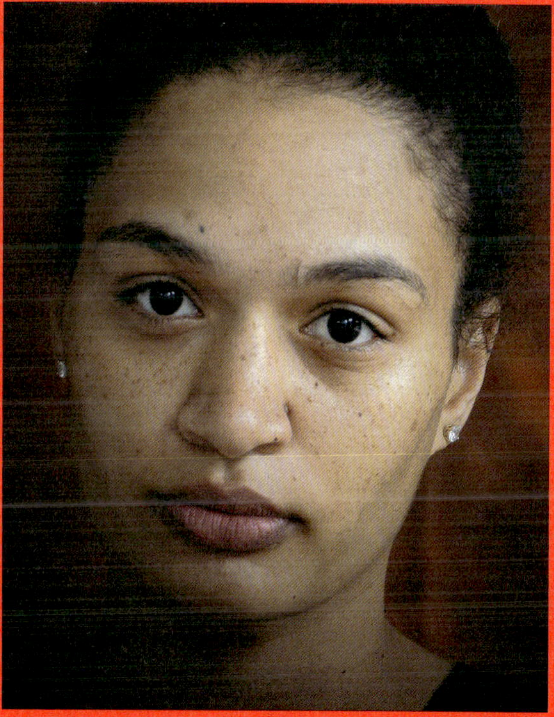

SHAAR BENDANON
SOLAR PANEL INSTALLER IN TRAINING WIJKENERGIEWERKT
Affordable energy for everyone in the district, that's what I want to contribute to.

CAROLINA CASTRO
CO-FOUNDER AND PROJECT LEADER VEERKRACHTIGE GEMEENSCHAP FOUNDATION
The energy of the community is indispensable for the realization of a successful and socially inclusive energy transition. We desperately need the minds, hearts and hands of residents, officials, and initiators.

RINI BIEMANS
CO-FOUNDER CREATIEF BEHEER / 'CITY DOCTOR'
Urban nature heals and teaches, free of charge. I work on an integrated maintenance practice that is good for both residents and urban nature: green, healthy, and sociable!

MELVA ROSARIA
ACTIVE RESIDENT, INVOLVED IN SCHOON & MOOI BOTU
How wonderful is it, to be part of a sustainable community? By combining our strengths, talents and inspiration to realize a healthy, clean and green living environment, we can achieve much more.

TONNY VAN SOMMEREN
INITIATOR DE BUITENBOEL AND ZELFREGIEHUIS
We widen the range of experiences available to women – and increasingly, to men. Because outside, that's where we meet!

ROTTERDAMSE MUNT

Open your senses and marvel at the beauty, smells and flavors of the edible urban nature. An edible oasis, in the middle of the city. Rotterdamse Munt works together with fellow city dwellers to create exciting picking gardens where the youth can discover the magic of plants, where organizations can host wholesome team days, and where Rotterdammers can find inspiration to create their own green, healthy spot while enjoying peace and liveliness in the middle of the city. The gardens are open to the public and include a terrace and a plant stall. Visitors can harvest their own food and there are various activities, such as workshops, tastings, music and educational programs for the 1,500 primary school-age children growing up in the neighborhoods around the garden. In addition, bespoke picking gardens are designed for all kinds of urban stakeholders, usually businesses.

photo: Edita

STICHTING SCHIEZICHT

The kitchen as a social hub, just like at a party at home: that's the Kadekantine at Schiezicht. With some tried and tested recipes: 'Schaften aan de Schie' (dinner parties), Cooking with Kids and Specials (brunches during holidays and other special moments, including NL Doet, King's Day and Neigbors' Day), and some new ones, like Cooking Club Kadekantine, Food and Creativity, Low-Cost Plant-Based and Healthy Cooking, and 'Horen-Zien-Schransen' (a program around food and art). It's precisely because of this abundance of activities that so many different people gather 'at the table' in the Kadekantine. Cooking and/or eating together is a great way to engage local residents in conversation on a variety of subjects. Significant outcomes are: mutual contacts between residents, greater involvement in what's going on in the neighborhood, interests and opportunities to follow, and increasing cooperation with other organizations in Delfshaven.

AGE OF BUILDING STOCK

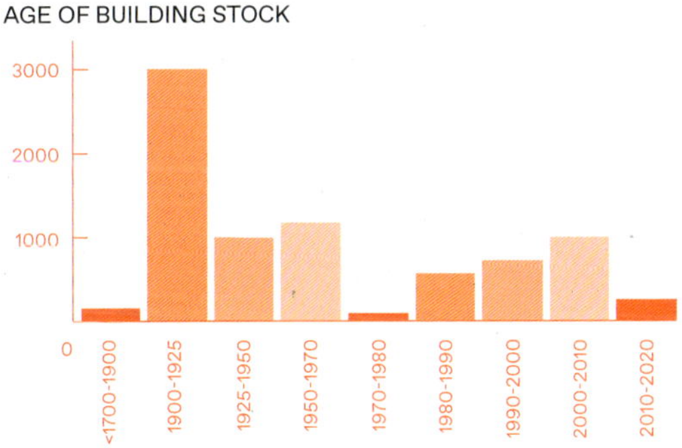

source: BAG–OBI

WIJKENERGIEWERKT

WijkEnergieWerkt wants renewable energy for everyone in the district and to make the energy transition inclusive, so that everybody benefits from it in different ways. It trains local residents to work at the WijkEnergieWerkt installation company. These employees help their neighbors realize renewable energy systems in their homes and at the same time start the conversation about energy, energy conservation and the current offer of WijkEnergie-Werkt (1) door-to-door sustainability in combination with a discussion about energy and savings for awareness and insight; (2) the installation of solar panels; (3) the installation of floor insulation; (4) the work that has to be done inside dwellings on the construction of a heat network. By linking sustainability and the energy transition to local education and employment, WijkEnergieWerkt wants to positively impact various Sustainable Development Goals.

POPULATION BY MIGRATION BACKGROUND

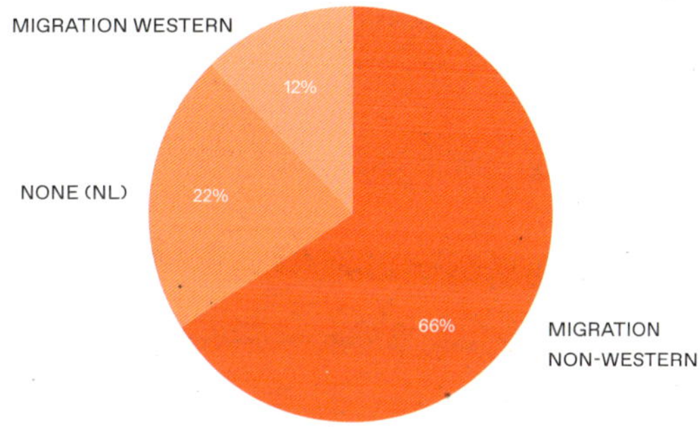

source: BRP–OBI

WMO RADAR

WMO Radar provides social management, supervises the Huizen van de Wijk and programs all kinds of activities for and by residents, in cooperation with network partners in Delfshaven. These include activities for senior citizens and vulnerable people, children and youths: language development, encounter, self-development, recreation, and assistance and services. WMO also offers residents space to organize their own activities and make use of the facilities of the Huizen van de Wijk.

photo: Ivo Montijn

WERKGROEP ENERGIE-TRANSITIE CO_2, HUURDERSRAAD WEST

Huurdersraad West is an association that aims to represent the interests of tenants, co-tenants and residents of houses owned by housing corporation Havensteder in Bospolder-Tussendijken. It maintains the relationship between the residents and the employees of Havensteder, in accordance with the laws on tenant participation. The working group Energietransitie CO_2 is specifically concerned with providing (legal) advice to the housing corporation on the energy transition and achieving gas-free homes. Huurdersraad West provides advice on, among other things, affordability, comfort, future-proofing and alternatives.

ENERGIE PERFORMANCE BOTU, THEATER FORMAAT

Where is the energy in Bospolder-Tussendijken? What will the district look like in 2050 if we live energy-healthy lives? On the basis of these questions, Theater Formaat conducts a theatrical investigation with residents of Bospolder-Tussendijken and creates a theatre performance that shows the position of residents today, the existing strengths and the changes that are necessary to live in an energy-efficient way. Workshops on energy are held at various locations in Bospolder-Tussendijken and people are invited to take part in rehearsals of the theater performances. As part of these performances, Theater Formaat talks to residents and professionals, emphatically seeking the connection between the energy challenge and the district's social issues.

HOME OWNERSHIP

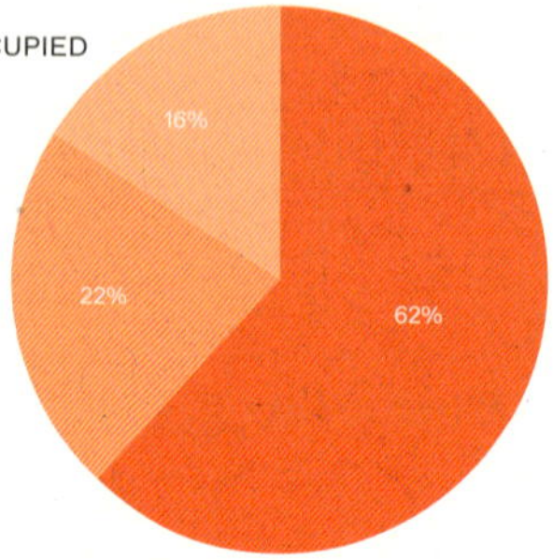

source: BAG–OBI

photo: Theater Formaat

STICHTING VOOR CULTUUR EN PARTICIPATIE (CCPR)

The Centrum voor Cultuur en Participatie is a foundation that focuses on the Moroccan community and aims to introduce people to Moroccan culture. This is achieved by organizing activities such as interreligious gatherings, workshops, information, lectures, and iftars. The foundation also offers, for example, weekly homework tutoring and language lessons. The foundation is a non-profit organization and tries to achieve its goals through activities in the fields of education, training, welfare, cultural participation and religion. It provides solicited and unsolicited advice in relevant areas within the scope of the foundation.

photo: CCPR

ZELFREGIEHUIS DELFSHAVEN

As environmental coaches, Tonny van Someren and Wilma van der Wilt organize as many activities as they possibly can about the environment and creating sustainable personal living conditions. Other activities include: (1) a permanent knitting group: grandmas knit for a good cause, while discussing the problems of ageing; (2) a sewing workshop: in the context of recycling and sales, the participants produce articles including aprons made of old jeans and textile bread bags and shopping bags of old T-shirts; (3) in collaboration with De Buitenboel, participants cook healthy meals and designate window sills for plant cultivation to help the neighborhood to become greener; (4) De Roze Brigade: this group focuses on keeping the outdoor area clean.

photo: Zelfregiehuis Delfshaven

DAKPARK SCHOOL

The public elementary school Dakpark is a small primary school that falls under the school group of Stichting BOOR. In addition to regular education, it is also an eco-school with an emphasis on green thinking, sustainability, a healthy lifestyle, and attention to citizenship. For example, the school is participating in the construction of a collective solar roof in collaboration with the Delfshaven Energie Coöperatie, Blijstroom, Stichting BOOR, the City of Rotterdam, and WijkEnergieWerkt. The solar panels on the roof of the school will provide electricity to some 120 families. In addition, the school is investigating ways to tackle the regular flooding of its low-lying inner courtyard and ways to collect or reuse rainwater for a new vegetable garden or for flushing its toilets.

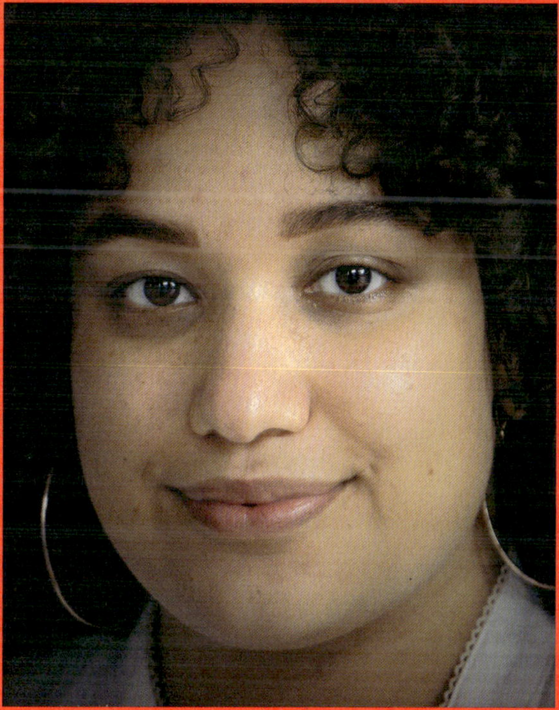

FATIMA DE JONGE
LANGUAGE-ENERGY COACH
Why I'm committed to the environment? Because a beautiful tomorrow is not guaranteed.

MICHAEL BOEVEE
SOLAR PANEL INSTALLER WIJKENERGIEWERKT
We humans have already polluted the Earth enough. It's time for us to help it. And we can't do that alone.

ANGELA RENFURM
CHAIRPERSON PARKRAAD 1943 AND RECEPTIONIST AT BOUWKEET
To get energy, you have to give energy. To others, to the neighborhood: working together for a better future. Then, hopefully, the energy transition will offer a solution for everyone, regardless of their living conditions.

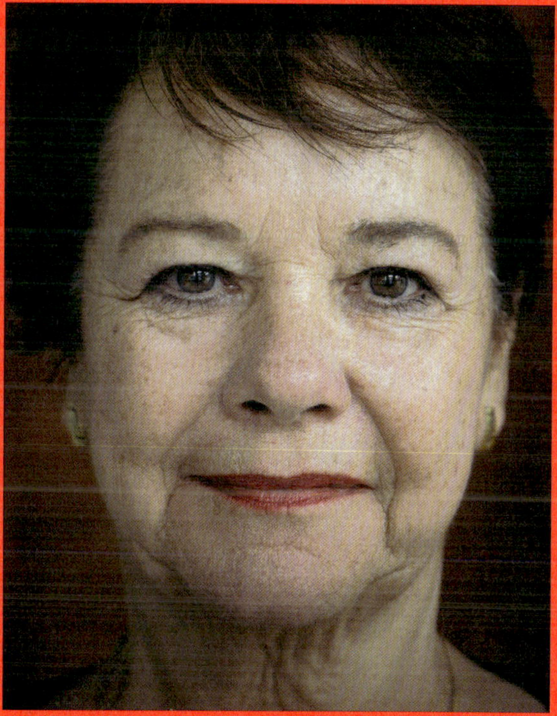

MIRJAM KROON
ENVIRONMENTAL COACH
Energy transition because our nature is worth it and needs our care now!

STICHTING DE VEERKRACHTIGE GEMEENSCHAP

De Veerkrachtige Gemeenschap, 'investigators of quality of life and society,' pays attention to the family as a community that can be very complex. The family can be a source of resilience, but also of suffering and pain, or a mixture of both. De Veerkrachtige Gemeenschap therefore works to raise parents' awareness of issues such as inclusion and empowerment with an emphasis on talent and strength, participation, and processes of co-creation of knowledge.

photo: Ximena Dávalos

DELFSHAVEN ENERGIE COÖPERATIE

The Delfshaven Energie Coöperatie wants to make renewable energy accessible to all residents of Delfshaven, by generating sustainable electricity in the district together with the residents, but also by linking up with and seeking added value in energy saving, work and other developments in the area. Preparations are currently being made to install 880 solar panels on the roofs of primary schools Dakpark (Bospolder) and De Boog (Schiemond). The special feature of these two collective solar roofs is that the installation will be pre-financed by Bank Nederlandse Gemeenten (BNG) according to the 'Op Rozen' model. According to this system, the panels are rented instead of purchased, which means that people who do not have a few hundred euros to spend can still have access to local sustainable electricity. Anyone can become a co-owner of the collaboration for a mere ten euros per solar panel.

photo: Robbert de Vrieze

AVERAGE INCOME PER RESIDENT

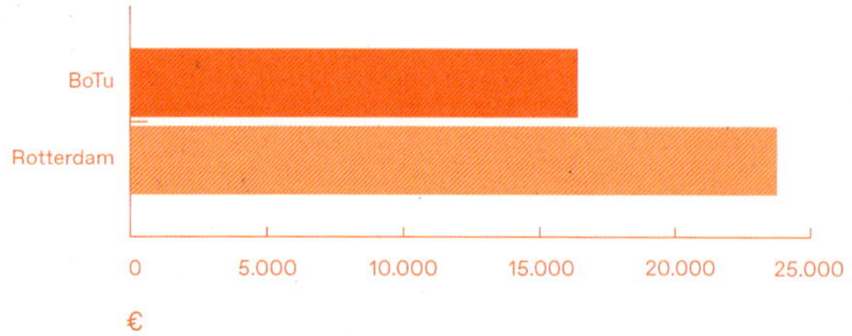

source: CBS

INTERCULTURELE STICHTING SALAAM (ISSALAAM)

Together with VluchtelingenWerk Nederland, ISSALAAM helps newcomers in the city with administrative matters, doctor's appointments, or interpreting services, among other things. ISSALAAM also runs an Islamic food bank that, during the corona pandemic, provided 400 families with a food package twice a month. In addition, with the winter homeless project, the organization provides warm meals to about 50 homeless people every Saturday evening from November to March. ISSALAAM is also active in four prisons, where it supports the imam and his work and with after-care following the release of detainees.

photo: Sanne Donders

POPULATION DENSITY PER KM^2

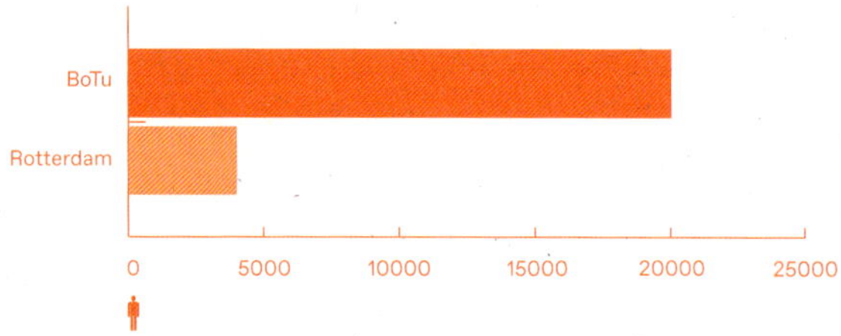

source: allcijfers.nl

portrait photos: Ximena Dávalos

SÁNDOR CSENKI
PROJECT COORDINATOR WIJKENERGIEWERKT, BOTU12
The energy transition has to be a social transition, too. An integral approach makes optimal use of the 'transition energy' of the people and the community.

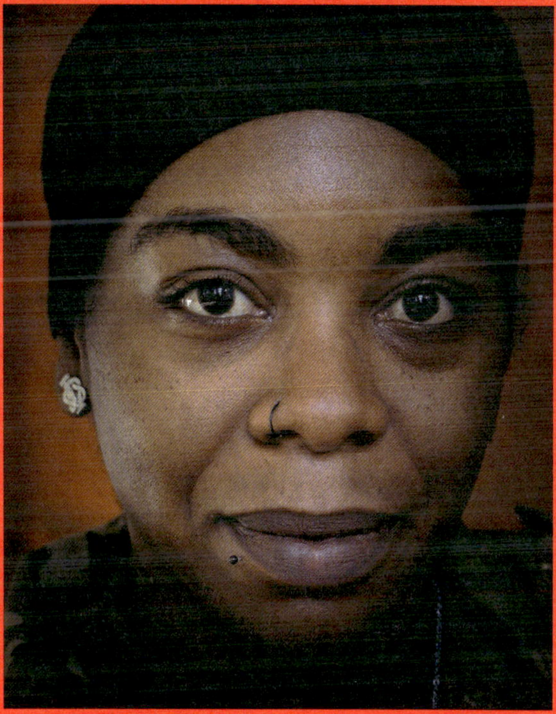

ALIDA ADRIAAN
SOLAR PANEL INSTALLER IN TRAINING WIJKENERGIEWERKT
Work on the future so that we can see the future.

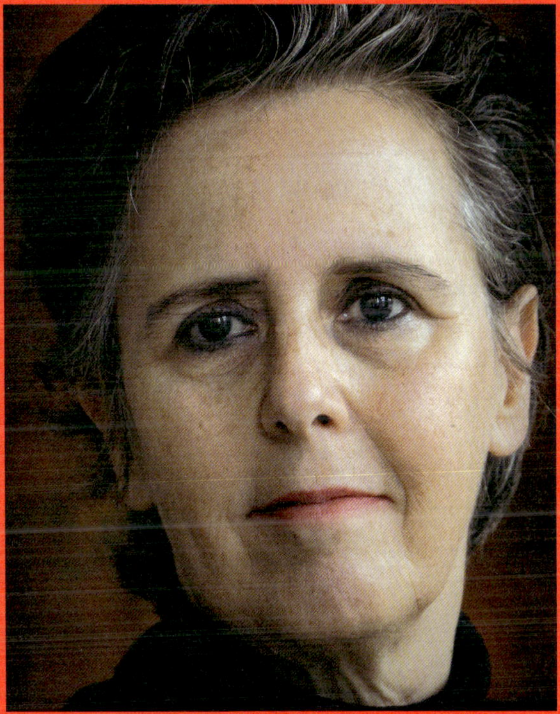

LYDIA PEES
OWNER OF A BUILDING WITH SOLAR PANELS
Putting solar panels on currently empty roofs will contribute to a more sustainable BoTu *and* a lower energy bill. Enjoy the sun twice!

WESLEY DOS SANTOS
ENTREPRENEUR, SUSTAINABLE YOUNG 100
Why make things difficult if you can do them together?

SOCIAL INITIATIVES IN BOTU

BOUWKEET
Daniel White, local residents, volunteers and staff

ATELIER DE KLEINE VIS
Juan Heinsohn Huala (poet, artist and organizer); Houman Esmal Nia (artist); Jana Beranová, Ineke Palm and Marco Nijmeijer (directors)

DE GROENE CONNECTIE
Meriam Beek, Nienke Bouwhuis, Tom van Geest, Philip Kuypers and Catherine Visser with residents, GGD, City of Rotterdam, Delfshaven, Hoogheemraadschap Schieland and de Krimpenerwaard, and Hoogheemraadschap Delfland

COOL DOWN CITY
Charlotte van der Heiden, various volunteers

CREATIEF BEHEER
Stadsgeneeskunde Karin Keijzer and Rini Biemans, VOF Creatief Beheer

CIRKEL SOCIAAL ONDERNEMER
Ximena Dávalos

DELFSHAVEN COÖPERATIE
Patrick Boel, Marte Kappert, Milja Kruijt, Madelon Stoele, Robbert de Vrieze (board)

DE VERBINDINGSKAMER
Marianne de Koning, Helma van den Bogert

HET TAALBEDRIJF
Stichting PAUW, Miriam Roelofs, Marieke Grund

HUIS VAN DE TOEKOMST
Melle Smets, in collaboration with several partners

LSA SCHAKELWIJKEN
Landelijk Samenwerkingsverband Actieve bewoners, Annerike Hekman (project leader)

MENEER VAN HOUTEN, PAMEIJER
Meneer van Houten, Pameijer

WIJKCOLLECTIE BOSPOLDER-TUSSENDIJKEN, MUSEUM ROTTERDAM
Museum Rotterdam and Veldacademie

STICHTING RIJNMOND MULTICULTUREEL CENTRUM (RMC)
Uğur Arisoy, Metehan Ozdemir (board members)

PARK 1943
Angela Renfurm, Dick van Wageningen, Tonny van Sommeren, Willem Beekhuizen, Ron van den Bovenkamp, Anneke van der Pol, Milja Kruijt, Wessel Klootwijk and Judith Dunsbergen

ROTTERDAMSE MUNT
Ingrid Ackermans, Ingrid Ruijgrok

STICHTING SCHIEZICHT
Core group (including Julia Hevemeyer) and a large group of volunteers

WIJKENERGIEWERKT
Josee van Linschoten, Sándor Csenki

WMO RADAR
Ivo Montijn

WERKGROEP ENERGIETRANSITIE CO_2, HUURDERSRAAD WEST
Huurdersraad West, Léon Richard and Ed Krebbers

ENERGIE PERFORMANCE BOTU, THEATER FORMAAT
Thamar Kemperman, Christy de Wit, Wilma van der Wilt

ZELFREGIEHUIS DELFSHAVEN
Tonny van Sommeren, Wilma van der Wilt

CENTRUM VOOR CULTUUR EN PARTICIPATIE (CCPR)
Vereniging de Oranje Horizon (Saïd el Koubai, Jamal Ajal)

INTERCULTURELE STICHTING SALAAM (ISSALAAM)
Rahma Hulsman, Maud Mahyou (founder)

STICHTING DE VEERKRACHTIGE GEMEENSCHAP
Carolina Castro (founder), Nuria Gonzalez, Til Duinker and Ben Lindeman (board)

DELFSHAVEN ENERGIE COÖPERATIE
Jessica Curta, Julia Hevemeyer, Robbert de Vrieze

DAKPARK SCHOOL
Stichting BOOR, Marja Damman (director)

→
WHOSE ENERGY IS IT, ANYWAY?
photo: Aad Hoogendoorn

SOCIALE INITIATIEVEN IN BOTU

A LOCAL ENERGY ACTION PLAN

If Bospolder-Tussendijken can provide the building blocks for a more sustainable, socially inclusive approach to the energy transition, how and by whom can these building blocks then be used in practice?
To explore this, a locally supported Local Energy Action Plan, a LEAP, is requisite. The social and spatio-energetic building blocks delivered ready-to-use by the IABR–Atelier form the basis of the LEAP. By working integrally and by continuing to link the spatial, social, administrative, financial, legal, and technical aspects of the transition, a picture emerges of how the various challenges can be connected and which joint actions at a local level are possible and promising.
The most crucial aim of the LEAP, specifically designed for BoTu by the Atelier, is to organize the energy transition at district level here in such a way that it also contributes to Rotterdam's ambitions to become a resilient city. And to boot, by realizing a CO_2-neutral district in the long term, the LEAP can even contribute to the United Nations' *2030 Agenda for Sustainable Development*.

Work session IABR–Atelier Rotterdam III, Summer 2019
photo: Frank Hanswijk

THE SUSTAINABLE DEVELOPMENT GOALS: A TOOLBOX FOR THE WORLD

In 2015, all of the member states of the United Nations signed the *2030 Agenda for Sustainable Development*. They committed to achieving the Sustainable Development Goals, the SDGs: 17 goals to ensure a 'better and sustainable future for everyone.' A call to action to tackle global challenges such as growing inequality, poverty and climate change integrally and collectively, because otherwise by 2030 the point of no return will have been reached and the climate goals will no longer be achievable.
Not only countries, but also cities, businesses, civil organizations and communities can join the *2030 Agenda* and use the SDGs as tools: as framework, compass and monitor for progress. It's important to always deploy all 17 in cohesion, to not just pick the low-hanging fruit, but to consciously make use of the interdependence between all domains and challenges. To apply systems thinking and leverage, being fully aware that investing in one domain can and must have positive consequences for all the others.

The IABR joined the *2030 Agenda* in 2016 and has been using the SDGs in its research by design ever since. They function as both a guide and a design tool, and are always the starting point in the search for maximum synergy between the various challenges in order to secure ecological and social surplus value. They help define priorities and minimum conditions for interventions and guide the design and implementation process. And last but not least, they are a yardstick for technical, social and environmental aspects along which progress and results can be measured.

The IABR–Atelier Rotterdam argued that when implementing the LEAP in BoTu, the 17 SDGs should be viewed through five lenses simultaneously: personal wellbeing, direct living environment, city and district, planet and global governance. This ensures a better understanding of the interdependencies at the individual, local and planetary scales. It helps people and initiatives to get a grip on the SDGs when it comes to making decisions in their own environment, and to arrive at concrete actions aimed at 2030. This strategy, a process of learning by doing, a step by step implementation of the LEAP in a neighborhood like Bospolder-Tussendijken, not only increases awareness of the importance of an integrated approach, but also of the relationship that exists between the district and the world and of how leverage works. Awareness will grow that without local change there can be no global change – and vice versa.

→
The Sustainable Development Goals, the planet, and the district
RECLAIMING THE COMMONS
photo: Aad Hoogendoorn

PLANET
A MORE RESILIENT
NEIGHBOURHOOD
CULTURAL
INSPIRATION
CASE STUDIES

WELL-BEING
IMPROVED
LIVING

THE LEAP: A TOOLBOX FOR THE DISTRICT

To realize the goal of a CO_2-neutral socially sustainable district, we need to act quickly and decisively in the next ten years. And in the understanding that this is impossible to achieve with technological solutions alone, such as a heat network and solar panels or making homes more sustainable – which will reduce our CO_2 footprint by less than 20 percent at best. Also, there is not a single approach that will work everywhere, and the solution will not come from one side or one party. It is a shared and cultural problem that is on all our plates and that will have to be solved integrally in each specific local situation by all stakeholders together – businesses, government, and civil society.

This is more difficult for residents than for the other, much better organized stakeholders. The IABR–Atelier therefore provided a toolbox for the LEAP: energy, climate adaptation, and policy instruments that can be used by residents to develop new case studies and test projects step by step. In this way, it is possible to proceed directly to implementation while slowly creating a process of learning by doing, in which the transition starts to program itself, as it were, building on feedback. Residents can lay claim to the transition and appropriate it, in consultation with businesses and the authorities. The financial risk for all investors will be reduced, and every step taken will bring Bospolder-Tussendijken closer to its objectives: a CO_2-neutral and socially resilient BoTu 2028.

The *Toolbox for the District* combines four principles of action: *build capacity locally, integrate all systems with each other, manage all resources together,* and *keep counting down to 2030*.

The performance target is based on calculating the maximum capacity of the district: the total of energy that can be produced and stored locally, benefits that can be achieved through efficient use, savings and smart sharing, and the social capacity to manage such a local system. The tools help to take steps together and build local capacity.

In addition, all systems need to be integrated with each other. In order to be able to deal with the drought and heat stress that awaits us in the coming decades, the management and administration of greening, water, and energy must be approached in conjunction with each other in order to achieve climate mitigation and climate adaptation. This will make the district healthier, more livable, more economically attractive, and therefore more valuable.

The resources (assets) that are built up in and by the district must be managed collectively, as in a commons. Only in this way can an increase in value benefit the district itself.

When making decisions and monitoring progress, the countdown is always to 2030. The most important steps have to be taken in the next ten years or the climate objectives will not be achievable. Thus the interests of the district and the world converge.

A LEAP FOR BOSPOLDER-TUSSEN-DIJKEN

1. Why the LEAP?

Planet Earth is at a critical tipping point, and that's why it is vitally important that, by 2050, CO_2 emissions reach net zero worldwide to avoid irreversible damage to the biosphere. We have to make sure that everything we do is leveraged effectively, and thus has an impact on the entire system. It's crucial to see the energy transition not just as a way to phase out fossil fuels entirely, but also as a lever, a necessary intervention to help reach all sustainable development goals as much as we can.

We are all in this together. Citizens, governments and corporations, the responsibility is a shared one. As citizens, associating and collaborating, there's a lot we can do, especially at the district level. The Local Energy Action Plan furthers the development of integrated and inclusive solutions for the energy transition. It helps us attain a carbon-neutral district that is also healthier, more just, attractive, and livable for all. Simultaneously, the LEAP helps to deliver on the commitments of the City of Rotterdam, the Paris Agreement, and the Sustainable Development Goals.

CO_2 EMISSIONS AND FOOTPRINTS

CO_2 is a greenhouse gas that is stored in fossil fuels and released through the burning of fossil fuels. It is emitted as a result of human activities, such as transportation and producing goods. A carbon footprint is the sum of all these emissions, caused by human activities within a specific timeframe. These can be *direct*, such as the CO_2 released during an individual car journey, or *indirect*, for instance the CO_2 released during the production of clothes.

Various 'emissions pathways' have been calculated showing how much we should decrease our emissions by, and by when. The Paris Agreement signed in 2016 binds countries worldwide to the aim of keeping the global temperature rise below 1.5 °C, to save the world from the worst consequences. Despite their big contribution to CO_2 emissions, aviation, shipping, and defense do not fall under the restrictions set by the Agreement.

WHY ALL THE NUMBERS??

Data help us to know where we are, and how far we have left to go. Numbers and data are necessary to hold governments to account, to see how they are keeping their promises. The numbers are important at every level: lots of small numbers add up. Data about reductions in the city are therefore just as important as those about reductions worldwide.

PERSONAL SCALE

SIMPLE SWITCHES

Individuals can make an impact with specific changes. Insulating homes and/or switching to renewable energy sources reduces energy consumption. Changing habits, for example, buying ethically or making greener transportation, consumption and investment choices, can promote sustainable local entrepreneurship and new organizational models.

DISTRICT SCALE

BOTU DOES IT BETTER

BoTu's energy consumption is below the national average. BoTu-inhabitants also consume less meat, make fewer long-distance trips, and enjoy walking to get places. BoTu'ers love their district, but they would like it to be greener, and to grow their food locally. There are already many resident-led initiatives that help improve the district.

DISTRICTS CAN MAKE AN IMPACT

As a collective, district residents can make an impact in a variety of ways, for example by building an awareness-changing movement. Managing local energy sources collectively will allow the district to take ownership of both the revenues and the decision-making processes; this in turn will allow the district to take more ownership of the local energy transition.

PLANETARY SCALE

THERE IS NO PLANET B

The Earth's resources are finite, and the precarious balance needed to provide all life forms with healthy ecosystems is in danger of being disrupted. To guard this balance, it is necessary to drastically reduce CO_2 emissions, achieving the necessary levels can only be done through collective action.

INFLUENCING DEMAND

Positive impacts of choices on the scale of the individual and the neighborhood trickle up and influence national policy, also contributing to the achievement of the SDGs. Growing demand for sustainable products and renewable energy drives investment and forces big polluters to adapt. Through targeted policies, governments can apply top-down pressure to guide industry in the right direction. Time is running out: each day of inaction make the necessary investments more expensive.

- BoTu footprint: 0.23 Mt CO_2: 15.8 t x 14,445 (average footprint per inhabitant of the Netherlands x population of BoTu)
- BoTu emissions: 0.15 Mt CO_2: 10.3 t x 14,445 (average emissions per inhabitant of the Netherlands x population of BoTu)
- NL footprint: 274.5 Mt: 812 billion euros x 0.338 kg (average GDP x CO_2 emissions per euro)
- Only 50% of the energy consumed is produced in the Netherlands

BoTu and the World
image: OOZE architects & urbanists

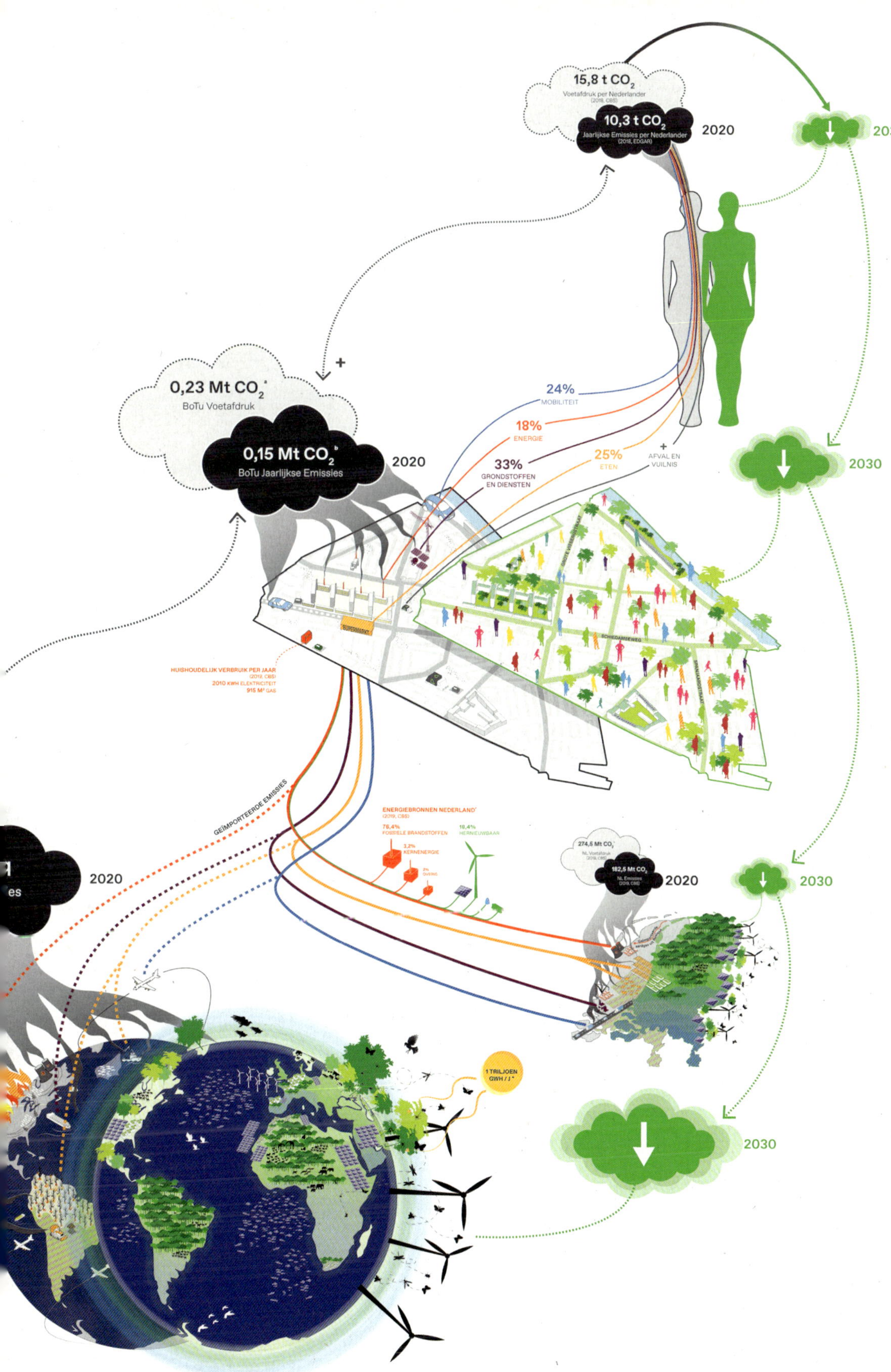
15,8 t CO_2
Voetafdruk per Nederlander
(2018, CBS)
10,3 t CO_2
Jaarlijkse Emissies per Nederlander
(2018, EDGAR)
2020
2030
0,23 Mt CO_2*
BoTu Voetafdruk
0,15 Mt CO_2*
BoTu Jaarlijkse Emissies
2020
2030
24%
MOBILITEIT
18%
ENERGIE
33%
GRONDSTOFFEN EN DIENSTEN
25%
ETEN
AFVAL EN VUILNIS
SUPERMARKT
SCHIEDAMSEWEG
HUISHOUDELIJK VERBRUIK PER JAAR
(2019, CBS)
2010 KWH ELEKTRICITEIT
915 M³ GAS
GEÏMPORTEERDE EMISSIES
2020
ENERGIEBRONNEN NEDERLAND*
(2019, CBS)
76,4%
FOSSIELE BRANDSTOFFEN
18,4%
HERNIEUWBAAR
3,2%
KERNENERGIE
2%
OVERIG
274,5 Mt CO_2*
NL Voetafdruk
(2019, CBS)
182,5 Mt CO_2
NL Emissies
(2019, CBS)
2020
2030
1 TRILJOEN GWH / J*
2030

2030
2030
COLLECTIVE
2023
2025
2030

2. Countdown to 2030

To achieve the goal of a zero-carbon district, quick and decisive action needs to be taken within the next ten years. The LEAP proposes step by step decision-making processes and actions linked to specific alternative designs and a district-wide program. This allows change to be incremental, a locally championed movement to be built, and investments needed for this transition to be broken down into tangible, low-risk segments, so that a mistake can be made, and lessons learned from it. Building on the wealth of existing initiatives, residents and networks are made aware of their potential roles within the greater structures and are placed at the heart of decision-making processes. Opportunities for new types of collective ownership are created, resulting in a genuine energy common, directly linked to the local economy.

The LEAP takes energy as its starting point: developing a low-temperature heat network comprised of many microgrids that ultimately become integrated into one system – a locally owned district grid. Coalitions focusing on specific initiatives and themes are built on this same scale, where the individual can exercise immediate influence. They become interlinked and part of wider district plans, maximizing impact.

Every decision and action taken is a 'no-regret' step forward, preparing homes, energy systems, the public realm and the community for the future. Each step should also lead to evident surplus value. Investment in new underground infrastructure is coupled with investment in a climate-adaptive public realm, in greener streetscapes that improve livability. Insulating homes lowers both energy consumption and monthly bills, while the insulating itself provides local job opportunities. Several of the first stepping stones, like solar panels on roofs, are already there to build on.

←
WHOSE ENERGY IS IT, ANYWAY?
photo: Aad Hoogendoorn

WHAT ARE COMMONS?

Commons are cultural or natural resources that are shared, managed, and governed by the community that uses them. In the context of the LEAP, this refers to locally generated, renewable energy that belongs to the commons. While in the current energy system, consumers have no influence on decision-making processes, the LEAP accomplishes that in the commons, locally generated energy is shared and managed by neighborhood coalitions. In the commons, a collective transition path emerges, and users gain tools and skills to contribute directly to democratic decision-making processes.

COALITIONS

Coalitions can be formed throughout the district, each choosing the goal and approach that best fits their context. Over time, the coalitions formalize into companies, increasing local ownership of energy systems. Inspired by neighbors, more coalitions are set up over time, becoming interlinked to form a resilient social network. As more coalitions form, the district grows toward a social tipping point: positive feedback loops in the neighborhood lead to increased awareness and adaptive power, which contributes to accelerated change.
By 2030 there will be many coalitions, each contributing to their immediate context and the building of a locally supported district grid.

THE ENERGY TRANSITION

Many homeowners have already invested in solar panels and there is already a local energy cooperative in BoTu. As the initiatives and coalitions grow and increase in number, more homes will be powered by the locally owned energy, decreasing the district's reliance on fossil fuels.
Different combinations of solar, wind and aquafer thermal energy sources are consolidated in ATES (aquifer thermal energy storage) networks.
By 2030 there will be many microgrids that have been set up by the many coalitions. They are interlinked and are therefore more resilient than the current, centrally regulated energy network.

CLIMATE ADAPTATION

As initiatives multiply, the capacity of the blue-green solutions will increasingly mitigate the negative effects of climate change. The more green infrastructure is found across the district, the more opportunities for nature and biodiversity can be created, and the more square meters of green per person can be achieved. It's possible that by 2030, local initiatives, in collaboration with the City of Rotterdam, will have transformed the public realm for leisure and cultivation purposes, in which 50 percent of the district's surface will be green, and up to 336 tons of CO_2 can be sequestered per year.

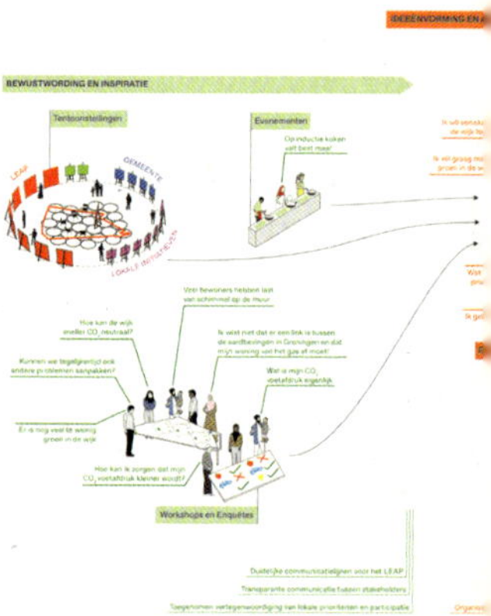

2020

many separate initiatives,
1 energy cooperative

0.02% local energy production

14% area is green

current CO_2 emissions

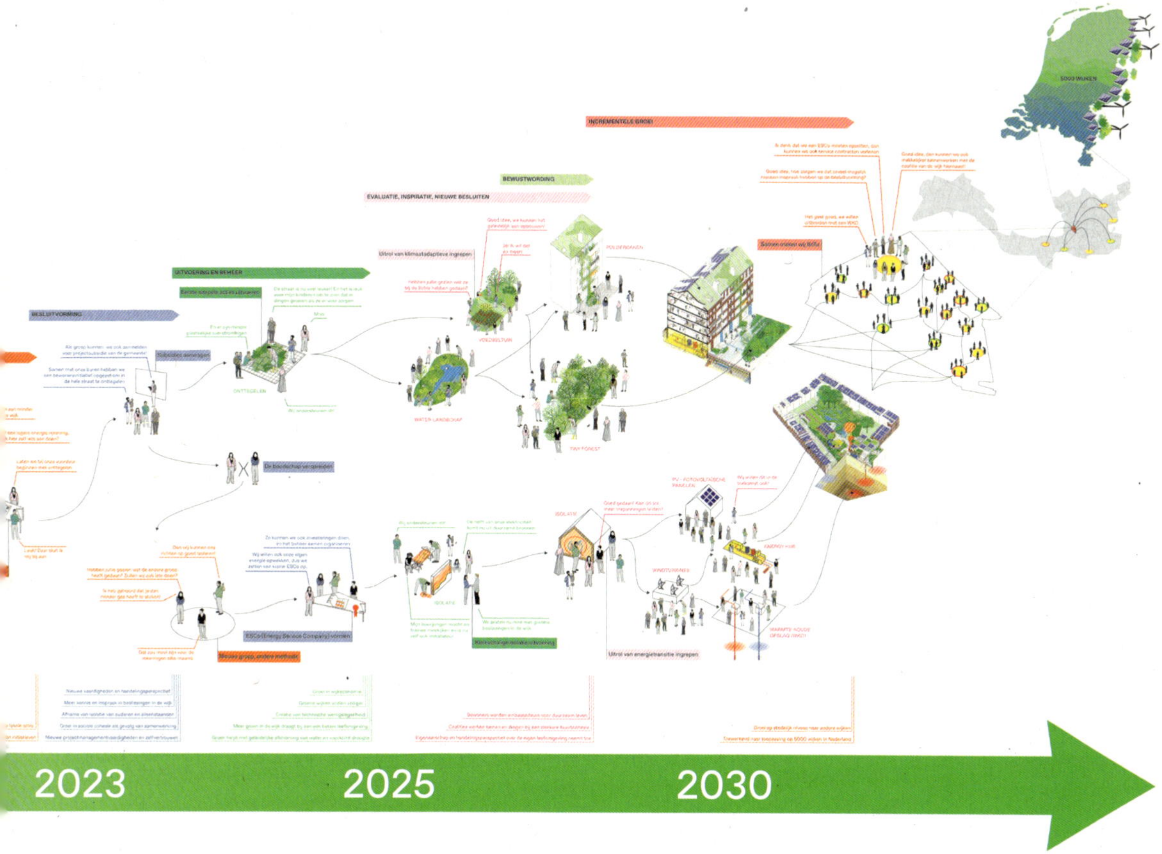

ny separate initiatives, 4 alitions with ground-coupled heat :hanger, 1 energy cooperative

many new initiatives, 15 coalitions of which 7 with ground-coupled heat exchangers, 1 energy cooperative

20 coalitions whose ground-coupled heat exchangers are connected, 3 energy cooperatives

% local energy production

20% local energy production

46% local energy production

% surface area is green

27% surface area is green

50% surface area is green

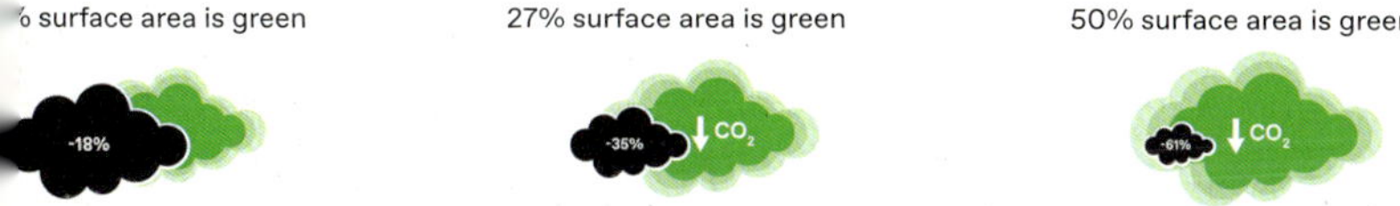

% lower CO_2 emissions

35% lower CO_2 emissions

61% lower CO_2 emissions

Zo kan er toch direct tot uitvoering worden overgegaan, terwijl er langzaam een proces van *learning by doing* ontstaat waarbij de transitie als het ware zichzelf gaat voeden en programmeren. De bewoners kunnen zich die transitie dan eigen maken én toe-eigenen, in samenspraak met bedrijven en overheid. Het financieel risico voor alle investeerders wordt kleiner en iedere stap brengt Bospolder-Tussendijken dichterbij de doelstellingen: een CO2-neutraal en sociaal Veerkrachtig BoTu 2028.
Het *Instrumentarium voor de Wijk* combineert vier handelingsprincipes: *lokaal capaciteit opbouwen, alle systemen met elkaar integreren, alle middelen samen beheren, en blijven aftellen naar 2030.*
to implementation while slowly creating a process of lea
doing, in which the transition starts to program itself,
building on feedback. Residents can lay claim to the trans
appropriate it, in consultation with businesses and the a
The financial risk for all investors will be reduced and ev
taken will bring Bospolder-Tussendijken closer to its ob
a CO_2-neutral and socially resilient BoTu 2028.
The *Toolbox for the District* combines four principles
build capacity locally, integrate all systems with each
manage all resources together, and *keep counting dow*
The performance target is based on calculating the ma
€€€€
HOUSE OWNERS

3. Collective Action and Shared Assets

When it comes to the transition, every district in the Netherlands faces the same challenges, but each has a unique set of urgencies, histories, and assets, as well as demographics, needs, and priorities.

What does a community need to turn the LEAP into concrete action, which instruments can be utilized, what are the possibilities? While there can be no one-size-fits-all solution, a set of tools can be provided for stakeholders to act in a way that suits a district best. A distinct combination of energy-related technological and blue-green innovations work hand in hand with distinct organizational and governance models, innovative policymaking, and shared decision-making processes. This helps to build assets over time, which are then owned and managed by the community. Community and capacity building are essential to identifying which tools to select. Through this process, the tools become instrumental to leveraging in the positive changes best suited to each district.

←
The LEAP: Toolbox for the District
RECLAIMING THE COMMONS
photo: Aad Hoogendoorn

MOVEMENT-BUILDING TOOLS

Different participatory processes can be explored and used to teach residents the skills they can use to help mitigate climate change and create awareness.
Possible methods for discovering shared priorities and common ground include neighborhood campaigns, group gatherings and neighborhood meetings, surveys and research, cultural events and action-led workshops.
Activities help individuals work together, in networks, toward the same goal. They can also help build the skills and action perspectives of residents, ensure they are well-informed and become equal partners at the negotiation tables.

ENERGY TOOLS

There are various tools that can help solve local challenges, related to the production, saving, storage of energy – or all three. The possibilities include insulating homes to lower energy use, electrifying mobility, installing solar panels, contributing to investments in wind energy, or setting up an ATES (aquifer thermal energy storage) per street.

GOVERNANCE TOOLS

New ownership systems are inclusive of all district stakeholders: residents, the municipality, and the business sector.
Different organizational forms, ranging in formality and degrees of democratic participation, can be chosen from to ensure true local ownership. Each step is part of a bigger process and unlocks a new scale with a bigger impact.

ORGANIZATION AND FINANCING MODELS

Different organizational forms allow groups to coordinate and apply for finances, formalizing the commons and driving investments.
Coalitions managing larger local energy assets can consider setting up an Energy Service Company (ESCo) to manage the services they provide.

POLICY MODELS

Governments at local and national levels can support district LEAPs by effective policymaking, not only regulating but also incentivizing and supporting new forms of ownership and using alternative indicators of economic development.
Examples of such policy models include the Zero-Growth Model, focusing on key indicators other than economic growth as indicating positive development; Doughnut Economics, prioritizing living within the planetary resources; the New Green Deal, placing climate adaptation at the heart of broader policy and using it as a means for economic development; and carbon reporting, making companies and countries accountable for their behavior.

CLIMATE ADAPTATION TOOLS

Blue-green interventions in districts have many other positive effects besides climate adaptation. Having lots of green spaces reduces drought and heat stress (by water storage, improving subsurface infiltration and shading) and sequesters CO_2. In addition, access to green spaces benefits our mental wellbeing. As the district's knowledge of this added value grows, so does the likelihood of residents getting involved in similar projects, such as planting trees, creating green roofs and façades, or even urban agriculture.

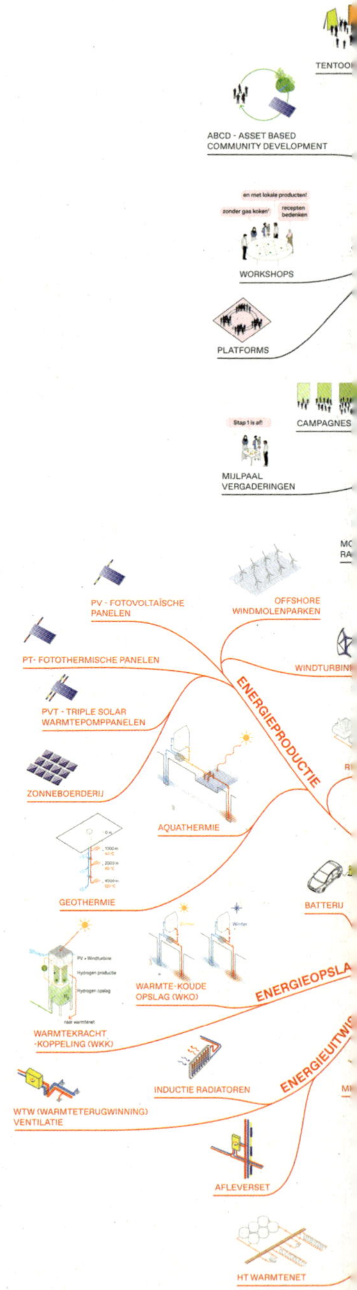

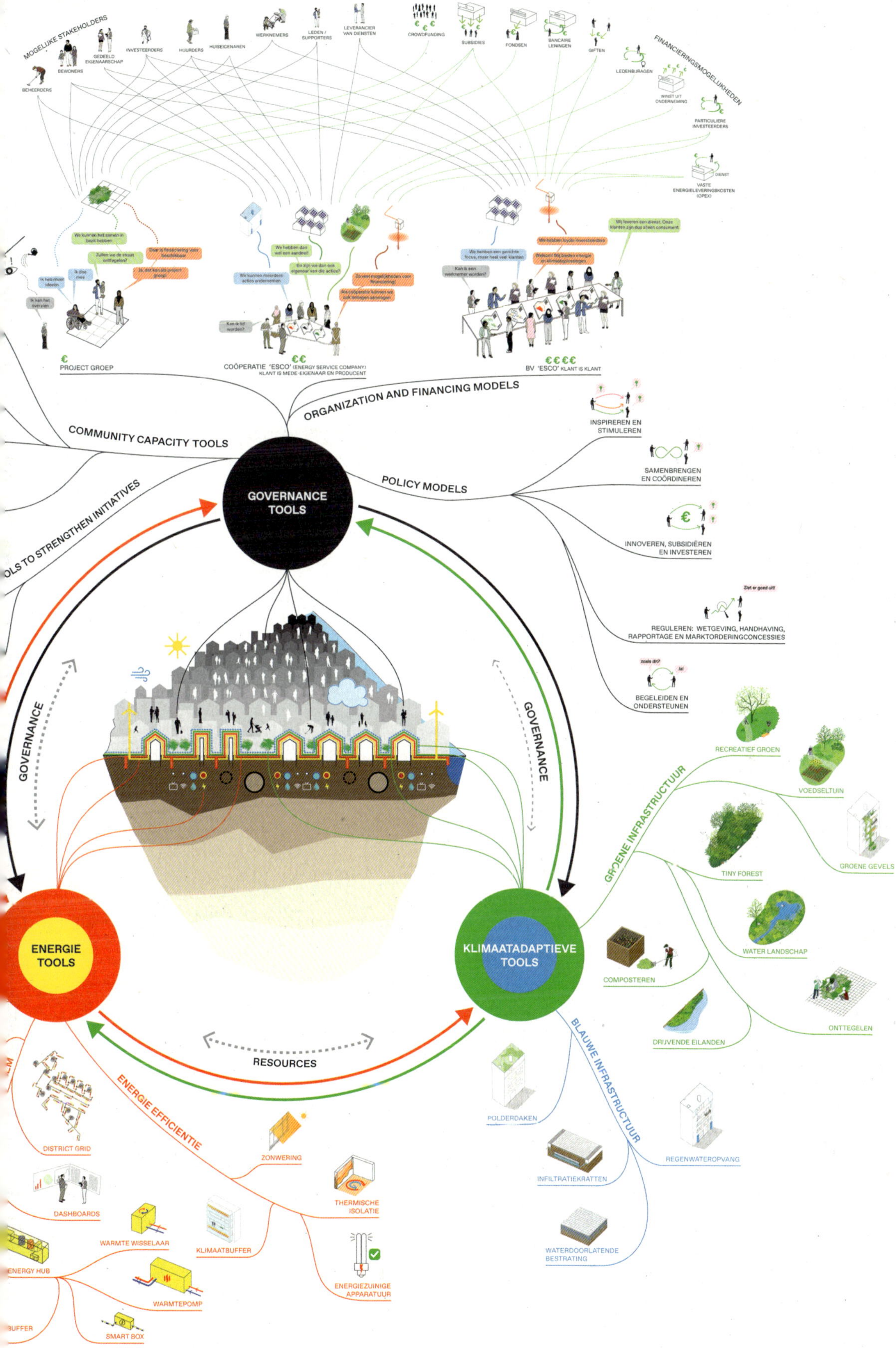
MOGELIJKE STAKEHOLDERS
BEHEERDERS
BEWONERS
GEDEELD EIGENAARSCHAP
INVESTEERDERS
HUURDERS
HUISEIGENAREN
WERKNEMERS
LEDEN / SUPPORTERS
LEVERANCIER VAN DIENSTEN
CROWDFUNDING
SUBSIDIES
FONDSEN
BANCAIRE LENINGEN
GIFTEN
FINANCIERINGSMOGELIJKHEDEN
LEDENBIJDRAGEN
WINST UIT ONDERNEMING
PARTICULIERE INVESTEERDERS
DIENST
VASTE ENERGIELEVERINGSKOSTEN (OPEX)
€
PROJECT GROEP
€€
COÖPERATIE 'ESCO' (ENERGY SERVICE COMPANY) KLANT IS MEDE-EIGENAAR EN PRODUCENT
€€€€
BV 'ESCO' KLANT IS KLANT
ORGANIZATION AND FINANCING MODELS
COMMUNITY CAPACITY TOOLS
OLS TO STRENGTHEN INITIATIVES
POLICY MODELS
GOVERNANCE TOOLS
INSPIREREN EN STIMULEREN
SAMENBRENGEN EN COÖRDINEREN
INNOVEREN, SUBSIDIËREN EN INVESTEREN
REGULEREN: WETGEVING, HANDHAVING, RAPPORTAGE EN MARKTORDERINGCONCESSIES
BEGELEIDEN EN ONDERSTEUNEN
GOVERNANCE
GOVERNANCE
ENERGIE TOOLS
KLIMAATADAPTIEVE TOOLS
RESOURCES
GROENE INFRASTRUCTUUR
RECREATIEF GROEN
VOEDSELTUIN
GROENE GEVELS
TINY FOREST
WATER LANDSCHAP
COMPOSTEREN
ONTTEGELEN
DRIJVENDE EILANDEN
BLAUWE INFRASTRUCTUUR
POLDERDAKEN
REGENWATEROPVANG
INFILTRATIEKRATTEN
WATERDOORLATENDE BESTRATING
ENERGIE EFFICIENTIE
DISTRICT GRID
ZONWERING
THERMISCHE ISOLATIE
DASHBOARDS
WARMTE WISSELAAR
KLIMAATBUFFER
ENERGY HUB
WARMTEPOMP
ENERGIEZUINIGE APPARATUUR
BUFFER
SMART BOX

4. What's in the LEAP for BoTu?

The energy transition is inevitable, but it's also a lever for change. Only an *integrated approach*, using all available data and technological, climate adaptative and governance tools, will enable the energy transition to leverage a more fair, just and resilient district, delivering on all the SDGs. By generating and storing energy locally, the resource loop is closed and the district becomes more self-reliant. Through local ownership, positive feedback loops are built into the social system that lead to increased awareness and accelerated change. A smart investment in the district's energy infrastructure is an investment in its residents, their wellbeing, their skills and economic position in the city, but also in its physical and economical capacity to withstand extremities caused by climate change.
The LEAP implementation phase starts in strategic locations where social, technical, and blue-green innovations meet in unique combinations. They are small enough for individuals to have a voice in their management, and large enough to have an impact on their environments.

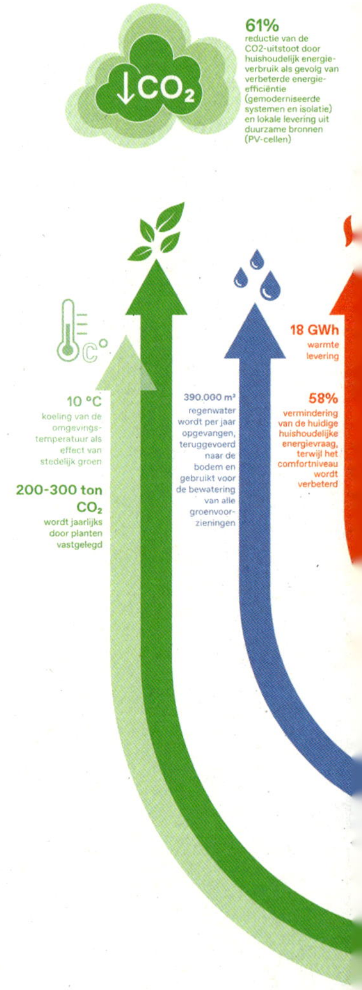

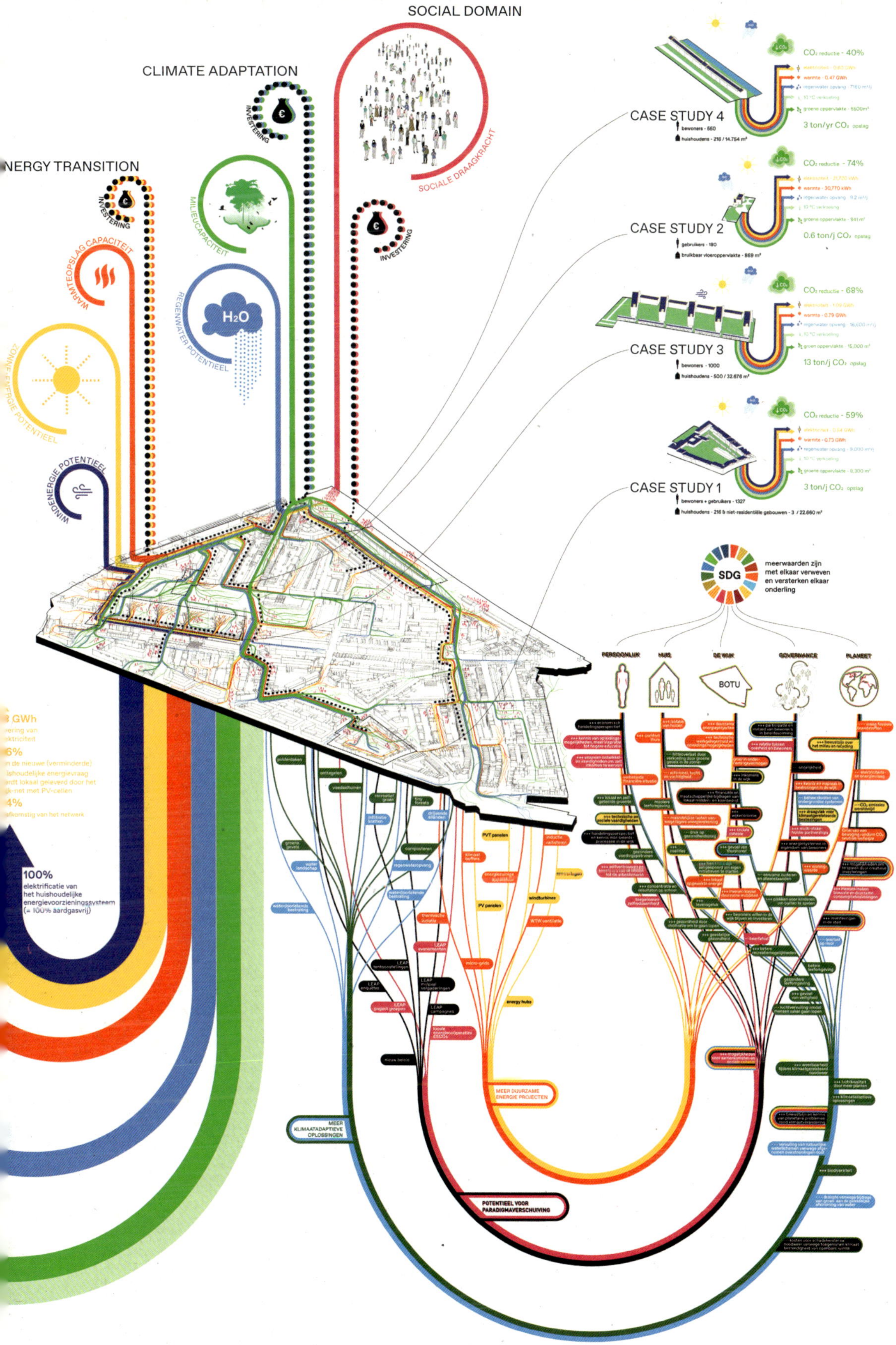
SOCIAL DOMAIN
CLIMATE ADAPTATION
NERGY TRANSITION
INVESTERING
SOCIALE DRAAGKRACHT
MILIEUCAPACITEIT
WARMTEOPSLAG CAPACITEIT
REGENWATER POTENTIEEL
H2O
ZONNE-ENERGIE POTENTIEEL
WINDENERGIE POTENTIEEL
CASE STUDY 4
bewoners - 550
huishoudens - 216 / 14.754 m²
CO2 reductie - 40%
3 ton/yr CO2 opslag
CASE STUDY 2
gebruikers - 180
bruikbaar vloeroppervlakte - 869 m²
CO2 reductie - 74%
0.6 ton/j CO2 opslag
CASE STUDY 3
bewoners - 1000
huishoudens - 500 / 32.676 m²
CO2 reductie - 68%
13 ton/j CO2 opslag
CASE STUDY 1
bewoners + gebruikers - 1327
huishoudens - 216 & niet-residentiële gebouwen - 3 / 22.660 m²
CO2 reductie - 59%
3 ton/j CO2 opslag
SDG
meerwaarden zijn met elkaar verweven en versterken elkaar onderling
PERSOONLIJK
HUIS
DE WIJK
BOTU
GOVERNANCE
PLANEET
100%
elektrificatie van het huishoudelijke energievoorzieningssysteem (= 100% aardgasvrij)
MEER DUURZAME ENERGIE PROJECTEN
MEER KLIMAATADAPTIEVE OPLOSSINGEN
POTENTIEEL VOOR PARADIGMAVERSCHUIVING

FOUR CASE STUDIES

The IABR–Atelier carried out four case studies, research that was, admittedly, speculative by nature, but at the same time had its sights set on feasibility and implementation, on what we *can* want. The starting point of each case study was the existing situation; the Atelier used the LEAP (Local Energy Action Plan) approach to 'stack,' as it were, the spatio-energetic and socio-civic building blocks the Atelier previously identified in BoTu.[16] Each case study thus involved a certain number of inhabitants, a clear spatial demarcation, and its own context and typology, representative of the Bospolder-Tussendijken district. They all involved a specific combination of stakeholders with shared objectives that enabled forms of self-governance and common ownership. After all, the goal was to increase the capacity to adapt to the effects of the climate crisis including heat and drought, while working as integrally and socially inclusively as possible, that is, maximally taking into account that which the Sustainable Development Goals ask of us.

[16] Also see page 34-35

Each case study is the result of research by design, translated into a spatial design. They are partly based on calculations and simulations that underpin the local capacity to produce, store and reuse energy (heating, cooling, and electricity) as accurately as possible. This provides clear insights into the local capacity to store carbon, and in ways to use social and spatial interventions to reduce CO_2 emissions and, as a district, contribute to achieving the city's climate goals and to the SDGs. Combined with projected installation and management costs, the research results offer residents a scenario for a realistic business case and ways to work together in their day to day lives.

Together, the four case studies form a framework that can serve as a basis for similar consistent approaches elsewhere, which can help to start a movement. Indeed, as collaborations multiply and grow, the benefits become greater: the argument for ever-new investments becomes stronger and the system more resilient. This collective approach makes the goal, carbon-neutral districts, achievable.

→
WHOSE ENERGY IS IT, ANYWAY?
photo: Aad Hoogendoorn

CASE STUDY 3: GIJSING
ENERGY ACTION PLAN
ENERGY ACTION PLAN
100% ELEKTRIFICATIE
66% VERMINDERING H
ENERGIEVRAAG
45% LOKALE ENERGIE
16.675 M³ REGENWATER
63% VAN DE TOTALE OPP
GROEN
10°C KOELING VAN DE OMG
TEMPERATUUR
13,3 TON CO2 WORDT DOOR
PLANTEN VASTGELEGD
1.000 BEWONERS
32.676 M²

Case Study 1: Residential Block and Dakpark School

The urban block that includes public elementary school Dakpark consists of 216 dwellings, 114 with energy label D-G, and three non-residential buildings (the elementary school and two community centers), all of which need to be upgraded to energy label A-C.

ENERGY ACTION PLAN

Three pairs of Aquifer Thermal Energy Storage (ATES) wells provide heat and cold storage for all buildings in the urban block, with an energy hub to raise the temperature when necessary. Photovoltaic panels on the roof meet part of the complex's electricity consumption, while the energy hub is powered by the energy grid.

The roofs that are not used to produce solar power and the shared courtyard are greened; four new landscape types respond to the needs of the urban block's users – schoolchildren, visitors to the community center, and residents of the surrounding apartments. The design includes new, educationally enriched play areas, food-growing locations, places of sojourn, and quiet places for rest and reflection that will not only offer support to face the negative impacts of climate change, but also provide room to learn and exchange knowledge about sustainable energy and nature-based solutions, together.

The systems will be managed and maintained by a coalition of local stakeholders – including the school, the two community centers, the housing association, and the owner's association active in the residential block – in collaboration with the energy cooperative, potential new resident initiatives, and the city. The coalition can decide to establish an Energy Service Company (ESCo) to enable the stakeholders to manage and jointly control the production and maintenance of the energy systems and blue-green interventions. This will create local jobs and bring people from across the district closer together.

OUTPUT OF THE INTERVENTIONS

— 100 percent electrification of household energy supply (= 100 percent natural gas-free)
— 63 percent reduction in household energy demand, while improving comfort levels
— 37 percent of the new (reduced) demand is supplied locally by the district grid of PV cells, 63 percent is supplied by the energy grid
— 16,675 m³ of rainwater collected annually is returned to the soil and used to irrigate green spaces
— 44 percent of the total area is green (compared with only 36 percent today)
— 10 °C cooling of ambient temperature as an effect of urban greenery
— 3.4 tons of CO_2 is sequestered in plants
— 58 percent reduction in CO_2 emissions from household energy use due to improved energy efficiency (more modern systems and insulation) and local supply from renewable sources (PV cells)

Case Study 2: Zelfregiehuis

This 1929 building has a total area of 1,086 m^2 and currently carries energy label G. It had an important community function for many years, but was recently sold by the owner, the City of Rotterdam.

ENERGY ACTION PLAN

Using simple insulation methods, the energy label of this prewar community center can be upgraded from label G to label A. To generate heat, a microgrid consisting of triple photothermal solar panels (PVT) is being developed that will be combined with a heat pump to raise the temperature if necessary. Any short-term excess heat is stored in a buffer tank. The same PVT panels will also meet the electricity needs of the energy hub, while electricity for the building, such as for lighting and appliances, will be provided by the energy grid.

Responding to local interest of residents in the growing of food, a food forest and greenhouses are developed in which they can also learn more about the carbon footprint of their food. Other blue-green measures include permeable pavement and geocellular water storage, which will counteract the flooding that is also a problem here.

The systems are managed by the building owners. However, they are linked to the surrounding energy systems, and the maintenance of the outdoor space is coordinated with the city and with local groups of supporters.

OUTPUT OF THE INTERVENTIONS

— 100 percent electrification of household energy supply (= 100 percent natural gas-free)
— 85 percent reduction in household energy demand, while improving comfort levels
— 100 percent local heat production
— 921 m^3 of rainwater collected annually is returned to the soil and used to irrigate green spaces
— 63 percent of the total area is green (compared with only 10 percent today)
— 10 °C cooling of ambient temperature as an effect of urban greenery
— 0.6 tons of CO_2 is sequestered in plants
— 74 percent reduction in CO_2 emissions from household energy due to the adoption of new systems and making them more sustainable

Case Study 3: Gijsingflats

The Gijsingsflats, a complex of 500 apartments built in the 1960s by architects De Nijs, Lucas and Niemeijer and owned by housing association Havensteder, all carry energy label D-G.

ENERGY ACTION PLAN

Improving the insulation of the apartments will immediately yield an energy label A-C.

Five pairs of ATES (Aquifer Thermal Energy Storage) wells will provide heat and storage, distributed to all apartments by a centrally located energy hub, and five booster pumps are located near the buildings to raise or lower the temperature as necessary. For domestic electricity consumption, modules that are a combination of photovoltaic thermal (PVT) panels and wind turbines are placed atop the tallest buildings, while standard PVT panels are mounted on the lower decks. In this case the electricity for the energy hub and booster pumps is supplied by the energy grid.

At this site, the new layout provides opportunities for food cultivation and recreation, while facilities such as geocellular water storage and permeable pavement ease flooding and sewer pressure. The northwest façades of the apartment buildings will be fitted with a climate skin in support of CO_2 sequestration and insulation. The green landscape connects to other existing green areas in the district, enhancing pedestrian routes and local biodiversity corridors.

The systems are managed and maintained by a coalition consisting of the housing association, local energy cooperative, local cultural and civic foundations, and resident initiatives. The coalition can decide to establish an Energy Service Company (ESCo) to enable the stakeholders to manage and jointly control the production and maintenance of the energy systems and blue-green interventions. This will create local jobs and promote social cohesion in the district.

OUTPUT OF THE INTERVENTIONS

— 100 percent electrification of household energy supply (= 100 percent natural gas-free)
— 66 percent reduction in household energy demand, while improving comfort levels
— 45 percent of the new (reduced) demand is supplied locally by the district grid of PVT cells, 55 percent is supplied by the energy grid
— 16,675 m^3 of rainwater collected annually is returned to the soil and used to irrigate green spaces
— 63 percent of the total area is green (compared with only 33 percent today)
— 10 °C cooling of ambient temperature as an effect of urban greenery
— 13.3 tons of CO_2 is sequestered in plants
— 68 percent reduction in CO_2 emissions from household energy use due to improved energy efficiency and local supply from renewable sources (PVT cells and wind turbines)

ATES wells at 150 m depth

Case Study 4: Housing Block along the Schie

The housing block along the Schie consists of 275 apartments with deck access built before 1945; some are privately owned, others belong to the housing association. Currently all of the dwellings carry energy label D-G.

ENERGY ACTION PLAN

Improving the insulation of the individual dwellings will immediately yield an energy label A-C.
Heat exchangers in the Schie can provide aquatic energy for heating and cooling, which is derived from surface water and is stored in three ATES (Aquifer Thermal Energy Storage) wells. The temperature is raised by a heat pump housed in an energy hub, to which all of the apartments are connected. Photovoltaic panels on the roof provide the apartments with electricity, while the energy grid supplies the electricity needed to power the energy hub.
To prevent flooding and mold, common problems in this area, rainwater is collected from the roofs. The permeable pavement and geocellular water storage system retain the water and allow it to gradually flow back into the empty aquifer. This waters trees and plants, and eases the pressure on the city's sewer system. Making 50 percent of the street green creates new landscape functions. There will be more room for recreation and biodiversity, which contributes to both CO_2 sequestration and improved livability.
The systems will be managed and maintained by a coalition consisting of a new energy cooperative, local owners' associations, local cultural arts organizations, and residents' initiatives. The coalition can decide to establish an Energy Service Company (ESCo) to enable the stakeholders to manage and jointly control the production and maintenance of the energy systems and blue-green interventions. This will generate local jobs and promote social cohesion in the district.

OUTPUT OF THE INTERVENTIONS

— 100 percent electrification of household energy supply (= 100 percent natural gas-free)
— 55 percent reduction in current household energy demand, while improving comfort levels
— 20 percent of the new (reduced) demand is supplied locally by the district grid of PVT cells, 80 percent is supplied by the energy grid
— 7,158 m^3 of rainwater collected annually is returned to the soil and used to irrigate green spaces
— 50 percent of the total area is green (compared with only 6.3 percent today)
— 10 °C cooling of ambient temperature as effect of urban greenery
— 3.1 tons of CO_2 is sequestered in plants
— 40 percent reduction in CO_2 emissions from household energy use due to improved energy efficiency (modernized systems and insulation) and local supply from renewable sources (PVT cells)

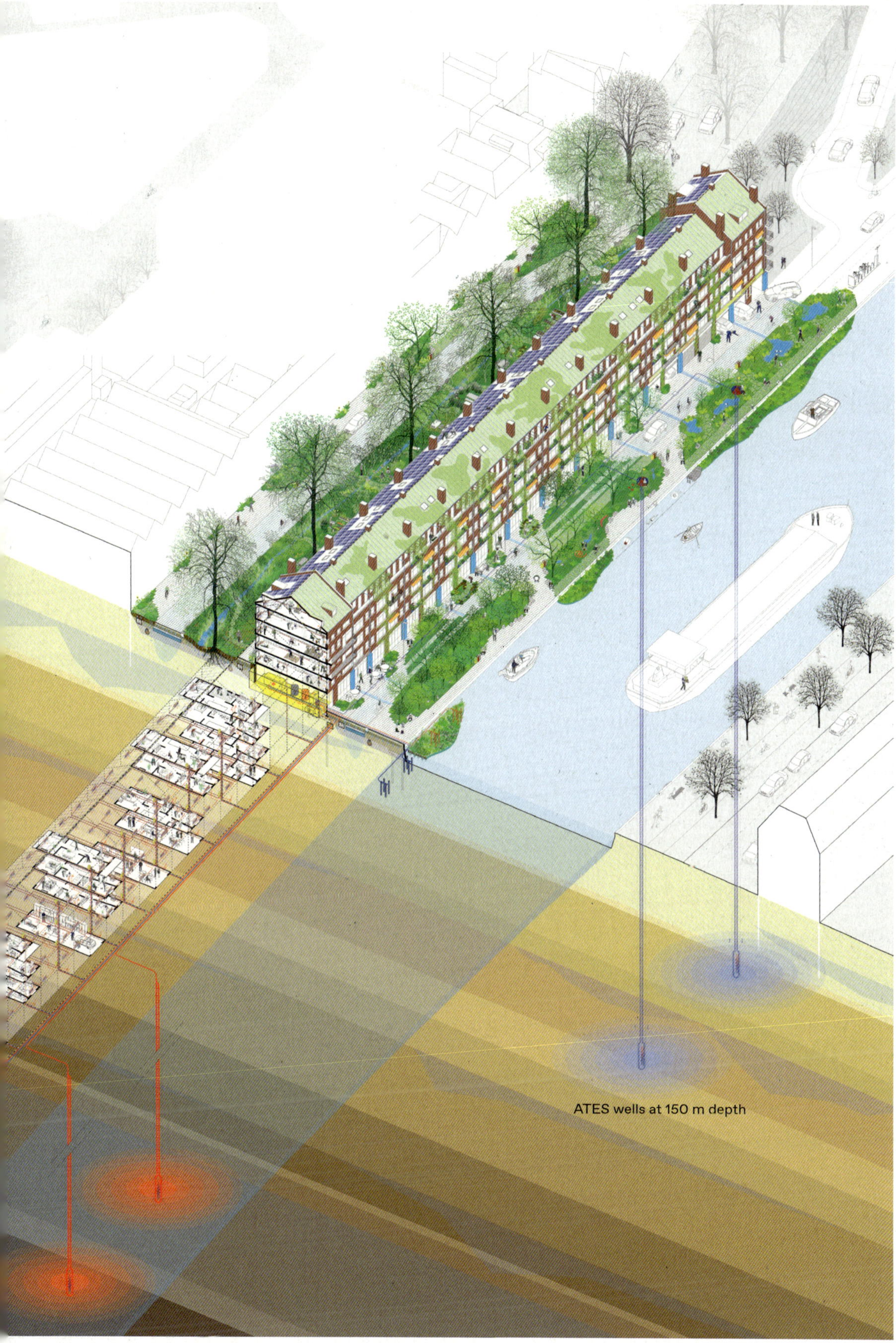
ATES wells at 150 m depth

INCREMENTAL TRANSITION

The case study 4 of the housing block along the Schie illustrates how the LEAP's instruments on policy, energy and climate adaptation can be used by residents to transition and how they can thus actively improve the climate performance and livability of the district.

The instruments will be implemented incrementally to transform the public space between the dwellings and the Schie River into a climate-adaptive area. In addition to quantitative benefits (water storage, CO_2 storage, and heat stress prevention), this scenario also visualizes qualitative benefits, such as development and management of common property, and social cohesion.

The local capacity to store rainwater and produce energy from natural resources, such as sun and wind, is increased step by step. The adaptation of individual dwellings, for example by adding insulation, PVT panels and heat recovery systems, improves their energy efficiency. Half of the public space will be greened. Rainwater collected on roofs is used to water the new planting. This relieves the municipal sewer system and reduces dampness and mold in the dwellings.

The management is in the hands of a coalition of new, local energy cooperatives, organizations and residents' initiatives. This way, both the CO_2 footprint of the neighborhood is reduced and the transition becomes visible, step by step. As awareness grows that common ownership also creates common values, more and more organizations and residents will join the transition to a resilient BoTu.

cartoons:
OOZE architects & urbanists

→
The climate goals and the district
RECLAIMING THE COMMONS
photo: Aad Hoogendoorn

2017
2018
2019
2020
Step 1 is completed!
And with local products!
Like this?
Yes!
€€
SERVICE
COMPANY
PROFITS
SCENARIO #1

DOWN
THE LEAP:
A TOOLBOX FOR
THE DISTRICT
TO EA
Looking good!
Looking good!
€€€€
SCENARIO #3
HOUSE OWNERS
RESIDENTS

A TOOLBOX FOR THE DISTRICT Energy and Climate Adaptation Tools

Residents and governments can use energy and climate adaptation tools to contribute to the transformation of districts into energy-neutral and climate-adaptive areas. Energy tools are means to increase local energy production and energy efficiency. Blue and green infrastructures can be used as tools for climate adaptation, such as the limiting of flooding and rising temperatures. This implies working toward a better living environment and a higher quality of life for residents at the same time.

cartoons:
OOZE architects & urbanists

FAÇADE WATER STORAGE

Roofs (without geocellular water storage) collect and store rainwater in storage tanks that are integrated in façades. The stored water can be used year-round, for example to irrigate (façade) gardens. The system also serves as a visual marker of climate adaptation in the built environment.

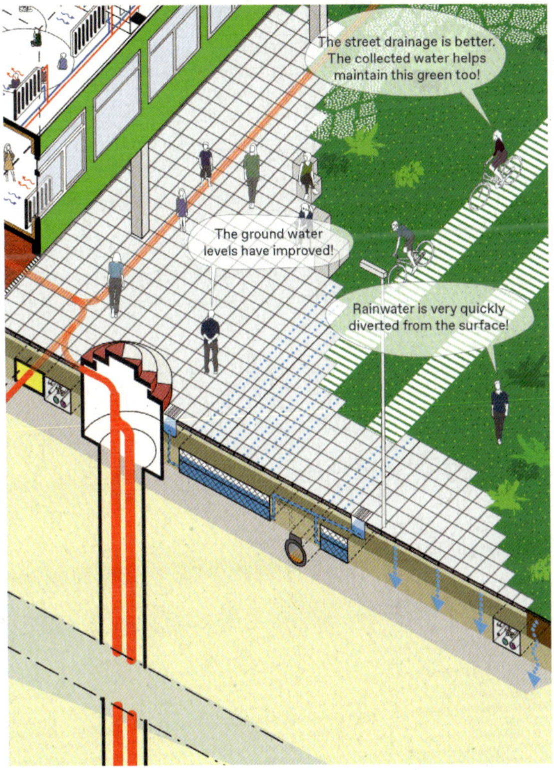

GEOCELLULAR WATER STORAGE

Geocellular water storage systems are a series of connected, porous crates placed under the pavement of the road and connected to street drains. The system relieves pressure on the combined sewer system (rainwater and wastewater) by collecting and redirecting rainfall. The water can be gradually infiltrated into the ground or stored for use in dryer months. Connections to street drains allow for overflow when the crates are filled to capacity, which brings down long-term costs for the municipality. When positioned alongside low-maintenance urban green, the stored rainwater can be reused locally.

PERMEABLE PAVING

Paved and hard surfaces will always be necessary in urban areas to facilitate mobility. By using pervious materials, these surfaces allow water to infiltrate into the ground, contributing to the drainage of rain- and stormwater. As such, they reduce the load on drains, recharge the groundwater table and prevent flooding. Possible locations are sidewalks, paved public (parking) spaces, and paving in private backyards.

GREEN ROOFS

Green roofs are either flat or sloped roofs equipped with technologies or planting to store water. Green roofs improve the building's thermal performance, offer green space for leisure, reduce the urban heat island (UHI) effect, and contribute to CO_2 sequestration. Examples range from simple designs, incorporating shallow soil depths and planted with sedum, to more intensive, heavier designs with complex and biodiverse vegetation and the potential to be used for urban farming projects. More intensive designs often incorporate geocellular crates and are referred to as *polderdaken*. On green roofs that facilitate rainwater storage, a rich, self-sufficient ecosystem can develop, thereby boosting urban biodiversity.

WATER LANDSCAPE

To deal with the increase in stormwater volume, public open spaces and/or green areas are dedicated to water attenuation and infiltration. These humid landscapes, in which water levels vary depending on rainfall events, strengthen biodiversity in the urban environment and lower the temperature of the local microclimate by up to 5 °C.

FLOATING ISLANDS

Water itself can be attractive for wildlife, but hard-surfaced river or canal sides are very detrimental to the thriving of animal species. Floating islands, made of a floating substratum planted with helophytes (perennial marsh plants), offer an ideal environment for fauna dependent on aquatic habitats and pollinators, which generally struggle in urban environments. In addition, floating islands contribute to CO_2 sequestration. They help to purify the water and as such can be combined with swimming facilities. They enrich the variety of vegetation in the district, with positive benefits on residents' health and wellbeing. In BoTu, floating islands could be realized in a segment of the Schie.

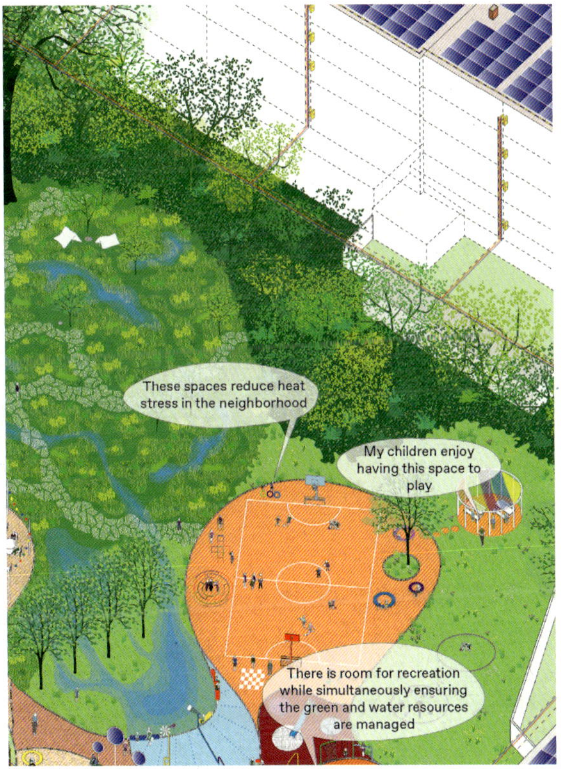

RECREATIONAL GREEN

Equipped with playgrounds, seating and other leisure-related elements, recreational green areas are specifically dedicated to improving the quality of the urban living environment of humans. In addition to their positive effects on the urban habitat, green areas can also be implemented as a climate adaptation tool. Soft surfaces allow rainwater to infiltrate into the soil. The green coverage, especially trees, contributes to reducing the urban heat island effect (UHI) and CO_2 sequestration.

MINI-FOREST

Mini-forests (*Miyawaki* forests) are fast-growing, densely planted, small-scale ecosystems that are very effective in carbon sequestration, have a cooling effect on the surrounding urban context, and offer refuge to a variety of animal species. Mini-forests have the potential to grow 10 times faster, be 30 times more dense, and 100 times more biodiverse than traditionally cultivated forests. Their area can be limited and have highly soil-regenerative characteristics. Therefore, they are ideal for climate adaptation in the urban context. Ideally, a variety of 30 or more native species are planted closely together, on average three per m^2, and are maintained for only the first three years after which they become an autonomous forest system.

FOOD GARDEN

Food gardens (*voedseltuinen*) are public or private areas dedicated to urban agriculture. Producing food locally fosters biodiversity and reduces the urban heat island effect (UHI). Food gardens can also sequester high amounts of CO_2. In some gardens traditional food production methods are implemented, while in others an uncultivated, stratified environment and less maintenance are preferred. Additional benefits are rainwater buffering and flood prevention.

GREEN FAÇADE

Green façades are building façades or walls covered by specific species of plants that are employed depending on the material and texture of the (façade) surface and the degree of exposure to sun and wind. Rough but resistant surfaces, for instance, are ideal for self-clinging plants. Application of this tool leads to higher green coverage and improves biodiversity in densely built neighborhoods. Green façades reduce the need for indoor heating and cooling and contribute to CO_2 sequestration.

DE-TILING

De-tiling (*onttegelen*) refers to the removal of paving tiles and replacing them with vegetation. De-tiling contributes to rainwater buffering and flood prevention, boosts urban biodiversity and CO_2 sequestration. It is easy for residents to carry out this intervention, which stimulates direct engagement with the LEAP transformation. They see the immediate results of the improvement of their living environment and, as such, experience that they are able to contribute to the social cohesion of their district.

COMPOST

Domestic organic waste like fruit and vegetable peels and organic waste from public green spaces can be composted in local compost bins. Composting reduces the pressure on urban waste processing and provides a useful product to be utilized as fertilizer in public and communal green areas, such as food gardens.

ENERGY HUB

An energy hub manages the flows of energy between storage and distribution systems, controlling the differences in supply and demand between night and day and different seasons. It is a technical room that serves as the central management point for a low-temperature Aquifer Thermal Energy Storage (ATES) microgrid. An energy hub consists of various components. A heat exchanger transfers heat from the source, for instance, aquathermal energy and seasonal heat, to the distribution (heat network) and storage systems (ATES). Hot and cold buffers facilitate short-term storage of temperature as an alternative to the ATES wells, which store temperatures long-term. A heat pump uses electricity to raise low-temperature heat to a higher temperature to supply heating and hot tap water. An energy management device regulates the flows in various parts of the energy hub to meet variable heating demands.

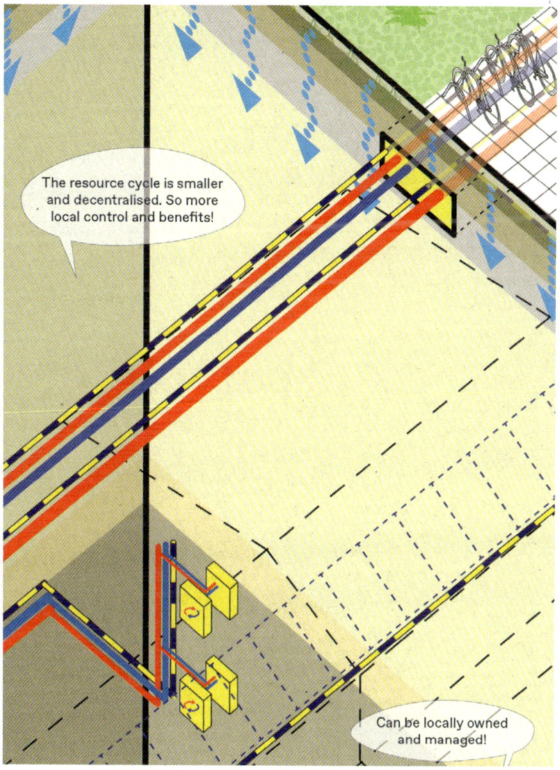

MICROGRID

A decentralized network integrating various renewable energy sources, used for multiple end-use needs simultaneously, such as heating, cooling, and electricity. Using local and renewable energy sources, such as aquathermal and wind energy, the microgrid reduces dependence on a centralized and privatized city-wide supply of heat and electricity. A microgrid is particularly beneficial in dense urban settings, as its capacity lies between 200 and 500 dwelling units. In the LEAP, the low-temperature Aquifer Thermal Energy Storage (ATES) microgrid provides low-temperature heating and cooling, high-temperature heating (hot water supply) and electricity distribution. Several microgrids combined form a district grid. A district grid can connect to a high-temperature heat network, exchanging energy with it.

DASHBOARD

The Dashboard is a live display communicating the production, availability, and use of energy in the district. It makes local energy data accessible to anyone. It encourages capacity-driven energy use by creating awareness of the energy availability in different seasons. As such, it increases the sense of ownership to manage and conserve the use of energy based on availability. The Dashboard is also accessible via a NeighborhoodApp (a LEAP governance tool), which anyone can install on their own device.

THERMAL INSULATION

Thermal insulation minimizes temperature loss from buildings. In doing so, it increases energy efficiency and reduces CO_2 emissions. Insulation improves the health, comfort, and wellbeing of residents and reduces their energy bills. There are various thermal insulation materials that can be applied to a variety of external surfaces, such as façades, roofs, and foundations. Interiors can also be insulated, for example by replacing single-glazed windows with double or triple glazing. Drafts can be prevented by sealing the edges of doors, window frames, and letterboxes and by adding brush seals to the bottoms of windows and doors. Together, these measures improve the value of the property and can create local jobs.

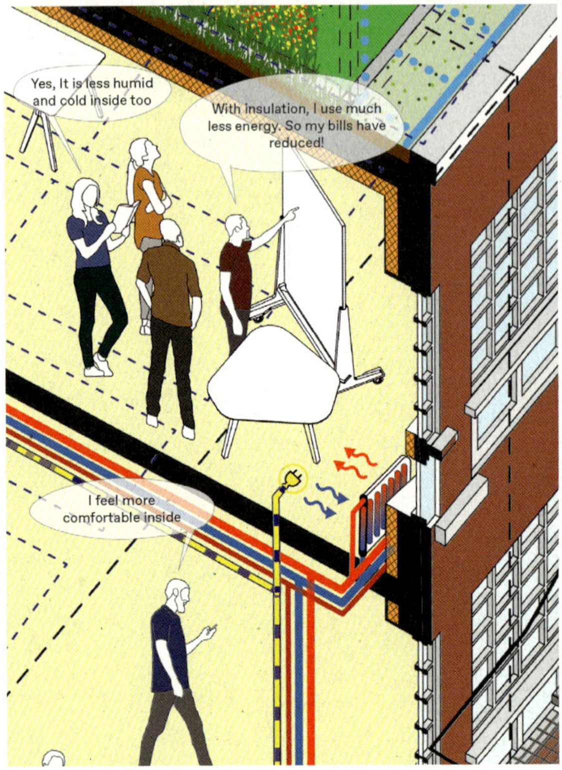

ENERGY-EFFICIENT APPLIANCES

Many older, sometimes gas-fueled appliances, such as whiteware, boilers, and lighting, consume more electricity than newer electric appliances. These goods are graded from energy label A to G; label A being the most energy efficient, label G the least. Creating awareness and stimulating the use of these energy-efficient appliances lowers electricity consumption and thus energy bills. For example, replacing a 60 W incandescent lightbulb with a 12 W LED light provides the same luminosity but consumes up to 80 percent less electricity.

CLIMATE BUFFER

Climate buffers or double-skin façades, that is, closed glass façades that are placed in front of interior façades, protect buildings against overheating due to solar radiation and against drafts by reducing wind pressure on the façade. They provide an efficient, self-regulating ventilation system to the building. To perform efficiently, the orientation of the climate buffer or double-skin façade needs to be considered. Generally, this system saves 15 to 70 percent of electricity compared to a single-skin façade with internal blinds.

Positioned above windows, shading canopies reduce heat generated by direct sun exposure in summer. In winter, they can be retracted to allow desired heat gain. By providing control of solar heat gain and reduction based on the weather, this system encourages participation, provides comfort, and reduces the residents' electricity bills.

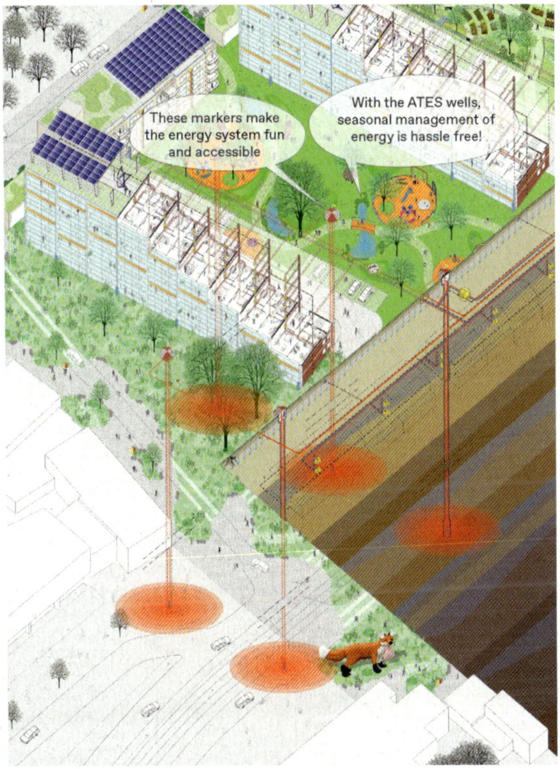

AQUIFER THERMAL ENERGY STORAGE (ATES)

The system stores naturally available seasonal thermal energy in underground aquifers to use at the right time for heating and cooling buildings. The system is designed in 'doublets', combining pairs of hot and cold wells. In the summer, the cold well provides cooling while heat is stored in the hot well. This system reverses in winter. Return thermal energy from indoor heating systems and aqua thermal energy from water bodies are examples of heat/cold sources for the system.

BATTERIES

Lithium batteries store surplus electricity generated by wind and solar energy for future use. This way, the maximum local energy capacity is utilized, and energy is available on demand. The daily surplus can be stored in homes or public buildings in the district. The battery capacity of electric cars can also be used for storage.

HYDROGEN MICRO-CHP

The hydrogen micro combined heat and power (micro-CHP) plant converts renewable energy into hydrogen fuel to be used on demand. It uses solar and wind energy to electrolyze water, generating oxygen and hydrogen. Hydrogen is then distributed as a fuel through the existing gas network. This system provides clean storage of solar and wind energy, which ensures consistent supply of hydrogen fuel across seasons. Steam, released as a by-product, is used to supply hot water or heating for a heat network. Large-scale storage is possible in the district or outside urban environments, but production and storage facilities need to be located at a safe distance from buildings.

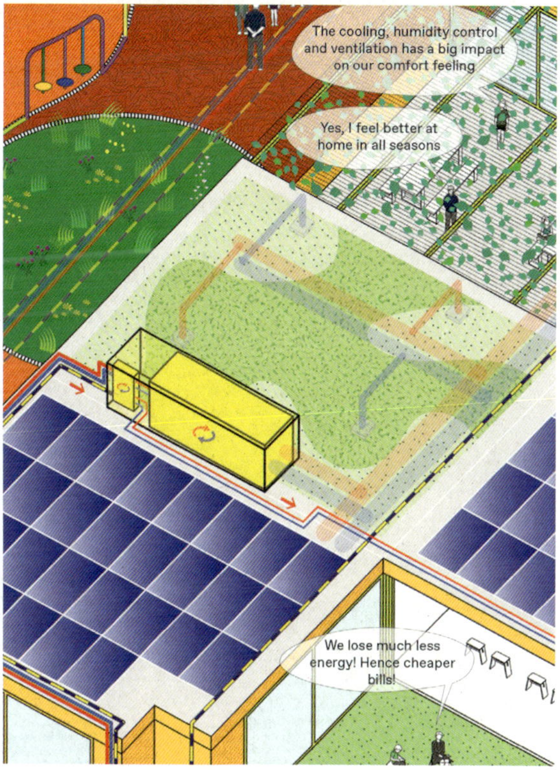

HEAT RECOVERY SYSTEM

This system provides temperature-conditioned ventilation by using building exhaust as either a heat source or a heat sink, depending on the climate conditions, time of year, and building requirements. The system recovers 60 to 95 percent of the heat in exhaust air, which significantly improves the energy efficiency of buildings and can also regulate indoor humidity. The system can be applied as a secondary heating system in various types of buildings, such as housing and offices.

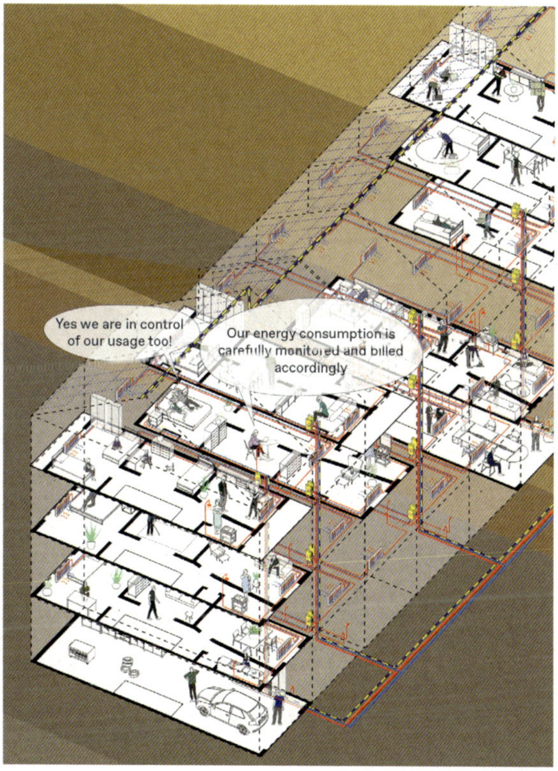

DELIVERY SET

This discreet box delivers heating and cooling, hot tap water, and electricity to its users. It is made for use in domestic situations, such as housing, and functions as the interface between the microgrid and the in-house energy network. A meter in the delivery set monitors the billing of electricity.
If used in an Aquifer Thermal Energy Storage (ATES) low-temperature microgrid, the delivery set receives the following supplies from the energy hub: hot tap water, low-temperature heating, low-temperature cooling, and electricity. From the delivery set, a return pipe feeds into the ATES system.

INDUCTION RADIATORS

Induction radiators can provide low-temperature heating and cooling in domestic environments, which is more efficient and generally more comfortable than high-temperature heating. The low-temperature radiators can only be used in well-insulated buildings (Energy Labels A to C). Thermal energy from the return pipe can be fed into Aquifer Thermal Energy Storage (ATES) wells through a low-temperature microgrid. Some models also integrate ventilation in the walls on which they are mounted.

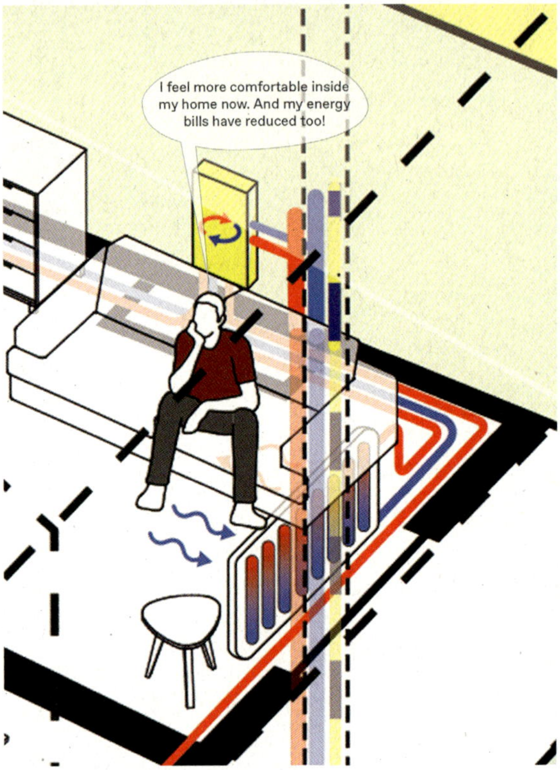

WIND TURBINES

Wind turbines can be places in urban settings and offshore. Wind turbines capture wind energy and convert it into electricity. They can be used in urban settings for local energy production to lower the dependency on centralized and corporate energy grids. The small turbines can be placed on flat roofs and combined with solar panels. This system is viable for roofs with a minimum height of 15 m and needs to be positioned free of obstacles. Rotterdam is close enough to the sea to connect the city's systems to those of large offshore wind turbines.

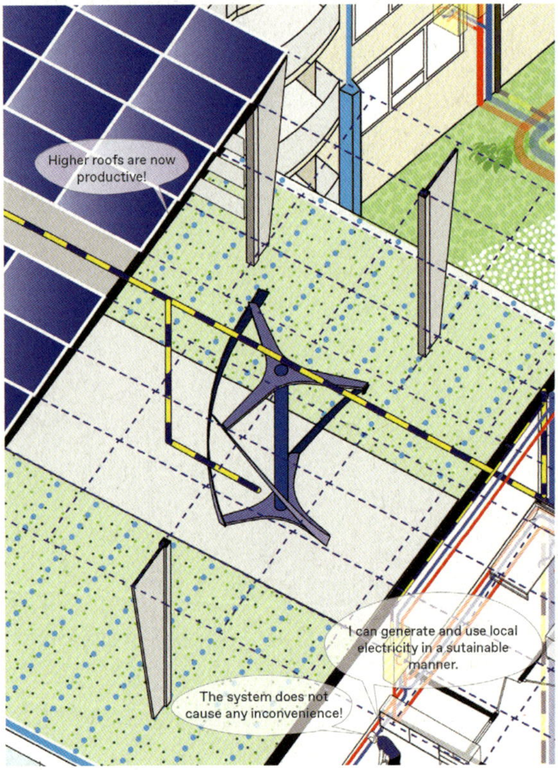

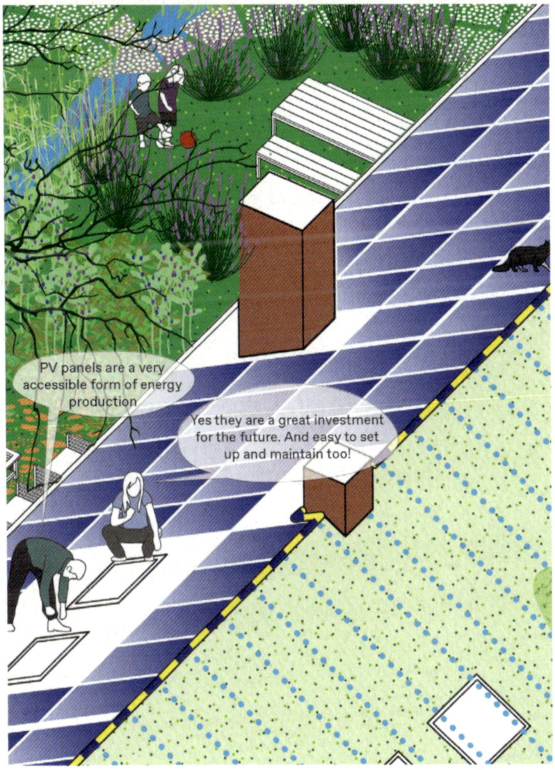

PV PANELS

Photo-voltaic (PV) cells convert solar radiation into direct current electricity. A collection of PV cells forms a PV panel that is easy to install. Depending on their orientation, PV-panels have the potential to serve as a primary energy source for local microgrids, which decreases the dependency on centralized and corporate grids. PV panels can be combined with green roofs.
Solar farms use solar panels for the low-cost, large-scale production of clean electricity. They are located in large open areas, such as the countryside and wastelands. Since urban settings have limited electricity production capacity on roofs, solar farms are essential to achieve 100 percent renewable electricity and to serve as an economical source of clean energy. Solar farms can be combined with vegetation, water retention or specific types of agriculture.

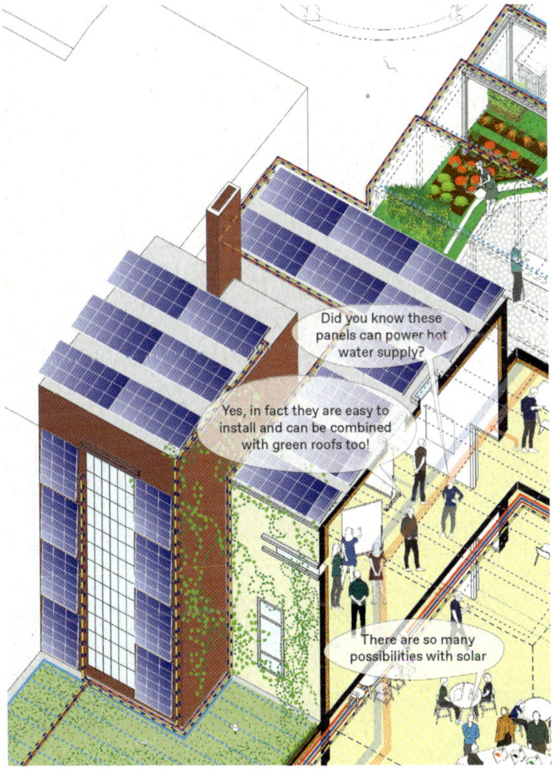

PT AND PVT PANELS

Two types of solar panels exist: photothermal (PT) and photo-voltaic thermal (PVT) panels. Photothermal (PT) panels absorb thermal energy from solar energy through a heat-conducting liquid. The heated liquid is used to heat tap water or is stored in water tanks that can support the local hot water supply. PT panels are feasible on well-oriented sloped and all flat roofs and can be combined with green roofs.
Triple Solar Photovoltaic Thermal (PVT) panels use a combination of photovoltaic and photothermal systems. They capture solar energy and convert it into heat and electricity. PVT panels are capable of recovering ambient heat when direct sunlight is unavailable. When combined with a heat pump and hot water buffer, these panels can supply heating year-round.

RESIDUAL HEAT DISTRIBUTION

This system captures residual heat generated by local supermarkets, bakeries and other heat sources in the district. The residual heat is inserted into an existing or new heating network. When combined with a heat pump, the system can be used to heat buildings and supply hot water.

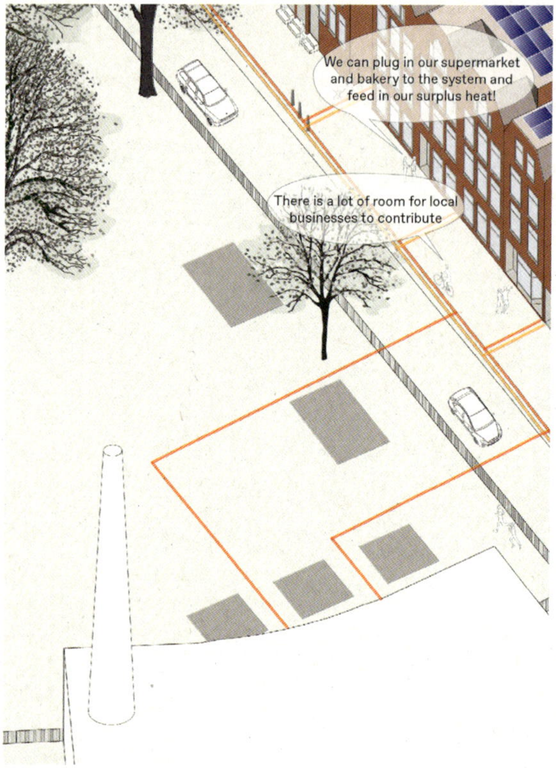

AQUATHERMAL ENERGY

Aquathermal energy is generated by capturing seasonal warmth and cold from surface water. Two fundamental systems exist and can be placed in open bodies of water: heat exchangers that capture heat from the water and systems that pump water to heat exchangers on land.
In the Netherlands, where surface water temperatures fluctuate between 7 and 25 °C, the system functions as a low-temperature heat source. At peak performance, which happens one or two weeks each year, the system can supply heat for direct use in a low-temperature Aquifer Thermal Energy Storage (ATES) microgrid.

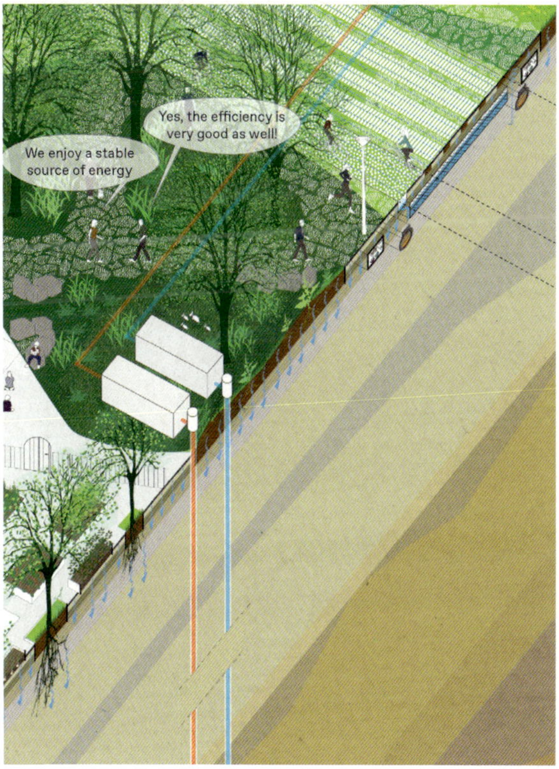

GEOTHERMAL ENERGY

Geothermal energy is generated by and stored in the earth. This energy can be extracted from geothermal wells that need to be at least 250 m deep and placed at least 1.5 km apart. Temperatures, and with that, the efficiency, increase with depth. Although greenhouse gases once trapped deep inside the earth are released near the wells, the released amounts are a lot lower per energy unit than those produced by burning fossil fuels.

A TOOLBOX FOR THE DISTRICT
Governance Tools

Governance tools enable stakeholders to transform a LEAP into concrete collective action in the district. By providing collaborative and financing models for the creation, ownership, and management of energy and climate adaptation tools, they support residents during the transition process to a socially inclusive and sustainable district. Governance tools can be used, for example, to create a roadmap for mobilizing and forming coalitions, like a project group or an Energy Service Company (ESCo).

COMMUNITY CAPACITY TOOLS

The activities below encourage individual residents and their networks to work toward a common goal. During these activities, they learn skills and gain action perspectives so that they can join the negotiating table with governments and private parties as equal partners.

EXHIBITIONS showcase community, research, results, and progress.

ABCD (ASSET BASED COMMUNITY DEVELOPMENT) develops assets in a collaborative process with the local community.

EVENTS build a sense of belonging through recreation and awareness.

WORKSHOPS facilitate collaboration by getting people together to work on ideas, visions, and aspirations.

SURVEYS gather qualitative and quantitative data and also capture consensus.

PLATFORMS facilitate learning and sharing information through an (online) space or forum.

MOVEMENT-BUILDING TOOLS

The activities listed below maintain the momentum of the transition process and facilitate the conduct of a continuous dialogue.

CAMPAIGNS communicate information, gather support, and create a gradual shift in consciousness.

At MILESTONE MEETINGS, progress is highlighted, transparency is ensured, feedback is exchanged, and potential optimization is discussed.

MONITORING AND REPORTING measure and validate progress, build trust, and inform decision making.

THE NEIGHBORHOOD APP is an open-to-all application for service management and resource sharing in the neighborhood.

POLICYMAKING

Governments at local and national levels can support district LEAPs through effective policymaking.

Policies can contribute to the:

— INSPIRING and STIMULATING of new ideas and REALIZING a positive environment in which citizens and businesses are encouraged to explore more sustainable practices.

— GATHERING AND COORDINATING of various initiatives that address specific issues, and to upscaling such initiatives and fostering knowledge exchange.

— INVESTING in and SUBSIDIZING of knowledge creation, experimentation and new ideas that benefit the green economy, and INVOLVING all stakeholders in the process.

— GUIDING and SUPPORTING of local action and making available knowledge gathered over time and through dedicated research.

— REGULATING and ENFORCING of and REPORTING on progress and decision-making, and NORMALIZING activities (for example, by capping the carbon emissions allowed by industry).

ORGANIZATION AND FINANCING TOOLS

stakeholder roles:

CARETAKERS maintain spaces in return for access to the commons.

USERS and RESIDENTS have access to the assets.

OWNERS own all assets JOINTLY; this is stipulated in an agreement.

INVESTORS invest through money, support, and in-kind.

RENTERS rent the assets for a set period in return for a fee or maintenance effort.

HOUSE OWNERS participate in setting up the assets on their property.

EMPLOYEES carry out work on a contract basis.

MEMBERS and SUPPORTERS of the cooperations provide (financial) support and keep the momentum going.

SERVICE PROVIDERS deliver a service on a contract basis.

finance models:

CROWDFUNDING allows voluntary financial contribution by interested stakeholders.

SUBSIDIES from the (local) government encourage activities that align with policy strategies.

GRANTS are awarded by organizations to specific activities that align with their societal or charitable goals.

BANK LOANS make it possible to borrow money on favorable terms.

DONATIONS are goodwill contributions by which individuals or groups give back to society.

MEMBERSHIP FEES are periodic payments made by interested members of a group.

PROFITS are income incurred through business activities that can be invested in future projects.

PRIVATE INVESTMENTS are funds granted by non-commercial parties with the expectation of a return over a period of time.

SERVICE FEE CONTRIBUTIONS are monthly fees that are charged in exchange for services.

organization types:

PROJECT GROUP
The project group can be applied to any grouping of residents and entrepreneurs to collectively carry out a local project. It is accessible to all, regardless of experience, income, or position in society.

COOPERATIVE/ESCO
In the Netherlands, cooperatives (*coöperaties*) take the legal form of members' associations (*verenigingen*). They are democratically owned by participating members, who also receive the profits made.
Compared with project groups, cooperatives access a wider range of financing options, including bank loans or third-party investments.

BV (COMPANY)/ESCO
A *BV (Besloten Venootschap)* is a limited liability company. In this context, it is the most formal organizational form, with access to the most financing options. Its primary goal is to make a profit in exchange for goods or services. This profit is returned to the company. For the energy transition, a BV's clients could be residents, homeowners' associations, or even housing corporations.

A COMMUNITY GAME

Imagine a room with a wall-to-wall game board, with a detailed map of Bospolder-Tussendijken showing the spatial and energetic data collected by the IABR–Atelier Rotterdam. The game pieces and strategy cards used are based on the LEAP and the Toolboxes for the World and the District. The aim of the game is to make the district more sustainable. Together, the players explore the possible applications of the energy and climate adaptation tools, while they have to choose between investments and ecological, social and financial returns. They also have to think about which governance tools they need to be able to realize proposals. In this way, an understanding is created of the interrelationships and everyone's position and role within them, and it becomes clear that the goal of increasing sustainability can only be realized by working together: in, with and by the district.

In its mobile game box, this Community Game will travel through the district. The game can be played anywhere: in community centers, classrooms, shop windows or at the library. Local game leaders ensure that the game is played regularly and in such a way that everyone can participate. Unhindered by the technical jargon of the energy transition, residents can thus exchange knowledge and experience in a playful manner. The safe but realistic environment of the game helps participants to put their roles, interests and wishes on the table, alongside those of other players, and to look for the common good together.

Resilient BoTu 2028: A Community Game was commissioned by the IABR and developed by Play the City to bring the results of the IABR–Atelier Rotterdam to Bospolder-Tussendijken. Residents, building owners, housing corporations, the city, grid operators and other stakeholders can explore together how the tools of the LEAP can be applied in the district, and residents can learn how to effectively own the transition.

Resilient BoTu 2028:
A Community Game
RECLAIMING THE COMMONS
photo: Aad Hoogendoorn

RECLAIM THE COMMONS!

By presenting the interim research results and thus stimulating reflection on them, the two DOWN TO EARTH exhibitions, WHOSE ENERGY IS IT, ANYWAY? and RECLAIMING THE COMMONS, were to become an active part of the step-by-step process of thinking and doing that should lead from the local energy *action plan* to local energy *action*. The aim was for the biennale, as a cultural organization, to create a free space for Bospolder-Tussendijken and provide it with a toolbox and a community game with which more and more residents can lay claim to the energy transition and eventually appropriate it – as such, but especially as a lever for integral change.

Everything Must Change

The four case studies convincingly demonstrate that residents can indeed take on new roles. The LEAP and the Toolbox for the District offer people who want to get started direction and support, and competencies are created. And if, with the Toolbox for the World in hand, the countdown to 2030 is kept in mind with every step that is taken towards reaching the goal of a socially sustainable CO_2-neutral district, then BoTu can land on Planet Earth.

But that won't just happen. Action perspective and action competence are one thing, acquiring ownership is another. In addition to action plans and tools, residents must also be given a real position and be taken seriously by the authorities and the business community as co-owners of the transition. After all, this is about *their* living environment. Private-public cooperation is imperative, but then residents have to be able to become real players, too. Residents will only be able to secure a real position if what they contribute is taken up seriously and considered real value. In other words, if not only economic but also social and ecological gains are considered as increases in value, as income added to the books.

Because everything must change. The way capitalism works and the relationships between government, businesses and civil society must change, especially the underlying power structures. We need a new balance of profit and loss that takes into account the importance of future generations and other forms of life without irresponsibly mortgaging the future. This requires profound transitions and a structural systems change. Only then will humans be harmless enough to safely land on Earth again. Only then can we reclaim the commons – that which belongs to us jointly and should remain so, and which we must take care of together – now and for the future.

THAMAR KEMPERMAN
theater maker
SILA SOEBDHAN
chairperson Huurdersraad West
"I want to help make life a little easier for everyone.
We can only hope to accomplish this if we join forces."
LYDIA PEES
owner of a house with solar panels

CREDITS
WHOSE ENERGY IS IT, ANYWAY? / RECLAIMING THE COMMONS

CURATORS
George Brugmans (chief curator)
Thijs van Spaandonk

ASSISTANT TO THE CHIEF CURATOR
Alexandra Sonnemans

CURATOR ASSISTANTS
Umut Türkmen, Leanne Hoogwaerts (WHOSE ENERGY IS IT, ANYWAY?)
Noortje Weenink (RECLAIMING THE COMMONS)

EXHIBITION DESIGN
Eva Pfannes, Thijs van Spaandonk, George Brugmans

GRAPHIC DESIGN
ARK
Roosje Klap, Loes Claessens, Nóra Békés, Nina van Tuikwerd

LEAP
OOZE architects & urbanists
Eva Pfannes, Sylvain Hartenberg, Leanne Hoogwaerts, Nilofer Tajuddin, Hsoc Mathai George, Federica Zatta, Elif Soylu, Felipe Gonzalez

EEKLO
PLUSOFFICE architects
Jitse Massant, Willem Hubrechts, Ward Verbakel
Studio Woudstra
Finn Meier, Adam Scales

please note that all credits for the research by design by the IABR–Ateliers Rotterdam III and OVK can be found on page 38-39 and page 45 respectively

PORTRAITS
Ximena Dávalos

DEVELOPMENT COMMUNITY GAME
Play the City
Ekim Tan, Txell Blanco, Asma Begdouri Achkari, Chia-Ju Lin, Hyunwoo Koo

EVENTS
Yonca Özbilge

PRODUCTION AND PLANNING
Jolanda van Dinteren, Lisa Lambert, Johanna Fuhler (WHOSE ENERGY IS IT, ANYWAY?)
Maartje Berendsen, Johanna Fuhler (RECLAIMING THE COMMONS)

COPY-EDITING AND TRANSLATIONS
InOtherWords translation & editing
D'Laine Camp, Gerda ten Cate, Maria van Tol

CONSTRUCTION, LIGHTNING, AND PRINTING
Bart Cuppens Tentoonstellingsbouw
Bouwer Bouwer
Keilepand bv
Nicari
Quintus Belichting
Rocka Art & Sign
Snijlab
Veenman+

←
RECLAIMING THE COMMONS
photo: Aad Hoogendoorn

HOW CAN WE LAND?

WAT R

THE IABR AND WATER

Ever since the 2005 biennale THE FLOOD, water has been the blue thread through many of the IABR's exhibitions and research programs. Over the past 15 years, we have been fostering the incremental development of the alternative practice of designing with water. This practice reserves a guiding role for research into ways to purposefully use the water challenge as leverage for a broad approach to alternative, sustainable urban development. These efforts fit in well with the IABR's intention to actively and to the best of its ability contribute to the realization of the climate goals of the global community. After all, water – too much of it, not enough of it, too polluted – creates some of the most challenging and complex dangers that humankind currently faces. More than 80 percent of all climate change-induced emergencies and disasters are water related. Everywhere and increasingly, floods and droughts, pollution, drinking water shortages, and water conflicts – in connection with population growth, increasing migration, rapid urbanization, and growing demand for food and energy – are causing problems and often even disasters. Water's almost constant potential for disruptive transitions has become far too great. But it is precisely this ubiquity and urgency of the water challenge that offers the opportunity to use water as a lever for the realization of research by design projects everywhere and at every level, aimed at integrated and true transformation.

New Challenges in the Delta of the Low Countries

Even the Netherlands, the country below sea level that believed it was home and dry, contends with serious flooding and, as of the summer of 2018, unexpected periods of severe drought – a completely new challenge in the Delta of the Low Countries.

In view of this double threat, in 2019 the IABR established two Ateliers in the context of the biennale DOWN TO EARTH. George Brugmans asked architect and urban designer Marco Vermeulen to lead the IABR–Atelier Drought in the Delta, which spent more than a year researching (causes of) drought in the area covering the Rhine, Meuse, and Scheldt River basins. Subsequently, the Atelier designed realistic, often regional solutions that, towards 2050, were to lead to a coherent approach to a new freshwater strategy for the entire Netherlands. And in the IABR–Atelier Dordrecht, five different design studios, led by landscape architect Adriaan Geuze, investigated whether and how, in a city at high risk of flooding, new preventive measures for water safety could be designed in such a way that they would also act as levers for truly sustainable area development. The results of the two Ateliers were presented in the exhibitions DROUGHT IN THE DELTA and THE HIGH GROUND.

The IABR Method: A Three-Stage Plan

In these two Ateliers, the IABR could build on what it had learned during previous research projects in which water challenges had turned out to play a frequently unforeseen crucial role at the local level. This had happened, first, in São Paulo, and later in Istanbul, the two metropolises in which the IABR established test sites together with the local city governments in the period 2008–2016 with the aim of offering what Brugmans called 'sabbatical detours.' These were multi-year research trajectories in 'free cultural spaces' in which administrators, designers, residents, stakeholders, and experts worked together concretely and purposefully. Jointly managed by city and biennale, they were designed as temporary in-between spaces, to beget true change by a three-stage plan comprising research by design, exhibition, and realization.[15]

From 2008 onwards, Brugmans formed an increasingly close pact with São Paulo's deputy councilor of Public Housing and head of the Social Housing Authority (SEHAB) Elisabete França, and architect and later councilor of Urban Development Fernando de Mello Franco (who was also a member of the curator team of the 5th IABR, MAKING CITY, in 2012). The pact proved strong enough to fulfill all three stages of the plan, from research to realization.

[15] For a detailed description and reflection on the IABR method and sabbatical detour, see: George Brugmans, 'It's the Culture, Stupid!,' in: George Brugmans, Jolanda van Dinteren, Maarten Hajer (eds.), *The Next Economy* (Rotterdam: IABR, 2016), p 115 ff.

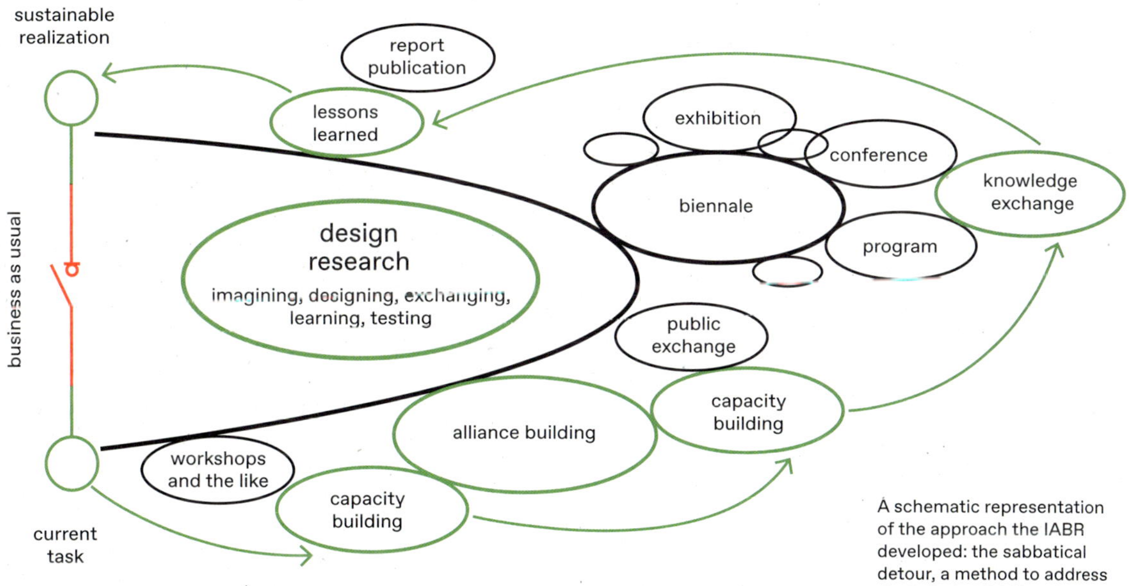

A schematic representation of the approach the IABR developed: the sabbatical detour, a method to address the 'missing link' in urban design, the gap between urgent challenges and sustainable implementation. © IABR

Experiences in Istanbul, however, went on to show how fragile collaborations between city administrators and designers in a free in-between space invariably are. In this metropolis, realization failed to materialize in spite of the first two stages having been quite successful.

→
Flooding in São Paulo, 2010
© George Brugmans

São Paulo: Investing in Both Infrastructure and the Living Environment

The collaboration with São Paulo, the largest metropolis in the southern hemisphere, started in Rotterdam, in 2007, during the 3rd IABR, POWER. The project Watery Voids, by the São Paulo-based design firm MMBB (led by Marta Moreira, Milton Braga, and Fernando de Mello Franco), which won the Rotterdam Biennale Award that year, argued that architects ought to focus much more on infrastructure because this always requires the largest investment in city making. The rule in São Paulo, a city carelessly constructed over thousands of creeks and small rivers, was to combat the perpetual problem of flooding by constructing an ever-expanding system of reservoirs to collect rainwater inside the city limits. However, as a purely technical solution – which, by the way, was inadequate: floods continued to plague the city – the functioning of these reservoirs was completely divorced from the fragile local living and housing conditions into which they were parachuted. Watery Voids wanted to show that the construction of a network of urban 'residual spaces' would make it possible to internally reconnect the city's periphery, especially if combined with policies in other sectors. Here, like in THE FLOOD, we are seeing the early contours of a *water-as-leverage* approach. The idea was to combine investments in major public (water) works at the level of the entire metropolis with social investments to improve the living environment at the local level.

Paraisópolis
© George Brugmans

MMBB's next project, Antonico, was part of the program to redevelop the favela Paraisópolis that was presented at the 4th IABR, OPEN CITY: DESIGNING COEXISTENCE. The project was commissioned by São Paulo's Social Housing Authority (SEHAB) in the context of the first collaboration between SEHAB and the IABR. It involved different, but related projects in Paraisópolis, in which Rainer Hehl (ETH Zurich), Urban Think Tank (Caracas), Christian Kerez (Zurich), Maciel, Boldarini and Dias (São Paulo) and Alejandro Aravena (Santiago) were actively involved as well. This collaboration challenged SEHAB to expand its activities in the *favelas* – which until then had focused solely on the development of social housing – for example by embedding social services, that is, by combining housing construction with projects in areas such as water (safety), mobility, public space, and public health.

The various projects carried out in the context of IABR–Test Site São Paulo
image: IABR

The specific goal of MMBB's project was to not only canalize the Antonico, a small river that intersects the *favela* and regularly floods, but to also improve the living environment of the residents in the process. As it turned out, the biggest challenge was the conception of a strategy that would ensure that the banks of the Antonico would be preserved as a public area once the work had been completed. The solution was drafting a covenant that specified the form in which each use of the space had to contribute to the strengthening of the public realm.

Paraisópolis exige respeito! In an animated meeting with designers and city officials, residents demand respect and a voice when it comes to changing their living environment. © George Brugmans

The Antonico project made it possible to realize the proposals conceived in Watery Voids. In addition, the IABR method introduced an element that was new to São Paulo's design processes, namely, to enter into dialogue with local stakeholders, neighborhood associations, and residents on approaches and interpretations of (re)development *while work is already underway*.[16]

To realize the first round of the plans the IABR and São Paulo jointly created for projects in the Paraisópolis *favela*, the SEHAB allocated the equivalent of about 220 million euros in 2010. Liftoff successful!

[16] Reflecting on the experiences of the first collaboration with the IABR, project manager of the Paraisópolis project on behalf of SEHAB Maria Teresa Diniz wrote: 'The collaboration proved to be much more intensive and productive than a mere exchange of ideas. We discussed the role of architects and urban designers, how their work might contribute to a better life in the city, to a much broader perspective. In the beginning we were not at all familiar with the IABR's working model: a test site where the work is already in progress? When Paraisópolis became a laboratory for the Open City, however, it proved extremely fruitful to discuss the way we work with experts from other parts of the world. Our methods were examined, and this forced us to reconsider and adjust them.' See: George Brugmans, 'It's the Culture, Stupid!', in: Brugmans et al., *The Next Economy* (Rotterdam: IABR, 2016), p 116.

The announcement of the São Paulo City Council's decision to invest R$400 million (the equivalent of over 200 million euros at the time) in the implementation of a number of IABR–Atelier projects, including Antonico. image: IABR

Istanbul: Closing the Water Cycle in Arnavutköy

The groundwork for the IABR–Atelier Istanbul was laid in 2010 in a series of informal conversations between the mayor of the Arnavutköy district located in northwest Istanbul, Ahmet Hasim Baltaci, professor at Istanbul Bilgi University Asu Aksoy, and IABR director George Brugmans. The question was whether and how to balance the ongoing urbanization that threatened Istanbul's verdant north, while at the same time addressing the increasingly urgent issue of preserving the water basins crucial to the drinking water supply and food production of the entire metropolis – and doing so in a way that benefited everyone and everything.

The solution the IABR–Atelier proposed, consisted of an integrated approach that was completely new to Türkiye. Water could be used as a formative strength in the design of Arnavutköy; in turn, the town would supply water for agriculture; the countryside would then purify water for use in the town. This closing of the water cycle, powerfully visualized in a computer animation, would not only provide Arnavutköy with promising yet realistic prospects, but also enrich the entire north side of the Istanbul metropolis with an alternative urban design practice.[17]

[17] The closing of the water cycle in Arnavutköy was persuasively visualized in a computer animation by H+N+S Landscape Architects and Tungsten.

See video *Closing the Water Cycle*

For those without a smartphone: an overview of all website addresses to which the QR codes in this book refer is provided on page 438.

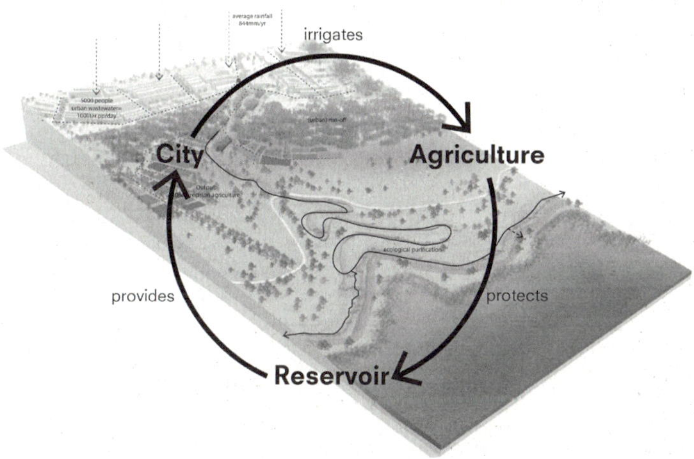

Closing the water cycle
Still from video *IABR–Atelier Istanbul: Arnavutköy*
image: Tungsten Studio, IABR

Atelier Istanbul was led by Aksoy, who was also asked to join the curator team of the 5th IABR, MAKING CITY. The research was carried out by H+N+S Landscape Architects, 51N4E, and Architecture Workroom Brussels (AWB). The Atelier drafted a Strategic Plan that laid the foundation for a sustainable interpretation of future developments in Arnavutköy. This was approved by the town in the fall of 2011 and subsequently further developed in an Action Plan and a number of pilot projects. The results were on show in 2012 in Rotterdam as part of the main exhibition of MAKING CITY. Next, the pilot projects were further developed on the basis of the Strategic Plan, and the results of the second stage shown in the exhibition 'Making City Istanbul,' curated by Brugmans and Joachim Declerck, which opened in October 2012 at the Istanbul Modern as part of the 1st Istanbul Design Biennale. Arnavutköy subsequently could and in fact wanted to start work on the pilot projects.

Istanbul: Space for Water in Beykoz

Meanwhile, a second IABR–Atelier Istanbul had been established in Beykoz, an Istanbul district located on the Asian side of the metropolis, where the Black Sea flows into the Bosporus. Beykoz is intersected by the Riva Caddesi, which regularly floods and causes problems. Its proposed canalization was meant to protect the valley from the water, but would also have a major impact on the scenic qualities as well as economic potential of this unique green area on the northern outskirts of Istanbul.

Flooding of the Riva Caddesi in Beykoz, Istanbul (2009)

Looking for alternatives to the threatening construction of a long, wide cement trough across the beautiful landscape, and inspired by the first research results of the Atelier in Arnavutköy, local administrators and entrepreneurs had gotten in touch with the IABR. After mutual explorations – during which the Turkish delegation had visited the Netherlands and become extra convinced by, among other things, the Room for the Rivers project – the two parties decided to enter into an agreement. Two design offices already active in Arnavutköy, H+N+S and 51N4E, were asked to develop an integrated plan. This would not only address water safety, but also the revitalization of the agricultural area and the ecological and recreational development of the forests, and conceive a new waterside city with a marina.

Field trip to Riva Caddesi, Beykoz, 2013
from left to right: Zeki Baran (IABR), Lodewijk van Nieuwenhuijze (H+N+S) and Türkiye's minister of Agriculture Mehdi Eker
photo: IABR

The Turkish Minister of Agriculture came to Beykoz in the summer of 2013 and was enthusiastic about the innovation – to Türkiye – of approaching water issues in such a way that agriculture would also benefit. After further research, the final presentation by the IABR to the Ministry's Water Directorate took place on 13 January 2014 in Ankara, after which the project was given the go-ahead.
The plan not only guaranteed water safety, but also facilitated a big step toward integrated area development. Beykoz was going to have room for high-quality agriculture as well as urban development projects; the tourist industry would have the opportunity to develop along the waterfront and recreational opportunities would be expanded to also benefit the city's other residents. Beykoz was going to develop into the green lung of the Istanbul metropolis – both its administrators and its entrepreneurs were raring to go.

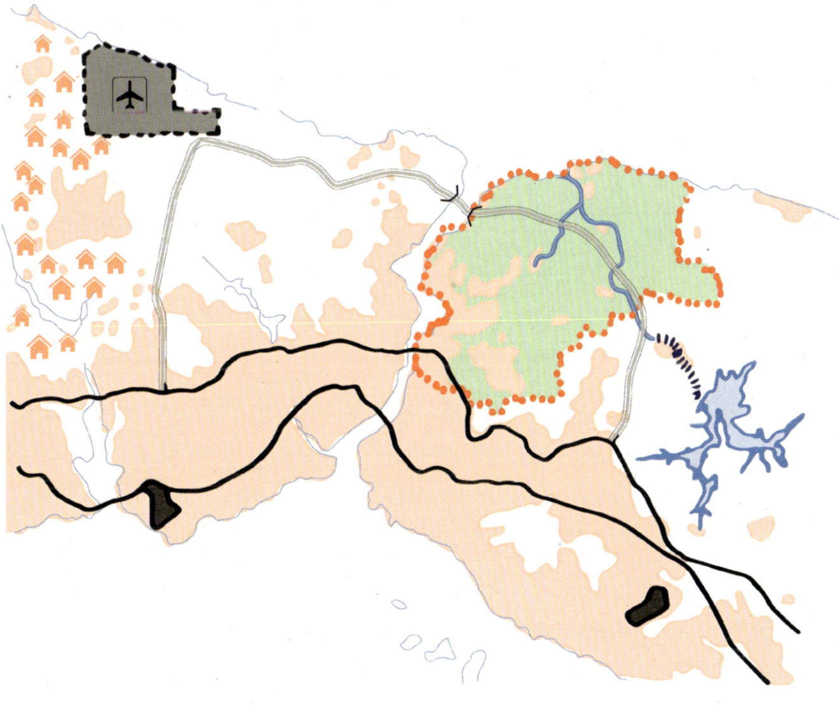

Beykoz as Istanbul's possible green lung, with the Riva Caddesi drawn into it. Above left is the later-constructed new airport, partly in Arnavutköy, a development that prevented the realization of the blue-green plans as proposed by the IABR-Atelier in Arnavutköy.
image: IABR–Atelier Istanbul

Nightmare

Although the plans of the two IABR–Ateliers in Istanbul could count on a great deal of enthusiasm and support both locally and at the distinct ministries, the third and decisive stage failed to materialize. Largely to blame for this was the Turkish government, which unexpectedly parachuted plans into the territory in which the blue-green north side of metropolitan Istanbul was sacrificed to new project developments. This involved a third bridge across the Bosporus, including a new highway to connect Europe and Asia on the north side as well; the construction of high-rise buildings and apartments directly on the (protected) Black Sea coast; a new, huge airport to the northwest, in Arnavutköy; and, possibly, a new canal connecting the Black Sea to the Sea of Marmara intersecting the European half of the city. No matter how eager local administrators in Arnavutköy and Beykoz were to move forward with sustainable projects that would help solve their local problems, the metropolis itself and, in the background, Ankara slammed on the brakes – larger, political, and business interests were at play.

The most publicly prominent result of the IABR–Atelier Istanbul was ultimately the 'Istanbul at the Crossroads' manifesto, signed by all curators of the 5th and 6th IABRs and the Istanbul Design Biennale, which was published in several media. In it, the issue was brought to a head: 'Will Istanbul become the next metropolitan nightmare, or will it become an inspiring example? That is the question.' [18]

At a later date, the IABR was approached by several Turkish local administrations, but by then it was clear that the close intertwining of politics and urban development in this country would always frustrate the approach advocated by the IABR. And in Istanbul, the nightmare has indeed come true; a large part of Istanbul's northern edge has now been sacrificed to ruthless developmentalism. [19]

[18] 'Istanbul at the Crossroads' manifesto (2012)

[19] We had been warned and had even issued warnings ourselves, see: Orhan Esen, 'Producing Inequalities by Producing Built Environment. Just in Case: Istanbul', in: Tim Rieniets, Jennifer Sigler, Kees Christiaanse (eds.), *Open City: Designing Coexistence* (Amsterdam: SUN, 2009), p 175-186, the book accompanying the 4th edition of the IABR.

Encroaching urbanization in the northern half of Istanbul © George Brugmans

Lessons Learned

So the IABR plans in and with São Paulo were more successful than those in Istanbul, also in the long term.[20] 'Critical reflection on what does or does not work in this "in-between space," on what the conditions are under which, during the sabbatical detour, design and politics can freely and at the same time truly engage with each other in a purposeful way, remains part of the method itself,' as Brugmans later wrote. 'The IABR is a learning organization,' there are no standard procedures, no short cuts: 'Ultimately, success depends on the way governments, but also designers deal with the potential of free space. Or rather, whether they *can* deal with it.'[21]
True transformative city making is and remains the work of humans. It not only involves designers and administrators, but also residents – who will only be actively involved in processes of change that cannot succeed without them if they feel they are being heard. It is this very condition that underscores the value of a free space – a safe place for dangerous ideas – that a cultural organization like the IABR can offer to everyone involved, with the aim of creating an alternative, yet goal-oriented approach to urban design challenges at all levels.

Nothing, however, kept the IABR from putting the lessons learned in Türkiye into practice elsewhere. After all, the Atelier Istanbul had amassed a great deal of knowledge, which the IABR could use to lay a solid foundation for further research. This started in the first IABR–Atelier Rotterdam, about the urban metabolism, and, in a broader sense, toward the 2014 biennale, URBAN BY NATURE. In Arnavutköy, landscape architect Dirk Sijmons, who had been actively involved in Atelier Istanbul, drew the (at the time) challenging conclusion that global environmental problems can and must be solved in cities. On the spot, Brugmans asked him to elaborate on that conclusion and become curator of URBAN BY NATURE and lead designer of the first three studios that the IABR wanted to set up in the Netherlands, in the City of Rotterdam, on the island Texel, and in the Province of North Brabant. Although all of the three Ateliers took the lessons learned abroad on board, IABR–Atelier BrabantStad is an especially good example of the unexpected effect that putting the water challenge at the center of the project can have. From this perspective, there is a very direct line between Istanbul and North Brabant.

BrabantStad, a Carpet Metropolis: Water as a Hidden Strength

BrabantStad, a partnership of the cities of 's-Hertogenbosch, Eindhoven, Tilburg, Breda, and Helmond, is in fact a dispersed city, or better still, an urban landscape. It is a mosaic as vast as it is motley, a carpet metropolis including many forms of high- and low-density land use. The post-2008 financial crisis had hit Brabant municipalities hard; many planned developments had to be abandoned. The question was, what approach would succeed in restoring momentum to the meeting of major socioeconomic

[20] De Mello Franco took his experiences with the Atelier with him when he became São Paulo's Urban Development councilor in 2013. In that capacity, in response to the ongoing collaboration between the Brazilian metropolis and the Dutch biennale, he wrote that – in general, but especially in the politically, often volatile conditions in a country like Brazil – it is necessary 'to ensure that the daily practice of government and autonomous research by design are nevertheless given ample space for a joint working process. Precisely there, in that shared space, lie the value and opportunities that the IABR approach offers.' Fernando de Mello Franco, 'Connect the Dots,' in: Brugmans et al., *The Next Economy*, p 129.

[21] Brugmans et al., *The Next Economy*, p 122. See also below, Dirk Sijmons, 'The System's Ceiling,' page 360 ff.

→
BrabantStad Carpet Metropolis (wall hanging, detail)
© Joep Vogels, Vogelvrij Vision

and ecological challenges at the regional level? The IABR–Atelier Brabant-Stad, established in 2013 by the IABR together with the Province of North Brabant, BrabantStad, and the North Brabant Water Boards, set out in search of the (hidden) strengths of Brabant's carpet metropolis, with the aim of devising an alternative spatial strategy and designing new development models in response to the standstill.

Spatial planning in North Brabant has always focused on strengthening and improving the urban environment, the water system, and the agricultural area as three separate worlds. This resulted in a lack of spatial and economic cohesion: the contact between city and country was weakened while the cities paid the most for the quality and safety of the water system. This, in fact, amounted to invisible investments in the water challenge made primarily in the countryside that continued despite the financial crisis. The IABR–Atelier, a collaboration of AWB (which was also involved in the Istanbul Atelier), Floris Alkemade Architect, and LOLA Landscape Architects, therefore investigated whether and how the water system could become a catalyst for the revival of the spatial and economic development of the region. Economic carriers for quality living, agriculture, recreation, and innovative enterprise were linked to the water challenge. This resulted in six regional development principles meant to jointly kick-start an accumulative development policy. The water challenge, including the underlying financial flows, was addressed with a view to creating a more attractive urban landscape, which would also improve health aspects and develop recreational city-countryside relationships. In addition, measures would contribute to the restoration of groundwater flow, reduction of droughts, and provision of opportunities for agriculture to produce more sustainably.

The report of the Atelier's research and results were presented in the publication *Reweaving the Urban Carpet*, [22] in the film *The Mosaic Metropolis of Brabant*, [23] and, of course, at the main exhibition of IABR–2014–URBAN BY NATURE in Rotterdam. As it turned out, the most powerful way to make the dynamic playing field of BrabantCity's urban carpet legible and tangible was literally by weaving a carpet, in this case a wall hanging.

[22] *Reweaving the Urban Carpet*

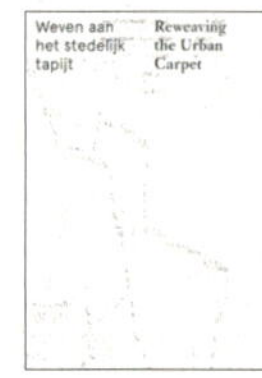

[23] film *The Mosaic Metropolis of Brabant*

BrabantStad Carpet Metropolis (wall hanging) IABR–2014–URBAN BY NATURE
photo: Maarten Laupman

After the biennale, the tapestry went on a six-month tour of the five cities of BrabantCity. In numerous encounters, a lively province-wide social debate about the future of North Brabant unfolded, culminating in concrete proposals that were included in the provincial Regional Environmental Vision presented in 2018. In a number of locations, including the Dommelvallei, Tilburg-Oost, and 's-Hertogenbosch, pilot projects continued to translate the six regional development principles into local project proposals, often in collaboration with the North Brabant Water Boards. Now, eight years later, the tapestry adorns the hall of the provincial government building in 's-Hertogenbosch still stimulating debate and exchange.

Water Worldwide

The Dutch Special Envoy for International Water Affairs Henk Ovink and IABR's president George Brugmans continued to cooperate closely after 2012, when they were both members of the curator team of the 5th IABR edition, MAKING CITY. They wanted to encourage and realize more *water-as-leverage* projects internationally and to that end, they signed a Memorandum of Understanding in 2016; it was extended for another four years in April 2020. [24] Brugmans thus cofounded, and was actively involved in, the Water as Leverage for Resilient Cities program spearheaded by Ovink. Together with a broad and powerful international alliance of partners including design offices such as FABRICations. and AWB, who were able to bring knowledge and experiences from previous IABR–Ateliers to the table, a first initiative, Water as Leverage Asia (WaL/Asia), was launched on the platform of the COP23 climate conference in Bonn in 2017. [25]

[24] *Memorandum of Understanding*

[25] WaL/Asia was launched on 19 November 2017 in Bonn by the Dutch Special Envoy for International Water Affairs together with the IABR, de Asian Infrastructure Investment Bank (AIIB), 100 Resilient Cities, UN-Habitat, FMO Dutch Development Bank, Pegasys, Partners for Resilience, Architecture Workroom Brussels, the World Wildlife Fund (WWF), the OECD, and the Water Youth Network, and with the support of the UN/World Bank High Level Panel on Water (HLPW), the Global Center on Adaptation (GCA), and RVO.nl.

Participants workshop *Water as Leverage Asia*, Singapore, 2019
© Cynthia van Elk | Water as Leverage

The first three projects were subsequently set up, in collaboration with local administrators and other stakeholders, in three cities in Southeast Asia: Chennai (India), Khulna (Bangladesh), and Semarang (Indonesia). What followed was a fascinating, demanding, and instructive process of thoroughly international knowledge exchange – The Hague and Singapore functioning as hubs – that developed incrementally. All steps were consistently supported by research by design carried out by internationally composed design teams and technical, administrative, and financial experts from all over the world. This made for a very rich but also vulnerable process – and an easy target for the Covid-19 pandemic and the ensuing lockdown. Unfortunately, the first, promising results of the explorations did not make it to the DOWN TO EARTH platform. From the spring of 2020, Covid-19 slammed all doors to international exchange with a bang. WaL/Asia could not really be rebooted until DOWN TO EARTH was over.

Floods in Semarang, Indonesia © Cynthia van Elk | Water as Leverage

THE FLOOD

Back to the beginning of this chapter, to Rotterdam, to the 2005 biennale: THE FLOOD, curated by Adriaan Geuze, which not only linked rising sea levels and urbanization, the water challenge and city making worldwide early on, but also and specifically proposed a change of perspective to the Rotterdam city council. At the time, Rotterdam, low-lying city in the delta, only saw water as a threat and an expense. But, the IABR suggested, water could offer opportunities as well.

The major conference organized by the IABR together with, among others, the Dutch water sector and all major developers was called Capitalize on Water for good reason. It was an appeal to consider the water challenge as a lever for integrated work on the sustainable city of the future. From this perspective, and in a series of workshops that took place during THE FLOOD, the IABR and the City of Rotterdam developed the project Rotterdam Water City 2035: the water challenge as the lever for an exploration of new opportunities for the urban development of Rotterdam.

The city council adopted the proposals of Water City 2035 in full in its Urban Vision Rotterdam 2030, and they became the inspiration for the Rotterdam Adaptation Strategy. Also, in 2005, the seeds were sown for several municipal initiatives and programs, which later crystallized as Resilient Rotterdam and Rotterdams Weerwoord.

- **800** The settlement of Rotta is founded.
- **1260** A dam is built in the Rotte River: the birth of Rotterdam.
- **1530** Peat extraction in polders around Rotterdam, creating the Kralingen Lake.
- **1705** Cruquius, hydraulic engineer and cartographer in Delft, starts measuring temperature, air pressure, moisture, and precipitation three times a day.
- **1854** Establishment of the Royal Netherlands Meteorological Institute (KNMI). After several outbreaks of Cholera in Rotterdam, Rose's Canal Plan improves hygiene in the city. Begin graven van de Nieuwe Waterweg.
- **1872** Construction of Nieuwe Waterweg commences. Start land reclamation, creating polder Prins Alexander (1874).
- **1883** Construction of the first sewer system in Rotterdam.
- **1890** KNMI starts with the measurement of sea levels on a regular basis.
- **1910** KNMI starts with the measurement of temperature on a regular basis.
- **1919** Rotterdam starts with the measurement of groundwater levels on a regular basis.
- **1940** Bombardment by German air force devastates the city center.
- **1953** Storm surge and spring tide caused the Great Flood, resulting in extensive damage and lives lost.
- **1954** Start of the construction of the Delta Works, the Netherlands' largest defense system against flooding from the North Sea.
- **1997** Construction of the Maeslantkering (Maeslant flood barrier) is concluded. After its construction, the Delta Works, which encompasses 5 storm surge barriers, 2 locks and 6 dams, were declared finished.
- **2001** Water Plan 1: a technical blueprint demonstrating how Rotterdam could arm itself against heavy rain.
- **2005** IABR–THE FLOOD: the water challenge as an instrument of an integrated approach to sustainable urban development.
- **2007** Water Plan 2: the municipality of Rotterdam and the three water boards of the city describe how they want to deal with the water in and around Rotterdam.
- **2013** Rotterdam Adaptation Strategy: vision of Rotterdam's adaptation to climate change.
- **2014** National Delta Program and the National Water Plan: outlines, principles, and direction of national water policy are established and implemented.
- **2019** Rotterdams Weerwoord: city-wide and district-driven program with the aim of making Rotterdam climate-resilient by 2025, an initiative for and by the people of Rotterdam.

water safety
subsidence
groundwater
precipitation
drought
heat stress

Timeline from the exhibition DOWN TO EARTH: METEOPOLIS image: Rotterdams Weerwoord

THE FLOOD was not only a milestone in Rotterdam's water policy, it also marked the beginning of a substantive collaboration between the city and the biennale – sometimes more loosely, sometimes more intensely – in which the latter, even apart from the IABR–Atelier Rotterdam, regularly acted as a – sometimes contrarian – think tank for the former. This partnership made it possible to act together at foreign conferences, in international collaborations, and at mayor meetings, and it offered municipal departments the opportunity to use the free cultural space of the IABR every two years, to use the platform of the biennale to present their own explorations and future plans in an open environment, and to discuss them in both a local and international setting.

DOWN TO EARTH

It was in keeping with this tradition that Brugmans, in his capacity as the chief curator of DOWN TO EARTH, asked Rotterdams Weerwoord to conduct new outlook studies, 15 years after THE FLOOD, on the way Rotterdam would have to deal with rising water in the long term. Because although 'climate crisis' may hardly have resonated in 2005, 15 years and many increasingly urgent climate reports later, it was high time for an update. These explorations were presented at METEOPOLIS, which was an integral part of DOWN TO EARTH as a partner exhibition.

Rotterdam's water challenge also plays a part in the Merwe-Vierhavens (M4H) city harbors, in which the IABR established its headquarters in 2020 and, since 2018, has been starting and/or supporting local initiatives under the banner of the IABR–Test Site M4H+. These involve a collaboration with the Programmabureau M4H, a joint effort of the city and Rotterdam Port Authority.[26] One of these initiatives is the Waterschool by M4H-based Studio Makkink & Bey, which already experienced its 1.0 version in 2018, as part of the program of THE MISSING LINK. Brugmans asked Rianne Makkink and Jurgen Bey to join the DOWN TO EARTH curator team, and to seize the principles and opportunities of this biennale edition to take their ongoing project to the next level: WATERSCHOOL M4H+.

[26] See page 26 and 246

In the context of DOWN TO EARTH, Brugmans intended the four exhibitions – DROUGHT IN THE DELTA, METEOPOLIS, WATERSCHOOL M4H+, and THE HIGH GROUND – to present a coherent picture of the ubiquity and urgency of the water challenge and of the way it can be leveraged at different scale levels in research by design trajectories aimed at integrated and true transformation.

IABR—ATELIER

DROUGHT IN THE DELTA

IABR–ATELIER DROUGHT IN THE DELTA

In the summer of 2018, for the first time the climate crisis asserted itself in the Netherlands not through an excess of water, but through a shortage of freshwater. To many, this came as a complete surprise. A great deal of hard work was necessary to keep the water machine running that year, and areas recovered from the drought only with difficulty. Yet, there was permanent damage, both in urban and in natural and agricultural areas.
That one dry summer was not the end of it, either. It soon became clear that drought was no longer incidental in the Dutch Delta. Preventing shortages by retaining water inevitably presented itself as a completely new structural challenge to a country that, for hundreds of years, had been cleverly designed to drain water as quickly and efficiently as possible with an eye to water safety and agricultural productivity.

Water Safety: Retaining Freshwater

As in many other places in the world, there is plenty of water in the Netherlands, just not always at the right time. The country has an annual surplus of precipitation, but the water that falls in wet periods is often no longer available in times of drought. Sometimes, too much freshwater is discharged straight into the sea while at other times, some places experience water shortages.
Expectations are that this mismatch between water demand and precipitation surplus will become more frequent and even worsen as a result of the climate crisis, not only because of changing weather conditions, but also because glaciers will melt and sea levels will rise. This calls for a complete transformation in thought and deed: a naturally wet delta geared towards discharging water as quickly as possible in order to survive needs to change into one that can retain freshwater so that it is available when it is needed.

Agricultural Productivity: Changing Land Use

Not only have we been setting up our water management more and more efficiently, we may also have become overconfident. We seem to have counted on innovative strength and water-technological ingenuity to create a rock-solid guarantee for lasting success – and not only at keeping our feet dry, but also and increasingly with an eye to the agenda of 'Holland Ltd'. However, we can no longer deny that prioritizing the economic interests of the agrocomplex contributes directly and substantially to the drought problem. Because of the maximization of agricultural productivity and the monoculture that results from it, the water boards, in which the interests of the agricultural sector are secured, have drained too much water and this causes problems that in fact could have been avoided. This is actually a flaw in the democratic setup of the water boards, a unique and ancient elected layer in our system of government, a flaw that is now exposed by global warming and climate change. To sustainably optimize agricultural productivity, land use must once again follow the logic of the water. Industrial agriculture, which has also led to soil depletion and nitrogen problems, is in need of radical change anyway, and solving the urgent drought problem that calls for retaining water until we need it can potentially leverage this.[27]

[27] According to figures of the Central Bureau of Statistics, the Netherlands is the second-largest agricultural exporter in the world and the largest meat exporter in the EU. However, to grow all the food we consume per Dutch citizen, our current eating pattern requires about 1,800 m^2 per person, and we do not have that much surface area in the Netherlands. Therefore, while according to the Netherlands Environmental Assessment Agency we export 75 percent of the food we produce, we are unable to produce what we use ourselves in the Netherlands. But not only is there not enough space, the space that is available is, in view of the climate crisis and the Sustainable Development Goals, used in an ill-advised way.

Space Shortage

That the Dutch, like no other people, know how to deal with water, is therefore suddenly no longer a certainty. Finding out how and where to store water until we need it is, as we realized in that dry summer of 2018, an unexpected and considerable challenge to the Rhine-Meuse-Scheldt Delta that, like other deltas in the world, is a densely urbanized and economically and ecologically crucial area in which space is extremely scarce.

There is more space available underground, where there have always been large reserves of freshwater, all over the world. This seems the most logical place to look for space to temporarily store freshwater. But the substructure constitutes a fragile system and has its own challenges. In many places in the world, underground freshwater lakes (aquifers) are under threat; they are being drained for irrigation or industry. In the Netherlands this kind of overuse is not as bad; in our delta, it is mainly salinization that puts pressure on the freshwater supply.

It is also very busy underground. There are more space claims than just those of water in need of storage, like those of the energy transition and of CO_2 storage. And due to the climate crisis, all of these claims are equally urgent. In the future, they will therefore either get in each other's way or have to share the space. Not to mention that claims made on the underground must be assessed against the potential risk of earthquakes.

IABR–Atelier Drought in the Delta

Taking all this into account, the IABR set up the IABR–Atelier Drought in the Delta in the autumn of 2018. George Brugmans asked architect and urban designer Marco Vermeulen to investigate opportunities and frameworks for the large-scale storage of freshwater, both above- and belowground. The Atelier was to map the situation and explore ways in which to increase the water-buffering capacity of the delta and the opportunities this could create, as much as possible in conjunction with other transition challenges, including the energy transition, food production and urbanization, not only to see where the different transitions touch on and influence each other, but especially to investigate where and how they can support each other.

As best it could, the Atelier took into account all the already available knowledge about topsoil and subsoil and purposefully mapped it out, which was a prerequisite for design activity. Initially, this provided insight into the opportunities and possibilities for the large-scale storage of freshwater, aboveground and underground, into how and where these intersect with other transitions and space claims, and subsequently into how those underground transitions are fundamentally linked to major aboveground transitions. After identifying the linking opportunities, it was possible to look ahead. How can the large-scale storage of freshwater also be a lever for adding social value in a wider sense? How can the underground storage of freshwater contribute to a resilient delta that is able to deal proactively with the major transitions ahead? [28]

[28] For its methodology the Atelier took a page from the IABR's earlier study Urban Metabolism (see page 21), following an approach that the IABR had previously fine-tuned in Atelier Rotterdam and that fits Studio Marco Vermeulen like a glove.

Atelier Drought in the Delta highlighted ten subareas representative of the drought problem and presented a vision of the future for each subsystem, in which measures to increase water buffering capacity are deployed as leverage for other transition challenges.
image: Studio Marco Vermeulen, IABR–Atelier Drought in the Delta
See also page 172 ff.

Building Blocks for a New Freshwater Strategy

The goal of Marco Vermeulen and his team was to come up with concrete building blocks for a new, common freshwater strategy to 2050 and to identify possible test projects that would be able to start working with these building blocks in specific locations. In that sense, this Atelier was an exception to the IABR rule. Past Ateliers were always set up in close collaboration with problem owners, with local or regional, and sometimes even national, authorities at home and abroad, who wanted to seize the opportunities offered by their collaboration with the IABR to work on their challenges using an alternative approach – in a free space, but always with an eye to actual realization.
Atelier Drought in the Delta took a different approach. It had to deliver solutions in search of problem owners. The research results not only had to be presented in a stimulating and convincing manner on the DOWN

TO EARTH platform but, even more importantly, the Atelier also had to ensure that after the biennale the results could be used as a toolbox for the delta, as it were, by local or regional authorities working on their own local assignments – and ready for use in such a way, that all local actions would fit optimally into the coherent transition of our entire delta.

Pandemic

Like the other IABR–Ateliers active in this period, Drought in the Delta did not escape the consequences of the Covid-19 pandemic. And like in the other Ateliers, this was mostly at the expense of the direct exchange of ideas and transfer of knowledge, of live meetings in which people can convince each other by generating mutual enthusiasm. Programmed work sessions with multiple stakeholders, which had been planned in conjunction with the Ministry of Infrastructure and Water Management, among others, fell through and as it turned out, webinars and Zoom sessions were not viable alternatives. Covid-19 caused a considerable delay in the work process and ambitions were gradually adjusted.
This made the exhibition itself, DROUGHT IN THE DELTA, all the more important. And because DOWN TO EARTH – as an antitypical biennale due to the pandemic – was a series of presentations that unfolded over time, each built around a single research project, rather than a compressed accumulation of many project presentations and international entries at the same time, a relatively large amount of exhibition space was indeed available for each Atelier.
The results of the research by design of Atelier Drought in the Delta were presented by Studio Marco Vermeulen in two panoramic cross sections of the Dutch Delta – anno 2020 and anno 2050 respectively. On the former, the problems resulting from the freshwater shortage were drawn; on the latter, the proposals for solutions to the current freshwater shortage and the linking opportunities that exist were shown. The two cross sections were then combined and computer-animated by Tungsten Studio. The result, a spectacular 30-m-wide and 3.5-m-high animation, was displayed in the Keilezaal. It looks in the direction of Germany, France and Belgium, upstream along the Rhine, Meuse and Scheldt Rivers, with the Alps in the distance. In 7 minutes it shows us how our delta now functions, what problems have arisen from land use and climate change both above- and belowground, and what possible solutions there are.
This animation portrayed the aim of this IABR–Atelier in a pertinent way, that is to persuasively present building blocks for a new freshwater strategy in conjunction with other transition challenges, which always involve the increasingly intensive use of the ground and the substructure, such as food production, energy transition and housing.

In addition, exhibition curator George Brugmans selected four exemplary projects – COASTAR, Panorama Waterland, Water Mosaic Groene Hart and Sponstuin – in which concrete solutions for a new freshwater strategy are already being explored locally, to frame the Atelier's presentation in broader research into solutions to the problem of drought. [29]

[29] For the panoramic cross sections of the Dutch Delta and the four exemplary projects, see page 172 ff.

DROUGHT IN THE DELTA was only allowed to stay open for one month, from 19 September to 18 October 2020. And due to Covid-19 measures taken by the Dutch government, few people got to visit it. It was therefore decided to have the huge animation translated into a video and a zoom box, a specially designed web application.[30] This made the research results of the Atelier and knowledge transfer accessible to everyone in the public domain and allowed work sessions to still take place at a later date.

[30] The video created by Tungsten Studio covers four of the ten subareas highlighted by the IABR-Atelier in the large animation.

The zoom box created by Maurits de Bruijn allows everyone to take a closer look at the cross sections of the delta in 2020 and in 2050, for instance by zooming in on the ten different subareas.

CREDITS

The IABR–Atelier Drought in the Delta was initiated by the IABR in 2018.

STEERING GROUP
George Brugmans, president IABR

LEAD DESIGNER
Marco Vermeulen

RESEARCH BY DESIGN
Studio Marco Vermeulen
Marco Vermeulen, Joost van der Waal, Bram Willemse

PROJECT MANAGEMENT
IABR
Jelte Boeijenga, Suzanne Tietema

PRODUCTION
IABR
Jolanda van Dinteren, Johanna Fuhler, Vivian Ammerlaan

WE THANK THE FOLLOWING PEOPLE FOR THEIR CRITICAL REFLECTION AND/OR THEIR CONTRIBUTION
Cees van de Guchte (Deltares)
Esther van Baaren and Roelof Stuurman (Deltares), Ruud Bartholomeus and Klaasjan Raat (KWR), Rob Bouman (Ministry of Infrastructure and the Environment), Ron Franken (Netherlands Environmental Assessment Agency), Karla Niggebrugge (Province of North Brabant), Jip Welkers (Vitens)

The IABR–Ateliers were initiated and executed nationally and internationally from 2008 to 2021 under the direction of George Brugmans. The IABR initiated and produced a number of IABR–Ateliers in the Netherlands, including the IABR–Atelier Rotterdam, as a lead partner of the Dutch National Government in the framework of the ARO, the Action Agenda for Spatial Design 2013–2016 of the Ministry of Infrastructure and the Environment and the ARO 2017–2020 of the Ministry of the Interior and Kingdom Relations.

DOWN TO EARTH

DROUGHT IN THE DELTA

CURATOR
George Brugmans

19 September – 18 October 2020
Keilezaal, Rotterdam

DROUGHT IN THE DELTA

CURATOR INTRODUCTION

If change is needed on a scale for which 'there is no documented historical precedent,' as the Intergovernmental Panel on Climate Change, the IPCC, convincingly claims, then nothing is self-evident anymore. [31] Even the fact that the Dutch, like no other people, know how to deal with water no longer offers any certainty. In the delta that we live in, the climate crisis is generating completely new problems. More and more often there is too much water, but we are also – and this is really new – now confronted with drought and shortages of freshwater.

For centuries, we've worked hard to make our country better at *draining* water as quickly and efficiently as possible for reasons of safety and agricultural productivity. But now we are unexpectedly facing a new challenge: how to *retain* a momentary water surplus in order to be able to use it when we have a shortage.

[31] See also the Curator Statement, page 14

DROUGHT IN THE DELTA
photo: Aad Hoogendoorn

Towards a New National Freshwater Strategy

The Dutch Delta consists of several subsystems, each with a characteristic soil and water system and its own landscape characteristics. The freshwater shortage therefore manifests itself differently in different places, with numerous consequences and therefore the urgent need to investigate diverse possible solutions.
The pressure on land use is great and the spatial claims of transition tasks in the areas of energy, water, food, and the built environment only add to it. But if we connect these tasks and use water as leverage, there are also many opportunities.

In a spectacular animation, IABR–Atelier Drought in the Delta highlights ten subareas. For each subsystem, the animation sketches a picture of the future in which measures to increase the water buffering capacity serve as a lever for other transition tasks. For example, a renewed freshwater system can contribute to robust nature (biodiversity and the reduction of natural fires, for instance), to the energy transition (aquathermia), to the reduction of CO_2 emissions (wetting peat meadows) and to sustainable urbanization (water plazas and retention parks).
By showing how we can deal with weather extremes, right down to the subsoil, the study points the way to how the freshwater challenge can be used as leverage to attain the comprehensive transformation of our delta. At the same time, an attractive picture of the future of the Netherlands is painted, with a wide variety of landscapes. Something that is certainly possible if we broker good international agreements about the water distribution in the Rhine, Meuse and Scheldt catchment area.

The results of the research by design done by the IABR–Atelier are a call for action, of policymakers in particular. The concrete building blocks for a new national freshwater strategy and, equally important, the identification of matching opportunities and the ensuing concrete proposals for integrated solution directions, are a ready toolbox for local and regional authorities. They demonstrate that specific urgent challenges can be dealt with locally in such a way that all actions seamlessly fit into the inevitably comprehensive transition of the entire delta.

BUILDING BLOCKS FOR A NEW NATIONAL FRESH-WATER STRATEGY

Incidental freshwater shortages are causing different problems in low and high parts of the Netherlands. The low parts of our delta primarily face rising sea levels. The sea exerts more pressure on the groundwater, which leads to increased salinization in the coastal regions. Due to insufficient precipitation and a low water supply from the Rhine, Meuse and Scheldt Rivers, there is not enough counterpressure. As a result, large sections of our agricultural land are becoming less and less suitable for the crops that are currently grown there. And although it is counterintuitive, water shortage is also posing a threat to water safety. About a quarter of the Dutch dikes are peat dikes. These contain a lot of water, and if this evaporates, they can collapse due to subsidence or shifting.

On the higher, sandy soils of the Netherlands, sharply declining groundwater levels resulting from prolonged drought present the greatest challenge. These cause welling – groundwater that slowly seeps up from the soil under pressure – to decrease and streams, springs, and fens to dry up. In addition, once soil has dried out, it is much less likely to become waterlogged again. Once the small pores in the soil are empty, water quickly runs through the larger cracks.

photo: IABR

In the lower parts of the delta, space is at a premium and water safety challenges are often greater. Here, agriculture and greenhouse farming alternate with cities and industry. Many freshwater measures are likely to be underground and more technical by nature. If industry, the city and agriculture make use of each other's purified residual water as much as possible, the freshwater can remain underground. Increasing the size of the dune landscape will yield additional resistance to salt water. Freshwater measures will also become visible in the city. Urban landscapes will include polder roofs, sponge squares and retention parks to buffer rainwater while providing coolness in the summer. The old meanders of the big rivers, together with dike reinforcement and river widening, will become part of the freshwater system to create a river landscape that is much more dynamic than that of today; sufficient water will be available when needed. Agriculture will not only feed people, but also the soil. A healthy soil can stock up on more rainwater for dry periods.

On the sandy soils in the higher parts of the Netherlands, nature will transform desiccated coniferous forest into an open infiltration landscape. A special landscape will develop, with large height differences, spring streams and deciduous forests. Spruce will make way for oak, birch, and beech; much less groundwater will evaporate and ecological and spatial diversity will be created. Brooks will meander once more and the return of watermill landscapes will ensure that surface water will have the time to replenish the groundwater. The resulting landscape will consist of both subsoil and topsoil and have a robust 'new freshwater level.'

Studio Marco Vermeulen translated drought problems in the delta anno 2020 and the building blocks for a new freshwater strategy towards 2050 into a leporello and a large computer animation (see left and following pages).

BUILDING BLOCKS FOR A NEW NATIONAL FRESH-WATER STRATEGY

2020

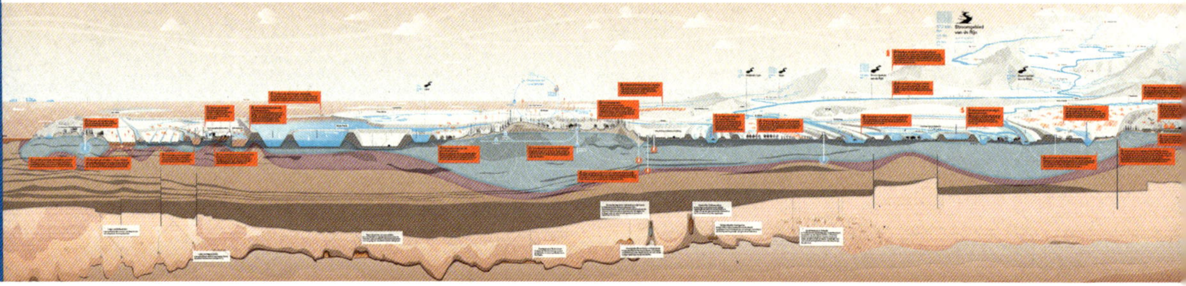

2050

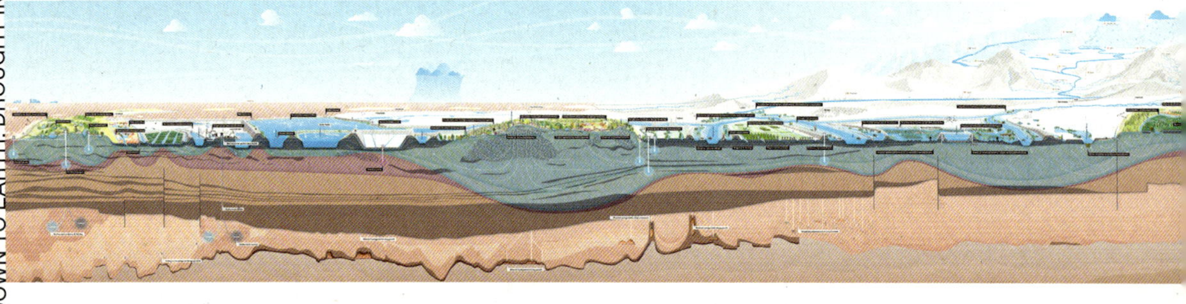

The viewer perspective of the 7-minute animation of Drought in the Delta is toward Germany, upstream along the Rhine, with the Alps in the far distance; to the right toward France and Belgium, upstream along Meuse and Scheldt with the Maasvlakte on the far right; and to the left along the dunes to the Wadden Islands.

2020

The Freshwater System of the Dutch Delta at a Time of Prolonged Drought

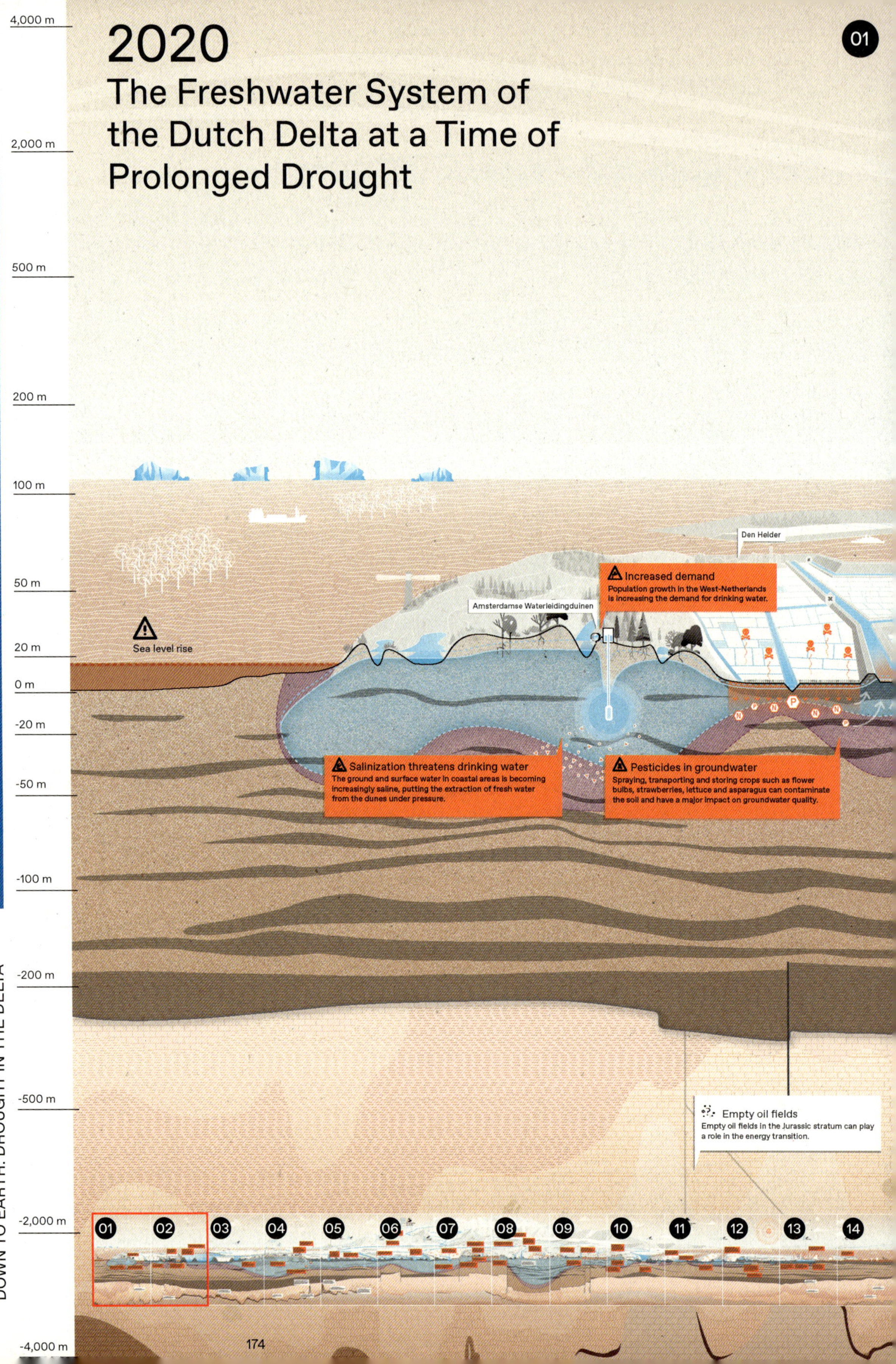

CHALLENGES FRESHWATER SYSTEM

- water quality
- water safety
- natural values
- salinization
- freshwater shortage
- drinking water extraction

GROUNDWATER SYSTEM

- average groundwater level
- extremely low groundwater level
- freshwater (Cl- < 150mg/l)
- brackish water (Cl- 150–1,000 mg/l)
- saltwater (Cl- > 1,000 mg/l)

SUBSURFACE

- geological fault line
- water separation layer, clay, loam, or peat
- water-permeable layer, sand
- push moraines, pushed layers
- river sediments

DEEP SUBSURFACE

- Tertiary, North Sea Group
- Late Cretaceous, Chalk Group
- Early Cretaceous, Rhineland Group
- Uppor Jurassic
- Lower Jurassic, Althena Group
- Triassic
- Permian, Zechstein Group
- Permian, Rotliegend Group
- Carboniferous, Limburg Group
- Carboniferous, Geul Subgroup

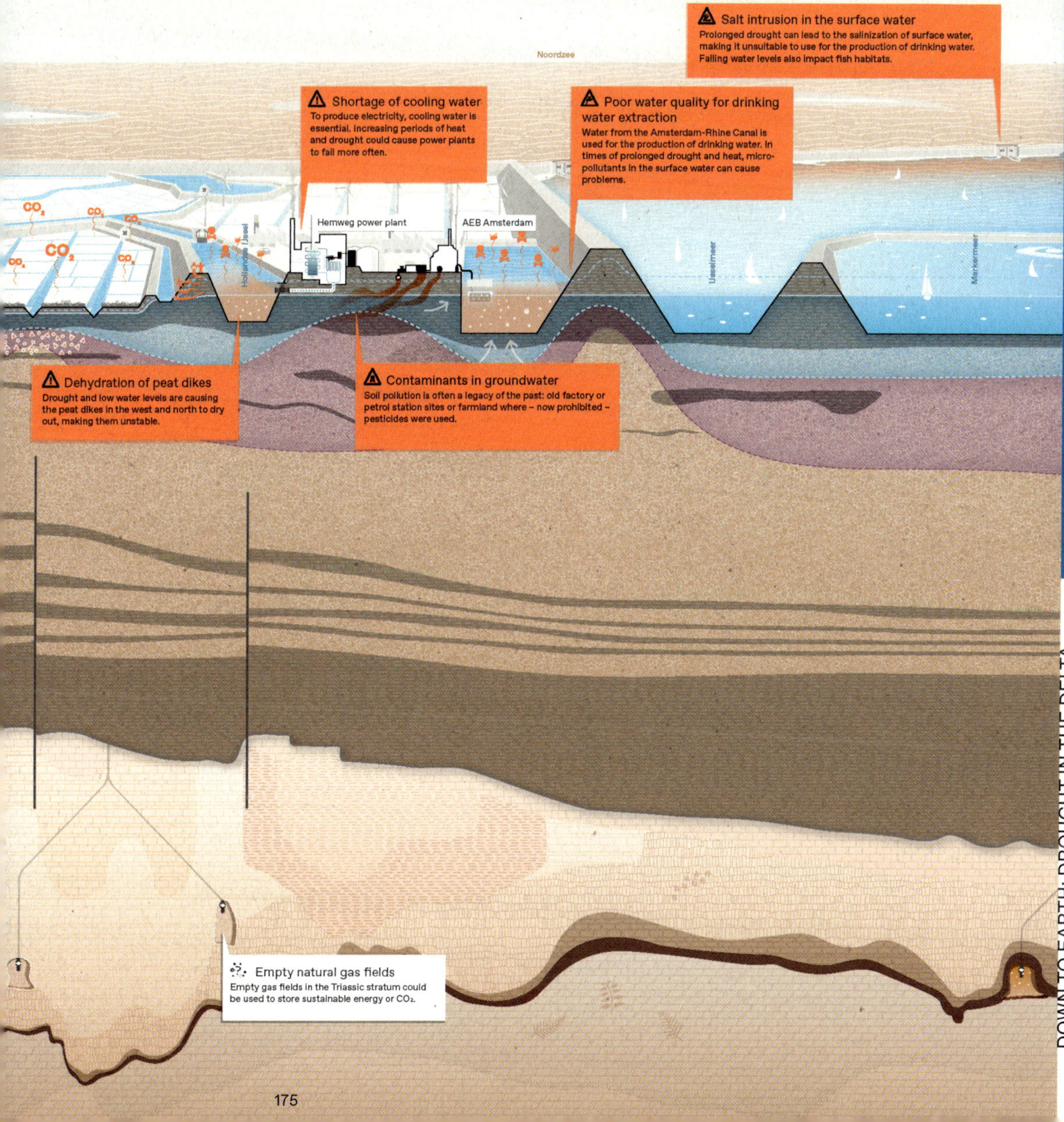

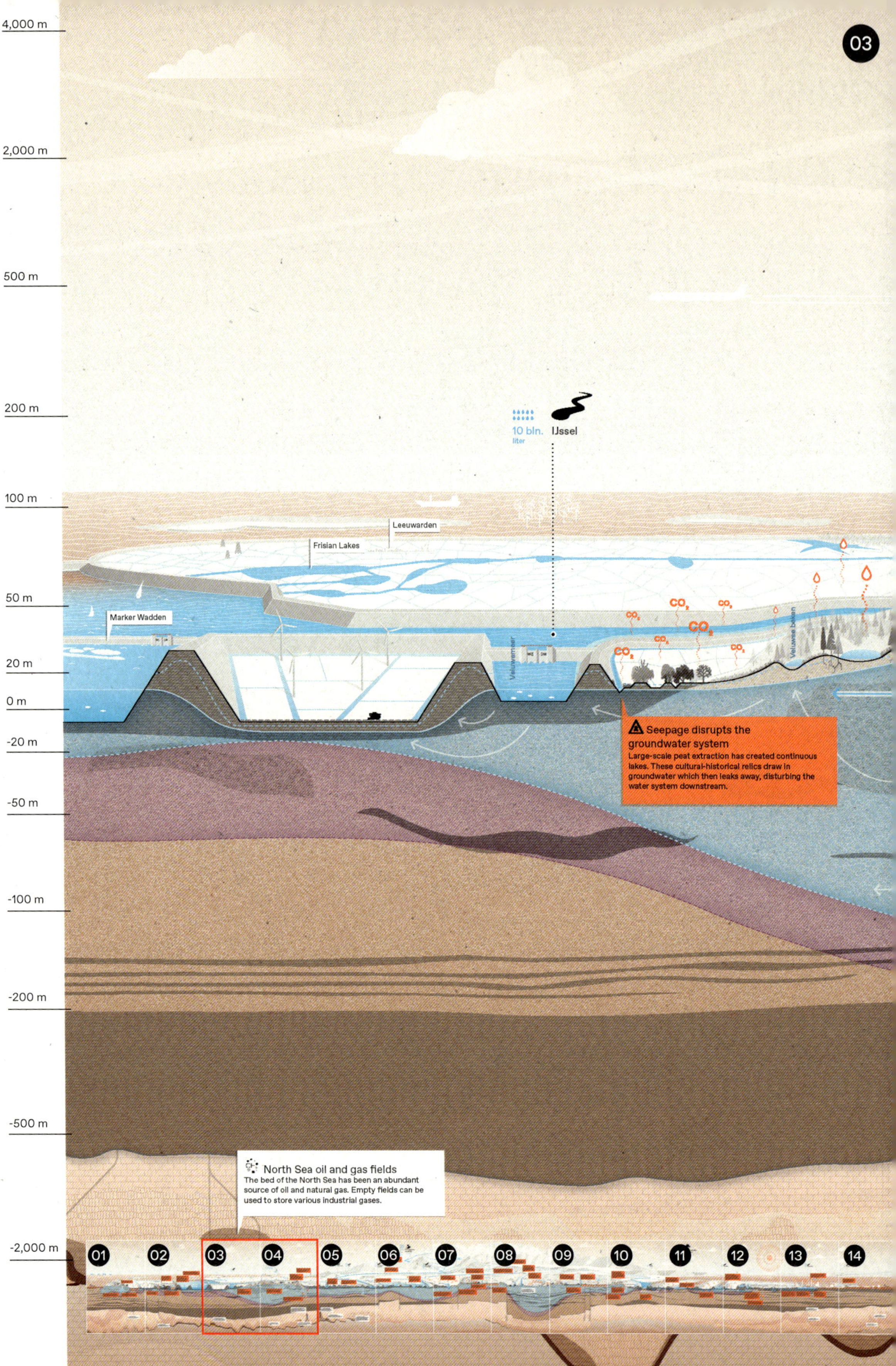
03
4,000 m
2,000 m
500 m
200 m
100 m
50 m
20 m
0 m
-20 m
-50 m
-100 m
-200 m
-500 m
-2,000 m
-4,000 m
10 bln.
liter
IJssel
Leeuwarden
Frisian Lakes
Marker Wadden
Veluwemeer
CO_2
Seepage disrupts the groundwater system
Large-scale peat extraction has created continuous lakes. These cultural-historical relics draw in groundwater which then leaks away, disturbing the water system downstream.
North Sea oil and gas fields
The bed of the North Sea has been an abundant source of oil and natural gas. Empty fields can be used to store various industrial gases.
01
02
03
04
05
06
07
08
09
10
11
12
13
14

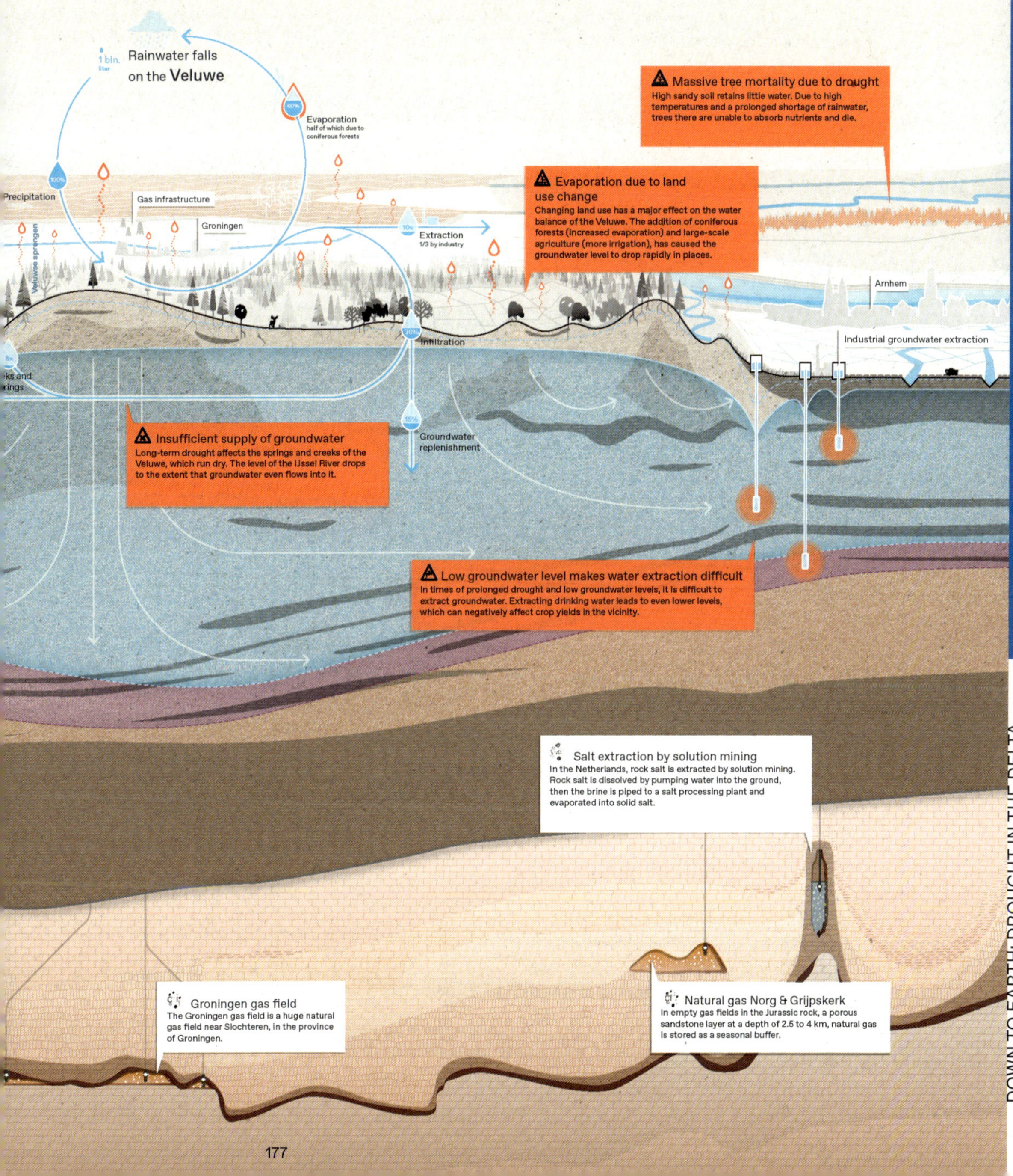
1 bln. liter
Rainwater falls on the Veluwe
60%
Evaporation
half of which due to coniferous forests
100%
Precipitation
Gas infrastructure
Groningen
Veluwse sprengen
10%
Extraction
1/3 by industry
30%
Infiltration
ks and
rings
15%
Groundwater replenishment
Insufficient supply of groundwater
Long-term drought affects the springs and creeks of the Veluwe, which run dry. The level of the IJssel River drops to the extent that groundwater even flows into it.
Massive tree mortality due to drought
High sandy soil retains little water. Due to high temperatures and a prolonged shortage of rainwater, trees there are unable to absorb nutrients and die.
Evaporation due to land use change
Changing land use has a major effect on the water balance of the Veluwe. The addition of coniferous forests (increased evaporation) and large-scale agriculture (more irrigation), has caused the groundwater level to drop rapidly in places.
Arnhem
Industrial groundwater extraction
Low groundwater level makes water extraction difficult
In times of prolonged drought and low groundwater levels, it is difficult to extract groundwater. Extracting drinking water leads to even lower levels, which can negatively affect crop yields in the vicinity.
Salt extraction by solution mining
In the Netherlands, rock salt is extracted by solution mining. Rock salt is dissolved by pumping water into the ground, then the brine is piped to a salt processing plant and evaporated into solid salt.
Groningen gas field
The Groningen gas field is a huge natural gas field near Slochteren, in the province of Groningen.
Natural gas Norg & Grijpskerk
In empty gas fields in the Jurassic rock, a porous sandstone layer at a depth of 2.5 to 4 km, natural gas is stored as a seasonal buffer.

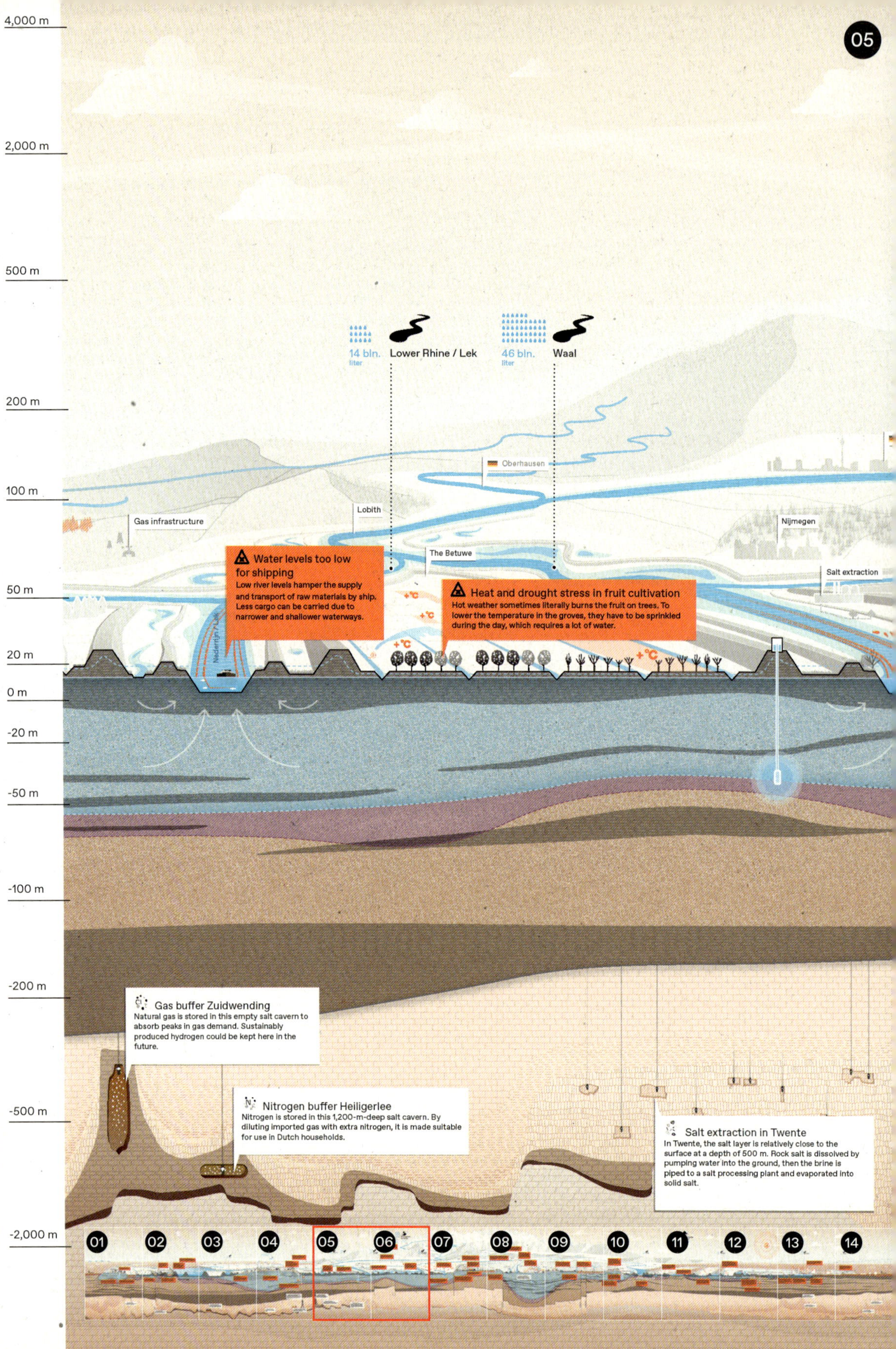

05
4,000 m
2,000 m
500 m
200 m
100 m
50 m
20 m
0 m
-20 m
-50 m
-100 m
-200 m
-500 m
-2,000 m
-4,000 m
14 bln. liter
Lower Rhine / Lek
46 bln. liter
Waal
Oberhausen
Lobith
Gas infrastructure
Nijmegen
The Betuwe
Salt extraction
Water levels too low for shipping
Low river levels hamper the supply and transport of raw materials by ship. Less cargo can be carried due to narrower and shallower waterways.
Heat and drought stress in fruit cultivation
Hot weather sometimes literally burns the fruit on trees. To lower the temperature in the groves, they have to be sprinkled during the day, which requires a lot of water.
+°C
Gas buffer Zuidwending
Natural gas is stored in this empty salt cavern to absorb peaks in gas demand. Sustainably produced hydrogen could be kept here in the future.
Nitrogen buffer Heiligerlee
Nitrogen is stored in this 1,200-m-deep salt cavern. By diluting imported gas with extra nitrogen, it is made suitable for use in Dutch households.
Salt extraction in Twente
In Twente, the salt layer is relatively close to the surface at a depth of 500 m. Rock salt is dissolved by pumping water into the ground, then the brine is piped to a salt processing plant and evaporated into solid salt.
01
02
03
04
05
06
07
08
09
10
11
12
13
14

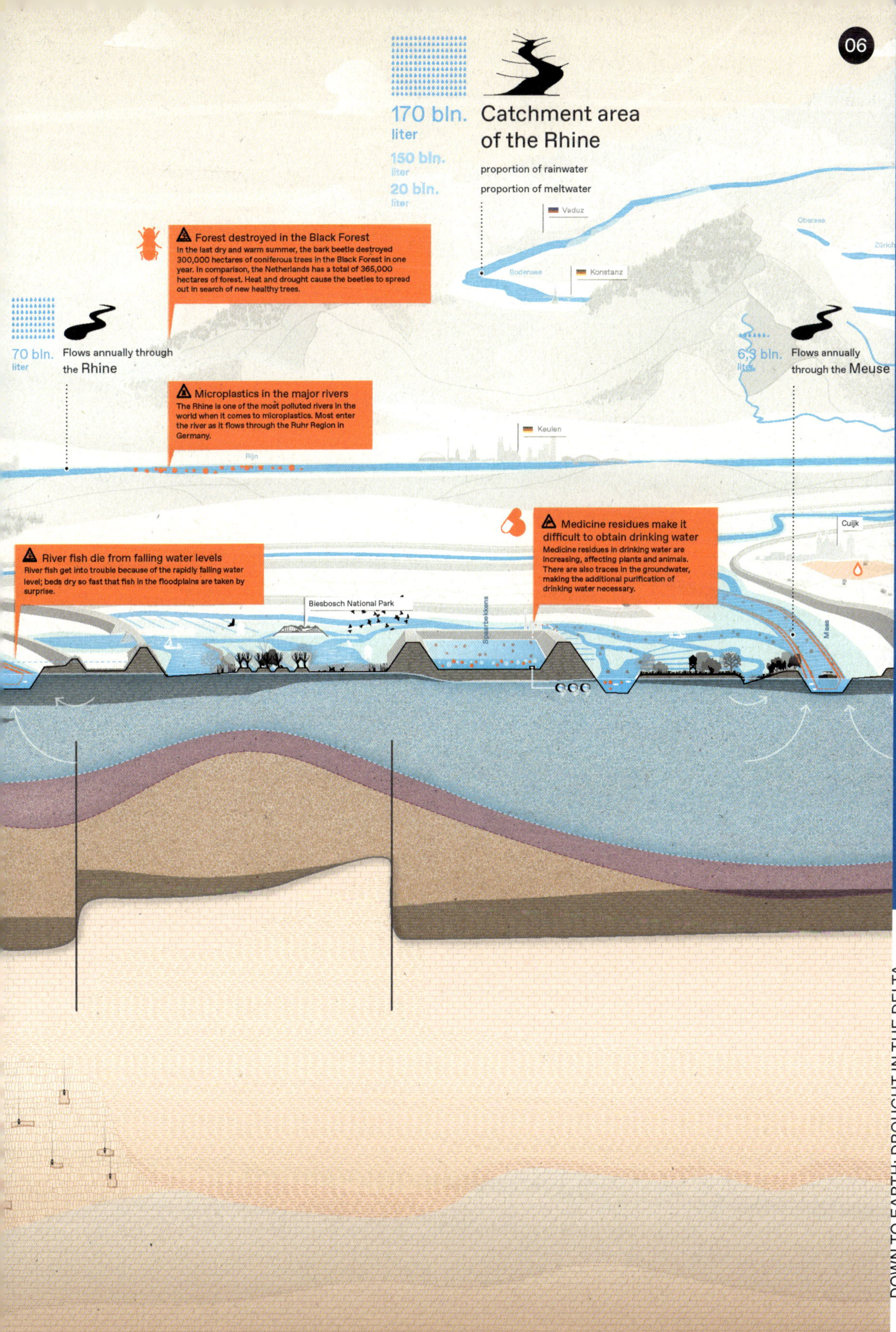
170 bln.
liter
150 bln.
liter
20 bln.
liter
Catchment area of the Rhine
proportion of rainwater
proportion of meltwater
Vaduz
Obersee
Zürich
Bodensee
Konstanz
Forest destroyed in the Black Forest
In the last dry and warm summer, the bark beetle destroyed 300,000 hectares of coniferous trees in the Black Forest in one year. In comparison, the Netherlands has a total of 365,000 hectares of forest. Heat and drought cause the beetles to spread out in search of new healthy trees.
70 bln.
liter
Flows annually through the Rhine
6,3 bln.
liter
Flows annually through the Meuse
Microplastics in the major rivers
The Rhine is one of the most polluted rivers in the world when it comes to microplastics. Most enter the river as it flows through the Ruhr Region in Germany.
Rijn
Keulen
Medicine residues make it difficult to obtain drinking water
Medicine residues in drinking water are increasing, affecting plants and animals. There are also traces in the groundwater, making the additional purification of drinking water necessary.
Cuijk
River fish die from falling water levels
River fish get into trouble because of the rapidly falling water level; beds dry so fast that fish in the floodplains are taken by surprise.
Biesbosch National Park
Spaarbekkens
Maas

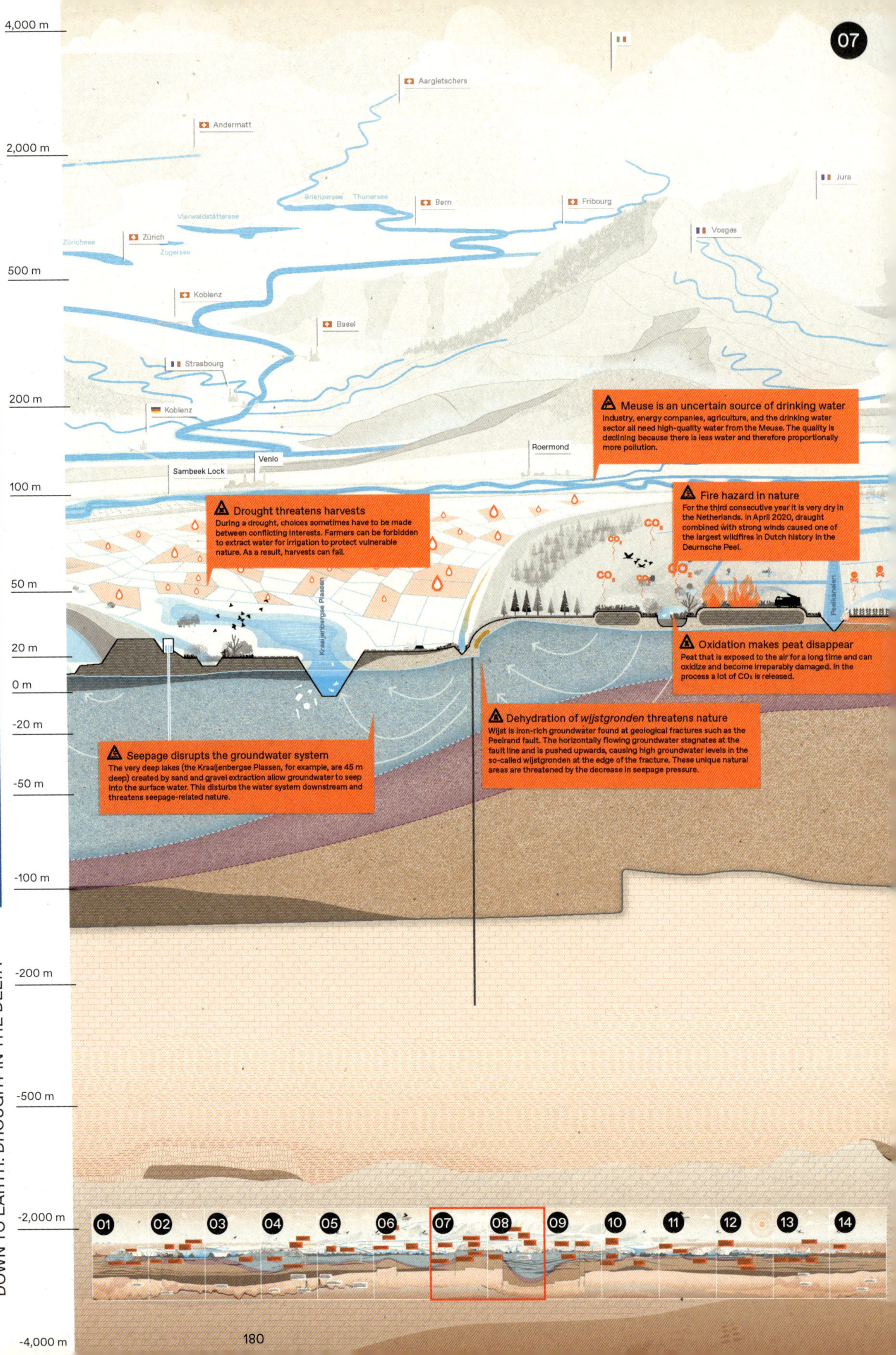
07
4,000 m
2,000 m
500 m
200 m
100 m
50 m
20 m
0 m
-20 m
-50 m
-100 m
-200 m
-500 m
-2,000 m
-4,000 m
Aargletschers
Andermatt
Brienzersee
Thunersee
Bern
Fribourg
Jura
Vierwaldstättersee
Zürichsee
Zürich
Zugersee
Vosges
Koblenz
Basel
Strasbourg
Koblenz
Roermond
Venlo
Sambeek Lock
Kraaijenbergse Plassen
Peelkanalen
Meuse is an uncertain source of drinking water
Industry, energy companies, agriculture, and the drinking water sector all need high-quality water from the Meuse. The quality is declining because there is less water and therefore proportionally more pollution.
Fire hazard in nature
For the third consecutive year it is very dry in the Netherlands. In April 2020, draught combined with strong winds caused one of the largest wildfires in Dutch history in the Deurnsche Peel.
Drought threatens harvests
During a drought, choices sometimes have to be made between conflicting interests. Farmers can be forbidden to extract water for irrigation to protect vulnerable nature. As a result, harvests can fail.
Oxidation makes peat disappear
Peat that is exposed to the air for a long time and can oxidize and become irreparably damaged. In the process a lot of CO_2 is released.
Dehydration of *wijstgronden* threatens nature
Wijst is iron-rich groundwater found at geological fractures such as the Peelrand fault. The horizontally flowing groundwater stagnates at the fault line and is pushed upwards, causing high groundwater levels in the so-called wijstgronden at the edge of the fracture. These unique natural areas are threatened by the decrease in seepage pressure.
Seepage disrupts the groundwater system
The very deep lakes (the Kraaijenbergse Plassen, for example, are 45 m deep) created by sand and gravel extraction allow groundwater to seep into the surface water. This disturbs the water system downstream and threatens seepage-related nature.
01
02
03
04
05
06
07
08
09
10
11
12
13
14

30 bln.
liter

Catchment area of the Meuse

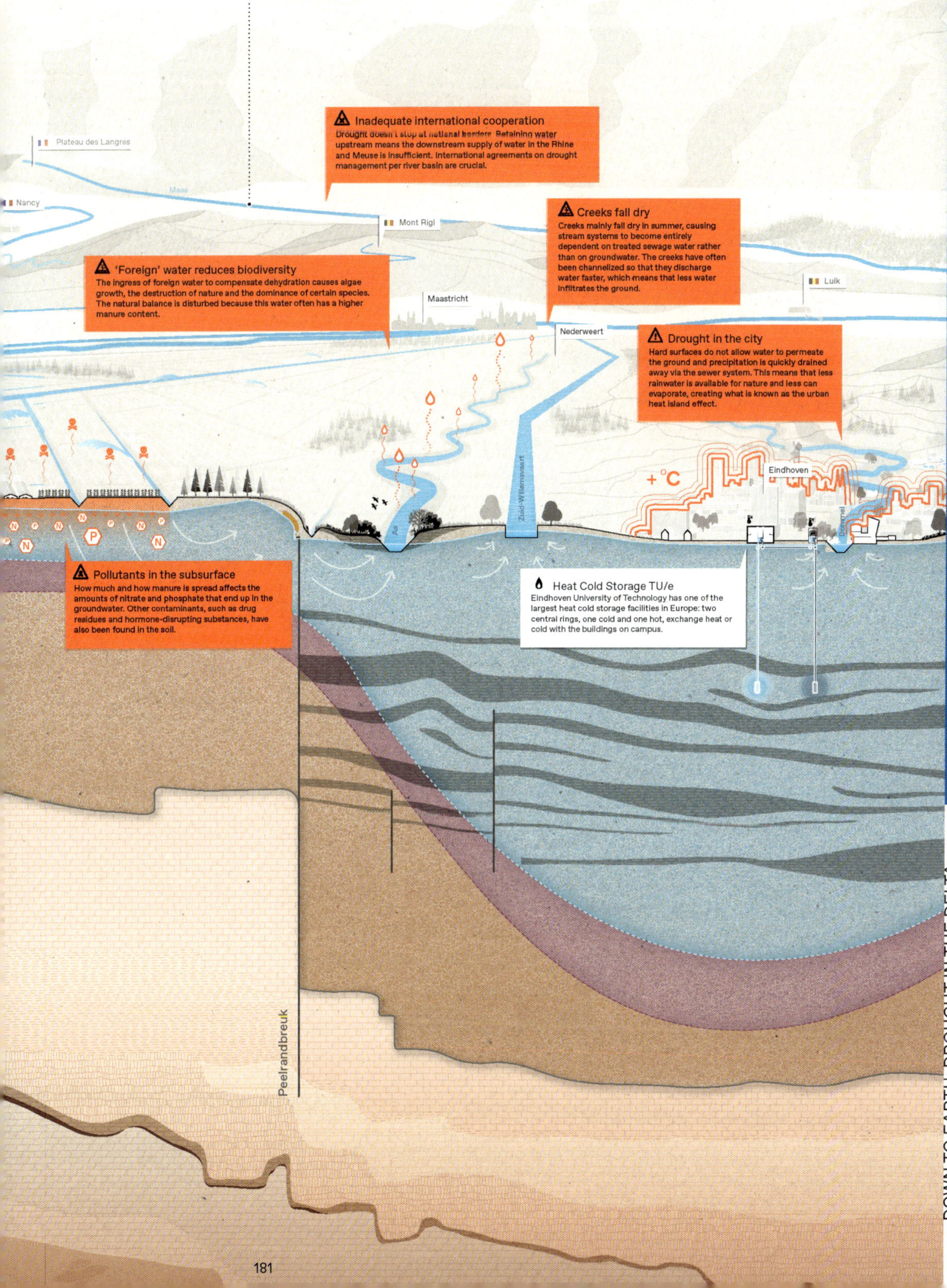

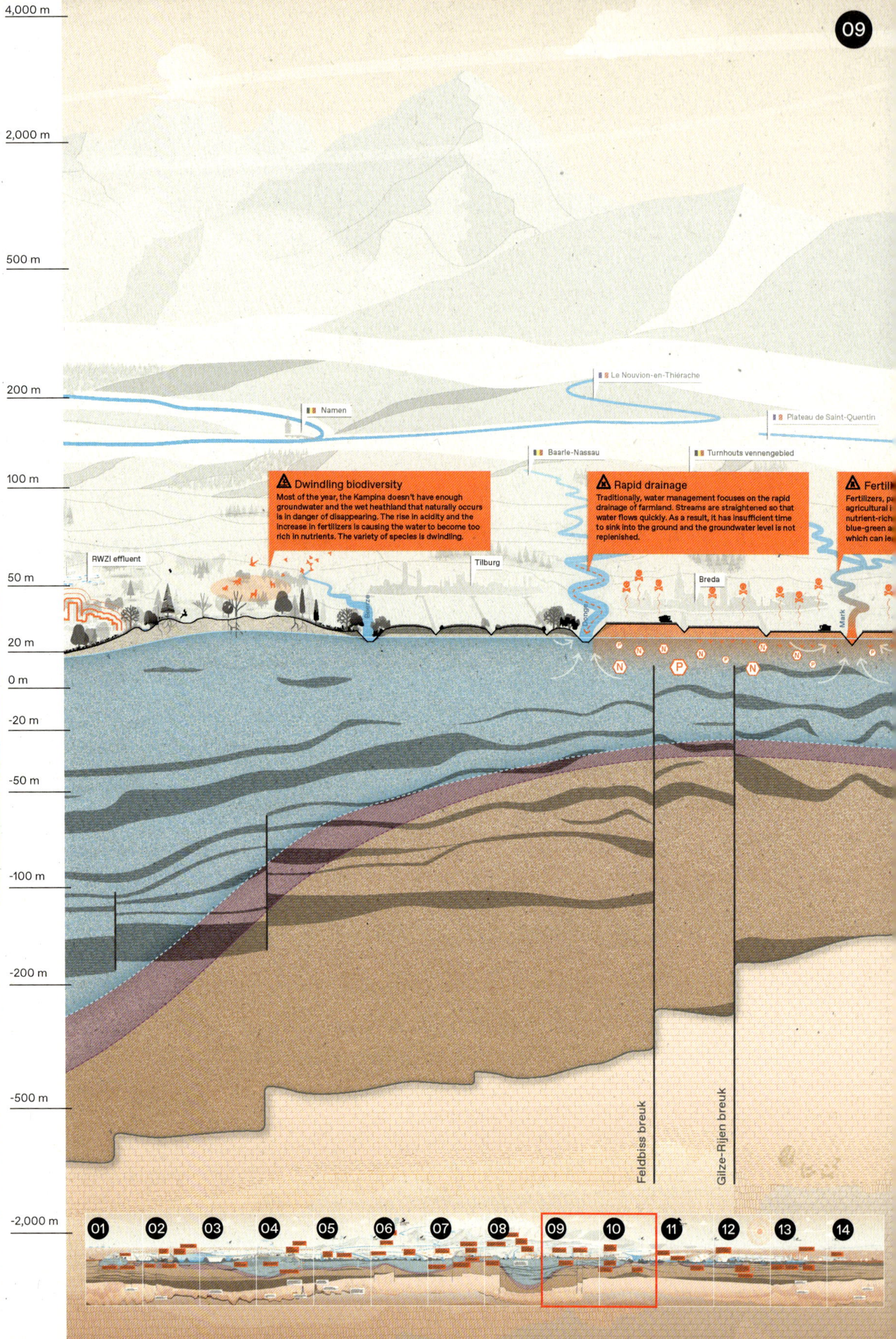

09
4,000 m
2,000 m
500 m
200 m
100 m
50 m
20 m
0 m
-20 m
-50 m
-100 m
-200 m
-500 m
-2,000 m
-4,000 m
Le Nouvion-en-Thiérache
Namen
Plateau de Saint-Quentin
Baarle-Nassau
Turnhouts vennengebied
Dwindling biodiversity
Most of the year, the Kampina doesn't have enough groundwater and the wet heathland that naturally occurs is in danger of disappearing. The rise in acidity and the increase in fertilizers is causing the water to become too rich in nutrients. The variety of species is dwindling.
Rapid drainage
Traditionally, water management focuses on the rapid drainage of farmland. Streams are straightened so that water flows quickly. As a result, it has insufficient time to sink into the ground and the groundwater level is not replenished.
RWZI effluent
Tilburg
Breda
Beerze
Donge
Mark
N
P
Feldbiss breuk
Gilze-Rijen breuk
01
02
03
04
05
06
07
08
09
10
11
12
13
14

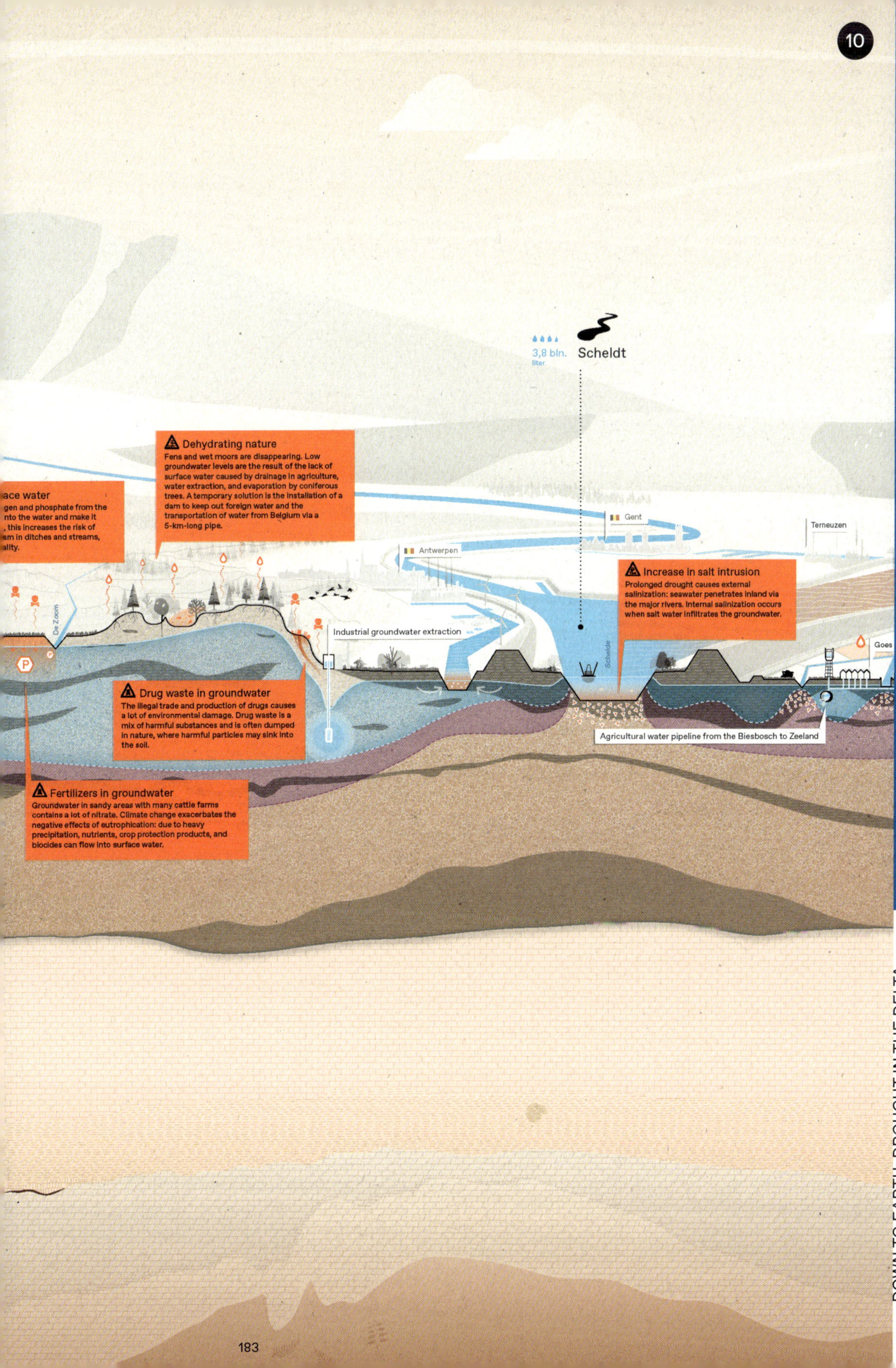
3,8 bln.
liter
Scheldt
Dehydrating nature
Fens and wet moors are disappearing. Low groundwater levels are the result of the lack of surface water caused by drainage in agriculture, water extraction, and evaporation by coniferous trees. A temporary solution is the installation of a dam to keep out foreign water and the transportation of water from Belgium via a 5-km-long pipe.
ace water
gen and phosphate from the nto the water and make it , this increases the risk of sm in ditches and streams, ality.
Gent
Antwerpen
Terneuzen
De Zoom
Increase in salt intrusion
Prolonged drought causes external salinization: seawater penetrates inland via the major rivers. Internal salinization occurs when salt water infiltrates the groundwater.
Industrial groundwater extraction
Scheldе
Goes
P
Drug waste in groundwater
The illegal trade and production of drugs causes a lot of environmental damage. Drug waste is a mix of harmful substances and is often dumped in nature, where harmful particles may sink into the soil.
Agricultural water pipeline from the Biesbosch to Zeeland
Fertilizers in groundwater
Groundwater in sandy areas with many cattle farms contains a lot of nitrate. Climate change exacerbates the negative effects of eutrophication: due to heavy precipitation, nutrients, crop protection products, and biocides can flow into surface water.

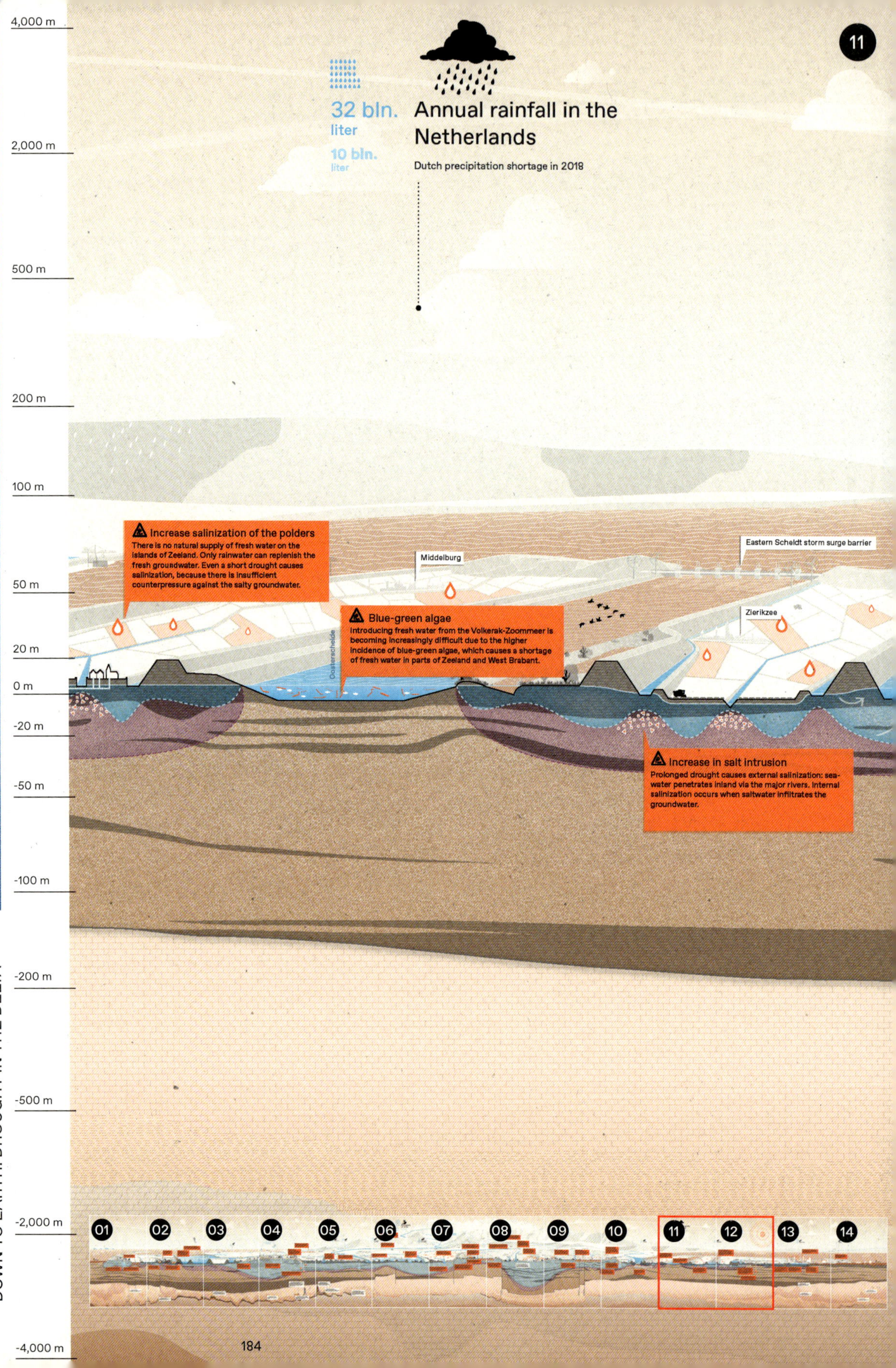
11
32 bln. liter
10 bln. liter
Annual rainfall in the Netherlands
Dutch precipitation shortage in 2018
4,000 m
2,000 m
500 m
200 m
100 m
50 m
20 m
0 m
-20 m
-50 m
-100 m
-200 m
-500 m
-2,000 m
-4,000 m
Increase salinization of the polders
There is no natural supply of fresh water on the islands of Zeeland. Only rainwater can replenish the fresh groundwater. Even a short drought causes salinization, because there is insufficient counterpressure against the salty groundwater.
Middelburg
Eastern Scheldt storm surge barrier
Zierikzee
Oosterschelde
Blue-green algae
Introducing fresh water from the Volkerak-Zoommeer is becoming increasingly difficult due to the higher incidence of blue-green algae, which causes a shortage of fresh water in parts of Zeeland and West Brabant.
Increase in salt intrusion
Prolonged drought causes external salinization: sea-water penetrates inland via the major rivers. Internal salinization occurs when saltwater infiltrates the groundwater.
01 02 03 04 05 06 07 08 09 10 11 12 13 14

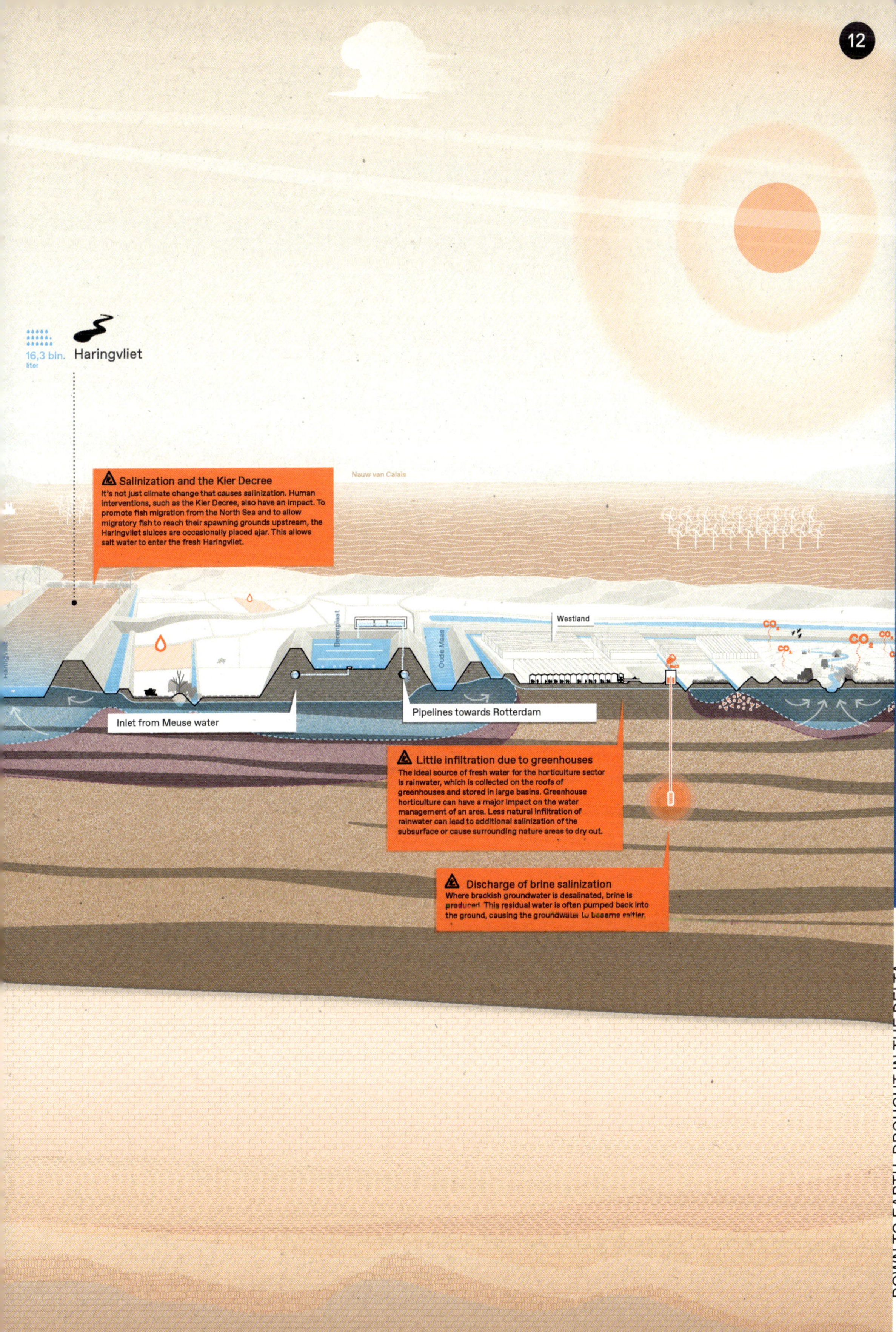
12
16,3 bln. liter
Haringvliet
Nauw van Calais
Salinization and the Kier Decree
It's not just climate change that causes salinization. Human interventions, such as the Kier Decree, also have an impact. To promote fish migration from the North Sea and to allow migratory fish to reach their spawning grounds upstream, the Haringvliet sluices are occasionally placed ajar. This allows salt water to enter the fresh Haringvliet.
Westland
Oude Maas
CO_2
Inlet from Meuse water
Pipelines towards Rotterdam
Little infiltration due to greenhouses
The ideal source of fresh water for the horticulture sector is rainwater, which is collected on the roofs of greenhouses and stored in large basins. Greenhouse horticulture can have a major impact on the water management of an area. Less natural infiltration of rainwater can lead to additional salinization of the subsurface or cause surrounding nature areas to dry out.
Discharge of brine salinization
Where brackish groundwater is desalinated, brine is produced. This residual water is often pumped back into the ground, causing the groundwater to become saltier.

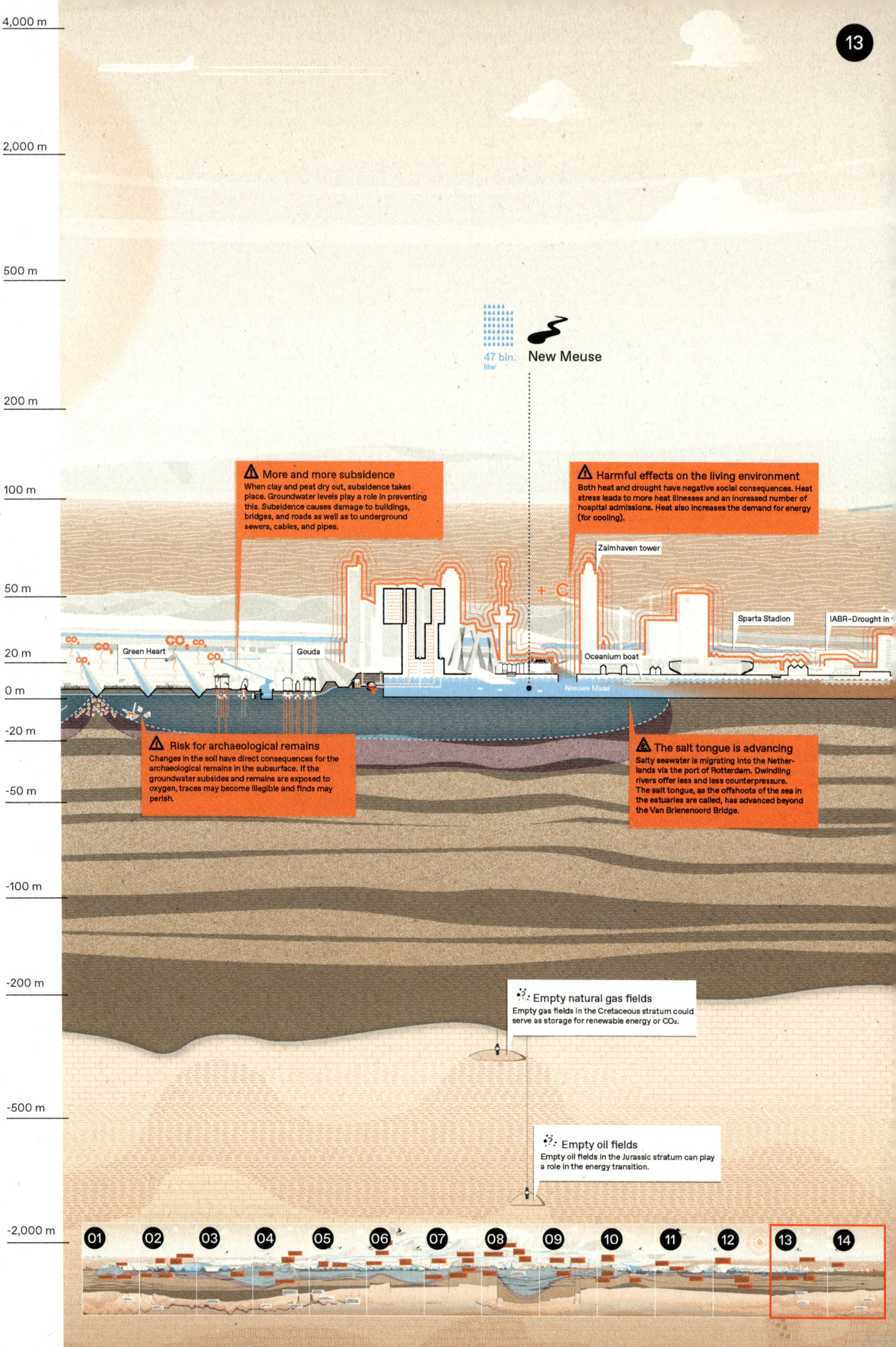
13
4,000 m
2,000 m
500 m
200 m
100 m
50 m
20 m
0 m
-20 m
-50 m
-100 m
-200 m
-500 m
-2,000 m
-4,000 m
47 bln.
liter
New Meuse
More and more subsidence
When clay and peat dry out, subsidence takes place. Groundwater levels play a role in preventing this. Subsidence causes damage to buildings, bridges, and roads as well as to underground sewers, cables, and pipes.
Harmful effects on the living environment
Both heat and drought have negative social consequences. Heat stress leads to more heat illnesses and an increased number of hospital admissions. Heat also increases the demand for energy (for cooling).
Zalmhaven tower
+ °C
Sparta Stadion
IABR–Drought in
Green Heart
Gouda
Oceanium boat
Nieuwe Maas
Risk for archaeological remains
Changes in the soil have direct consequences for the archaeological remains in the subsurface. If the groundwater subsides and remains are exposed to oxygen, traces may become illegible and finds may perish.
The salt tongue is advancing
Salty seawater is migrating into the Netherlands via the port of Rotterdam. Dwindling rivers offer less and less counterpressure. The salt tongue, as the offshoots of the sea in the estuaries are called, has advanced beyond the Van Brienenoord Bridge.
Empty natural gas fields
Empty gas fields in the Cretaceous stratum could serve as storage for renewable energy or CO_2.
Empty oil fields
Empty oil fields in the Jurassic stratum can play a role in the energy transition.
01
02
03
04
05
06
07
08
09
10
11
12
13
14

2 bln.
liter
Thames
Londen
Theems
Water shortage in industry
Various industrial processes require (cooling) water. A shortage can temporarily shut down these industries, with far-reaching economic and social consequences.
Port of Rotterdam - Maasvlakte
Sea level rise
Empty natural gas fields
Empty gas fields in the Cretaceous stratum could serve as storage for renewable energy or CO_2.
Empty oil fields
Empty oil fields in the Jurassic stratum can play a role in the energy transition.

2050 A Vision of the Future for a Robust Freshwater System

SUBSURFACE
- geological fault line
- water separation layer, clay, loam, or peat
- water-permeable layer, sand
- push moraines, pushed layers
- river sediments

DEEP SUBSURFACE
- Tertiary, North Sea Group
- Late Cretaceous, Chalk Group
- Early Cretaceous, Rhineland Group
- Upper Jurassic
- Lower Jurassic, Althena Group
- Triassic
- Permian, Zechstein Group
- Permian, Rotliegend Group
- Carboniferous, Limburg Group
- Carboniferous, Geul Subgroup

GROUNDWATER SYSTEM
- average groundwater level
- extremely low groundwater level
- freshwater (Cl- < 150mg/l)
- brackish water (Cl- 150–1,000 mg/l)
- saltwater (Cl- > 1,000 mg/l)

4,000 m
2,000 m
500 m
200 m

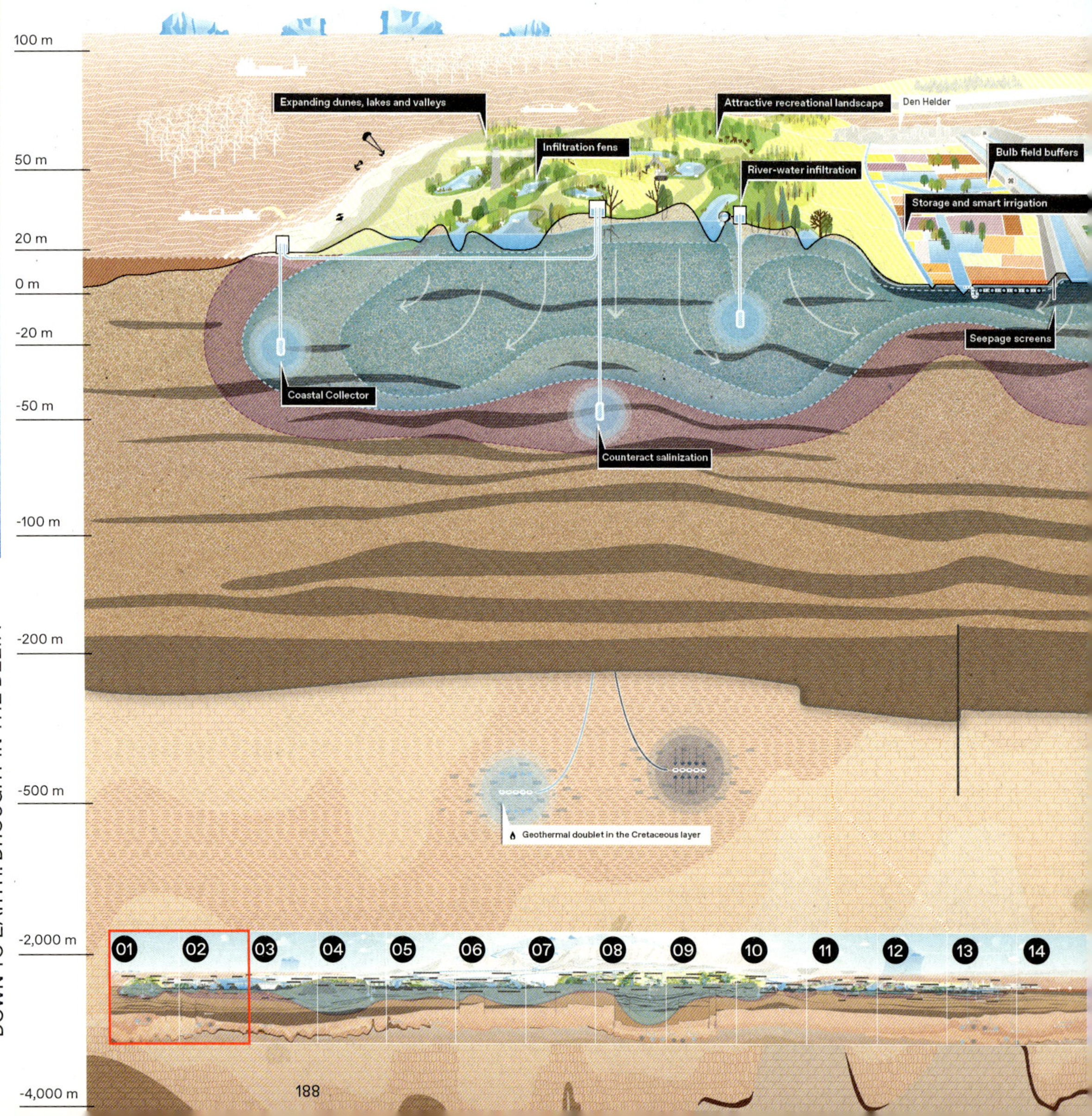

XL FRESHWATER DUNES

Durable Protection against Salinization

The freshwater bubble underneath the dunes protects agricultural land from salinization. Increasing this freshwater supply keeps saline groundwater out of the polders. The dunes are also important for the production of drinking water. Through long pipes, river water is transported to the dunes, for example to the Amsterdamse Waterleidingduinen. The dunes filter and clean the water, which is subsequently pumped up and purified into drinking water.

In 2050 the dunes will have been laid out to maximize the fresh-water bubble, building on gradients and transitions of beach, dunes, dune lakes, valleys, heath, and forests. This will create a dynamic landscape with a robust freshwater system and a biodiverse, attractive, and varied area for recreation and sojourn. The dunes are widened and heightened and as a result, the groundwater level rises. A larger freshwater bubble provides counterpressure against saltwater seepage (groundwater that escapes from the soil to the surface under pressure). With great effect: for every 10 cm of groundwater level rise, the freshwater lens increases by 4 m due to the pressure. During high water levels in rivers, excess water can be pumped to the dunes. Moist dune hollows allow the water to infiltrate slowly.

Flower bulb cultivation will become more drought-resistant and nature-friendly through underground storage and drip irrigation. When bulb fields are flooded more often, they require fewer chemical pesticides. If this environmentally friendly technique is used more often and for longer periods of time, bulb fields can also contribute to freshwater infiltration and counteract salinization.

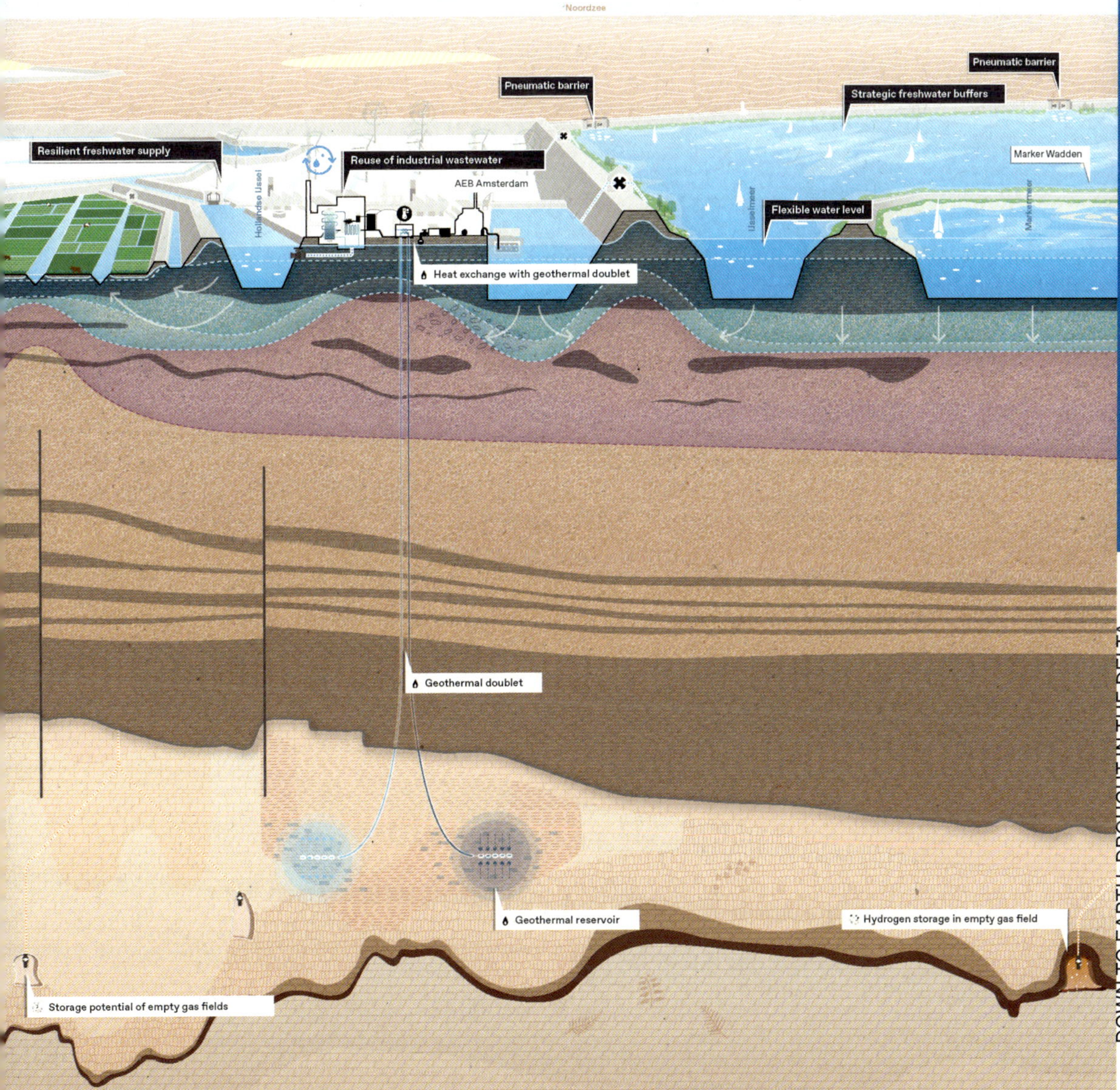

THE BLUE HEART

Flexible Equals Robust

The IJsselmeer and Markermeer are the largest freshwater reservoirs in the Netherlands. From these lakes, water is let into the surrounding polders in the summer through gravity drainage and used in agriculture for flushing and to prevent salinization; in nature, as cooling and processing water; and for drinking water. The increasing weather extremes call for a flexible water level management. The region and the Dutch national government are establishing rules to this effect in the *Peilbesluit* (Dutch Water Level Ordinance). The IJsselmeer, Markermeer and Veluwerandmeren will each have their own target level, creating a freshwater buffer of 400 million m³.

By 2050 the water level in the Wadden Sea will be a lot higher due to rising sea levels. The water level in the three lakes will also rise as a result, so gravity drainage will still be possible. A higher water level will also counteract the salinization of coastal areas by the Wadden Sea. During droughts, the raised water level in these lakes will create a freshwater supply. The three compartments each have their own level, depending on the water demand and supply from the IJssel River. By using a clever system of dams and sluices to distribute the water, the northern provinces will continue to dispose of freshwater in the future.

The IJsselmeer is currently bordered by steep dikes. The construction of sloping, nature-friendly banks of sand, clay, and silt from the Markermeer will ensure that small changes in the water level will lead to a great diversity of conditions and thus to richer nature development, with reed belts for birds and fish.

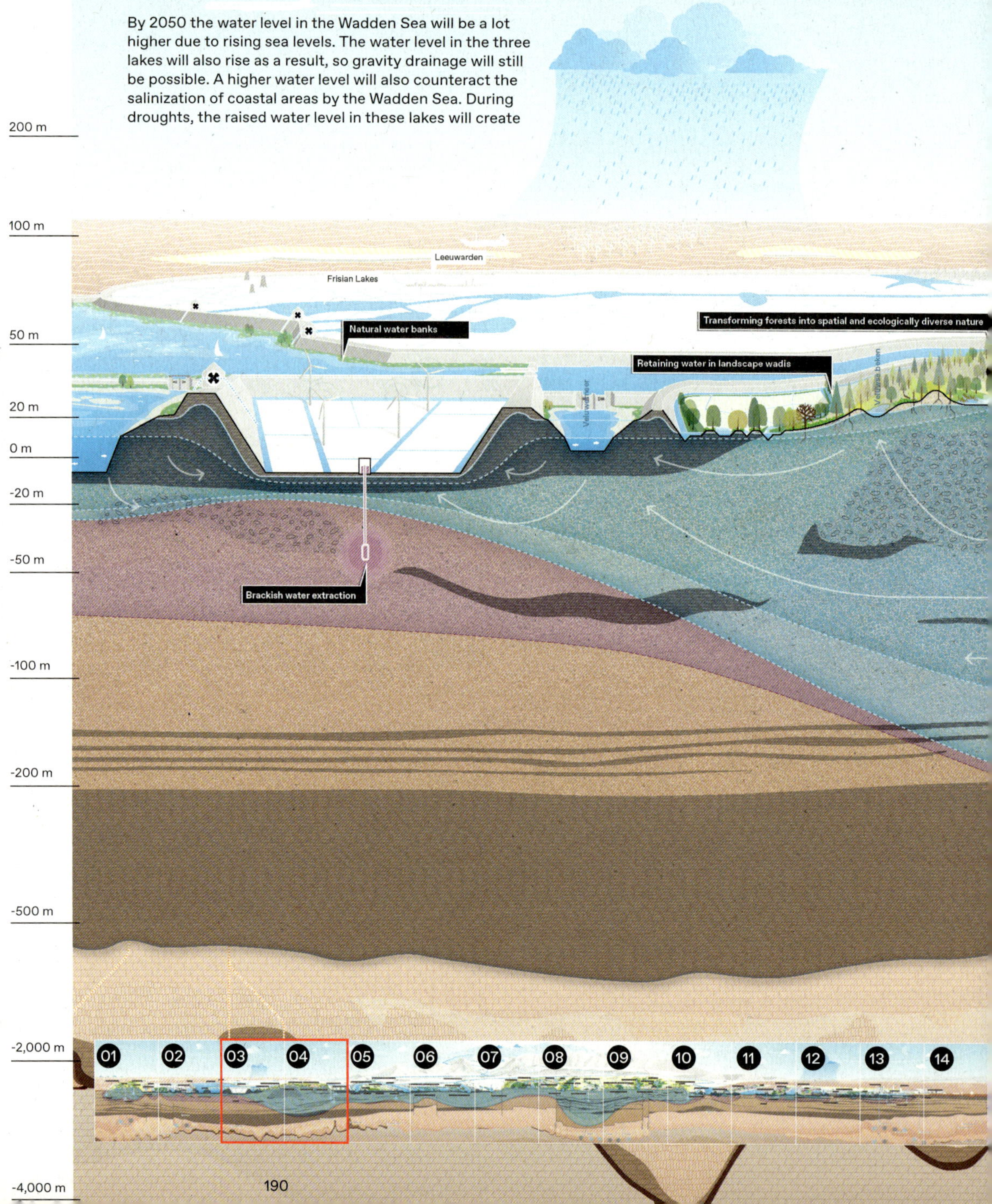

THE VELUWE AS A SPONGE
An Open Infiltration Landscape

The Veluwe depends on rainwater to supplement its groundwater. But once the soil has dried out, it becomes less porous and can absorb less moisture. It is therefore important to prevent the soil from drying out; also, healthy soil is less prone to drying out. Most of the forests in the Veluwe area were planted in the late nineteenth and early twentieth centuries. They mainly contain coniferous trees, which prevent sand drift caused by the overgrazing of heathland and can be used for timber production. But conifers also evaporate a lot of water, up to 60 percent of the rainwater that falls on the Veluwe, and this dries out the soil. The reclamation of the Flevopolders has also proved disastrous for the groundwater level: the counterpressure from the IJsselmeer fell away, and as a result the Veluwe has been able to store less water and many springs have dried up. These springs are typical of the Veluwe and were created by people digging holes in slopes, down to the groundwater level, in places where there was sufficient water pressure. Water flowing from such 'spring heads' flowed to a canal system that powered the water mills used in the paper industry or for laundering.

In 2050, the Veluwe will have transformed from a parching coniferous forest into an open infiltration landscape. This landscape will have height differences, wet valleys, and spring creeks. Part of the coniferous forest will be changing into drifting dunes with pools, which will improve the infiltration capacity of the thick sand bed and create spatial and ecological diversity. In addition, the monotonous coniferous forests will have been enriched with mixed, deciduous forests of oak, birch, and beech that evaporate less groundwater, create better soil quality, and offer more variety.
Agriculture will contribute to a healthier soil by the use of compost and grass or strip cultivation. Soil containing more organic matter can retain water better; the subsurface of the Veluwe will become a sponge; once vanished springs and special seepage nature become visible again.

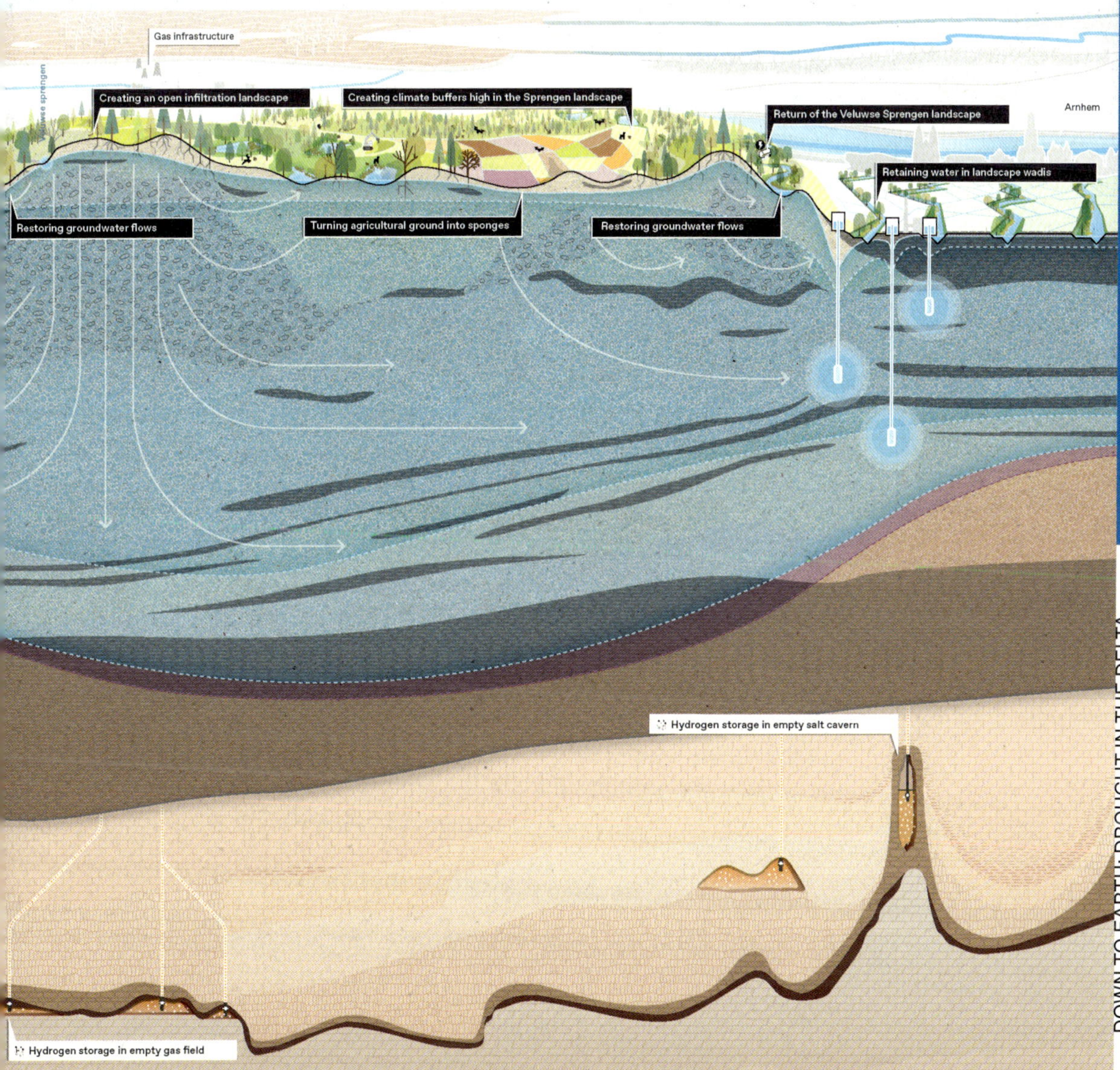

SLOWING DOWN THE RHINE

Rich and Dynamic River Landscape

05

Along the Rhine, the groundwater level is determined by the level of the river, partly because rivers dissect the top layer. When water levels are high, seepage from the rivers often occurs. When water levels are low, lateral spread occurs: groundwater is drained by the river. If it is very dry for a long time and the river water level is low, the flood-plains and polders dry out.
Nutrient-rich river deposits have provided the fruit cultivation characteristic of this area with fertile soil, ideal for cherries, apples, and pears. Longer periods of heat and drought threaten these crops. To make sure fruit does not burn on the tree it has to be sprayed during the day, which takes a lot of water at a time when little is available.

In the 2050 river landscape, various freshwater buffers will be created using river basins and banks. Old meanders, such as the Rijnstrangen, remnants of the river course from the seventeenth century that have been disconnected from the river since the 1960s, are particularly promising. If the water level is too high or the river flows too quickly, the old meanders will be filled by means of valve culverts or small water windmills and so-called ram pumps – pumps that use the flow of the river to pump water to higher areas without using an additional energy source. When the river level is low and groundwater can be replenished, the stored water slowly infiltrates the soil. This way, the former river basins absorb weather extremes and sufficient water remains available at all times, making the river landscape much more dynamic: it changes constantly in accordance with wet and dry periods. The result is a much richer landscape, with extensive river swamps and meanders that are part of the natural DNA of the Rhine and the fruit orchard of the Netherlands.

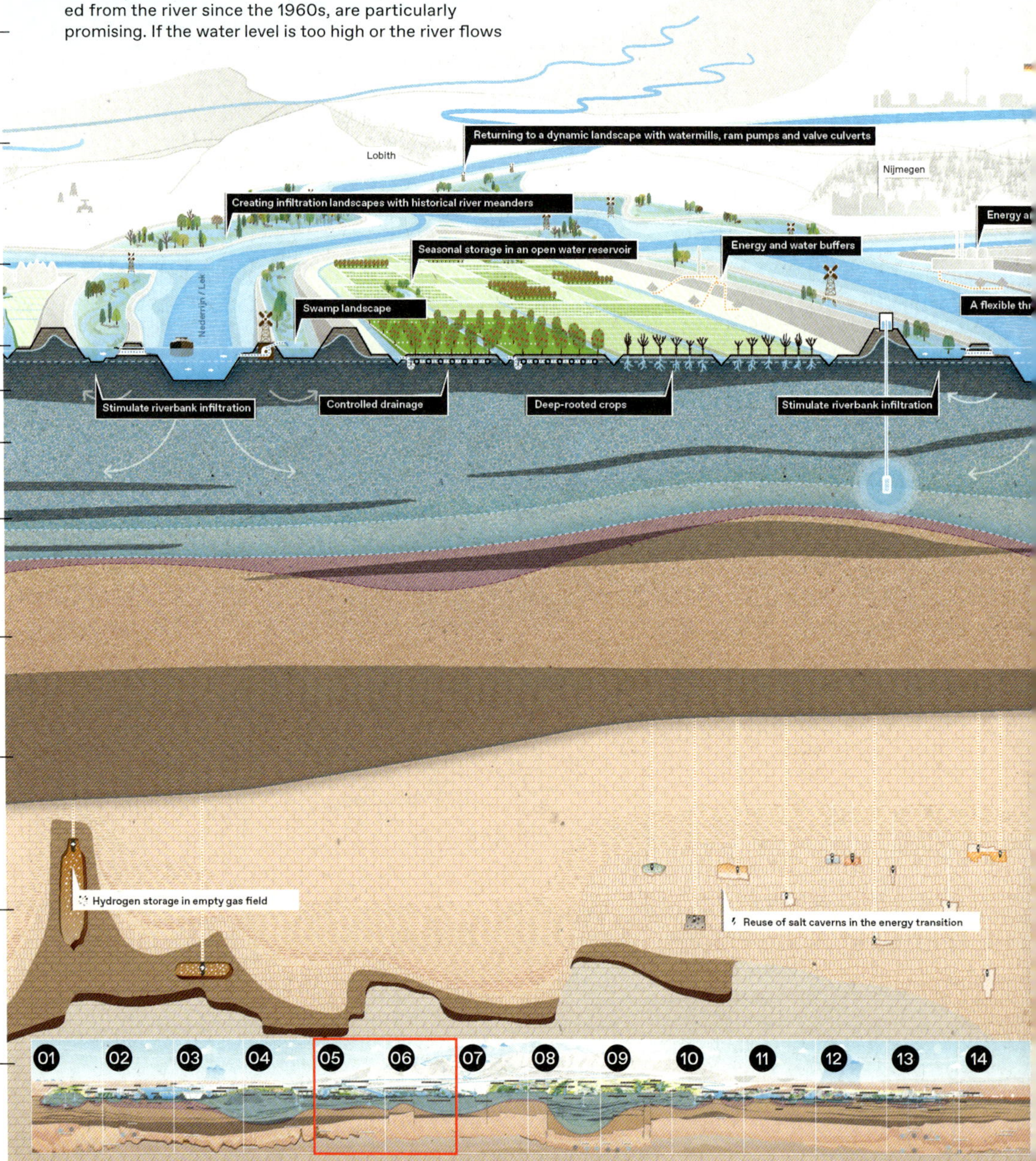

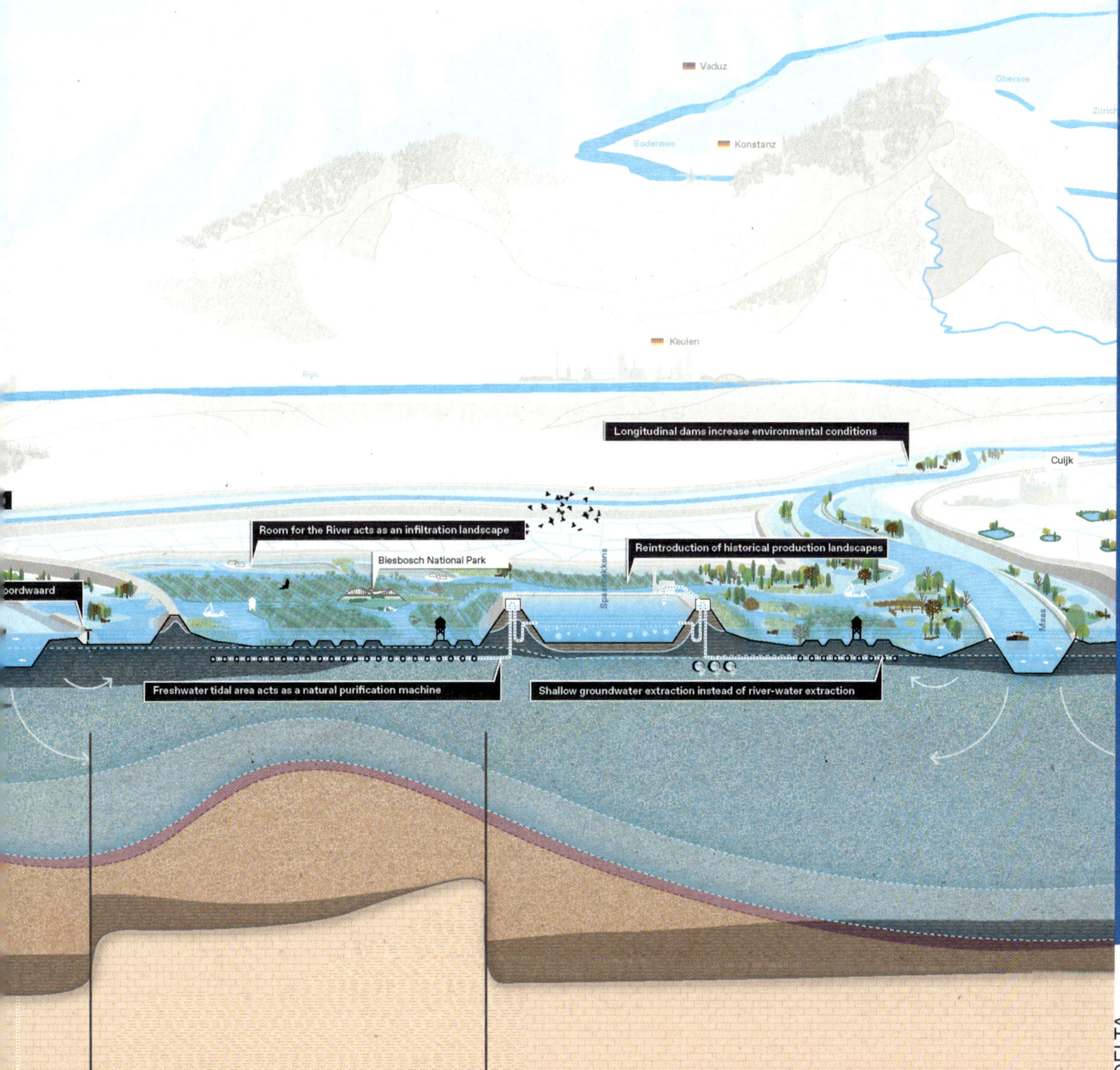

THE DRINKABLE MEUSE

Natural Purification Machines

It is no longer certain the Meuse will continue to be a source of drinking water. Due to increasing drought, the water level in the Meuse is falling and 4 million Dutch and 3 million Belgians are threatened with a shortage of drinking water. When there is less water, its quality deteriorates because the Meuse is more polluted and the river flows slower and therefore changes less often.

The Meuse is a rain river. If it does not rain for a long time, river water previously stored in reservoirs is used for drinking water production. The Meuse is also an important transport axis for shipping as well as a route for recreational boating. If the river is too low, fewer ships can use it, with all the economic consequences that this entails.

Like the Meuse, the Biesbosch is an important water landscape. Now a national park, it has a rich history of harvesting and processing natural materials and can be seen as an early 'biobased production landscape.'

Freshwater is the gold of the future. In 2050, to make sure the river as a source of drinking water survives, the banks of the Meuse and the Biesbosch area will function as natural (pre)purification machines: instead of river water, groundwater will be extracted just below the banks. Riverbank plants such as reed, rushes, and willow filter the river water. This makes water extraction more efficient and stable and it requires fewer chemicals and consumes less energy. Reeds can be used for roofing, rushes for insulation, willows and other fast-growing wood for building materials.

By reintroducing historic cultural landscapes that both purify water and produce raw materials, the tradition of natural production in the Biesbosch is continued.

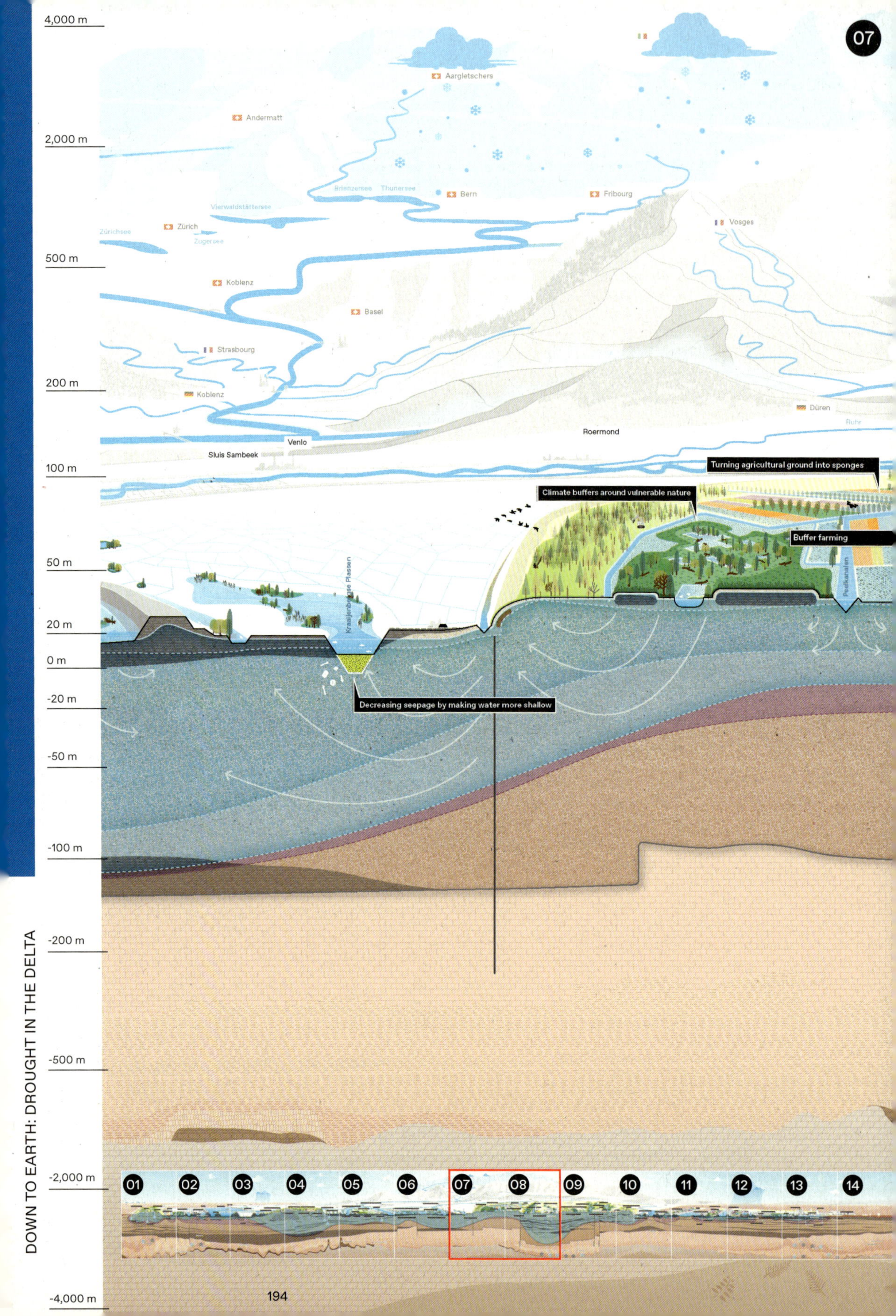

07
4,000 m
2,000 m
500 m
200 m
100 m
50 m
20 m
0 m
-20 m
-50 m
-100 m
-200 m
-500 m
-2,000 m
-4,000 m
Aargletschers
Andermatt
Brienzersee
Thunersee
Bern
Fribourg
Vierwaldstättersee
Zürichsee
Zürich
Zugersee
Vosges
Koblenz
Basel
Strasbourg
Koblenz
Düren
Ruhr
Roermond
Venlo
Sluis Sambeek
Turning agricultural ground into sponges
Climate buffers around vulnerable nature
Buffer farming
Peelkanalen
Kraaijenbergse Plassen
Decreasing seepage by making water more shallow
01
02
03
04
05
06
07
08
09
10
11
12
13
14

In the past, De Peel was 1,000 km² of swampy, inaccessible peatland; reclamation turned it into large plots of agricultural land. Today, De Peel is the most important food-producing region of the Netherlands, with thousands of agricultural companies. The remaining peatland is one of the most bird-rich areas of Western Europe; here, thousands of migratory birds gather every autumn. If De Peel does not stay wet, the peat will disintegrate and release a lot of carbon into the air.
Because De Peel is higher than the surrounding area, water drains away. In addition, the agricultural land is laid out to drain the water as quickly as possible. Often, water from the Meuse has to be brought into the arid area via the canals of De Peel. The current monotonous agricultural production has resulted in an ecological desert. Thanks to artificial fertilizer, the productivity of the soil has increased enormously, but soil life has largely disappeared.
In addition to animal protein, cattle breeding produces ammonia, methane gas, particulate matter, and manure. Manure still contains many nutrients and by applying it to the land the soil is overburdened. As nitrogen and phosphate enter the ground and surface water, the natural balance is disturbed.

In 2050 the area will have changed into a wet, open production landscape that will feed people as well as the subsurface and soil life. It is a landscape with a living soil, rich in organisms and with many organic substances, important to soil fertility. A living soil captures rain, retains water, and reduces the amount of fertilizers leaking into the ground and surface water. The agricultural production landscape and its environment are balanced, more diverse and small-scale, including food forests, algae beds, duckweed pools, willow forests, and strip farming.

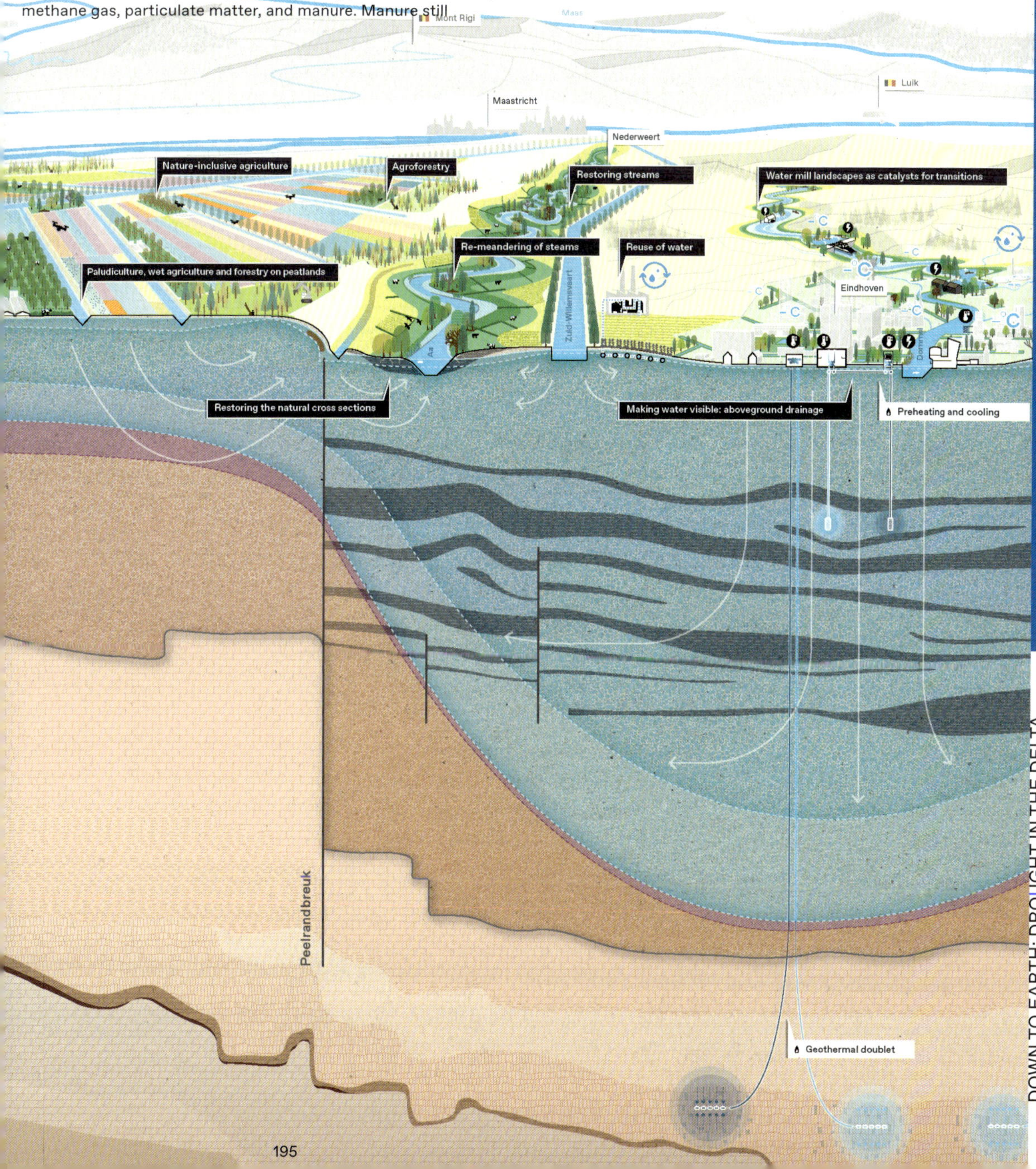

A RESILIENT STREAM VALLEY LANDSCAPE
Historical Interaction of Culture and Nature

Stream valley landscapes consist of low-lying areas with creeks that transect the higher sandy areas. Stream valleys are very gradient-rich, which offers many opportunities for nature development. The soil is part of an integrated water system, which is particularly evident in the event of flooding or prolonged periods of drought. The balance between soil, water, and agriculture needs to be restored, for example by increasing the organic matter content of our soil and allowing stream valleys to meander once more.

In 2050, creeks will form the backbone of the water system in the high sandy areas. The stream valley of the future will have different effects on the upper, middle, and lower parts of the stream, in which the flow rate will slow down. The historical route of the stream valley will be followed as much as possible; there will be no agriculture that ignores the soil. Downstream, the restoration of water meadows alongside hay meadows will increase the infiltration of groundwater. The creation of waterlogged wooded terrain along the creeks will contribute to carbon sequestration. To create a robust water system, the flanking nodes that connect the stream valleys with the natural and forested areas on sand ridges will be strengthened.
For centuries, many of these stream landscapes consisted of chains of water mills and dammed-up streams – these are among the earliest energy landscapes. They can be refitted on the basis of historical elements to allow them to buffer, retain, and infiltrate freshwater, which is good for nature, water safety, and agriculture. In addition, these watermill landscapes can be used for the production of sustainable energy (aquathermal or hydropower). The historical interaction between culture (farmers and watermills) and nature (original stream with dammed-up areas and flood plains) is strengthened.

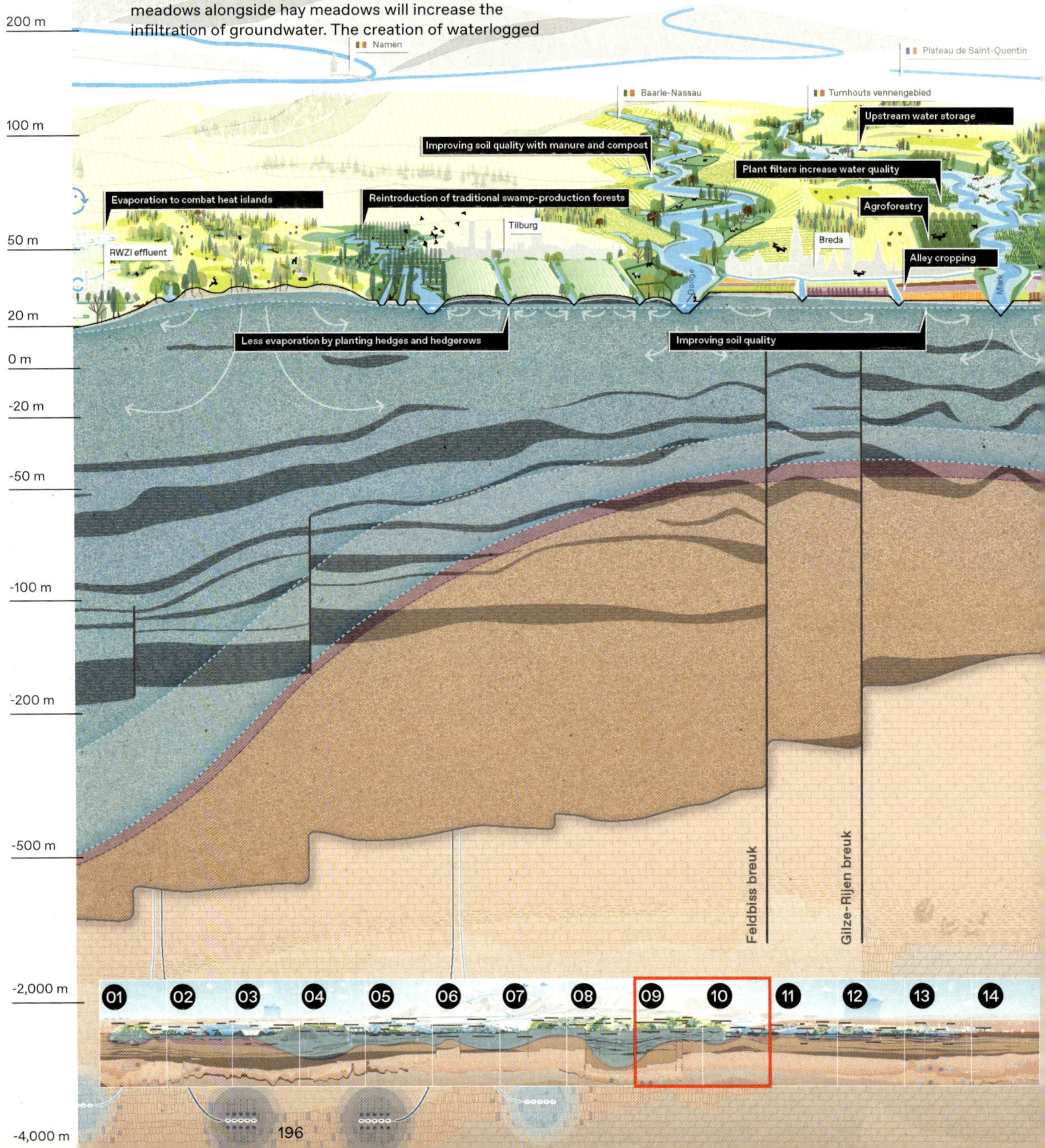

Wuustwezel
Transforming forest into spatially and ecologically diverse nature
Infiltration fens
Precision agriculture
Antwerpen
Gent
Terneuzen
Reuse and storage of industrial wastewater
Making water visible: aboveground drainage
Schelde
Extraction at end of groundwater cycle
Storage in Boom clay layer

11

THE DYNAMIC ISLANDS OF ZEELAND
Varied Conditions, Varied Landscape

Low tide and high tide, land and water, nature and culture, past and present, dry and wet: on the islands of Zeeland they are all found within a short distance of each other. Much of the soil is alternatingly drenched in freshwater and in saltwater. Salt-loving glasswort and sea lavender grow in the low mudflats; willow, elder, and bush grass grow in the saltmarshes. The sea gates have deepened considerably in recent centuries, causing salinization to move inland. The freshwater problem caused by the salinization of groundwater is acute in the islands, which depend entirely on rain for their freshwater supply. The alternative supply of freshwater via high-pressure pipelines unnecessarily cost energy and infrastructure. The islands are currently on a freshwater drip; the salinization pressure is increasing further due to sea level rise.

By 2050, saltwater will be pushed as far out to sea as possible to protect the inland freshwater bubbles, for example by installing bubble screens in sluice gates. Freshwater will be led as deeply into the polders as possible. Marsh areas inside the dikes in the polders along the Western Scheldt will provide counterpressure against salinization.
Large parts of the Province of Zeeland's agricultural land will have to contend with increasing salinization. By means of precision agriculture, farmers will be able to adapt to the changing conditions, according to specific situations. The diversity of fresh- and saltwater gradients will create different landscapes and allow corresponding agriculture. At the plot level, local freshwater storage can also be considered, both above- and belowground.
Freshwater is led as deeply into the polders as possible.
In Zeeland's creeks, the water level can possibly be raised.

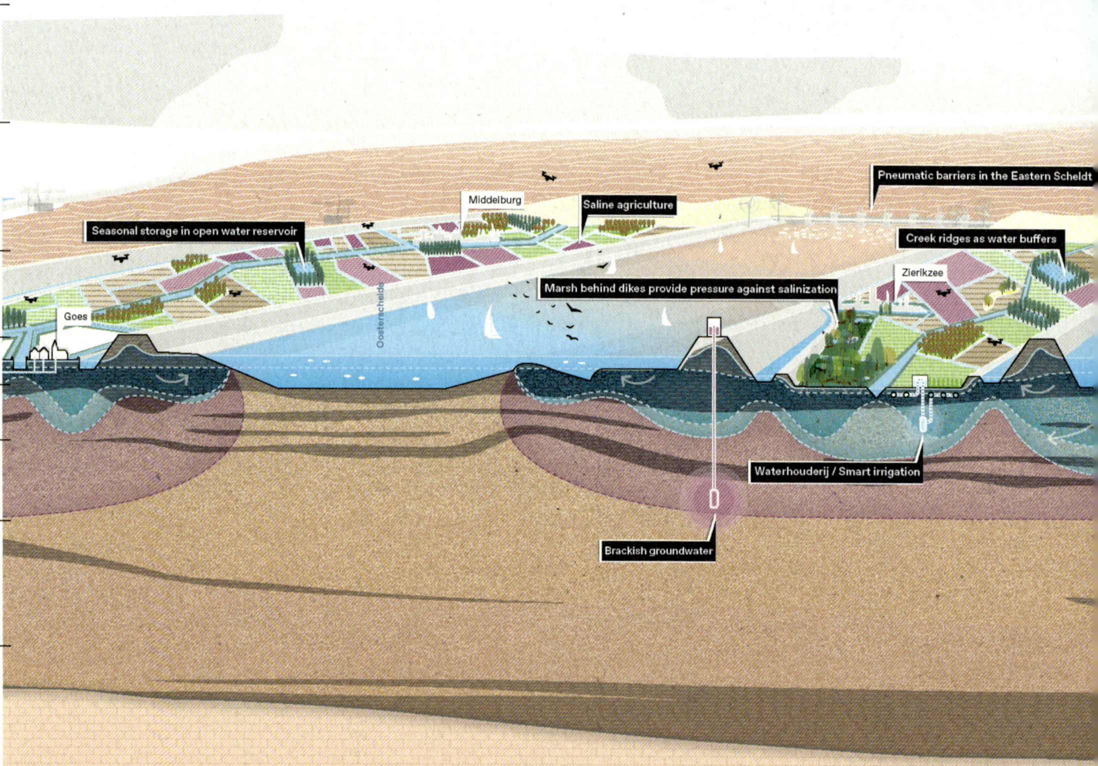

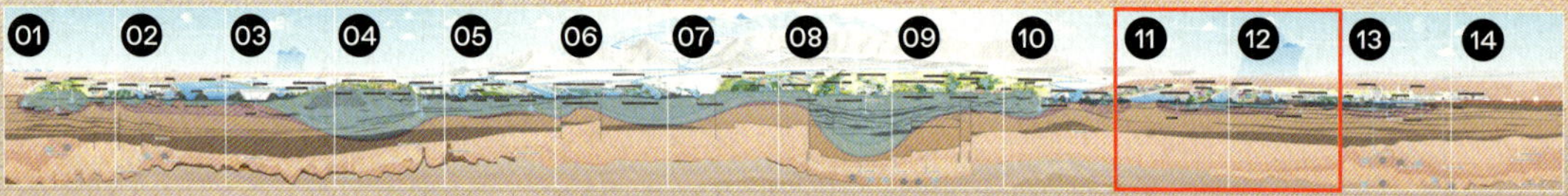

Centuries of land reclamation have turned the Netherlands into a rich production landscape. But if we continue to raise our dikes and drain the land artificially, subsidence will turn the western part of the Netherlands into a dangerously large bathtub. Due to dehydration, the peatland is subsiding by 1 cm per year. The result is increased salinization, which means that more and more freshwater has to be used to flush the system; in the peat meadow area, cattle breeding is becoming less and less profitable. The higher parts of the peat meadow area face damage to crops during prolonged periods of drought. Finally, as the peat dries out it releases high levels of greenhouse gases into the air, as much as 2 million cars emit per year. A fixed water level management, with fragmented water level sections, directed by the demands of agriculture, which, as a result of saltwater seepage, continuously needs to be flushed, is an undesirable and unaffordable situation.

By 2050 the water level will be raised, subsidence halted, and peat oxidation reduced or stopped. The peat meadow area is full of relics from the reclamation days: mill streams, quays, ring dikes, raised polder water storage basins, watercourses, and canals. These historical elements will be revitalized and used to transport freshwater to the right place and to buffer.
Traditional agriculture on deep peatlands will give way to the cultivation of wet crops such as cat's tail (building material), cranberry (food), waterfern (protein-rich fodder crop), and reed (energy/biomass). Livestock farms will have changed into more extensive, nature-inclusive, circular dairy farms with flower-rich grasslands and cattle that are more resistant to higher water levels, such as the Dutch *blaarkop* cow. Some traditional peat meadows are maintained through underwater drainage. In places that become too wet, water and nature recreation will take over from agriculture and cattle breeding as an economic carrier.

A LANDSCAPE OF SPONGE PARKS AND POLDER ROOFS

Resilient Cities

In combination with the increasing paving of urban surfaces, the effects of climate change are causing more and more drought problems and damage in cities. Water is important for the prevention of (accelerated) subsidence, pile rot, and heat stress, and to create a vital green structure. Opportunities to replenish groundwater in the city are limited by hard surfaces; the water system has traditionally been designed to drain water as quickly as possible to prevent flooding, not to retain freshwater.

In 2050, city residents will use water sparingly and reuse it as much as possible. In industry, different sectors and production processes will use each other's residual water. Reduced water consumption also has an energy advantage: if hot process water is reused, there is no need to heat cold groundwater to production temperature.

Water will not only be stored in the existing, underground water storage facilities, but also buffered in the public space in water squares, wadis, and infiltration points that help green the city. Sponge parks will be constructed to support infiltration. Rainwater will no longer be discharged via the sewer system, but visibly led to these parks through open gutters. Surface water and greenery provide much-needed cooling in the city. Absorbing and retaining rainwater in the city reduces heat stress, increases biodiversity and creates a beautiful and pleasant environment. Parking lots are paved with semi-open stones so that water can infiltrate here as well. Green 'polder roofs' will have a water-buffering function. In short: as much public and private space in the city as possible will be 'soft-surfaced.'

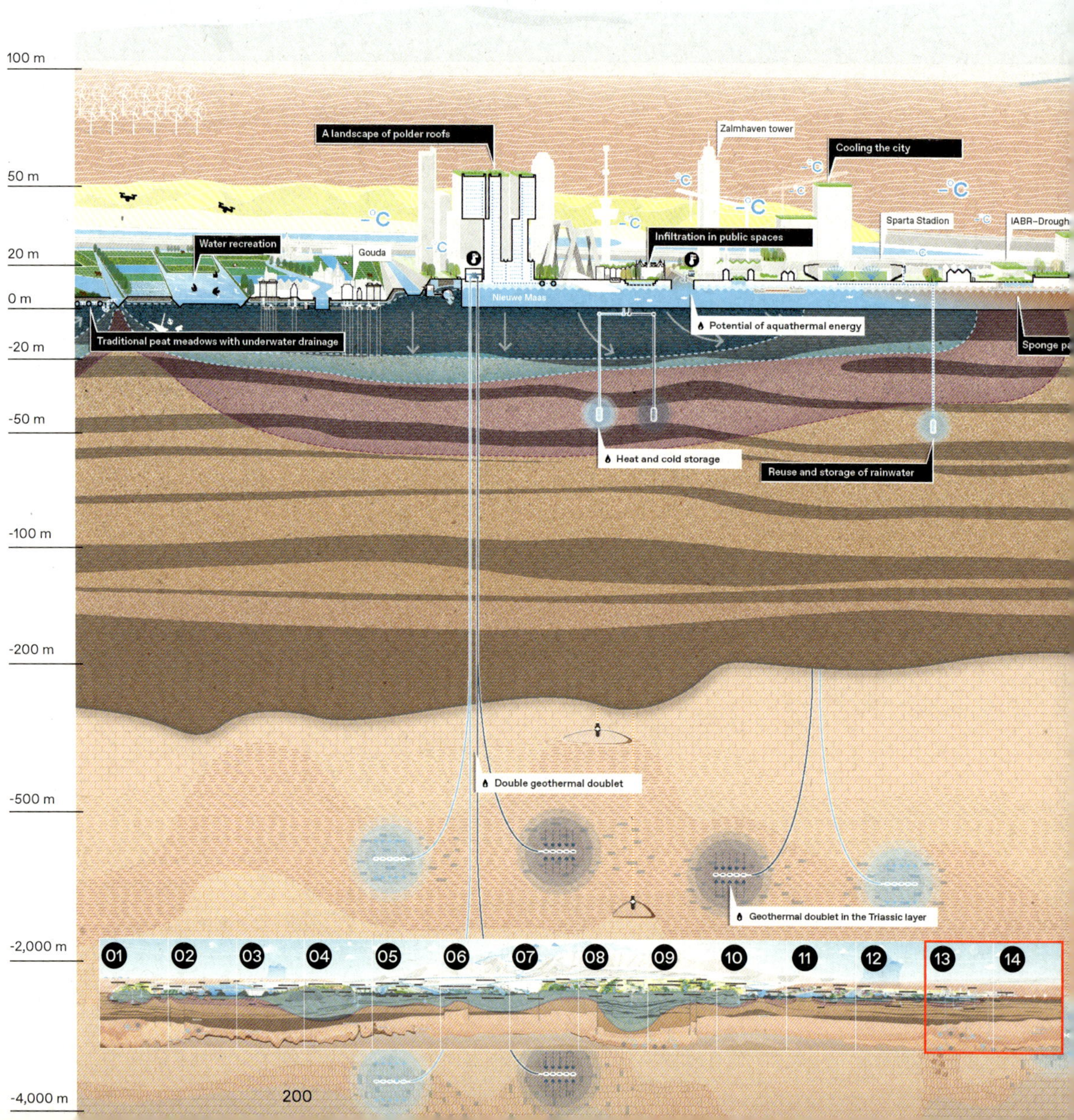

Londen
Theems
Port of Rotterdam - Maasvlakte
Reusing wastewater: industrial symbiosis
Pneumatic barrier
Underground storage in empty gas fields
Underground storage in empty gas fields
Geothermal doublet in the Triassic layer
Storage and extraction of gas from coal beds

2050
DOWN

DOWN TO EARTH: DROUGHT IN THE DELTA

FOUR EXPLORATIONS

In four exemplary Dutch projects, Sponstuin, Panorama Waterland, Water Mosaic Groene Hart, and COASTAR, solution directions proposed by the IABR–Atelier are already being concretely explored on specific locations.

Field trip to the Sponstuin
DROOGTE IN DE DELTA
photo: IABR

←
DROUGHT IN THE DELTA
photo: Aad Hoogendoorn

1. Sponstuin

Many Dutch cities are built on wet soil, composed of peat or clay. Excess water has to be drained away, but in combination with intensive urbanization this generates risks such as flooding, drought and subsidence. Climate change exacerbates these risks, so it's time for a new, sustainable approach to water management in an urban context.

'Stad als spons' (Sponge City) is such a new approach. A sponge can absorb water, retain it for a long time and then release it for reuse. That is why the urban designers and landscape architects of design office De Urbanisten are investigating how Rotterdam can function as a sponge on the scale of the entire city.
De Urbanisten, the designers of Rotterdam's world famous water square, have translated the results of the research into concrete applications in specific locations. The Sponstuin (Sponge Garden) is one of them, realized in and together with the Voedseltuin (Food Garden), right next to the Keilepand – where the IABR is located. There, experiments are being carried out to find out which soil mixtures and plant species are most suitable for the application of the sponge technique. De Urbanisten are testing how an attractive green outdoor space can also function as a sponge on site: as a green space that is able to absorb and retain water during periods of heavy precipitation, and so that flooding is avoided. The retained water can then be released in dry periods, which have become increasingly common in the Netherlands in recent years.

RESEARCH, DESIGN AND REALIZATION
De Urbanisten

SPONSORS AND SUPPORT
Water Sensitive Rotterdam, Stichting Voedseltuin Rotterdam, Municipality of Rotterdam, Water Authority of Delfland, Province of South Holland, EFL Stichting, Binder Groenprojecten, Kim Kogelman, Lapinus

Sponstuin
© De Urbanisten

SPONGE PLANTING

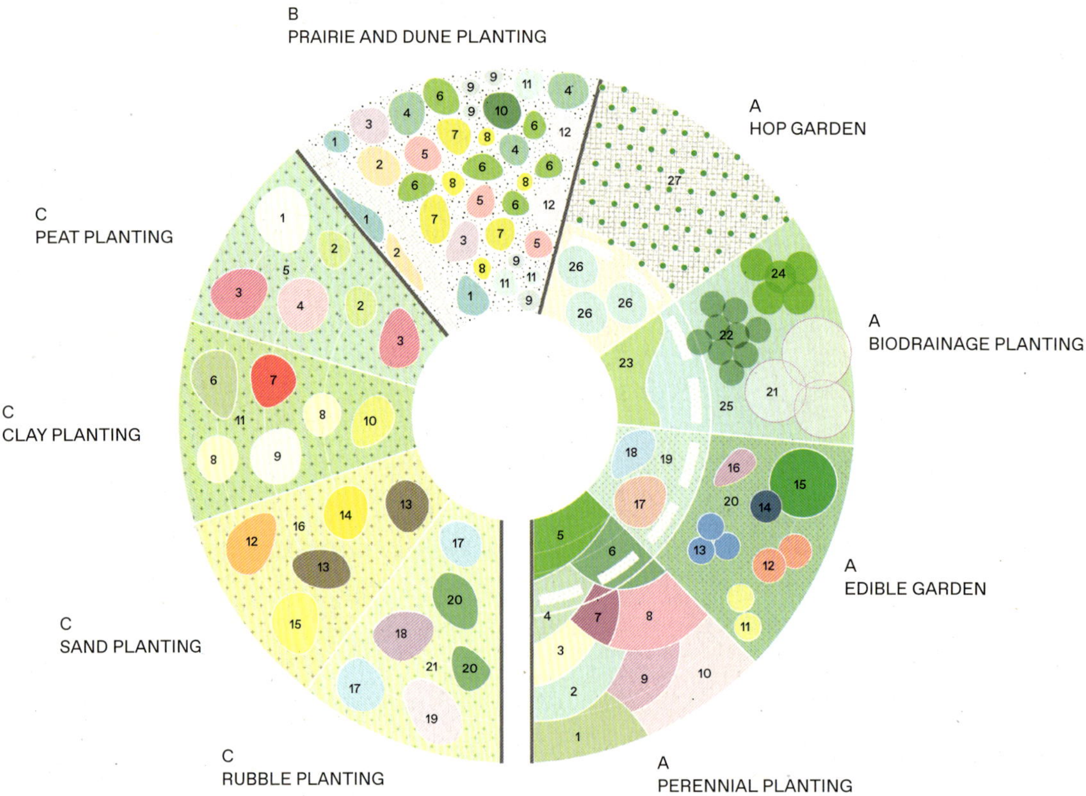

A

PERENNIAL PLANTING
1. Chinese fountaingrass 'Hameln'
2. Purple coneflower 'Alba'
3.Feather reed-grass 'Karl Foerster'
4. Meadowsweet
5. Palm sedge
6. Japanese forest grass
7. Purple loosestrife 'Robin'
8. Common bistort
9. Stonecrop 'Matrona'
10. Aster 'Asran'

EDIBLE GARDEN
11. Gooseberry
12. Japanese quince
13. Blueberry
14. Purple chokeberry
15. Juneberry
16. Bronze fennel
17. Common valerian
18. Common comfrey
19. Water mint
20. Borage + Coriander + Lucerne + White clover

BIODRAINAGE PLANTING
21. Tamarisk 'Pink cascade'
22. Purple willow 'Nana'
23. Silvery creeping willow
24. Narrow-leaved rose-mary willow
25. Native grassland flowers

HOP GARDEN
26. Northern sea oats 'River mist'
27. Common hop

B

PRAIRIE AND DUNE PLANTING
1. Sea lyme-grass 'Blue dune'
2. European beach grass
3. Lupin
4. Pearly everlasting
5. Red valerian
6. Mexican feather grass
7. Tickseed
8. Great mullein
9. Umbelata yarrow
10. Dwarf mountain pine
11. Hairy hawkweed
12. Russian sage

C

PEAT PLANTING
1. Aster 'Starshine'
2. Purple moor-grass 'Heidebraut'
3. Heather
4. Japanese spiraea 'Gen-pei'
5. Snow rush

CLAY PLANTING
6. Chinese fountaingrass 'Hameln'
7. Red bistort
8. Feather reed-grass 'Karl Foerster'
9. White bistort
10. Coneflower 'Early Bird Gold'
11. Lady's mantle

SAND PLANTING
12. Butterfly flower
13. Stonecrop 'Chocolate'
14. Yarrow
15. Tickseed
16. Mexican feather grass + Silver feather grass

RUBBLE PLANTING
17. White sage 'Valerie finnis'
18. Sea aster
19. Russian sage
20. Prairie dropseed
21. Lavender cotton + Green lavender cotton

SPONGY SOIL

HYDROPONICS
wood chips
peat soil
vermiculite
perlite
planting soil

PEAT
A peat soil
B peat soil, woodchips
C peat soil, perlite, vermiculite
D peat soil, lapinus fibers

flowsand
sand
planting soil

asphalt
sand
planting soil

sand
planting soil

BERM SAND
sandy soil
planting soil

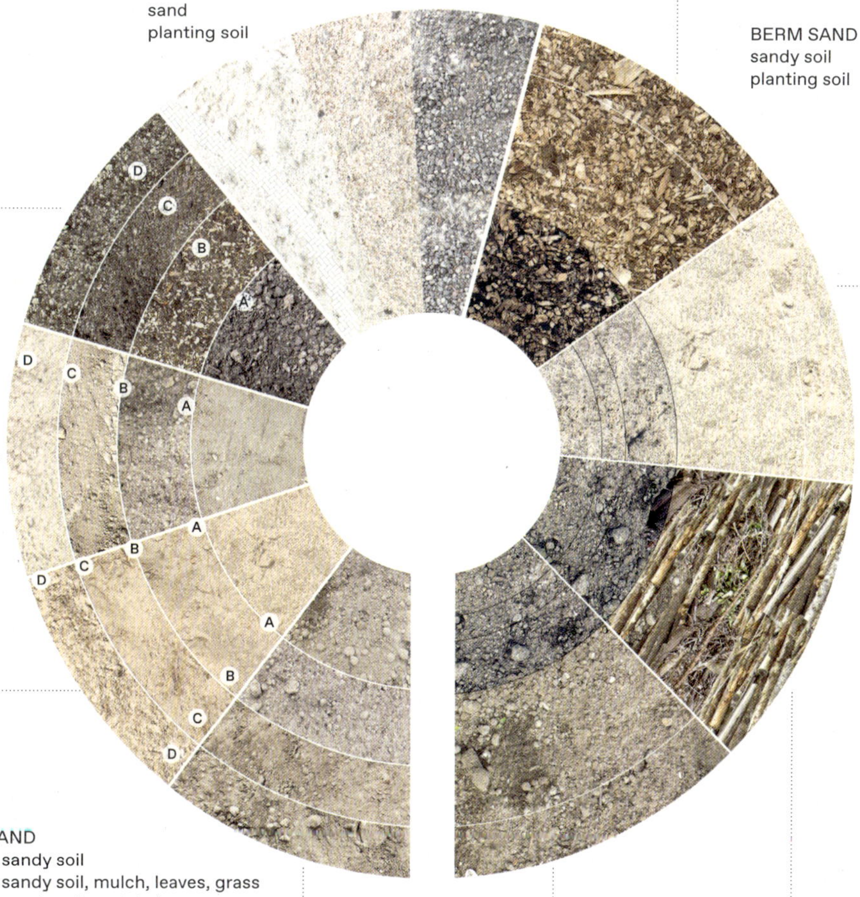

SAND
A sandy soil
B sandy soil, mulch, leaves, grass
C sandy soil, mulch, leaves, grass, vermiculite
D sandy soil, mulch, leaves, grass, super absorbent polymer

PLANTING SOIL

HÜGELKULTUR
logs
branches
compost
leaves
planting soil

RUBBLE
A rubble soil
B rubble soil, compost
C rubble soil, compost, vermiculite
D rubble soil, compost, super absorbent polymer

CLAY
A clay soil
B clay soil, compost
C clay soil, perlite, vermiculite
D clay soil, lapinus fibers

MONITORING

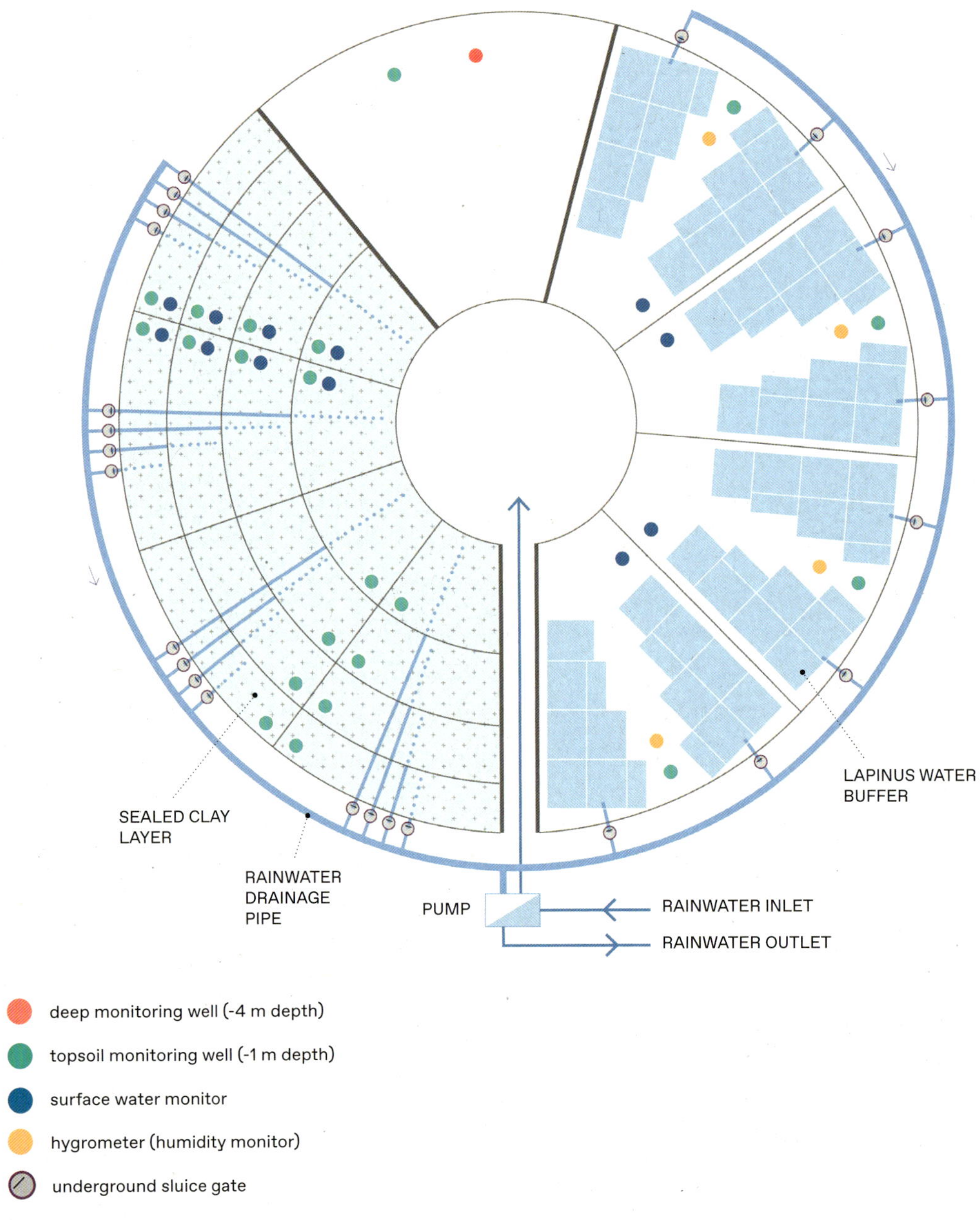

SEALED CLAY LAYER
RAINWATER DRAINAGE PIPE
PUMP
RAINWATER INLET
RAINWATER OUTLET
LAPINUS WATER BUFFER
deep monitoring well (-4 m depth)
topsoil monitoring well (-1 m depth)
surface water monitor
hygrometer (humidity monitor)
underground sluice gate

URBAN APPLICATIONS

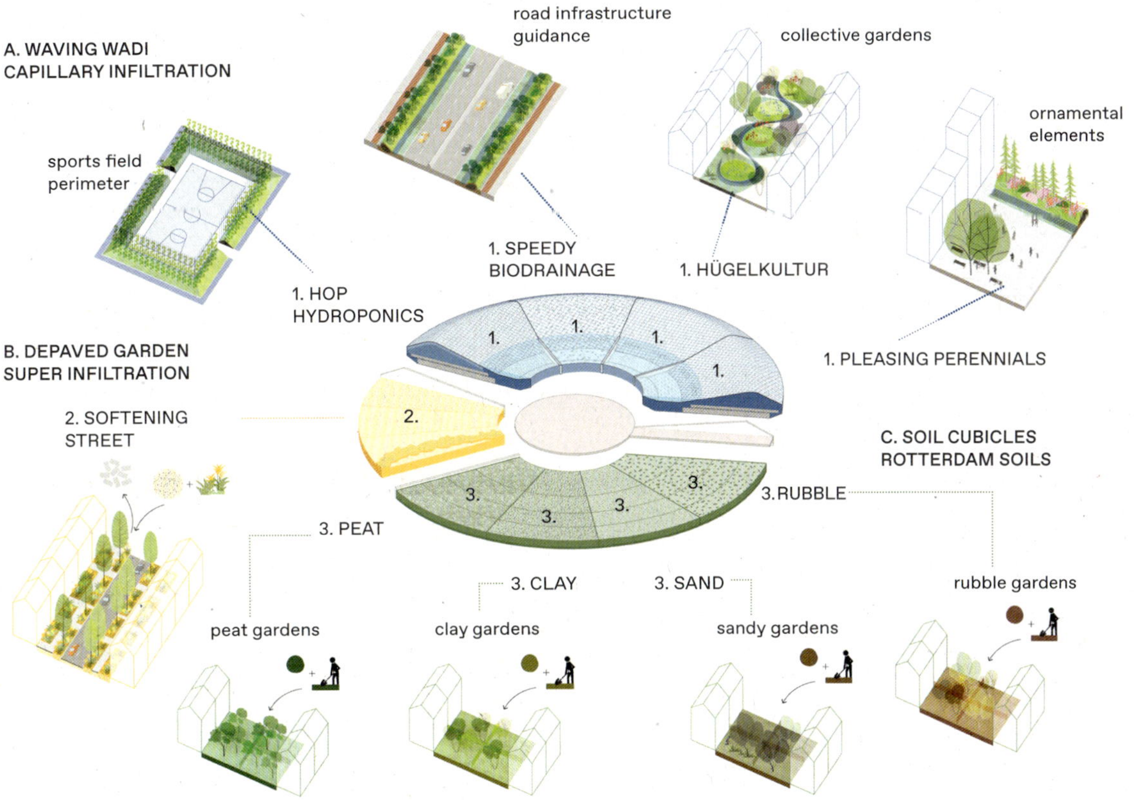

A. The Waving Wadi: Capillary Infiltration

A *wadi* (the name comes from the Arabic word for a stream that only fills after heavy rain) is a type of swale that stores water, retains it in its recess, and lets it slowly soak away. The Waving Wadi builds on this, testing how the water can be absorbed in the berm that makes up one of the wadi's sides. The water is drawn higher into the berm by capillary action, adding water storage capacity above the water line, behaving like a sponge.

The Waving Wadi goes no deeper than 80 cm below ground level, making it ideal for use in areas with high groundwater levels. The design of the Waving Wadi has four different variations, tailoring it for use in different environments.

B. Unpaved Garden: Super Infiltration

This setup is suitable for the reuse of paved roads whose subsoil consists mainly of sand, which was used as a base when the road was built. The asphalt is removed and a small amount of soil is mixed into the sandy foundation, making it a perfect home for drought-resistant plants. The setup has three zones with slightly different soil compositions: regular fine sand (standard application), a mix with crushed asphalt (to recycle the road surface), and extra-absorbent 'flow sand' (sand with basalt grit).

C. Soil Cubicles: Rotterdam Soils

This is an experiment in which various soil compositions are used, based on four different types of soil that are found in Rotterdam: peat, clay, sand, and a rubble mix. All four types come from the Rotterdam Soil Bank and represent the various conditions found in the city. As such we can investigate how to improve the water-absorbing performance of the city's subsurface.

Water struggles to permeate peat and clay, while it runs straight through sand and rubble without being absorbed. For each type of soil there are three compartments where the base material is mixed with a variety of additives. The planting in these compartments is tailored to the different soil types. The depth of the soil is only 50 cm, making this test location easily applicable in small-scale environments such as private gardens.

2. Panorama Waterland: The Search for an Eternal Source of Clean Drinking Water

Water company Vitens is faced with the challenge, now and in the future, of providing its 5.7 million customers in the (north)eastern part of the Netherlands with sufficient drinking water. Weather extremes, climate targets, the energy transition and the transition to circular agriculture are all upping the pressure on the current water system – which is reaching its limits. In 2020, the third extremely dry year in a row in the Netherlands, it had become altogether clear that new perspectives needed to be explored.

Panorama Waterland, in which Vitens collaborates with landscape architects and other partners, explored such a new perspective: a spatial concept that takes the retention of the available water as its starting point. The water system and soil determine the spatial design and land use: areas are approached as eternal, clean sources of water.

To test the principles of Panorama Waterland, the Sallandse Heuvelrug was used as an exemplary test case.
From now on, the precipitation that usually drained away from the area will be retained. The idea of a landscape *wadi* has been elaborated in combination with strengthening the capacity of the soil to absorb water. Recirculation of the water gives it added value in different places. Sufficient water will be available year round, for agriculture but also for the extraction of drinking water. Functions are integrated and combined in such a way that they benefit optimally from the water system and fit in with its conditions *and* are compatible with drinking water extraction. Instead of subjecting land users to strict rules, opportunities for cooperation are created.

But it is also clear that Panorama Waterland can only exist by the grace of fundamental changes in land use. The transition to circular agriculture, which doesn't leach harmful substances into the soil and groundwater, is crucial. Guaranteeing enough clean water at all times is important, because it gives farmers something to hold on to in the transformation to sustainable business operations. Only then can new environmental values, greater ecological significance, improved biodiversity, and the possibilities to meet social needs in terms of housing, health, sustainable energy generation, and recreation emerge.

INITIATED, RESEARCHED AND REALIZED BY
Vitens, H+N+S Landscape Architects, Ruimtevolk, and Roosemalen & Savekoul

A CONNECTING CONCEPT

Panorama Waterland is an integrated spatial development perspective for the high sandy areas. It is a response to the dramatic decline in biodiversity and increasing water demand in times of drought, and it places thinking about agriculture versus nature in a new perspective.

A new water system serves as the basis for land use in high sandy areas and creates unique conditions for a symbiotic relationship between all forms of land use.

The system provides a continuous water cycle that guarantees sufficient water. The collected water is for agriculture, drinking water, and nature. Clean (drinking) water is thus a lever for new economic processes, spatial planning, and innovation.

The Sallandse Heuvelrug as a hydrological 'island' is divided into several basins, which form the basis for further elaboration. The water production on the sandy ridge is maximized by gearing the water system entirely to infiltration and storage in the sandy subsoil, and no longer draining the water.

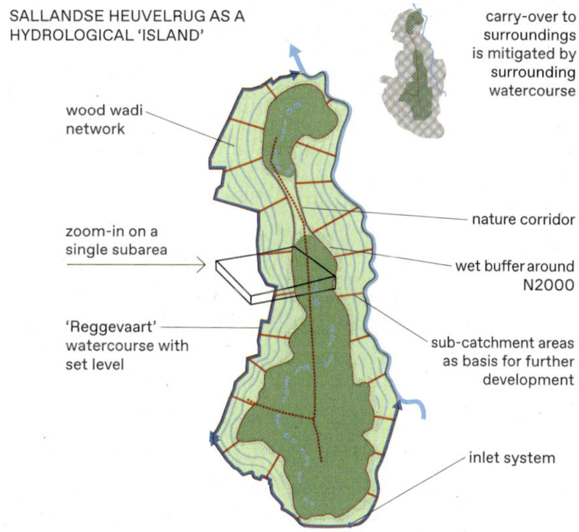

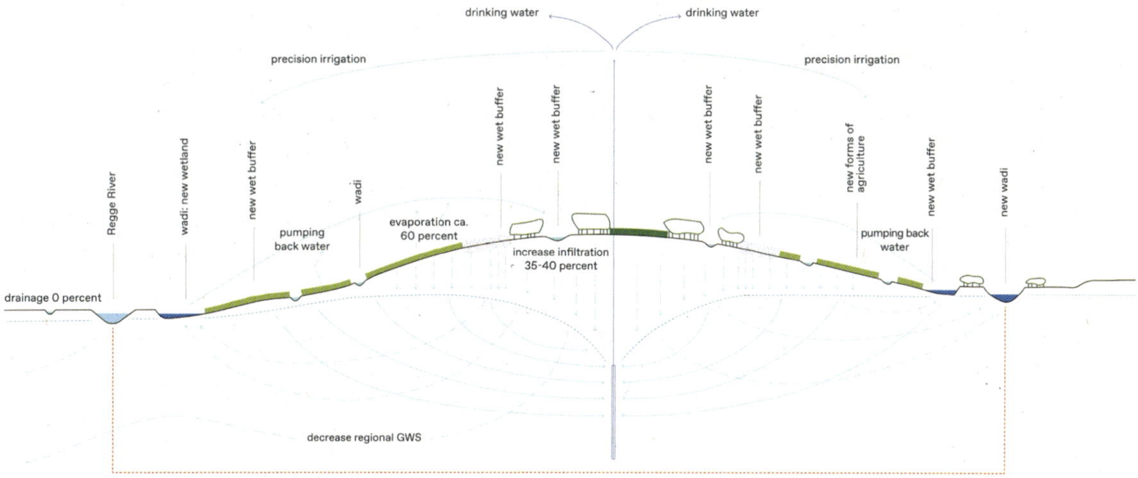

RUN-OFF TO ZERO

NOW: deep drainage in the agricultural area: aimed at draining excess water, while there are water shortages in the summer.

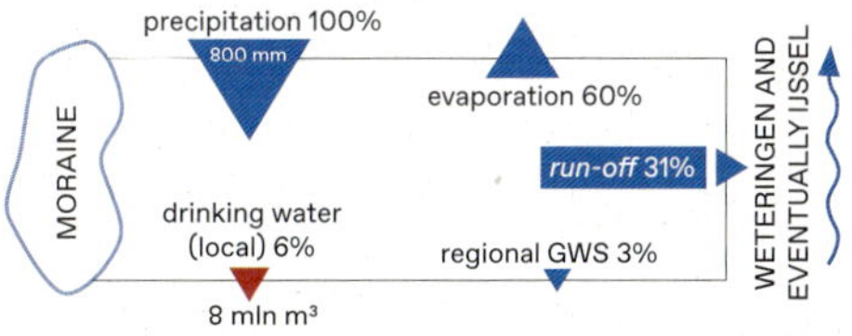

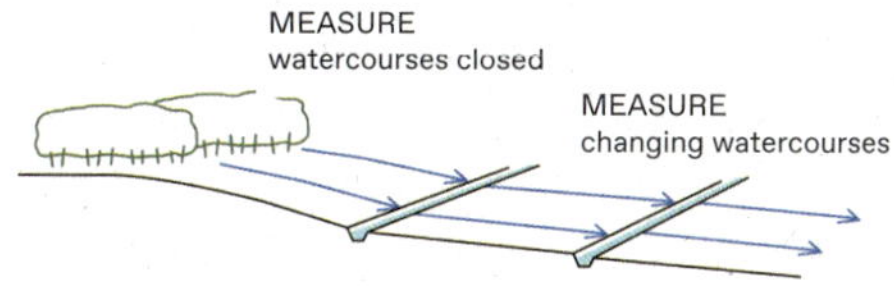

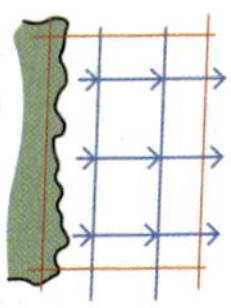

FUTURE (WOOD WADIS): maximum storage of the precipitation surplus in the sandy ridge, with reserves for dry periods. The wood wadis, the 'hedgerows of the twenty-first century', are part of the agricultural business model.

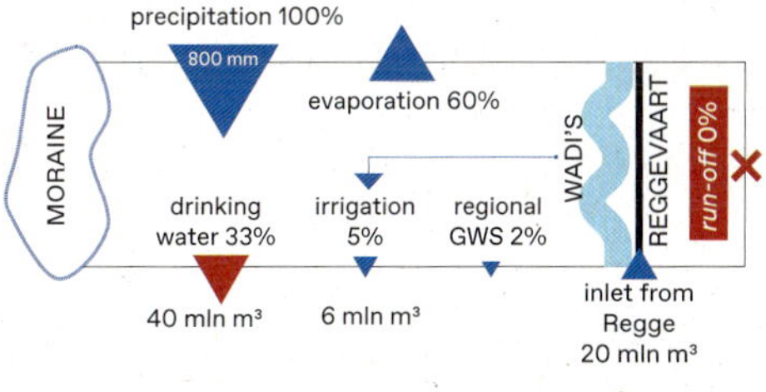

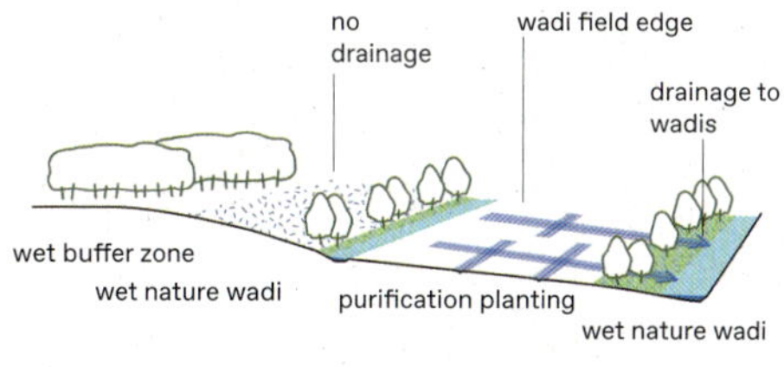

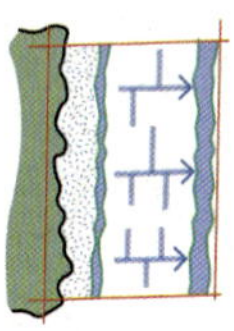

NEW WATER SYSTEM

Transforming the water system on the flanks of the ridge makes it possible to retain the run-off (the drainage of precipitation) in the area. Ditches will be filled in a buffer zone around the nature reserve. The ditches around agricultural plots are widened and new 'wood wadis' are introduced. These will collect the water so that it can infiltrate. In this way, up to five times as much (drinking) water becomes available, also for agriculture and nature, without the agricultural areas becoming too wet.
The new water system presents opportunities for enrichment with new wet environments. New networks connect dry and wet nature. This creates a robust nature full of gradients, and enhances habitat quality.

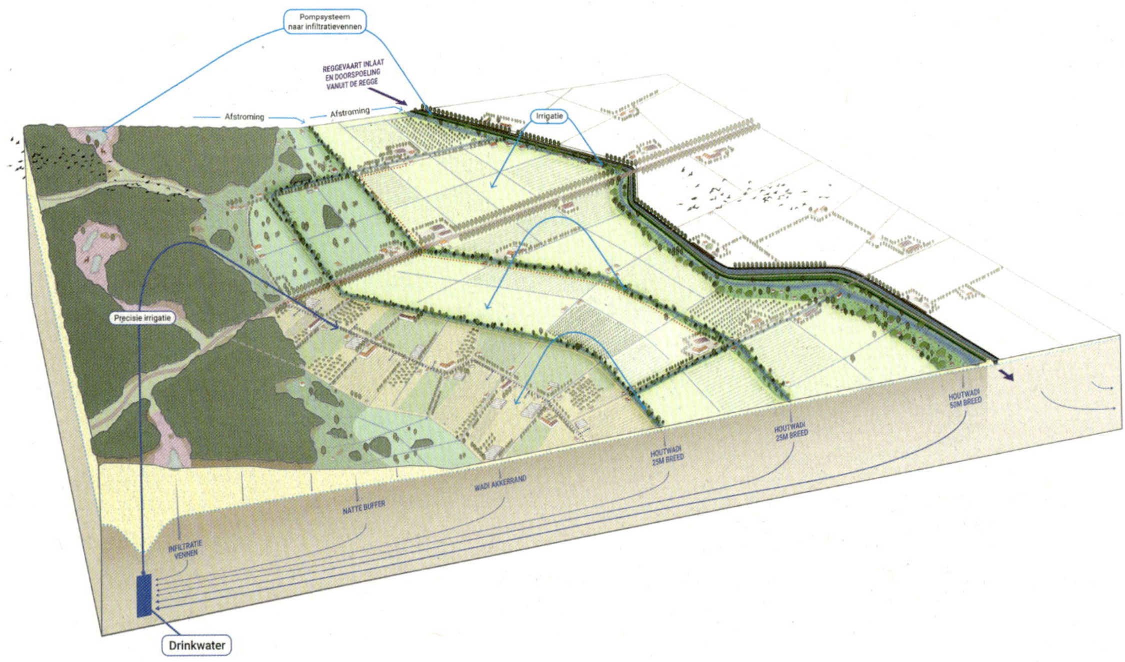

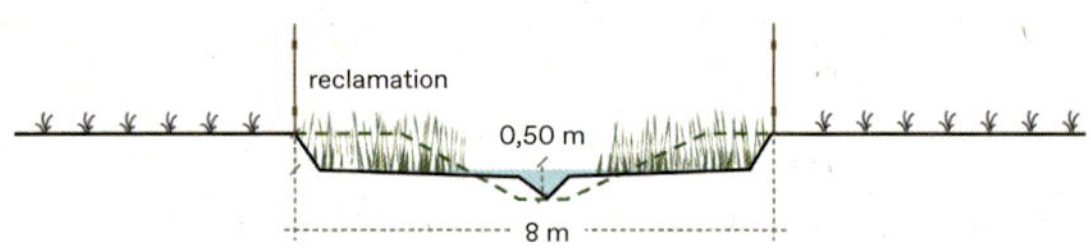

WADI FIELD EDGE

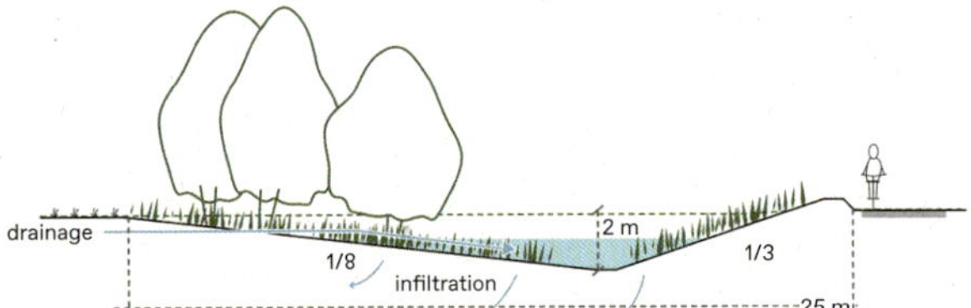

WOOD WADI 25 m

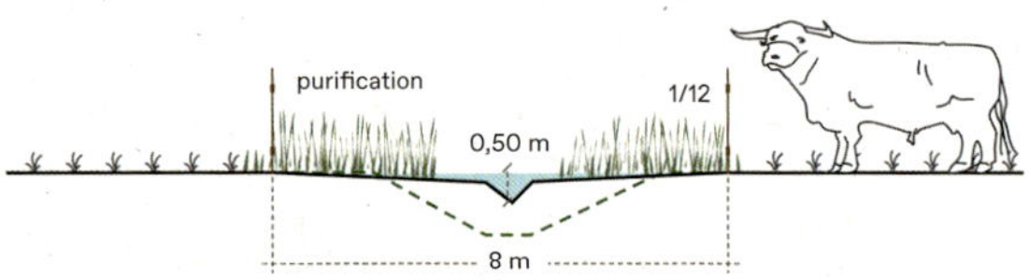

DRAINAGE-PURIFICATION SYSTEM (NATURAL BUFFER)

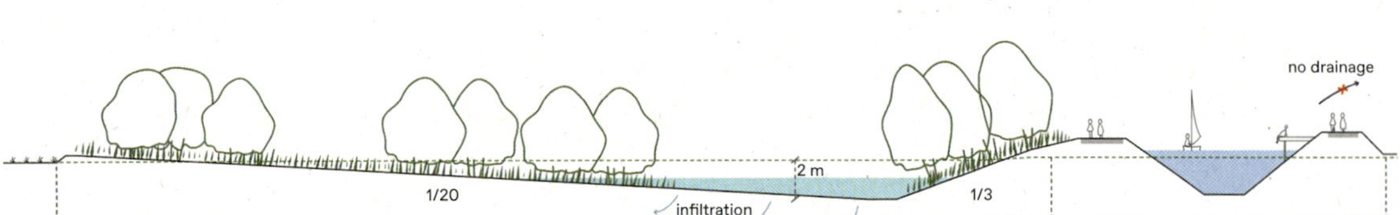

WOOD WADI 50 m

TRANSITION TO BUSINESS MANAGEMENT

The unique conditions in Panorama Waterland can act as a catalyst for the agricultural transition. Traditional agriculture in this new water landscape will have to transform into clean business operations, without fertilizers and pesticides leaching into the soil and groundwater. Various agricultural business practices are suitable: from nature-inclusive agriculture to high-yield precision agriculture in a closed system. Operational reliability through, among other things, clear regulations with a long-term perspective, a guarantee of sufficient and clean irrigation water, a soil restoration program, and cooperation within an 'area brand' make investments possible. In addition, Panorama Waterland offers farmers a bridging mechanism in this turnaround of business operations, by enriching their revenue model by harvesting sustainable energy, for example.

Clustered agricultural businesses dot the area, like islands. The farmyards are incorporated in a green way. Readable boundaries mark the area inside a 'delightful landscape' with opportunities for recreation, care, and residential environments. Attractive routes make the landscape accessible.

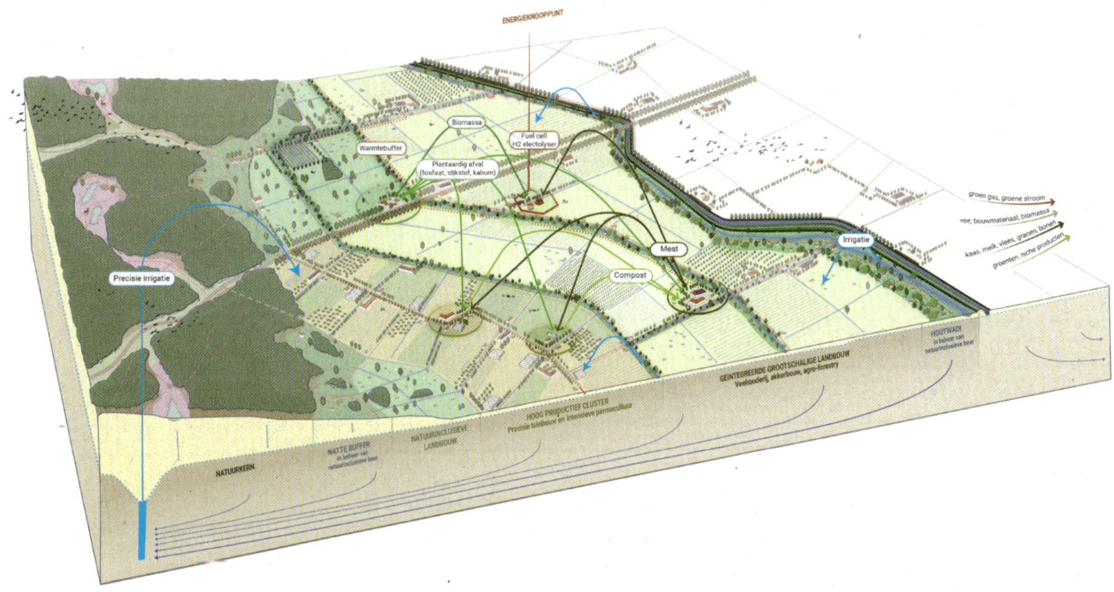

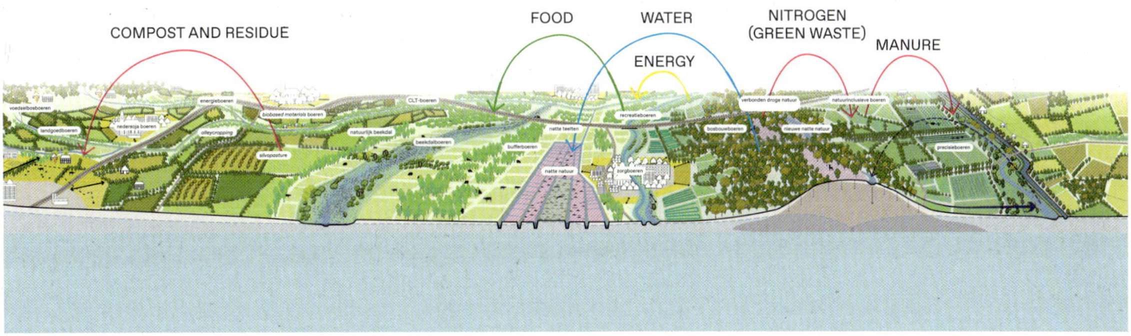

CLEAN AGRICULTURE AND ENERGY

THREE EXAMPLES OF CLEAN BUSINESS MODELS

HIGHLY PRODUCTIVE IN CLUSTERS
high production in closed system on small number of hectares: horticulture, intensive permaculture and food forests

products: vegetables and fruits, niche products; exchange crop residues with imported farmyard manure and compost from nearby farms

INTEGRATED LARGE-SCALE
mixed (combination) farms with maximum soil resilience: (dairy) cattle farming, agriculture and agroforestry

products: cheese, milk, meat, grains, beans (contribution to protein transition); farmyard manure for arable farming exchanged for crop residues from arable farming for livestock farming

NATURE-INCLUSIVE AND BROAD
extensive agriculture with various functions

products: livestock, biomass, building materials

secondary functions: care and recreation; landscape management of wadis; organic matter supplier for livestock, agriculture and horticulture

HIGHLY PRODUCTIVE IN CLUSTERS

WATER
reduce irrigation and evaporation with permanent cover

ENERGY
minimal use of energy

LANDSCAPE
strengthen green structure

ENERGY
solar panels on commercial buildings, local heat grid

WATER
drip irrigation with drone control

SOIL
crop rotation, import of compost

INTEGRATED LARGE-SCALE

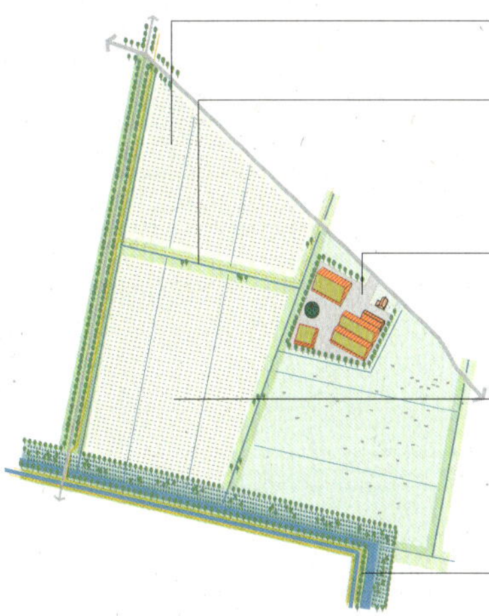

LANDSCAPE
new green structure and green-blue network

WATER
irrigation support
water retention by ditches
underground irrigation (reverse drainage)

ENERGY
fermentation of manure to green gas
heat grid
solar panels on roofs of stables

SOIL
crop rotation, rotational grazing, high-tech soil analysis, deep-rooting crops to improve soil structure, dry manure instead of fertilizer and slurry, organic matter storage (from permaculture, village or nature)

ENERGY
biomass (cane cultivation) in wadis
low consumption
temporary solar fields

NATURE-INCLUSIVE AND BROAD

SOIL
addressing nitrogen, intensive grazing (sheep and cows, rotational grazing), manure disposal (via deep litter houses), cultivation of certain plants and so-called 'catch crops' (e.g. alders, product for biomass or building material), testing ground for new nature development

WATER
minimum water demand

LANDSCHAP
wadis as a quality landscape and green-blue network

FROM IDEA TO A FRAMEWORK FOR ACTION

FINDING A BALANCE BETWEEN CONCEPT DEVELOPMENT AND AN OPEN REGIONAL PROCESS

The goodwill of landowners and users is essential for the realization of Panorama Waterland. That is why the concept is an open invitation to parties to commit themselves to it and to jointly realize it area-specifically. This will create a basis for new coalitions and unexpected cross-pollinations and allow the concept to be developed into applicable designs for each subarea. Next, planning measures can be used to select the desired implementation practice.

RESEARCH BY DESIGN FROM A NATIONAL/REGIONAL PERSPECTIVE

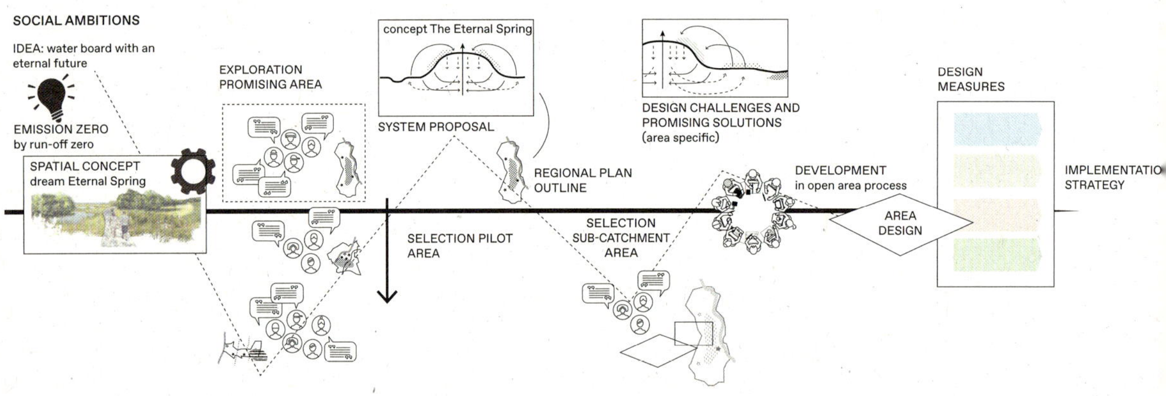

LOCAL KNOWLEDGE AND INTERESTS INPUT FROM STAKEHOLDERS AND FACTORS

URGENCY
extent to which parties feel problem ownership, leading to increasing the pace of (sub) projects

TRACTIVE POWER
extent to which a party is able to take on the leading role in (sub)projects

RESOURCES
extent to which parties can make financial resources, but also land, available

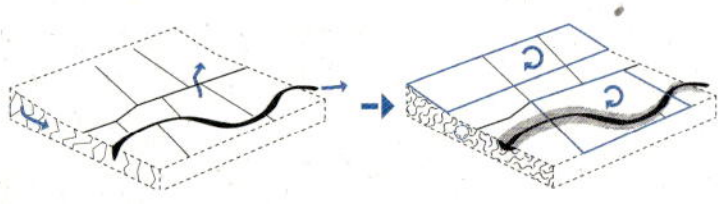

a robust soil and water system is a prerequisite for a future-proof food supply

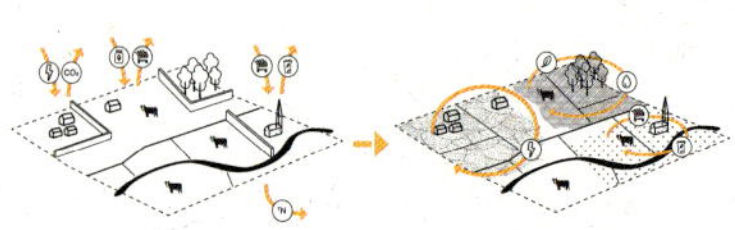

region- and site-specific cycles offer opportunities for sustainable land use

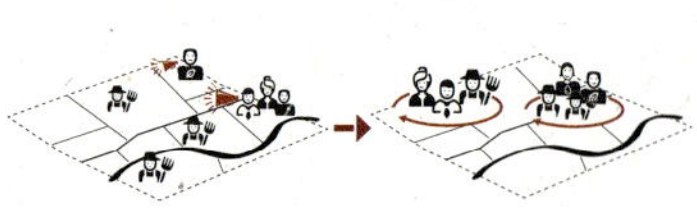

inclusive concepts connect people with various interests

PLANNING MEASURES

THREE POSSIBLE GOVERNANCE AND COLLABORATION MODELS WITH ACCOMPANYING INSTRUMENTS

Three governance models provide a framework for a strategic approach at the area level, each with its own financial and legal instruments, ranging from firm steering (active land policy and the deployment of planning frameworks) to facilitative and seductive (based on public-private and cooperative partnerships). The models can coexist: each subbasin can set up a suitable form of cooperation and determine the right mix of tools.
The possible palette of instruments grows incrementally: 'Waterlandgoed' has access to a limited number of tools, which steer quite firmly (planning). The 'Pact' adds a number of instruments to this. 'Waterport' has access to the entire range, including more enticing and facilitating instruments, which start from light public-private or cooperative partnerships.

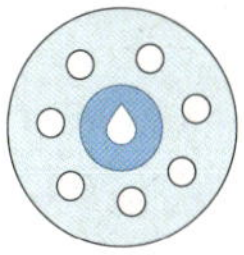

I. WATERLANDGOED OF THE TWENTY-FIRST CENTURY
the water company as steward: opportunities for indirect involvement and third-party management

II. THE CLEAN SOURCE PACT
water-oriented development: the clean source as a guiding principle for symbiotic area development

III. WATERPORT
water ecosystem: water as a catalyst for a sustainable innovation environment, with network steering and space for bottom-up projects

LEGEND

 ● water estate

 ■ the Pact

 ▲ Waterport

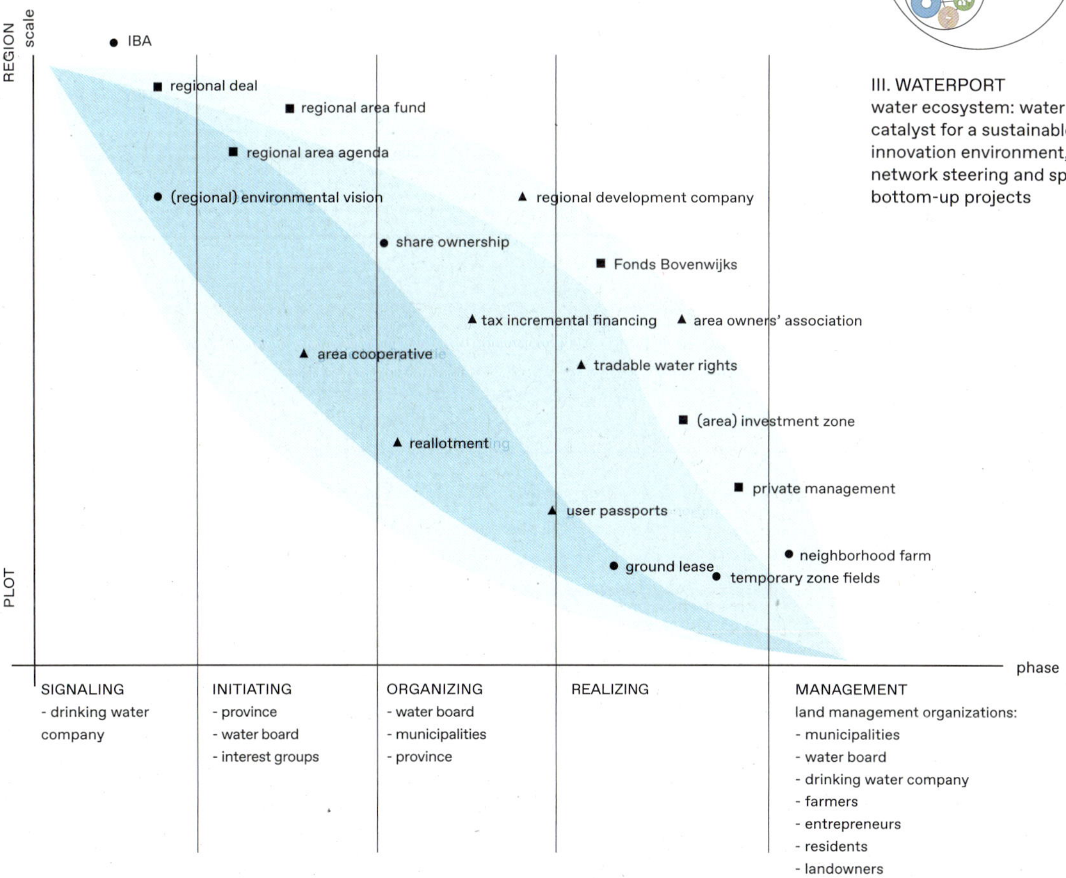

PANORAMA WATERLAND
PANORAMA WATERLAND

PANORAMA WATERLAND
PANORAMA WATERLAND
PANORAMA WATERLAND

3. Water Mosaic Groene Hart: The Condition of the Soil as a Yardstick for Water Management and a Prerequisite for Land Use

The Netherlands' *Groene Hart*, the Green Heart of the Randstad, is an icon. It's one place where the Dutch have taken control of the water over the centuries. Complex water management has led to a rich cultural landscape. The long and narrow plots, the striking palette of ditches and lakes, the open meadow landscape and the many quays, infrastructural works, and windmills form a unique cultural identity.

However, subsidence, salinization and dehydration caused by climate change are putting the Groene Hart under pressure. Increasing drought exacerbates soil subsidence and salinization, resulting in higher CO_2 emissions and lower crop yields. Seawater penetrates inland via the rivers, causing the freshwater intake points to become too saline to allow water to enter.

The Water Mosaic Groene Hart project states that, in order to cope with these problems, we have to say goodbye to the image of the Groene Hart as a homogeneous landscape where the current form of land use determines the management of water levels.

The design research shows the effects of a more future-proof water management that starts by determining the underlying soil conditions. For each soil type, the best water-level management to combat subsidence, CO_2-equivalent emissions, salinization and the consequences of drought was investigated, from which followed the appropriate form of land use. Not land use, but water-level management and soil conditions will be the guiding factors on the way to a new and sustainable perspective for the Groene Hart. The water-management instruments that make this transition possible are largely based on the existing cultural-historical landscape elements. Thus, the centuries-old tradition of 'Nederland Waterland' will be continued resulting in a prolific and distinctive Green Heart of the Randstad.

LEAD DESIGNERS
Paul Plambeck, Rens Wijnakker

RESEARCH BY DESIGN
Paul Plambeck, Nina de Munnik, Jie Yang, Joanna Krolak (Buro Sant en Co)
Rens Wijnakker, Marianne LaFontaine (FABRICations.)

INITIATED BY
Stuurgroep Groene Hart

COMMISSIONED BY
Provinciaal Adviseurs Ruimtelijke Kwaliteit of the provinces of South Holland, Utrecht and North Holland: Harm Veenenbos, Paul Roncken and Steven Slabbers

WE THANK THE FOLLOWING PEOPLE FOR THEIR CONTRIBUTIONS
Gilles Erkens and Huite Bootsma (Deltares), Erik Jansen (Veenweide Innovatiecentrum), Theo Vogelzang, Henri Prins and Bert Smit (Wageningen Economic Research), Edwin ter Hennepe (Waternet), Dolf Kern (Water Authority Rijnland), Charles Aangenendt (Ministry of Internal Affairs), Michiel van Dongen and Pim Kimenai (Province of Utrecht), Joke Schalk and Caroline Ammerlaan (Province of South Holland), Michiel Veldkamp (Province of North Holland), and Patricia Braaksma and Marlies Ferringa (Programmabureau Groene Hart)

←
DROUGHT IN THE DELTA
photo: Aad Hoogendoorn

THE GROENE HART

Long and narrow plots, a palette of ditches and lakes, an open meadow landscape and the many quays, infrastructural works and windmills have been typical of the rich cultural identity of the Groene Hart. Over time, however, the use of space has deteriorated into a carpet of turf for the benefit of dairy cattle.

LANDSCAPE OF PROBLEMS

The Groene Hart is under great pressure due to subsidence, salinization, and dehydration caused by climate change. Increasing drought intensifies soil subsidence and salinization, resulting in higher CO_2 emissions and lower crop yields. At the same time, salt water from the sea enters the area via the rivers and freshwater intake points become too saline to continue to allow water in. More and more measures have to be taken to maintain the existing land use.

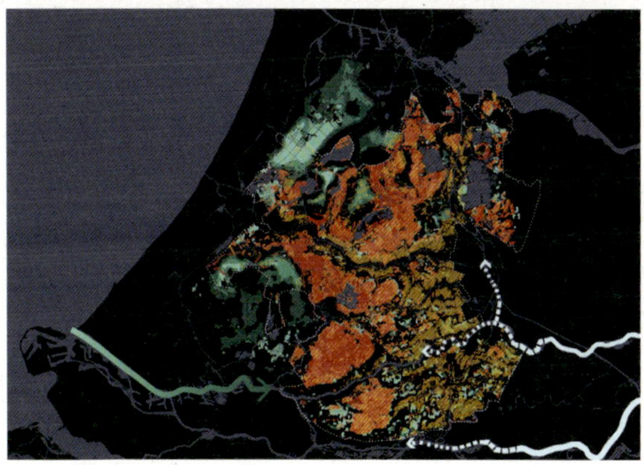

SUBSIDENCE
source: Subsidence 2016–2050, Climate Impact Atlas

- 3–10 cm
- 10–20 cm
- 20–40 cm
- 40–60 cm
- > 60 cm

SALINIZATION
source: Essink, G.H., Baaren, E.S., & Louw, P.G. (2010)

- salinization of 20% to 50% in 2050
- salinization of 50% to 100% in 2050
- salinization from 100% in 2050

DROUGT DAMAGE
source: Wageningen Environmental Research (2018)

- forecast > 20% yield loss due to drought in 2050

A RICH PALETTE OF SOIL TYPES

Where which problem occurs is strongly related to the soil conditions beneath the Groene Hart. In contrast to the land use and related water management, these conditions are very diverse. Taking the soil conditions as a starting point for possible land use paves the way to new approaches for dealing with drought and subsidence, transforming the Groene Hart from a monoculture to a rich spatial mosaic.

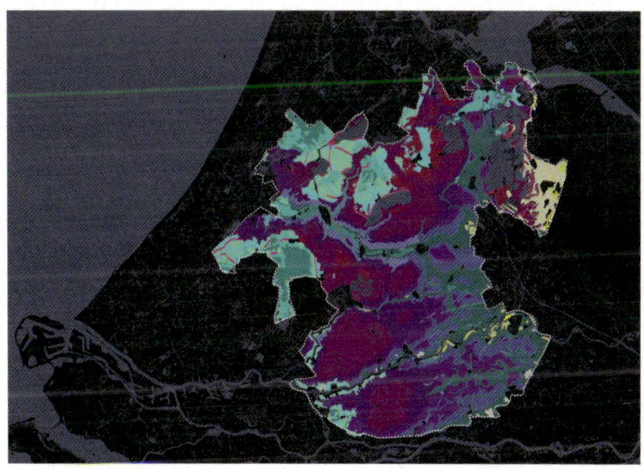

PEAT SOILS
- 'meer' peat
- 'aar' peat
- 'made' peat
- 'vlier' and 'vliet peat'
- 'koop' peat
- 'weide' peat
- 'waard' peat
- upstream land
- peat pits

PEATY SOILS
- on sand
- on light clay or clay

MARINE CLAY SOILS
- 'lied' earth
- non-calcareous drecht vague
- 'leek' 'woud' earth
- 'tocht' earth
- polder vague

RIVER CLAY SOILS
- 'lied' earth
- drecht vague
- 'leek-woud'
- earth
- 'ooi' vague
- heavy river clay

SANDY SOILS
- 'enk' earth
- non-calcareous
- calcareous
- podzol

OTHER SOILS
- silt deposits
- vegetable farmland

THE CONDITION OF THE SOIL AS A YARDSTICK FOR WATER MANAGEMENT AND A PREREQUISITE FOR LAND USE

POSSIBLE FORMS OF PRODUCTIVE LAND USE

Broadly speaking, there are three approaches for dealing with soil and land use. The three perspectives each offer an innovative and future-proof image for the Groene Hart, with a greater diversity of productive landscape and – not unimportant – a profitable future perspective for farmers.

Current Land Use

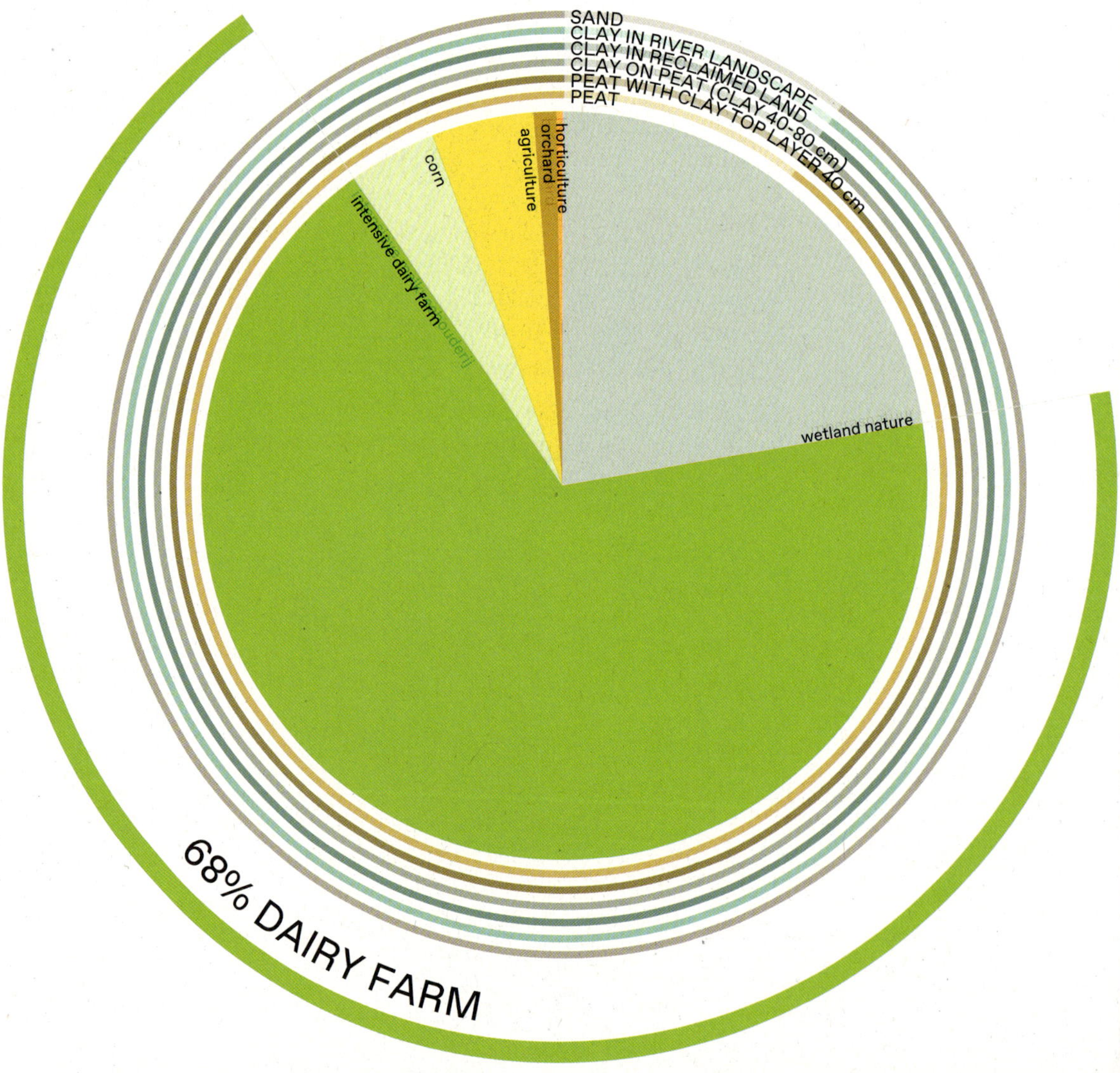

Scenario 1: Facilitate

Facilitate existing land use for as long as possible; areas will only change if the current land use cannot be sustained by technical means such as pressure drainage.

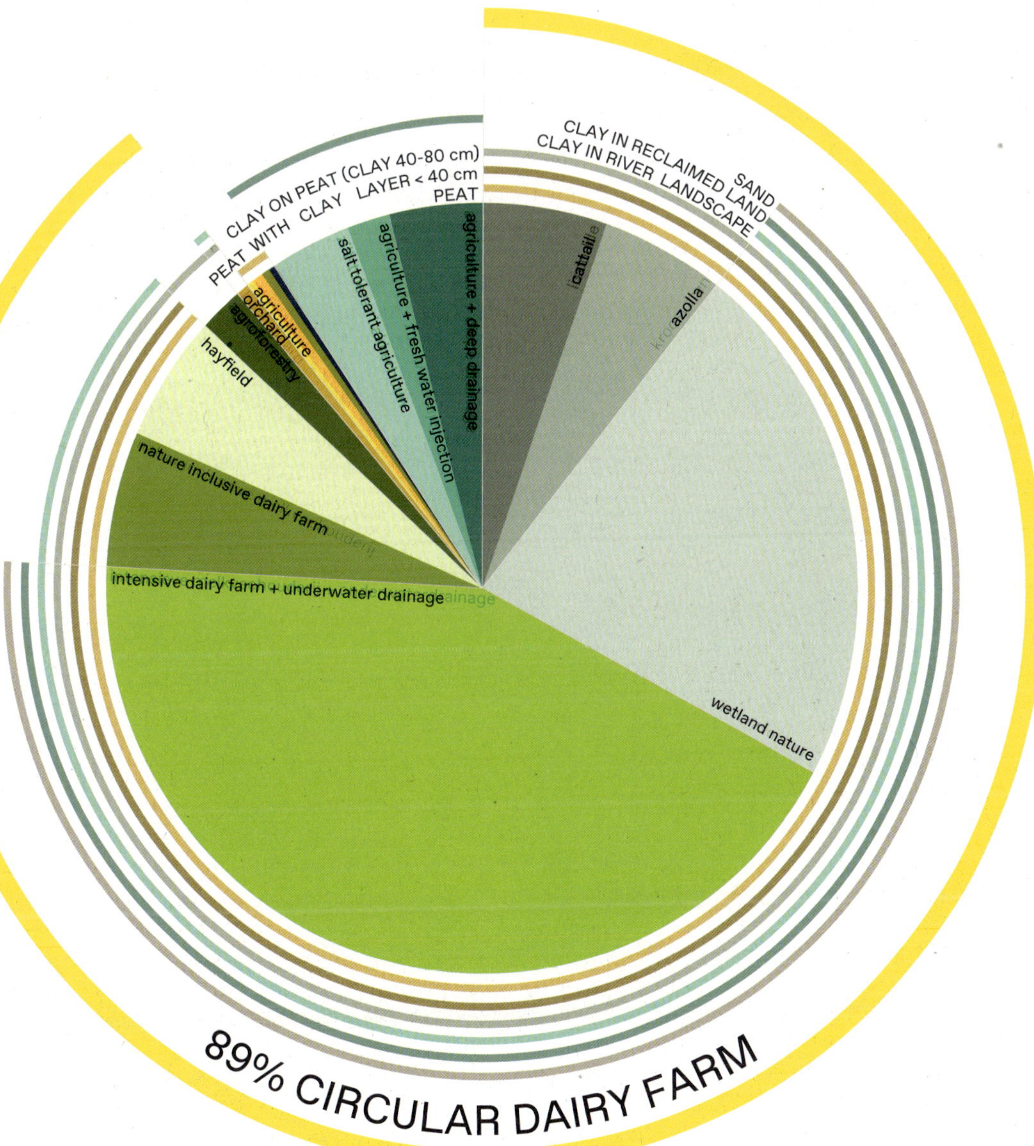

Scenario 2: Balance

Use the soil as a starting point in search of new productive landscapes; land use follows the state of the underlying soil, with wet crops in the wettest places, for example.

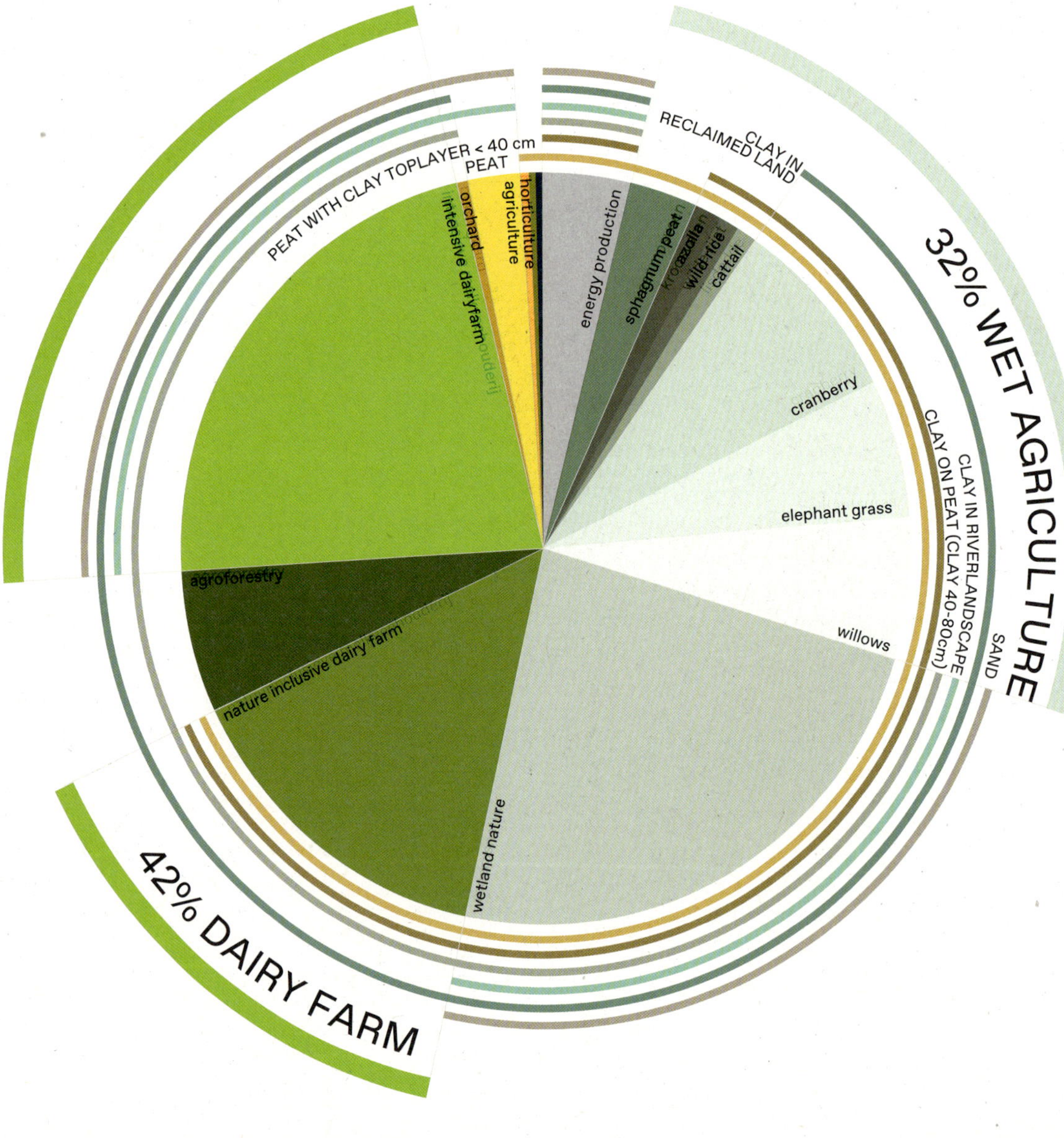

Scenario 3: CO_2-Positive

Transform to a landscape that does not breathe out CO_2, but records it. The focus is on biomass production and peatland growth, while outside the peatlands pastureland gives way to arable farming and fruit cultivation.

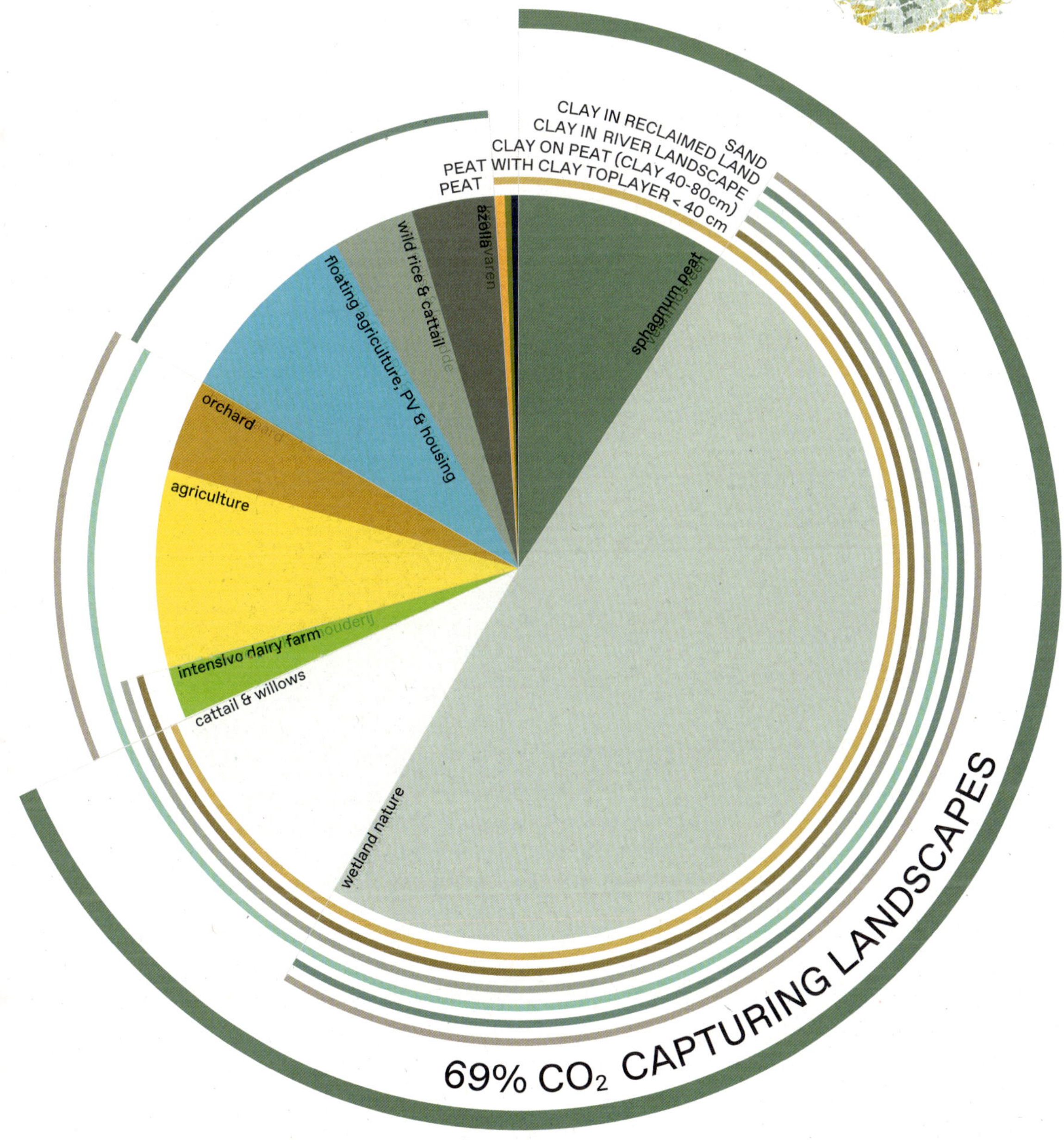

LANDSCAPE-FORMING WATER BUILDING BLOCKS

A series of new landscape-forming water building blocks are grafted onto the existing historical water system. By storing more water in the soil and on the surface, water surpluses can be used in times of drought. The water level management can be customized.

Transport of Water

1. AQUIFER EMBANKMENT

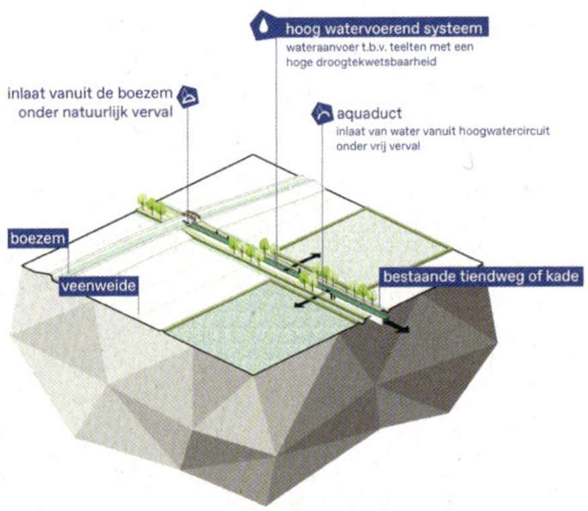

2. WATER PURIFYING SEPTIC DRAIN FIELDS

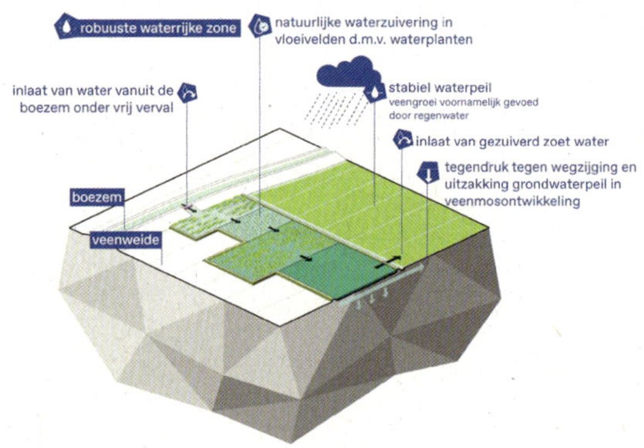

Protection of Buildings and Infrastructure with Water

3. ROBUST BACKWATERING

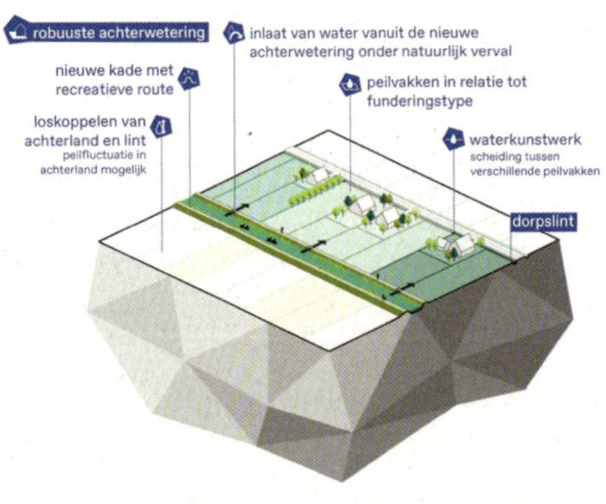

4. VILLAGE POLDER DRAINAGE POOL

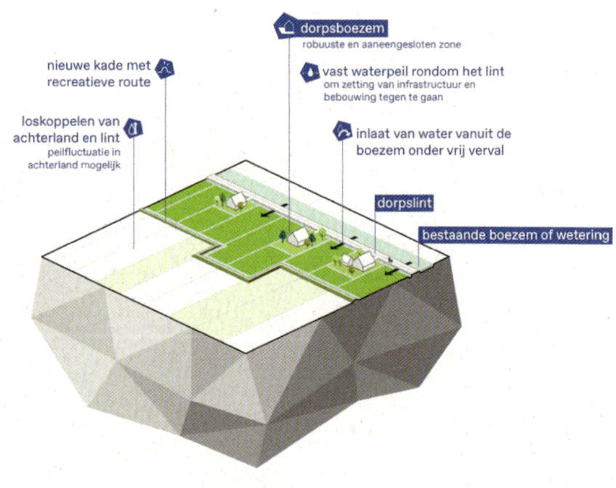

Storage of Water

5. STORAGE IN THE SOIL

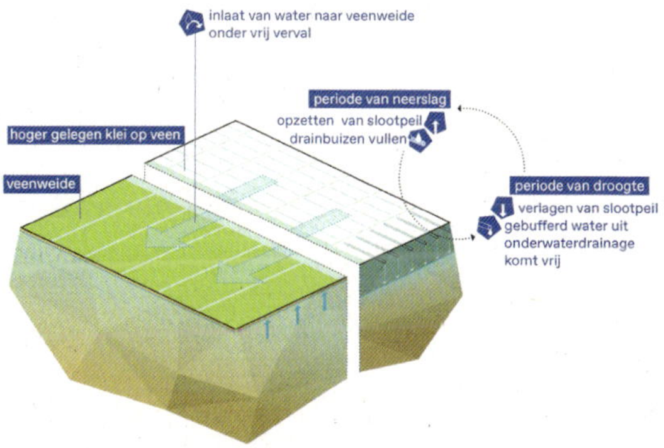

6. RESERVOIR ON GRADIENT FROM HIGH TO LOW: HIGH POLDER DRAINAGE POOL

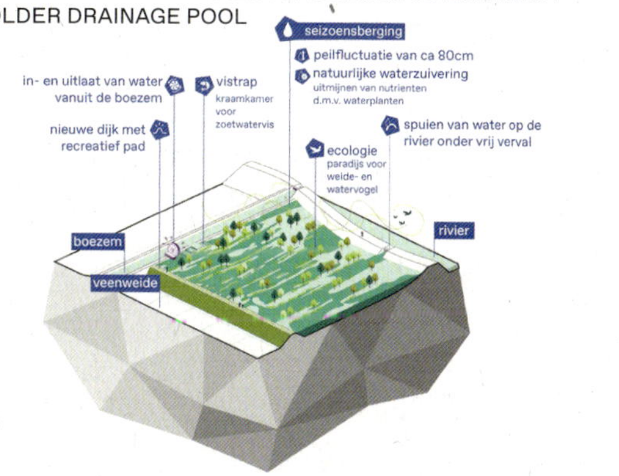

7. (NEW) SAND EXTRACTION POND

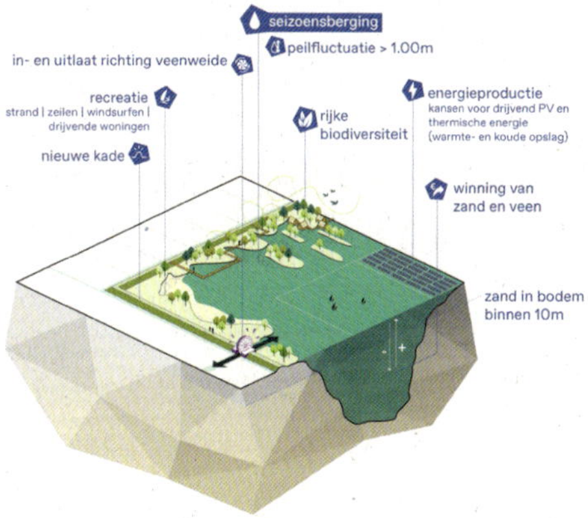

8. RESERVOIR ON GRADIENT FROM HIGH TO LOW: ON RECLAIMED LAND

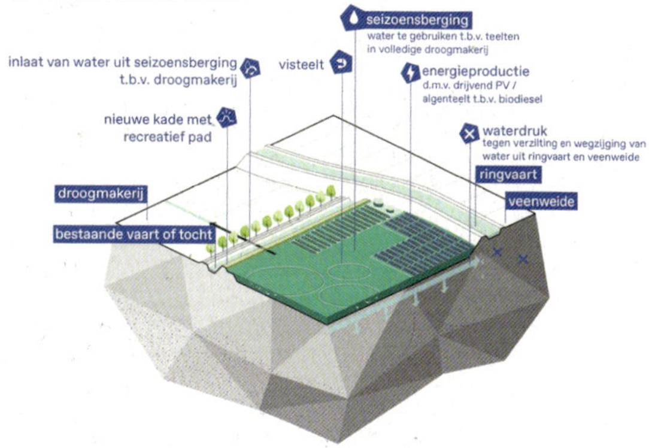

9. PEAK STORAGE OF THE POLDER DRAINAGE POOL

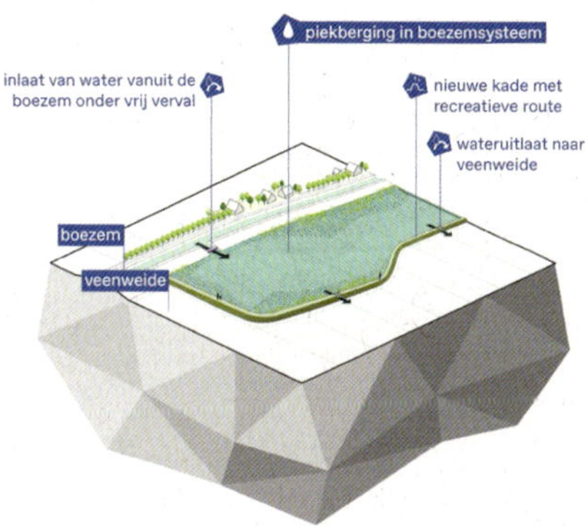

10. RESERVOIR ALONG TIENDWEG OR THE EMBANKMENT

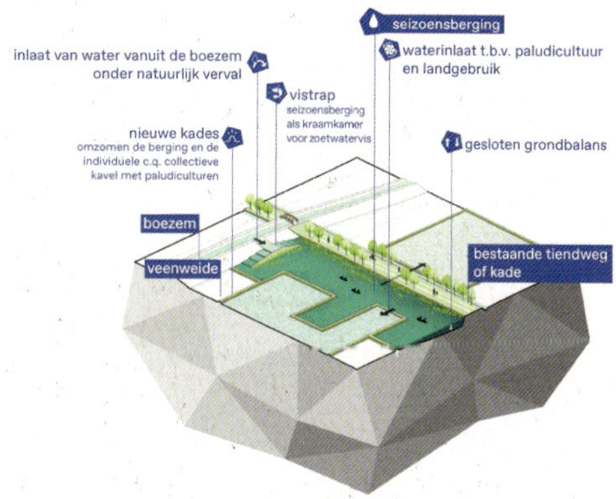

11. WIDEN AND ADD DITCHES

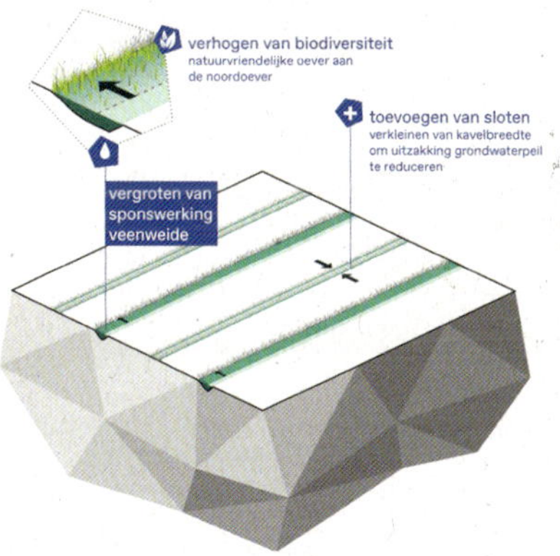

12. WIDEN CANALS AND/OR DITCHES ON RECLAIMED LAND

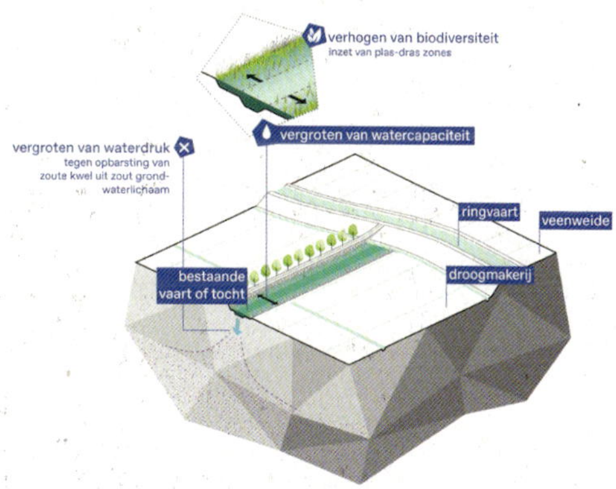

WATER MOSAIC GROENE HART
TRANSPORT VAN WATER
Energieopwekking en natte teelten
Energy generation and wet crops
THE NORTH FACE

Naar een gediffe
biodivers en CO2
landschap: Wate
Groene Hart
Towards a differe
biodiversified, ar
CO2-negative lar
Water Mosaic Gr

4. COASTAR: Smart Use of the Subsurface Leads to a Sustainable Freshwater Supply

Coastal areas are among the most densely populated areas in the world. And where there are people, there's a need for freshwater – to drink, but also for use in agriculture and horticulture. Inevitably, the freshwater supply in many coastal areas, including the Netherlands, is under pressure due to the high demand for water, but also because of salinization, subsidence, rising sea levels and longer dry periods.

In the mid-twentieth century, Dutch water companies started to replenish the freshwater reservoirs under the dunes with river water. Along our coast the groundwater is brackish in many places, making it unsuitable for direct use. It also rains regularly in this region and it's where the large rivers flow into the sea. Since that time, the subsurface has been expertly used to store and filter water.

More recently, however, the demand for freshwater has increased considerably. Opportunely, new techniques and insights offer prospects for new solutions. The COASTAR approach is one example: create a robust freshwater supply through the large-scale, organized and smart use of the subsurface for the storage and supply of freshwater. Research institutes are working together with private companies and government authorities to develop this approach. Tailor-made solutions are being devised for a variety of local issues. For example, brackish groundwater can be desalinated for use as drinking water. Extracting this groundwater in the dunes can contribute to increasing the freshwater reserves, and to reducing the risk of salt damage in agriculture in the polders. In cities or in greenhouse horticulture, the storage of rainwater in the subsurface can help lessen both flooding and the salinization of the groundwater. At the same time, pressure on other water sources can be alleviated.

COASTAR interventions have been explored in four locations in South Holland. Once elaborated, the next steps are pilot projects and eventually implementation. Thus, a valuable set of instruments is being developed that can be employed in other regions in the Netherlands as well as in coastal areas worldwide.

REALIZATION
Allied Waters, KWR, Deltares, Arcadis

PROJECT PARTNERS
Topsector Water en Maritiem, Dunea, Oasen, Evides, Mos Grondwatertechniek, municipalities of Rotterdam, Westland and Maassluis, Glastuinbouw Nederland, water authorities of Rijnland and Delfland, Province of South Holland, Deltaprogramma Zoetwater, Ministry of Infrastructure and Water Management

←
DROUGHT IN THE DELTA
photo: Aad Hoogendoorn

COASTAR TEST PROJECTS AND APPLICATIONS
Playing with Fresh and Saline Groundwater

For almost 70 years, Dutch water companies have been using the subsurface as a storage depot for freshwater by infiltrating river water into the coastal dunes. It is a game of managing fresh and saline groundwater that has increasingly been played behind the dunes over the past decade – at first as trials, but more and more concrete applications are now taking place. Horticulturists, for example, collect the rainwater that falls on the greenhouses and to create freshwater aquifers in the otherwise brackish subsoil, as a buffer for the dry summer. The rainwater that falls on and around Rotterdam's Sparta Stadium is stored and later used to water the football pitch. 'Not a drop of freshwater may leave the city unused' is Rotterdam's new credo.
COASTAR thus builds on decades of experience with fresh and saline groundwater management in the dunes and new, as yet small-scale applications in horticulture and the city, on the way to a robust freshwater supply for our saline delta through the large-scale, organized use of the subsurface.

LEGEND

WATER USE
- domestic use
- agricultural use
- industrial use

WATER SOURCE
- waste water
- rain and surface water surplus
- brackish groundwater
- groundwater on the island (including reclaimed islands)

CHALLENGES
- flooding
- saltwater intrusion
- drought
- overexploitation
- sea level rise
- land subsidence

A. Brackish Water Extraction from Coastal Dunes

The demand for drinking water is growing in The Hague. In addition, there is a need for larger freshwater reserves, to be able to bridge periods of poor river-water quality. By extracting the brackish groundwater beneath the fresh groundwater reserves in the dunes, the reserves are enlarged. In addition, the extracted water can be desalinated and used for drinking water.

CHARACTERISTICS
important source of drinking water; sandy ridge between sea and hinterland; fresh groundwater cavity in saline subsurface; robust existing system of river-water infiltration and fresh groundwater extraction

CHALLENGES
increasing drinking water demand and wish to enlarge water resources; sea level rise; river-water intake interruptions due to contamination

PROPOSED MEASURES
extraction of brackish groundwater (new source); enlarging the freshwater cavity: larger bridging period in case of calamities; protection of the hinterland from future salinization

STATUS
practical research with field experiment

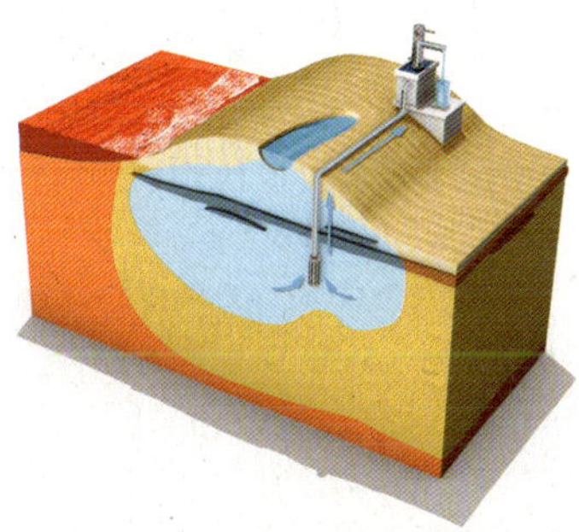

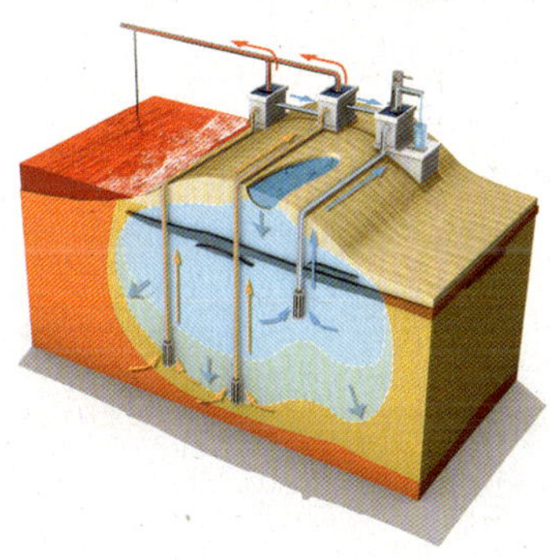

B. Brackish Water Extraction in (Deep) Polders

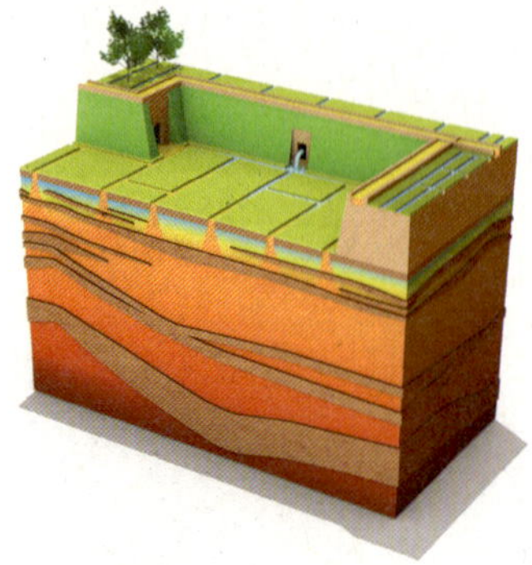

In polders that are below sea level, brackish groundwater flows towards the surface. This causes problems for farmers and lowers the quality of the surface water. By extracting this brackish seepage, desalinating it and using it as a source for drinking water, salinization on the surface is counteracted, while a high-quality source for drinking water is gained.

CHARACTERISTICS
polder below sea level; shallow brackish groundwater (incl. nutrients) reaches surface water; saline-sensitive agricultural crops

CHALLENGES
autonomous salinization; increasing salt damage to agricultural crops; increasing freshwater shortages in dry periods; increasing drinking water demand

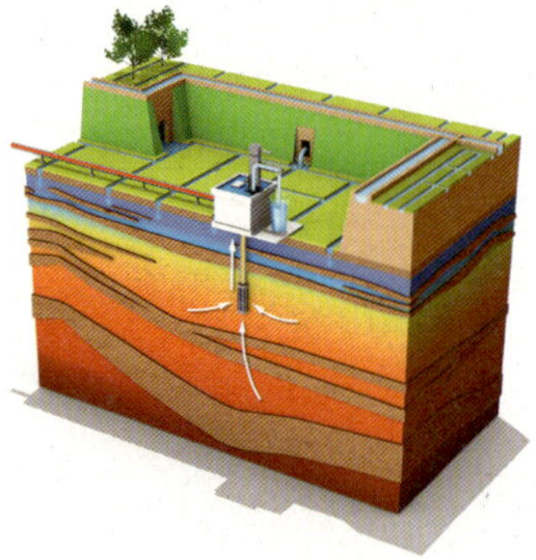

PROPOSED MEASURES
brackish groundwater as source for drinking water; reverse osmosis on brackish groundwater; decrease seepage, salt load and eutrophication; decrease salt damage to crops in the polder and its environment

STATUS
pilot preparation: various exploratory studies in North and South Holland
practical experiment: Horstermeerpolder

C. Westland: Dry Feet, Sufficient Irrigation Water

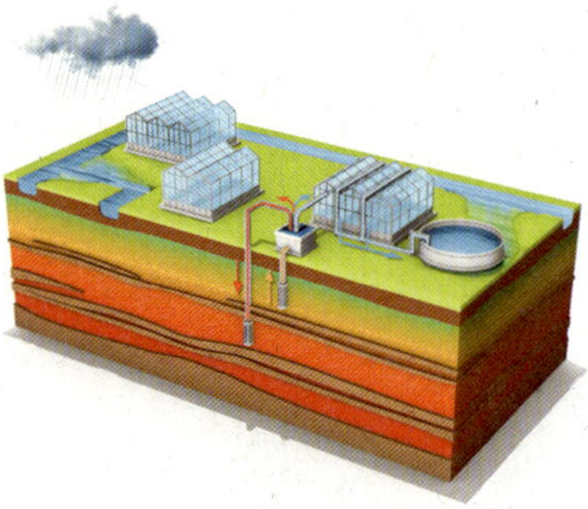

Horticulturists in the Westland use groundwater to irrigate their crops. But the groundwater reserves are under pressure. At the same time, excess rainwater is discharged into the sea in the winter, while heavy rains in the summer can cause flooding. By storing excess fresh rainwater in the subsurface, the horticulturists can compensate their groundwater use. They also clear out space in their rainwater basins to fully capture heavy rains, so that every drop of rain is used.

CHARACTERISTICS
4,000 ha greenhouse area Greenport, high-quality crops; brackish aquifer, desalinated groundwater used for irrigation; imbalance of rainwater availability and the demand for irrigation water

CHALLENGES
pluvial flooding; aquifer salinization due to extractions and deep polders inland, enforced by brackish water extractions including infiltration of membrane concentrate

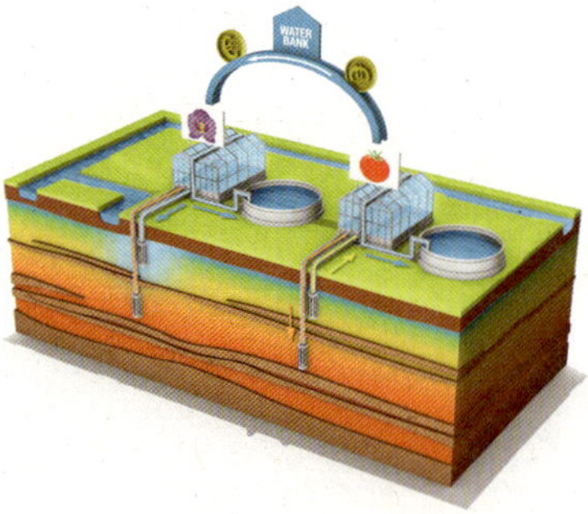

PROPOSED MEASURES
balance aquifer recharge and extraction by infiltrating precipitation surplus; aquifer management through water banking: (financially) promote infiltration, pay-per-use for groundwater extractions

STATUS
practical research with field experiment (start 2023)

D. Cities to Recharge

In a city like Rotterdam, with a lot of paved surface, heavy rain can easily lead to flooding. And quickly draining off the rainwater is a shame – that water is badly needed in parks and for sports fields, especially in the summer. By collecting the rainwater and storing it underground, pluvial flooding is prevented and the water remains available for reuse in the summer. It is crucial to prevent mixing of this precious freshwater with the ambient brackish groundwater during storage. Smart pumping and the shrewd use of existing knowledge of groundwater movement can do the trick.

CHARACTERISTICS
densely built-up urban area; local water demand; local flooding

CHALLENGES
climate adaptation in the city; drought; flooding

PROPOSED MEASURES
drain the water surplus in the city to deeper subsurface for groundwater replenishment and possible later use; an additional disposal option for water surpluses

STATUS
in progress: applications at Sparta Stadion and Het Nieuwe Instituut
design stage: Rotterdam Ahoy

COASTAR IN THE NETHERLANDS

All along the Dutch coast, the smart management of fresh and brackish groundwater can help improve the freshwater supply. Like in the deep polders in North Holland, where upward seepage of brackish groundwater causes water quality problems for surface water and for farmers. Storing water in the subsoil for later use can help industries in the Eems-Dollard Delta to become more circular. And brackish groundwater may well be a new source of drinking water for the young and growing cities in Flevoland. Everywhere, underground solutions contribute to a robust freshwater supply for agriculture, horticulture, drinking water and industry.

POTENTIAL AREAS FOR COASTAR
dune areas
shallow brackish groundwater (< 50 m below ground level)

COASTAR WORLDWIDE

Coastal areas are the most densely populated and economically vibrant regions of the world. But as in the Netherlands, freshwater reserves are under pressure while the demand for water is ever growing. Innovative thinking in the management of freshwater resources can help to sustain the water supply in a world facing climate change and sea level rise. COASTAR concepts are adaptable to local conditions and can be applied in coastal areas worldwide – from urban deltas to agricultural areas and small islands.

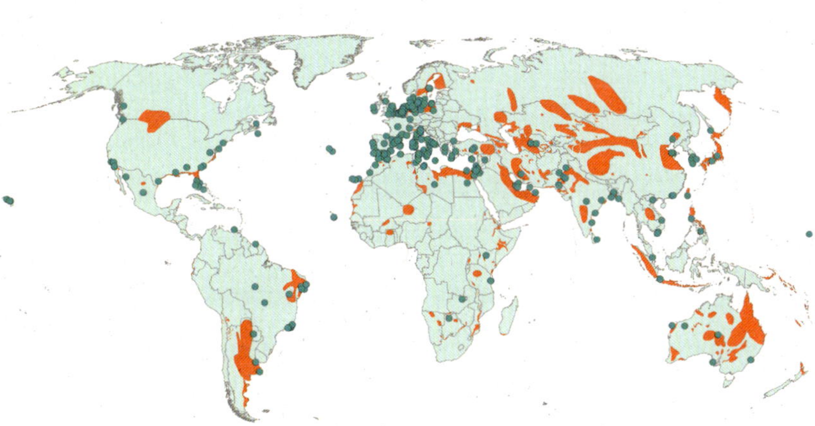

POTENTIAL AREAS FOR COASTAR
case studies saltwater problems
areas with saline groundwater

LEARNING DELTAS

Freshwater is crucial to just about every natural ecosystem on Earth. But while the world's population continues to grow, almost all our natural freshwater resources are diminishing at an alarming rate. The production of food, which is dependent on freshwater, cannot cope with the rising number of people. Not even in the world's deltas, the most fertile – but because of the climate crisis progressively vulnerable – areas where more than half a billion of the world's citizens live.

The large-scale irrigation of farmland is increasing the concentration of salt in the soils of these deltas. The further salinization of the coastal areas, which house almost half of the world's population, exacerbates this problem. Reservoirs everywhere are drying up, while aquifers are drained but inadequately replenished. One billion people have no access to safe drinking water. In the absence of proper water management, rationing and the battle for freshwater have already begun.

The good news is that the problems faced by the deltas, such as our own Rhine-Meuse-Scheldt Delta and the Mekong Delta, the Sundarban Delta and that of the Mississippi, are similar. The main differences are the magnitude of the problems and the extent to which integrated water management is in place. In many locations, the complex overview of the interrelationship of all of the transition challenges is lacking, causing opportunities to be missed. The potential offered by and consequently the conscious management of the subsurface is also usually a forgotten factor.

Lessons learned in the Dutch Delta, in the IABR–Atelier Drought in the Delta and other projects, can be applied to deltas all over the world. And it works the other way around as well: if we openly and constructively share our knowledge, the water challenge can be used worldwide as leverage to instigate the sustainable development of resilient deltas.

Sundarban Delta, Bangladesh
courtesy of ESA

CREDITS
DROUGHT IN THE DELTA

CURATOR
George Brugmans

COMPUTER ANIMATION
Studio Marco Vermeulen
Marco Vermeulen, Bram Willemse,
Joost van der Waal
Tungsten Studio
Martin Grootenboer, Sara Orfali

please note, the credits for the research by design by the IABR–Atelier Drought in the Delta can be found on page 165

GRAPHIC DESIGN
ARK
Roosje Klap, Loes Claessens, Nóra Békés

CURATOR ASSISTENT
Alexandra Sonnemans

TEXT AND NARRATIVE
George Brugmans

PRODUCTION AND PLANNING
Jolanda van Dinteren, Johanna Fuhler,
Eva Knollenburg

EVENTS
Lisa Lambert, Yonca Özbilge

COPY-EDITING AND TRANSLATIONS
InOtherWords translation & editing
D'Laine Camp, Gerda ten Cate, Maria van Tol

CONSTRUCTION, LIGHTNING, AND PRINTING
Bart Cuppens Tentoonstellingsbouw
Keilepand BV
Quintusbelichting
Rocka

←
DROUGHT IN THE DELTA
photo: Aad Hoogendoorn

DOWN TO EARTH

METEOPOLIS

partner exhibition curated by
Rotterdams Weerwoord

19 January – 28 February 2021
Keilezaal, Rotterdam

METEOPOLIS

Worldwide, Rotterdam is now among the vanguard in terms of implementation and innovation of climate adaptation measures, with the water squares, canals, and underground water storage to prove it. But the effects of climate change will become increasingly frequent and extreme in the coming decades. Trends identified by the Royal Dutch Meteorological Institute (KNMI) confirm a more than 80-cm sea level rise and a more than 30 percent increase in precipitation in winter versus a 23 percent decrease in precipitation in summer. The number of sunny days with temperatures above 25 degrees Celsius will grow from 12 to 30 days on average per year. Rotterdam – which includes the lowest inhabited area of the Netherlands at 6 m below sea level inside its city limits – not only consists of buildings, but also of polders, level areas, pumping stations, canals, open water, dikes, and rivers, and is surrounded by water on all sides. In the future, some of this infrastructure, the effectiveness of which we now take for granted, will no longer be adequate. It is conceivable that dikes will have to be raised; also the Maeslantkering, the storm surge barrier at Hoek van Holland, at the mouth of the Meuse that flows right through Rotterdam, may no longer meet safety requirements. At the same time, there is plenty of construction going on in the city, including outside the dikes. How can we reconcile these two trends? For the near future the city has an implementation agenda to address these challenges, but what will come next?

Fifteen years after the 2nd IABR, THE FLOOD, Rotterdam is ready for the next step. The increasingly obvious consequences of global warming make Rotterdam's water problems ever more urgent. Soil subsidence, water safety, extreme precipitation, heat, and drought are major and acute challenges.

At the invitation of the chief curator of DOWN TO EARTH, George Brugmans, Rotterdams Weerwoord therefore carried out a new future study. Its research by design as well as the ensuing METEOPOLIS exhibition focused on the year 2060 – not to put a realistic plan on the table, but to make an opening bid. The idea was that looking 40 years ahead was the best possible way to ensure that the discussion about what course to take and about the kind of city in which the citizens of Rotterdam want to live, work, and recreate in 2060 and beyond, would be conducted as openly as possible.

Dreaming is allowed, building castles in the sand isn't.
Sterker door/dan strijd, Walden Studio
METEOPOLIS
© Jan de Groen

Four Travel Guides for Rotterdam in 2060

To initiate the conversation, four design teams were asked to explore as many scenarios, with climate as a central starting point. After all, the city knows what to expect when it comes to climate change. The real questions and uncertainties concern the way to deal with it, that is, concern themes such as ownership, integrality, inclusiveness, and responsibility. Is climate adaptation only a public problem, or also a private problem? Do we opt for a grand gesture *with* or for pinpricks *in* the city? Will the city government enforce or encourage measures?
In the four scenarios, the designers had to elaborate on such questions and uncertainties from as many different angles: go with the flow collectively or individually; prevent collectively or individually. Each scenario had its own position on the axes separating collective and individual responsibility, and preventing or moving with the flow of the rising water. Basing their stories on the same climate assumptions on the one hand, but on one of four different perspectives on the other, the design teams produced, as it were, four different travel guides to Rotterdam in 2060.

In 'Nieuw Rotterdams Peil: Rotterdam zonder Dijken,' (Rotterdam without Dikes), Team Marieke Vromans and Buro Bergh conclude that we have to learn how to live with water again. We have to replace our fear of water with increased knowledge about its added value. Perhaps one single intervention, embracing and following the movement of water, can solve all climate effects and improve the quality of life in the city.

In 'Flatten the Curve,' Team De Zwarte Hond/Strootman Landschapsarchitecten rely on technology. Their central assumption is that humankind will succeed in decelerating the rise in water levels by doing everything possible to slow down global warming from this moment on. In that case, Rotterdam can still protect itself with dikes in 2060, and life in the city will not be radically different than in 2020. Crucial to this process is the role of the port, because this is where the difference has to be made when accelerating the transition away from fossil energy to sustainable alternatives.

In 'Sterker door/dan strijd,' (Stronger through/than Struggle), Team Walden Studio follows the rhythm of a flooded city that has stopped trying to keep the effects of climate change at bay. The water has come to stay, the underground has become brackish, and violent storms and peaking temperatures are the rule. It's a grim view of a future in which increased social inequality is very likely. Still, Team Walden Studio designed an alternative scenario in which the city is livable for everyone, despite drastic changes due to ecological disasters and the elimination of central government. It has become an urban community that is even fairer, more sustainable, and better functioning than the current one.

Finally, Team Verveeld & Verward wondered whether it was possible to enrich the belief in a sustainable and equal world with such substance and strength that it would spark a broad movement. The team therefore conceived a new 'religion': Het Nieuwe Fundament (HNF). In physical terms, HNF prescribes that city dwellers become co-owners of the land – 'hallowed ground,' safely behind the expected new waterfront to begin with. In spiritual terms, HNF provides guidance in the form of four ground rules, one of them a rock-solid trust in science.

Nieuw Rotterdams Peil/
Rotterdam without Dikes,
Studio Marieke Vromans and
Buro Bergh
METEOPOLIS
© George Brugmans

No Castles in the Sand

Climate change is an extremely complex problem, a so-called *hyperobject*: a conceptual event so large and complicated in scope and/or time that our human brain can never fully comprehend it. This requires an equally complex approach to the design process. In METEOPOLIS, designers had to consider many issues, from ownership to climate inequality, and mold their answers into futures: they were not to build castles in the sand, but to design a future city, constructed on the solid ground of present-day Rotterdam while facing the challenge of the climate crisis.

METEOPOLIS wanted to create space for the citizens of Rotterdam to collectively ask themselves: What will come next? Unfortunately, Rotterdammers were never able to visit the exhibition. Built during the winter of 2020–2021, at the height of the Covid-19 pandemic, it remained closed to the public due to the government's extremely strict lockdown measures at the time. It was therefore completely digitized, so that anyone who wanted to visit could at least take a virtual tour of the exhibition.

CREDITS

CONCEPT AND EXECUTION
Rotterdams Weerwoord
Emiel Arends, John Jacobs, Esther Barfoot, Marjolijn van Eijsden, Mariéne Vermeij, Rosemarie van Ham, Hanneke van der Heijden, Nora Prins, André Rodenburg

DESIGN OFFICES
Nieuw Rotterdams Peil/Rotterdam zonder dijken
Studio Marieke Vromans (Marieke Vromans), Buro Bergh (Floor van den Bergh), Ruut van der Beele, Anton Dautzenberg

Flatten the Curve
De Zwarte Hond (Daan Zandbelt, Thijs de Boer, Mike van Staten, Rosa Stapel, Richter Dallinga), Strootman Landschapsarchitecten (Joran Lammers, Marco Overdevest)

Sterker door/dan strijd
Walden Studio (Laurens van der Wal, Sebastiaan van Kints, Lena van der Wal, Bob de Boer, Marcella Wong, Willemijn Sneep, Govart van der Heijden)

Het Nieuwe Fundament
Verveeld & Verward (Jonas Martens-Baars, Dorine Martens-Baars, Riek Bakker, Maarten Bel, Laetitia Bosma, Daniëlle Huisman, Aletta Martens, Aniek de Rooij, Laura van der Steen, Renee Trijselaar, Paula Zwitser)

EXHIBITION DESIGN
Avenue & Plume

GRAPHIC DESIGN
Things to Make and Do
Lemmy Hoogendoorn, Lian Aelmans, Rogier Rosema Stella de Windt

CONSTRUCTION AND LIGHTNING
Vink standbouw, Bart Cuppens Tentoonstellingsbouw, De Creatieve Fabriek, AP Solutions, Quintus Belichting

PRODUCTION AND MARKETING
Andrea van Bussel, Elise de Fooij, Simone Rentmeester

WE THANK THE FOLLOWING PEOPLE FOR THEIR CRITICAL REFLECTION AND/OR THEIR CONTRIBUTION
Henk Oosterling, Nora Prins, Renée Rooijmans, Ruth Höppner

Rotterdams WeerWoord was initiated by the City of Rotterdam, Hoogheemraadschap van Schieland en de Krimpenerwaard, Waterschap Hollandse Delta, Hoogheemraadschap van Delfland, and Evides Waterbedrijf

DOWN TO EARTH

WATERSCHOOL M4H+

CURATORS
Rianne Makkink and Jurgen Bey

9 June – 30 July 2021
Studio Makkink & Bey, Rotterdam

A WATER-SCHOOL FOR IABR–TEST SITE M4H+

The Port of Rotterdam, a global player, has a symbiotic relationship with the city. Like Siamese twins, they are inseparable and unconditional parts of the Metropolitan Region's urban metabolism. While this relationship had become somewhat more fragile as the port was automated and relocated towards the North Sea, recently the areas in which the city and port meet, the so-called 'city harbors', have been receiving more and more attention. These now have room for new live-work areas, in which the inevitable transition in the fields of energy, water, and raw material use can be linked to the broader socioeconomic development of both residents and their urban industriousness. In these city harbors, concepts like the circular port and the circular economy are now tested in practice.

From Fruit Transition Hub to New Live-Work Typologies

One of the city harbors in which port and urban development come together is in the Merwe-Vierhavens area (M4H). Once home to one of the largest fruit transition hubs in the world, the area is now transforming incrementally into a new live-work area for – eventually – 6,300 makers/residents. M4H is in a strategic location, adjoining a number of vulnerable residential districts like Oud-Mathenesse and Bospolder-Tussendijken, in the middle of an economically active harbor area and yet close to the city center. It's also directly opposite knowledge campus RDM Rotterdam located across the Meuse River. Together, RDM and M4H form the Rotterdam Makers District, which is to become the Metropolitan Region's innovative manufacturing industry hub. The old industrial buildings, the space that M4H offers and the new dynamics that have quickly emerged here offer many opportunities for new live-work typologies, innovative maker spaces, test facilities, and knowledge platforms. By linking these to the surrounding districts, the opportunity presents itself to create new employment opportunities and to familiarize the 'workforce of the twenty-first century' with new knowledge and skills.

An Interactive Learning Environment

Following IABR–Atelier Rotterdam's 2015 and 2016 research into the possibilities of bringing the small manufacturing industry back to the city, [32] the IABR set up the IABR–Test Site M4H+ in collaboration with Programmabureau M4H. The Programmabureau, a joint initiative of the City and the Port of Rotterdam Authority, already knew that the makers, companies, and knowledge institutions that were settling in the area actually saw M4H as a learning environment: as a promising testing ground for the new economy. The challenge was to find a way to turn M4H into a truly interactive learning environment, in which the development, preservation, and dissemination of existing and new knowledge and skills could be concretely used for a purposeful area development with new live-work environments, and also to actively involve all parties in such a process, to include everyone's knowledge and to take steps jointly. And – after all, that's what the plus in M4H+ stands for – to involve adjacent vulnerable neighborhoods to this learning environment – districts like Bospolder-Tussendijken, in which the IABR–Atelier has been exploring how to link the energy transition to a broader transition agenda since 2018.

Model of Test Site M4H+ Work session during IABR–2018–THE MISSING LINK
photo: Hans Tak

[32] See publication IABR–Atelier Rotterdam, *The Productive City*

What Will It Take?

In 2018, at the test site, the IABR–Atelier started by conducting research by design into exactly what circular area development for the city harbor was or could mean, and what conditions and coalitions were needed to get such a process started. [33] This resulted in, among other things, guiding principles for a sustainable transition, which were subsequently integrated into the Spatial Framework for M4H approved by the City and the Port Authority of Rotterdam in 2019, serving as a guiding framework for the further development of the area. These principles promoted the values for policy in and development of M4H that were shared by all parties, and steered toward a progressively more circular, inclusive, and sustainable future.

[33] *Wat heb je nodig?*

Also see page 27

In 2018, the IABR also partnered with Studio Makkink & Bey, located on the western edge of M4H. The IABR supported the Studio's Waterschool initiative, an exploration of M4H as a learning production landscape developed on the basis of the water challenge. The initial results became part of the program of the biennale of 2018, THE MISSING LINK, in the form of a small exhibition, WATERSCHOOL 1.0.

Suiting the Action to the Word

By then it was clear to the IABR that the transition challenge at hand in M4H could benefit greatly from an approach that it had been applying since the very first IABR–Ateliers: continuing to test and adjust in a location where the work was already in full swing. [34] A multi-year research process of *learning-by-doing* area development also dovetailed perfectly with the IABR's ambition to contribute locally, in Rotterdam, by working on major challenges. In this testing ground for the circular economy, it could perfectly combine its objectives and its functions as an international platform and research and development institution.

[34] See also page 26-27

This is why in early 2020, the IABR settled in the Keilepand, centrally located in Test Site M4H+. It ensured that the Keilezaal, which was an excellent location for the biennale in the future anyway, would be funded and ready for use in time for DOWN TO EARTH. It was a process that got off to a bumpy start because of the Covid-19 pandemic, but by walking the talk the IABR managed to take its collaboration with Programmabureau M4H, the Keile collective, Studio Makkink & Bey, and other partners in the area to the next stage. This way, the IABR articulated its ambition to play a permanent part in the adaptive, partly culturally driven process of making a more sustainable M4H+ – the city harbor in conjunction with surrounding neighborhoods such as Bospolder-Tussendijken.

The Waterschool

Chief curator George Brugmans asked Rianne Makkink and Jurgen Bey to join the curator team of DOWN TO EARTH to further develop their Waterschool initiative in the context of both Test Site M4H+ and DOWN TO EARTH. With their Waterschool, Studio Makkink & Bey aims to promote the dialogue between science, culture, and the small-scale manufacturing industry by a program which allows the school to land permanently in M4H, as the driver of a learning production landscape that connects Rotterdam's former harbor area, the Meuse River and the North Sea in a dynamic and sustainable district that responds optimally to the needs of its new residents. The school addresses research questions, including: How can we collectively, as a collaborative commons, develop an ecological intelligence aimed at living a meaningful life in balance with this specific environment? How do we realize equal interaction between all organisms, living communities, and their environments? How can we concretely continue to build on a learning, sustainable, and circular production landscape, taking into account the water challenge and reasoning towards the optimal ecological footprints of 6,300 new residents?

This way, the Waterschool is developing guiding principles for a *cultural* framework that supplements and adds value to the earlier guiding principles that the IABR–Atelier Rotterdam formulated for the *spatial* framework for the redevelopment of the Merwe-Vierhavens area.
And in keeping with the objectives of the IABR, the Water School deliberately underwrote the United Nations' *2030 Agenda for Sustainable Development* and the municipality's *Resilient Rotterdam* agenda in this context.

A Working Exhibition with Five Future Scenarios

On the DOWN TO EARTH platform, the Waterschool manifested as a working exhibition, WATERSCHOOL M4H+, which was open to visitors from 9 June to 30 July 2021, during the summer break of the pandemic, and took place in Studio Makkink & Bey's own workspace.
WATERSCHOOL M4H+ not only showed how the city harbor could be (re)-developed into a better-balanced, sustainable, and dynamic ecosystem, but also what new live-work environments could look like spatially and culturally, with an eye to housing 6,300 future residents and their sustainable individual use of resources in approximately 3,000 (live-work) dwellings.

WATERSCHOOL M4H+: intro
photo: George Brugmans

WATERSCHOOL M4H+:
Merwe-Vierhavens in transition
photo: Aad Hoogendoorn

Five future scenarios depicted new relationships among all living organisms, including all residents, representing five new production landscapes in an area in which the energy transition, water management, and food production were central. The scenarios were represented in five different outdoor locations in which stories about, research into, and impact of alternative resource consumption were illustrated by publicly accessible spatial installations. Through a QR code that accessed a web application, visitors could discern direct relationships between locations and what they might look like in the future. They were also introduced to the pioneers of M4H, including the makers and entrepreneurs already living and working there and the future residents.

Water Use as a Lever

In all scenarios, water (use) plays an important part. This is why Makkink and Bey wanted to initiate a process that would, first of all, raise awareness of water issues, especially of our huge individual water footprints and of ways to reduce it. The program included tours of the area and small workshops about the production and consumption of water, talk shows with experts about the possibilities of using and producing biobased materials in M4H+, and live radio talks with experts on architecture and the applications of the five raw materials – all to fuel this process during the biennale.

Growing Public Archive

The approach allowed the Studio to ongoingly include the results of the process in the working exhibition. During DOWN TO EARTH, the collection and network of the Waterschool continued to grow into a public archive rich in (references to) existing and innovative work by more than 30 artists, designers, and (local) companies. A 'living' arsenal that feeds M4H with new insights and developments on different scales: from mushroom chairs to seaweed tableware, from wooden houses to duckweed clinkers. WATERSCHOOL M4H+ was, in short, a working exhibition that mutated into a public archive that fit in very well with M4H+'s ambition to be a learning production landscape. [35]

[35] For the introduction of the curators Makkink and Bey, see the Waterschool publication *IABR–DOWN TO EARTH: WATERSCHOOL M4H+ #0: Introduction*

WATERSCHOOL M4H+:
a developing public archive
photo: Aad Hoogendoorn

→
WATERSCHOOL M4H+
photo: Aad Hoogendoorn

DOWN TO EARTH: WATERSCHOOL M4H+

WATERSCHOOL M4H+

INTRODUCTION CHIEF CURATOR

Water Use as Leverage

Rotterdam is a low-lying port city in the delta. In times of climate crisis, the city has to face up to acute challenges such as subsidence, water safety, extreme precipitation, heat, and drought. But what about water use? The average Rotterdammer consumes 119 liters of water per day – 43,435 liters per year – *directly*, for everyday use. That same Rotterdammer consumes another 4,000 liters of water per day – 1.45 million liters per year – *indirectly*, as a consumer of mostly imported goods such as food and clothing. This constitutes 99 percent of their water consumption, with 95 percent of their water footprint being left in foreign countries where the water conditions are often much worse than they are in the Netherlands.

The goal of WATERSCHOOL M4H+ is to raise our awareness of our huge water footprint and of the ways we can reduce it. And to take this as the starting point for the alternative *learning-by-doing* area development of city harbor Merwe-Vierhavens. The (awareness of) water use becomes leverage for the collaborative exploration of a *learning production landscape*, of a future that we can want in a district in which the city plans to build some 3,000 (live-work) dwellings for approximately 6,300 people in the near future. Focusing on three challenges that are central to this (re)development – the production of food, the generation of energy and the design of innovative live-work environments – the water challenge is coupled with broader questions about the development of a future delta city with water used as leverage to create an integrated long-term vision for M4H+.

A Catalyst for New Cultures of Living

WATERSCHOOL M4H+ investigates how a range of resources can contribute to building a sustainable and circular learning environment, in order to meet the water challenge and ensure an optimized ecological footprint for the area's future residents. It illustrates what this new living and working environment could look like when its development is guided by a resource use that ensures a fair interaction between all organisms, communities, and their environment.
Insects, duckweed, seaweed, wood, and fungi are the five highlighted resources that shape the future of living in M4H+, impacting all areas of life. Starting from the basic needs of the individual and her body, such as nutrition and water use, these resources contribute to a new diet by sug-

gesting the use of alternative and less water-intensive protein sources, and thus a minimized water footprint. And when expanded to dwelling, working, and living and to energy and water consumption, they also generate new sustainable building materials and energy supplies, while suggesting new types of building typologies and cultures of living.
Also, examples of other (research) projects by designers, artists, institutions, and the green industries into the potential of the material and cultural uses of the selected resources strongly suggest that a new cultural framework for the area is feasible. Adhering to a *learning-by-doing* approach, the future production landscape M4H+ blends living and working while being designed around the prospective use of the five resources.

The Waterschool program for Merwe-Vierhavens, which Studio Makkink & Bey initiated in 2018 for THE MISSING LINK, aims to promote a dialogue between science, culture and the small-scale manufacturing industry and to superimpose a cultural framework onto the spatial framework for the area. In this way the Waterschool will be able to take permanent root in Merwe-Vierhavens as a driving force behind a networked learning production landscape and as a curator of a dynamically growing future-oriented public archive that can continue to feed M4H with new insights and developments. By gathering as well as distributing knowledge, WATERSCHOOL M4H+ operates as a catalyst for the sustainable (re)development of the area.

WATERSCHOOL M4H+

(RE)DEVELOPING WITH FIVE RENEWABLE RESOURCES

To reduce the overall ecological footprint of the M4H District, the future production landscape presented in WATERSCHOOL M4H+ had to focus on the manufacture and development of sustainable housing, biobased materials, renewable energy sources, and new food staples. This is why Makkink and Bey examined ways of life they expected to minimize the CO_2 footprint and water footprint of the future residents.

The Garden of Delight
WATERSCHOOL M4H+
photo: Aad Hoogendoorn

The Garden of Delight

Taking into account the three challenges that were already central to the (re)development of the Merwe-Vierhavens District and the adjacent Bospolder-Tussendijken area – food production, energy transition, and live-work environments – Studio Makkink & Bey mapped out, as concretely as possible, ways for 6,300 new residents to live sustainably, healthily, and in much better balance with the environment and other life forms. Inspired by a Hieronymus Bosch triptych, in an exhibition section called 'The Garden of Delight', Makkink and Bey explored the ingredients of such a better-balanced system, starting from the basic needs of each individual. What are the elements of which the human body consist? What does it need, at least, to be able to start afresh, so to speak, to be able to land on Earth, but functioning in a much better balance with the environment and other life forms? [36]

Next, they asked how the basic needs of the individual body could come to play a part in the challenges facing the M4H area, and which new forms of renewable resource production were potentially interesting and how these could be set up in M4H. Which essential raw materials are required for the production of food and building materials, for example?

[36] More about 'The Garden of Delight' in the Waterschool publication *IABR–DOWN TO EARTH: WATERSCHOOL M4H+ #1: The Garden of Delight*

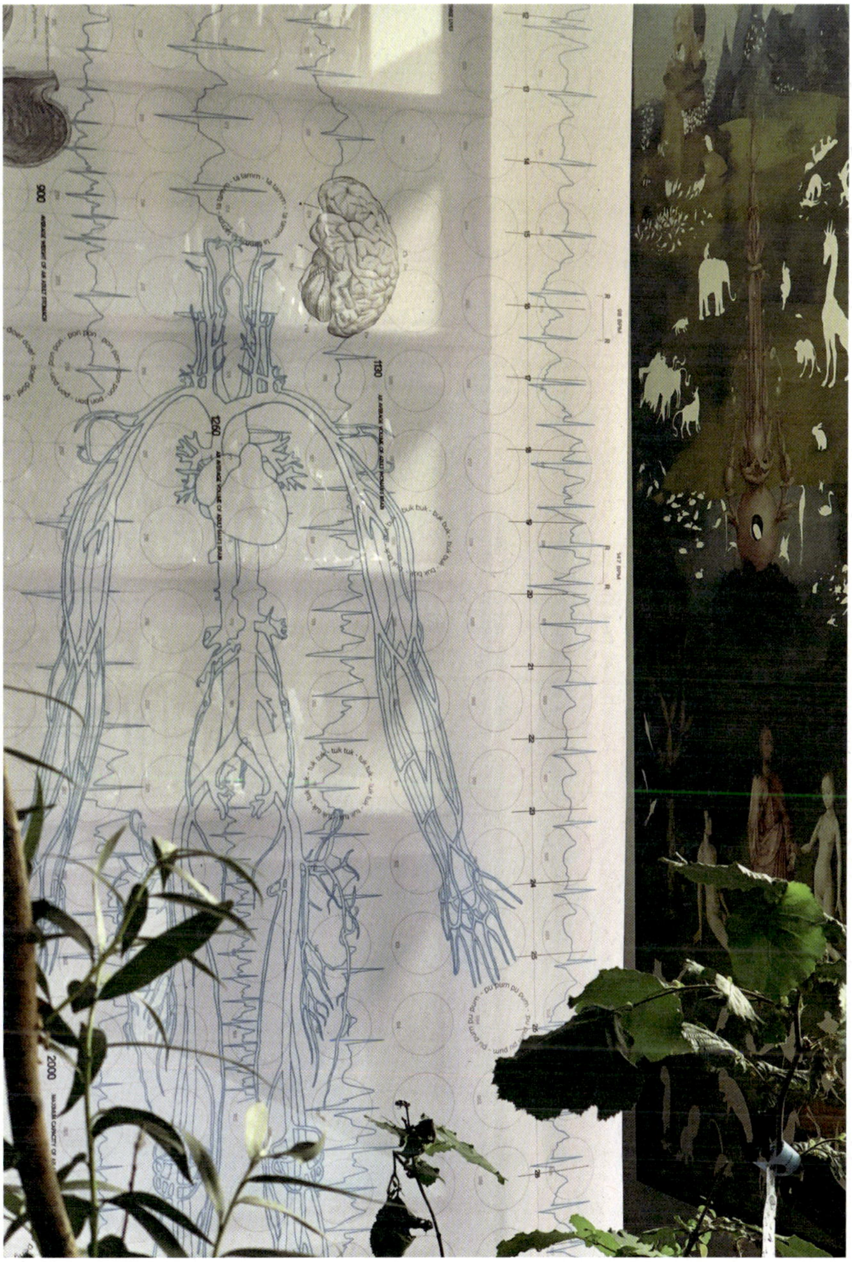

One basic human contains: Magnesium 35 g, Sodium 105 g, Sulfur 175 g, Potassium 245 g, Phosphor 1.05 kg, Calcium 1.05 kg, Nitrogen 2.1 kg, Hydrogen 7 kg, Carbon 12.6 kg, Oxygen 45.5 kg – 70 l of water is contained by an adult human body – 182.5 kg of sugar can generate the required energy for an adult human for a year – 250 l of compost creates an adult human based on the amount of nitrogen in a body – 40 trees are needed to compensate the CO_2 exhaled by one person – 45 kg of mealworms contains 50% of the required amount of protein per person per year – 7.5 m^2 of duckweed yields a weekly harvest of 50% of the required amount of protein per person per week – 0.72 m^2 of mushrooms yields a harvest of 6.15 kg, grown on the coffee grounds from the coffee consumption of one person in one year – 1 m^2 yields a harvest 8 kg of seaweed per week.

WATERSCHOOL M4H+
© George Brugmans

Five Production Landscapes

The five 'renewable' (or perhaps: 'living'?) raw materials Makkink and Bey chose as the starting point for (re)development of as many production landscapes were fungi, seaweed, insects, wood, and duckweed. These are potential sources of food and raw materials, each with their own potentially positive impact on the sustainable fulfillment of basic physical needs. The production of insects, for example, can indirectly reduce the amount of water used to produce meat: insects are an alternative source of protein and their production requires much less water than that of beef, pork, or chicken. In M4H they are also welcome as co-residents, and even as the new live-work culture's maintenance personnel. Fungi are a food source that can also support humans in other ways during various stages of existence – ranging from making fast-growing clothing and wall insulation to breaking down human remains in the earth. Duckweed can be used as a potential protein source and as a water treatment facility by both households and agriculture.

WATERSCHOOL M4H+
photo: Aad Hoogendoorn

The production of such renewable resources leaves a smaller water footprint than the production of conventional food, but requires new forms of (urban) agriculture, architecture and energy supply. Each of the five raw materials was examined to find out how they could be used as building materials, how they could concretely contribute to food and energy production, and what this would mean spatially in the specific environment of the M4H+ District. How many gallons of water would they save compared with more traditional approaches? How much space would they take? What was the annual consumption and production capacity in the area? Approximately how much duckweed would it take to provide residents with oxygen? And how many trees, to absorb the CO_2 emitted per resident? What initiatives in the area were already contributing to its sustainable (re)development? What part could existing harbor architecture play in these new forms of urban development? And what does this all mean to the building challenge and the energy and food supply in the future M4H District?

WATERSCHOOL M4H+:
a developing public archive
photo: Aad Hoogendoorn

Five Installations in the Public Space

At five different outdoor locations in the Merwe-Vierhavens District, the results of research into and the possible impact of each of the five production landscapes as introduced in the working exhibition were presented in as many spatial installations. Each installation presented a drawing of a future scenario that depicted the potential of the symbiosis between the individual basic need for a specific raw material and its translation into the future live-produce landscape. Five plots, five stories about ways to live and work in M4H in the future.

WATERSCHOOL M4H+:
Plot 001, the fungi production landscape
photo: Aad Hoogendoorn

Strategically placed between already existing small-scale initiatives, workshops, maker spaces, and cultural practices, the interventions invited visitors to make connections between the future scenarios of WATERSCHOOL M4H+ and the knowledge and expertise already present in the area. Exemplary architectural projects showed which innovative building methods could be applied in (re)development, and in what way. Each installation also illustrated the water footprint of the average Rotterdam resident – who *directly*, that is, personally and daily, taps 119 liters per day, equivalent to 43,435 liters per year. If they used rainwater, each Rotterdam resident would need their own 'vat' of circa 60 m^2, with a height of 72.4 cm.

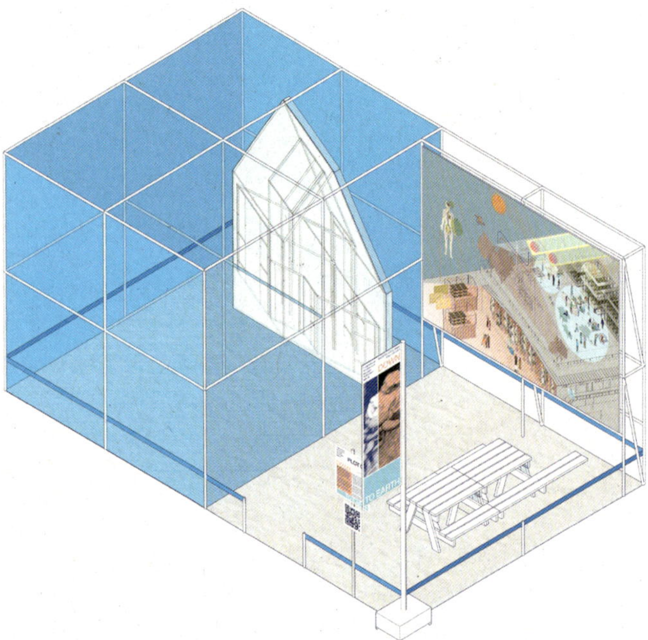

In each outdoor installation, the water footprint for each future resident of M4H+ was spatially visualized, always in relation to the specific production landscape addressed in the installation. A blue and white striped pipe at 72.4 cm in height indicated how much rainwater each resident must collect annually to cover their direct water consumption. A blue net gave insight into the indirect water consumption required to, say, produce a loaf of bread, a steak, or light a standard single-family home. A black-and-white drawing illustrated how designers can contribute to realizing the relevant future production landscape.
image: Studio Makkink & Bey

A QR code gave each visitor access to a web application that presented makers and entrepreneurs already active in the area.[37] This was based on a portrait series in which 14 M4H residents share their personal stories about activities and production in the constantly evolving community that is M4H.

[37] web application WATERSCHOOL M4H+

Using these five spatial interventions, which in a very concrete, visionary, and future-oriented way link M4H's status quo with its potential, Studio Makkink & Bey introduced a cultural framework that adds color and value to the spatial framework previously approved by the municipality and the Port Authority. By responding optimally to the needs of the future residents in this way, the Studio wanted to very directly influence the chances of actual incorporation of its future scenarios.

→
WATERSCHOOL M4H+: Plot 002, the seaweed production landscape
photo: Aad Hoogendoorn

1. FUNGI PRODUCTION LANDSCAPE

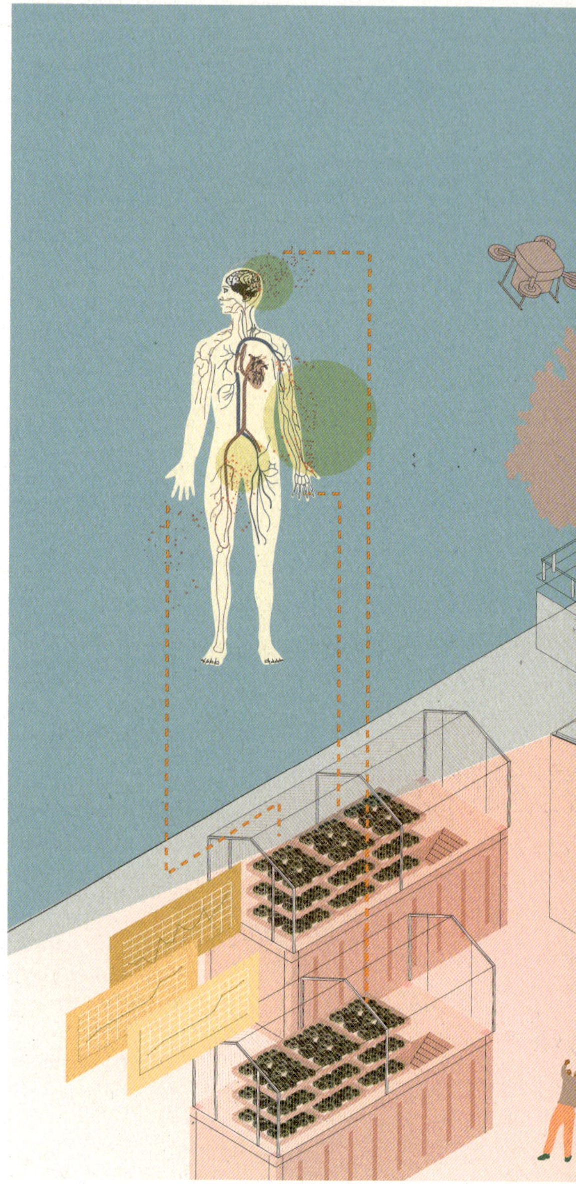

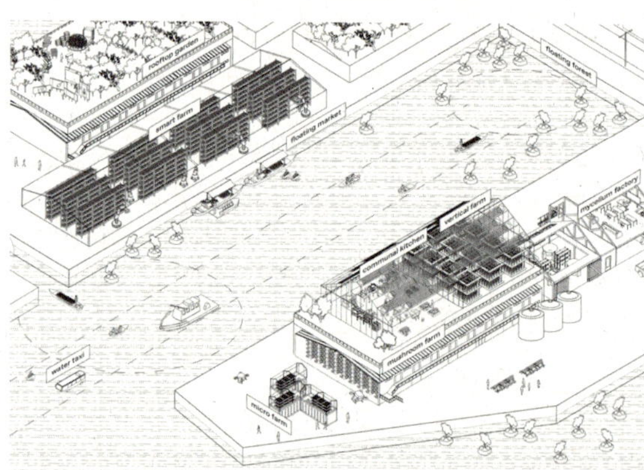

image: Studio Makkink & Bey

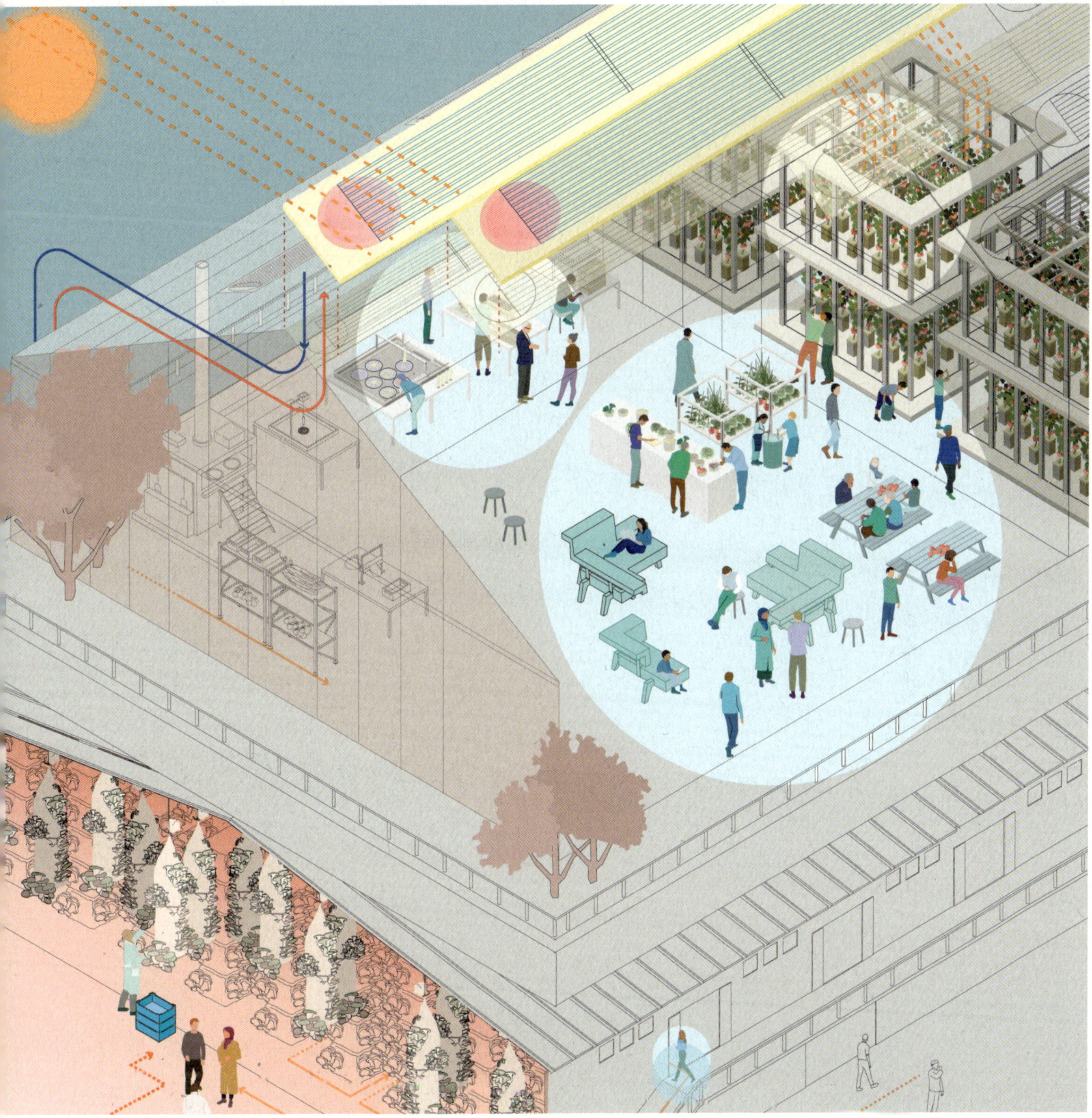

image: Juhee Hahm, Studio Makkink & Bey

Innovative fungi production involves more than just growing mushrooms, as fungi have many more possible uses. They facilitate numerous ecosystem cycles, convert human bodies and pollutants into richer soil through decomposition, and are a valuable source of nutrients in (urban) agriculture. Mushrooms, the fruit bodies of mycelium, the network of hyphal threads, are an alternative source of protein and vitamin D already embedded in Western diets. It is quite possible to integrate the use of fungi into this emerging maker district, with its food gardens and restaurants. [38]

[38] For more, see: *IABR–DOWN TO EARTH: WATERSCHOOL M4H+ #2: Fungi*

2. SEAWEED PRODUCTION LANDSCAPE

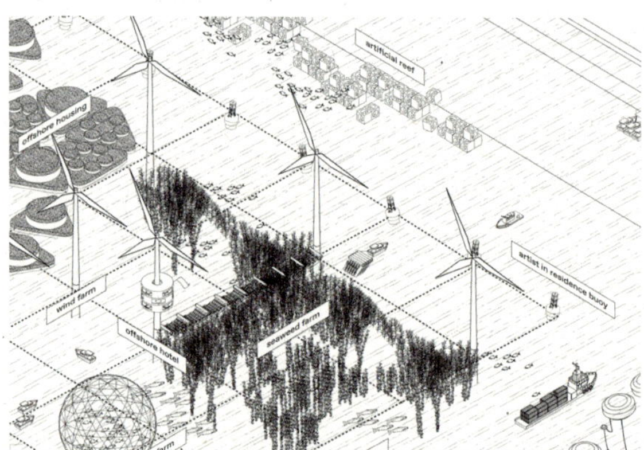

image: Studio Makkink & Bey

Seaweed production can connect the North Sea to M4H+. Otherwise unusable areas in close proximity to offshore wind farms can be utilized to grow seaweed, which can subsequently be used as biofuel in Rotterdam's city harbors. Other options, like using seaweed as a basis for bioplastic production or as a source of protein, can also contribute to the success of future seaweed production landscapes. A seascape of seaweed farms is not only a must-see in itself, but also a new habitat for fish and other lifeforms.[39]

image: Juhee Hahm, Studio Makkink & Bey

IABR–DOEN TO EARTH: WATERSCHOOL M4H+ #3

SEAWEED

[39] For more, see: *IABR–DOWN TO EARTH: WATER-SCHOOL M4H+ #3: Seaweed*

3. INSECT PRODUCTION LANDSCAPE

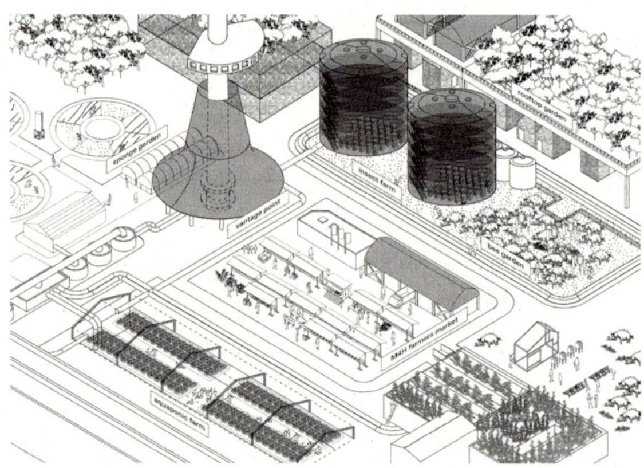

image: Studio Makkink & Bey

Insects are essential to the functioning of all ecosystems and a valuable source of protein. Their production in an insect production landscape requires ten times less water than beef production. Insect production not only adds value to the food chain, it also questions the stand-offish way in which we currently treat insects. An insect production landscape anticipates a transition to lighter forms of agricultural architecture. An insect presence actively promoted by humans will help ensure the city's food supply by stimulating innovative urban agriculture in M4H.[40]

image: Juhee Hahm, Studio Makkink & Bey

[40] For more, see: *IABR–DOWN TO EARTH: WATERSCHOOL M4H+ #4: Insects*

4. WOOD PRODUCTION LANDSCAPE

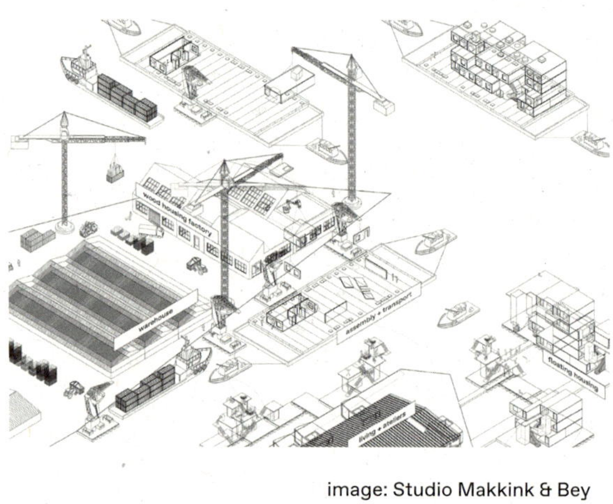

image: Studio Makkink & Bey

image: Juhee Hahm, Studio Makkink & Bey

In a balanced wood production landscape, growing wood absorbs CO_2 from the atmosphere; biobased buildings store CO_2 throughout their life span. The proposal is, therefore, for M4H+ to start a wood manufacturing laboratory to develop its own wood and to use it for local construction. Visualizing the potential of wood for M4H+'s live-work landscape, as a sustainable alternative to that of today's resource-intensive, concrete-dependent construction industry, will encourage the local construction industry to adopt a different approach and new architectural typologies.[41]

[41] For more, see: *IABR–DOWN TO EARTH: WATER-SCHOOL M4H+ #5: Wood*

5. DUCKWEED PRODUCTION LANDSCAPE

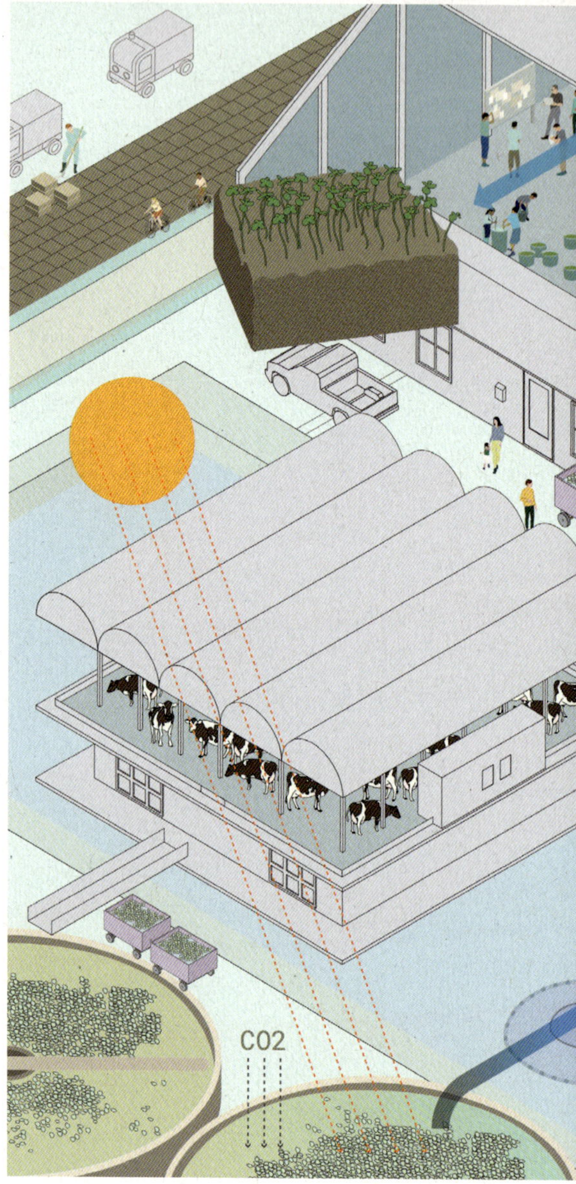

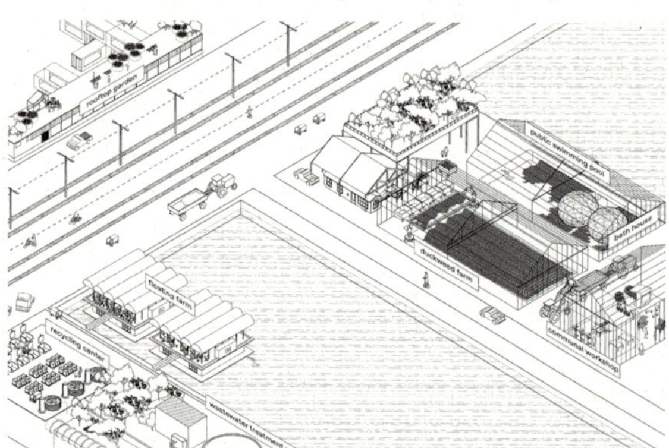

image: Studio Makkink & Bey

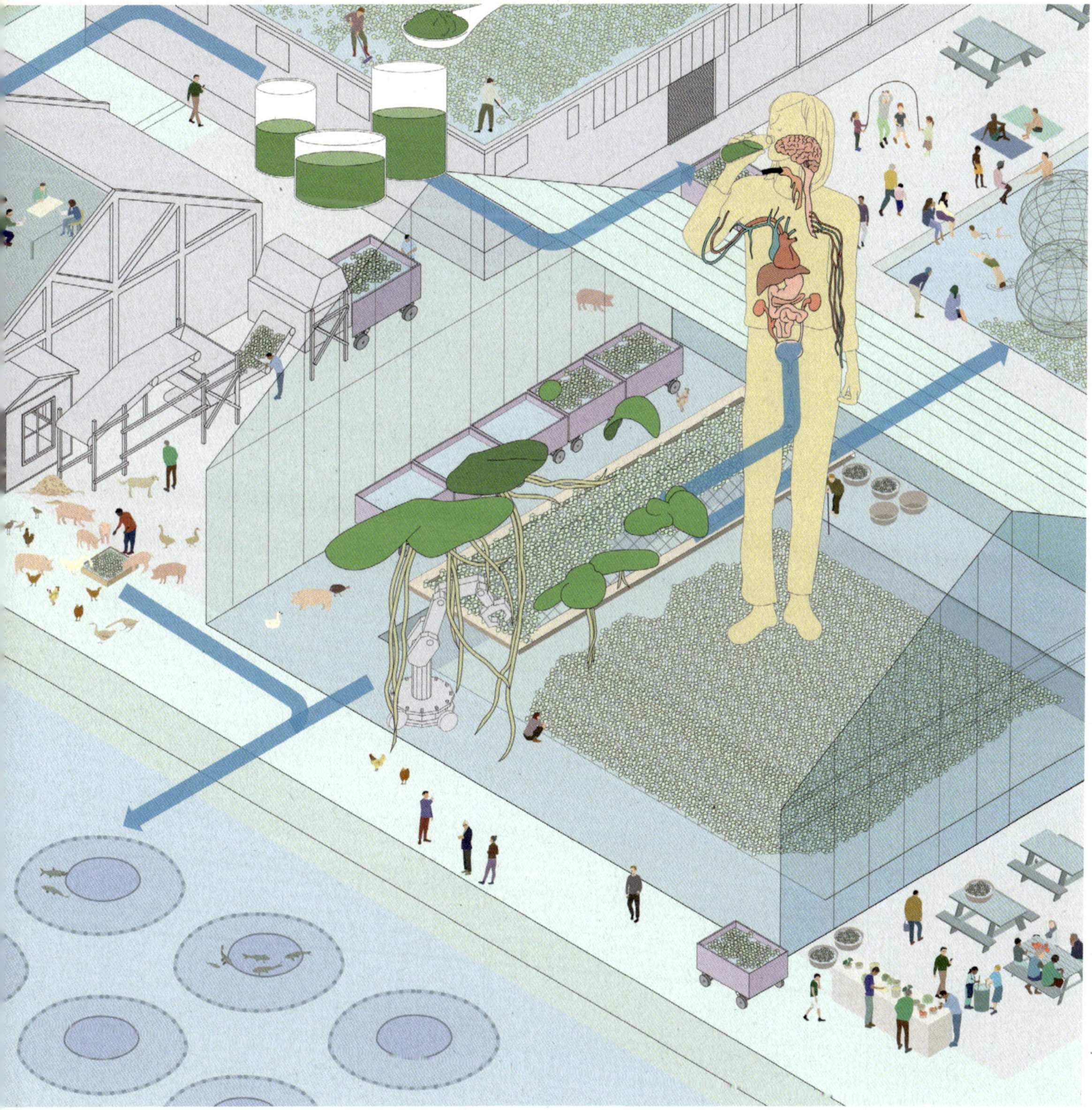

In a duckweed production landscape, human and non-human animals live together more effortlessly. Because duckweed provides a natural wastewater treatment, such a landscape can function as a water treatment plant for households and livestock. It also provides both humans and animals with food. Duckweed is a valuable source of plant protein, which can be used to feed herbivorous fish, chickens, cows, and pigs, and is considered a potential food source for humans. Integrating a duckweed production landscape into a work-live area strengthens the relationship between humans and animals, and raises awareness about the consumption of animal products.[42]

image: Juhee Hahm, Studio Makkink & Bey

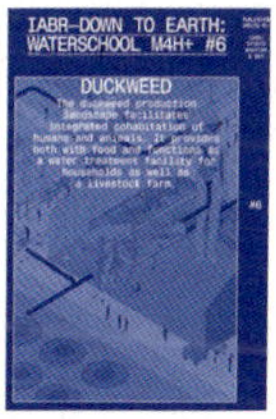

[42] For more, see: *IABR–DOWN TO EARTH: WATERSCHOOL M4H+ #6: Duckweed*

DOWN TO EARTH: WATERSCHOOL M4H+

CREDITS
WATERSCHOOL M4H+

CURATORS
Rianne Makkink
Jurgen Bey

EXHIBITION RESEARCH AND DESIGN
Studio Makkink & Bey
Rianne Makkink, Jurgen Bey, Anja van Zoomeren, Michou de Bruijn, Nai-Dan Chang, Hsiang Ching Chuang, Daan Veerman, Pichaya Puapoomcharoen, Timothy Liu, Juhee Hahm, Jules van den Langenberg, Anna Bolt, Gerard Lukken, Louis Moeckel, Tabitha Mosterdijk, Frédérique van Tilborg, Raphaël Flipo

DESIGNERS IN RESIDENCE
Studio Corvers with Carla Herrewijnen
Philipp Kolmann with Suzanne Bernhardt and Liza Witte
Michael Varga

COMMISSIONS
Metabolic - Sustainability Consultancy Data Science
Arjang Tajbakhsh

EXHIBITION TEXTS
Studio Makkink & Bey
Rianne Makkink, Daan Veerman, Anastasia Eggers
IABR
George Brugmans (introduction chief curator), Alexandra Sonnemans

GRAPHIC DESIGN
ARK
Roosje Klap, Senka Milutinović

WATERSCHOOL M4H+ APP AND WEBSITE DESIGN
Studio Makkink & Bey
Jurgen Bey, Nai-Dan Chang
ARK
Roosje Klap, Senka Milutinović, Bente van Bourgondien

EVENTS
Studio Makkink & Bey
Rianne Makkink, Jurgen Bey
IABR
Yonca Özbilge

PRODUCTION AND PLANNING
Studio Makkink & Bey
Rianne Makkink, Anja van Zoomeren
IABR
Maartje Berendsen

MARKETING AND COMMUNICATION
IABR
Melany van Twuijver, Dewi Baggerman
Studio Makkink & Bey
Antoinette Veneman

COPY-EDITING AND TRANSLATIONS
InOtherWords translation & editing
D'Laine Camp, Gerda ten Cate, Maria van Tol

CONSTRUCTION EXHIBITION
Bart Cuppens Tentoonstellingsbouw

PRINTING
Rocka Art & Sign

CONSTRUCTION INTERVENTIONS IN THE PUBLIC SPACE
LENN.eu, Gigant, Jasper van der Made

WITH THE SUPPORT OF
Programmabureau M4H Rotterdam

WE THANK THE FOLLOWING PEOPLE FOR THEIR CRITICAL REFLECTION AND/OR THEIR CONTRIBUTIONS
Isabelle Vries, Ilka Blok, Anne Koetsenruyter and Walter de Vries (Programmabureau M4H), Martijn van Halem (City of Rotterdam), Martin van Rijn (Coöperatieve Vereniging Marconia), Ester van de Wiel and Joost Adriaanse (RE-/place), Dolf Broekhuizen and students (Delft University of Technology), Maurik Stomps, Jack Bardwell, Matilde Patvelli, Roberta di Cosmo, Marta Rios Piza, GTBT Good Times Bad Times Radio

←
WATERSCHOOL M4H+
photo: Aad Hoogendoorn

IABR—ATELIER

DORDRECHT

IABR–ATELIER DORDRECHT

WATER SAFETY AS LEVERAGE FOR SUSTAINABLE AREA DEVELOPMENT

In 2021, it was 600 years ago that Dordrecht was hit by what was most likely the biggest water disaster in the history of the Netherlands: the Saint Elizabeth's Flood. The city has been an island ever since, and remains very vulnerable to flooding to this day. Dordrecht has always had to be prepared for the worst: extreme storms that can only be predicted a short time in advance. The fact that, due to global warming and its effects on the climate, water safety is now an even higher priority to Dordrecht than before is therefore unsurprising. After all, in the event of a calamity, the city needs to bring some 120,000 people to safety in less than 24 hours.

Arnold Houbraken pinxit; Romeyn de Hooge sculpsit: Devastation caused by the Saint Elizabeth's Flood of 17–18 November 1421 from: Matthys Balen Jansz, *Beschryvinge der stad Dordrecht* (1677), collection The Royal Library of The Netherlands

This means that, day in day out, Dordrecht has to be armed to the teeth, ready for an emergency that could occur at any time, but only actually happens once in so many years. Every single year, however, water safety eats up a substantial portion of the municipal budget while the city also faces other challenges that require public resources, such as housing, employment, mobility, health, sustainability, and the energy transition. Is it possible to forge synergy between the water issue and these other challenges, and to adopt a smart approach that can make a virtue of necessity?

Water Safety as Leverage

Because the IABR had actually been applying a *water-as-leverage* approach, and because in 1421 not only Dordrecht, but also its neighbor Rotterdam was affected and the cities wanted to commemorate the Saint Elisabeth's Flood together, the two parties found each other effortlessly. In 2019, the IABR and the City of Dordrecht jointly set up the IABR–Atelier Dordrecht; the starting point was to bring research by design into play to arrive at new, concrete solution directions to meet the existing challenges in the city. Integrated, sustainable, and socially inclusive area development was the primary goal, water safety was the lever: the means by which sustainable urban development would be stimulated.

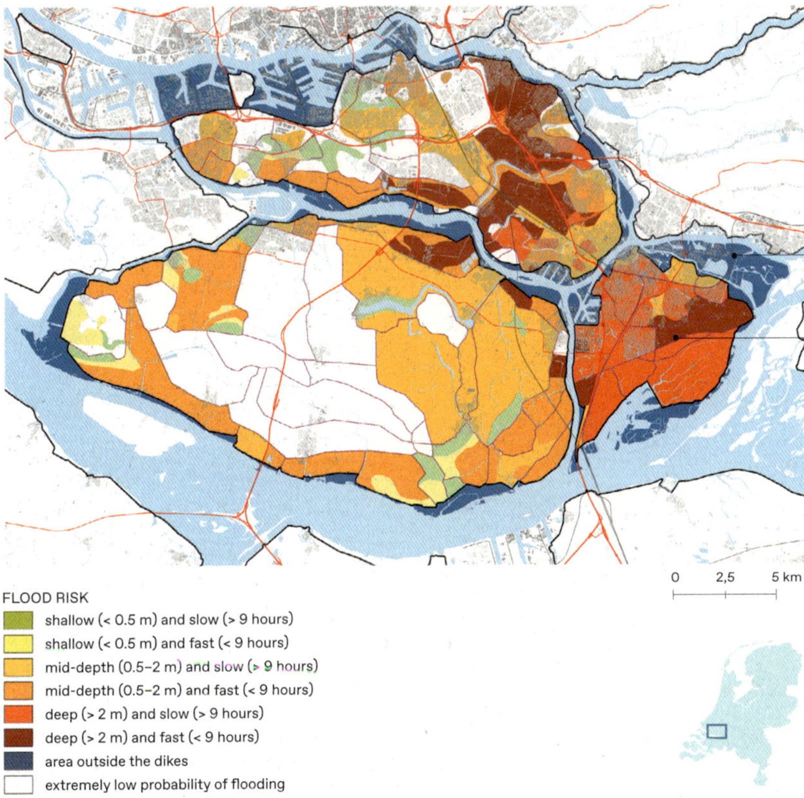

The Hazard Map of the Island of Dordrecht and surrounding area clearly shows that in the event of a flood, almost all of Dordrecht will be covered by a deep layer of water. The water will rise rapidly in most locations. The Staart, located outside the dikes, will remain dry.
source: Netherlands Environmental Assessment Agency (PBL), The Hague/ Bilthoven, 2009.

The Staart

George Brugmans asked Dordrecht-born Adriaan Geuze, the curator of THE FLOOD, the 2005 water biennale in which the tension between ongoing urbanization and rising sea levels was the central theme, to lead the Atelier's research by design.

This study started with an initial systems analysis and the broad mapping of the opportunities that the *water-safety-as-leverage* approach could produce, carried out by Geuze's design office, West 8. It soon became clear that the Staart, an area located outside the dikes on the city's northern edge, could play an unexpectedly important role in realizing Dordrecht's water safety agenda. The Staart is currently facing many problems and has little perspective; it is a socially vulnerable residential area partly located on a former toxic waste dump. After a polluted land affair and an environmental scandal, the district saw facilities leave and livability deteriorate, after which residents felt increasingly abandoned.[43] But the Staart is also uniquely situated, between the Wantij and Beneden-Merwede, surrounded by water but relatively elevated, and with the historical city center nearby and the Biesbosch nature reserve just around the corner. Dordrecht faces a huge housing challenge and it's beyond question that the Staart is a potentially attractive location. What's more, if the city were to decide to go for sustainable and inclusive urban development here, for new live-work environments, and for the establishment of good connections with both the city and the surrounding natural reserves, it would generate opportunities that would not arise were they to choose a different, more traditional approach.

[43] 'I'm sick and tired of it. I pay 600 euros rent to live here under the worst possible circumstances. . . . The general idea is: if you need to get rid of something, just dump it on the Staart,' said a resident in the newspaper *Algemeen Dagblad* of 8 December 2018.

Aerial photo of the Staart, with the Dordrecht city center, background left
© Cees Schilthuizen

From Necessity to Virtue

The *water-safety-as-leverage* approach requires that the Staart has space available to quickly realize the extra square meters needed to shelter people during a flood at all times. Designing the district as a large-scale shelter location, creating a design that includes spaces for the sheltering of evacuees from other Dordrecht districts, as well as other emergency facilities to be used in the event of a flood, makes it possible to create an urban environment in which people not only live and work, but in which there is also ample space for recreation, education, and other public facilities.

To allow this, the Staart always has to be easily and quickly accessible. This requires new connections in and with the city and between the city and the region, which will make its green areas and waterfronts more accessible in the process. The Wantij, the river that flows past the Staart, can be turned into a Tidal Park: good for nature, for the recreational options of local residents, and for the quality of life in the district. In addition, living on the water, in nature and with space for nature, becomes a serious option.

Broad Collaboration

Pandemic or not, the research by design of the IABR–Atelier gained momentum in the spring of 2020. The new package of measures for the EU's Water Framework Directive came just in time, as it ensured closer collaboration between the various stakeholders in the area, including Rijkswaterstaat (RWS, the national Department of Waterways and Public Works). The quest for new tidal nature, to better protect the stony and steep banks from the wash of passing ships, culminated in a workshop the Atelier organized in the Sliedrecht part of the Biesbosch, during which the City of Dordrecht, the IABR, RWS, Staatsbosbeheer (the Dutch government organization for forestry and the management of nature reserves) and the Wantij Foundation were able to effectively compare their agendas for the future.

The City of Dordrecht also asked West 8 to create a Vision Map for the area, linked to the assignment of the IABR–Atelier. This prevented fragmentation and created a solid and integrated spatial framework in which both urban and landscape developments could be embedded. This made it possible, in collaboration with Staatsbosbeheer and RWS, to design an Environmental Vision for the entire area that all stakeholders wanted to move forward with. In turn, the Map of Opportunities for the Staart, which the Atelier would present a year later during DOWN TO EARTH, was partly based on the Vision Map.[44]

[44] Also see page 293-294 and 303 ff.

Achieving Socio-Civic and Climate Goals

In the spring of 2020, the IABR–Atelier decided to highlight five aspects that were not only of interest to the Staart and Dordrecht, but could also be applied in other, similar locations in the Netherlands and abroad, in places where water safety themes such as good escape routes and optimal peak collection can be combined with sustainable urban development.

Five closely related substudies were put out to design offices with relevant expertise – VenhoevenCS architecture+urbanism, PosadMaxwan, EGM architects, Studio Donna van Milligen Bielke, and West 8 – while Geuze formulated the research assignments, in close consultation with the IABR and the City of Dordrecht.

Brugmans asked the five offices to place the 17 Sustainable Development Goals (SDGs) at the center of the program of requirements, and – and this was a crucial ground rule – as cohesively as possible. The research goal was to explore, in design practice, whether and how these global goals could be deployed locally, that is, bottom-up, and with water (safety) as leverage, to sustainably make city.[45] By fully integrating the SDGs into the research by design of the five substudies the Atelier, in line with the IABR's main objectives, wanted to actually contribute to the exemplary design of inclusive and sustainable cities and thus help realize the socio-civic and climate goals of Dordrecht and the global community.

[45] In effect, the programs of the different IABR editions since 2009 meet in the formula (Making City + (Open City + Next Economy)) * Urban by Nature – Missing Link = Down to Earth. In other words, sustainable city making with a socioeconomically inclusive and integral working agenda leads – if the missing link is found and forged – to landing on Earth.

Research by Design: Five Substudies

1. CITY WITH HIGH DENSITY

The first research question was about designing a new, high-density city district, with subcultures and corresponding facilities, connected to the public transportation network and with the SDGs at the center of the program of requirements. The aim was to ensure that this district would be able to function self-supportingly (in terms of electricity, food, water, and waste disposal, for example) in the event of a disaster, taking into account the 60,000 people that would need to be housed there for at least a week. To maximize chances of realization, this assignment specifically focused on the part of the Staart that the city of Dordrecht was expected to develop first.

Studio Donna van Milligen Bielke (DVMB), a young office that approaches urbanity and the use and the users of the city in an innovative way, was asked to include as a starting point for research the fact that designing a high-density, multifunctional city that is also water-safe begins with designing its open-to-sky space. Such a public space must not only be designed for daily use, but also for use as a 'machine' that can be quickly and purposefully activated in case of an emergency. It must be possible to instantly transform the different functions that enhance the diversity of the space in its day-to-day use into functions that are literally vital in case of flooding: a kiosk becomes an information point, schools become emergency hospitals, squares become food markets, and sports fields become helipads. To achieve this, DVMB opted for what the office calls 'reverse Hausmanning': advance-designing the public space and urban fabric for the kind of circulation it would see during an evacuation, but without this being visible during everyday use. So first making an analysis of what it takes to realize an evacuation and, subsequently, projecting the design of the everyday public space onto it.

Sustainable mixed city with green roofs, polder roofs and PV panels
left: daily use; schools, healthcare and hospitality outlets clustered around the high-quality public transportation station
right: peak demand; food market, emergency hospital, helicopter platforms and goods distribution around the high-quality public transportation station
image: DVMB, IABR–Atelier Dordrecht

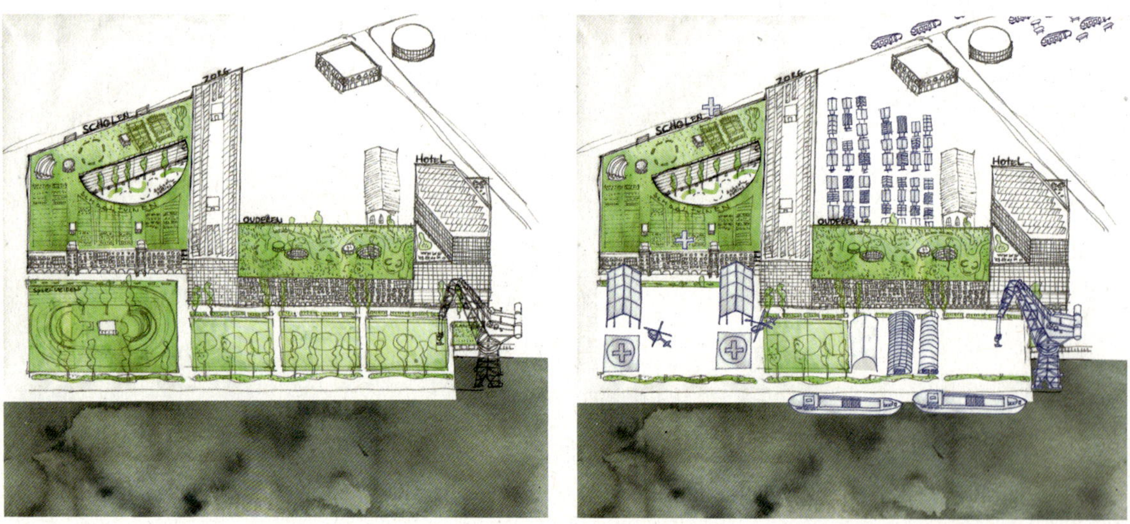

If, instead of the demands of the market, water safety requirements and the Sustainable Development Goals were made leading for area development on the Staart, and the design would start from the public space, this would result in a new type of urbanity in Dordrecht, in a district with a thoroughly Dordrecht identity in which the built environment and nature were better connected and contact between different subcultures encouraged, with more opportunities for small-scale developments, and including a great variety of functions and a good mix of living and working.[46]

[46] Research report DVMB

Dordrecht's new urbanity: a sustainable city with diverse waterfront identities
image: DMVB, IABR–Atelier Dordrecht

Dordrecht Waterproof

Complementing the DVMB study, students from the Eindhoven University of Technology's Faculty of Architecture participated in the master studio Dordrecht Waterproof, investigating how diverse urban life with a maximum mix of functions could emerge on the Staart. Looking for an effective response to the current flood threat, the students explored new, alternative approaches. After analysis and research, they worked in groups to create three master plans for the Staart in anticipation of a possible water disaster. Additionally, each individual student chose a specific location in which they integrated the worlds of living and working in hybrid building complexes providing safety from rising water.

2. CLIMATE-ADAPTIVE ESCAPE ROUTE

In the event of an extreme water emergency, the residents of Dordrecht have two options: flee vertically, to their attics, or, and this would be better, flee horizontally – first, to a more elevated urban district and from there, away from the city. However, there are currently no fast and direct routes from the historical city center to the suburbs. This means that only some 20 percent of the population would be able to flee the city by car; most residents would be advised to seek refuge in their attics.
New water safety policies need to ensure that in the future, some 60,000 people can flee the city and the other 60,000 can reach the Staart in time. The Staart is located outside the dike, on higher ground, and is therefore in principle a suitable refuge area, but people currently do not identify it as a place of refuge, and it is difficult to reach. In the absence of a fast, direct connection to the city center, residents now often prefer using their cars over using their bicycles. Is it possible to construct a new route for micro mobility that functions as the main route to and from the city center on a day-to-day basis but can also, in the event of a disaster, serve as an easily identified walking and cycling route from the city center to the safe haven of the Staart? And is it possible, through frequent usage and with an attractive program, to ingrain the existence of such a future escape route in the collective consciousness without confronting users with the threat of a possible disaster on a daily basis?

The office VenhoevenCS architecture+urbanism, an authority on infrastructural developments and new forms of urban mobility led by former state infrastructure advisor Ton Venhoeven, investigated the feasibility of a long micro corridor, elevated above the city center, between the Staart and the new Stadspark XL. This would comprise a raised cycling and walking route that residents would experience as attractive in everyday use, with entrances and exits at popular, recognizable locations that would be able to serve as the first ports of refuge in the event of a disaster and from which it would be possible to reach the Staart quickly.

Mindful of the assignment to place the SDGs at the center of the program of requirements, VenhoevenCS's research was mainly aimed at socioeconomically vulnerable neighborhoods. These often have fewer facilities, and are precisely the most suitable locations for the corridor entrances and exits as these can increase the accessibility of social functions such as public transportation, schools, and health care providers. Both small interventions like public inflaters as well as larger ones like neighborhood hubs or media centers would increase the appeal of the corridor. This would render existing and new social functions more accessible. The 15-minute-city concept was used as a starting point: all facilities people need for a good living environment must be accessible in 15 minutes at the most. This way, the corridor would soften the boundaries and differences between districts.
The corridor also breaks down existing barriers in the urban fabric, such as the railroad line and the N3 highway. At crucial points, it is linked to existing and new mobility networks, for example at railway stations, to

DAILY USE

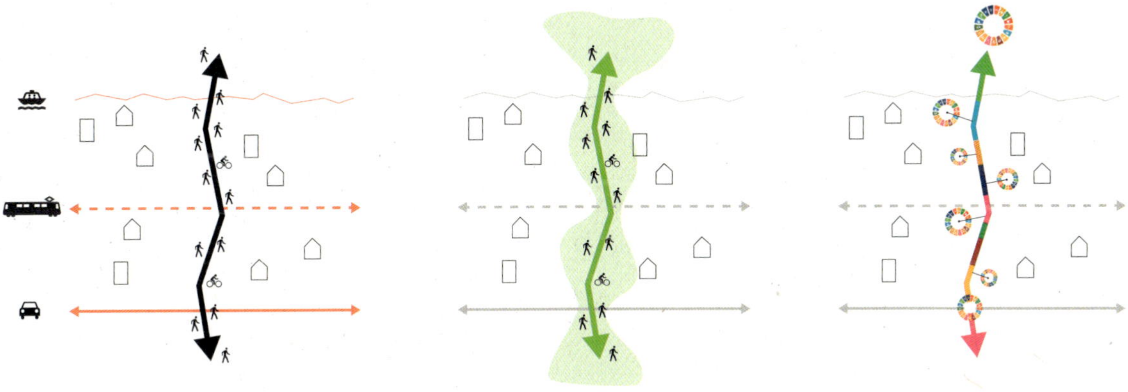

bridging of barriers created by roads/N3/ railroad/Wantij

ecological connection SportparkXL

social connection: strengthening accessibility between neighborhoods

CALAMITY

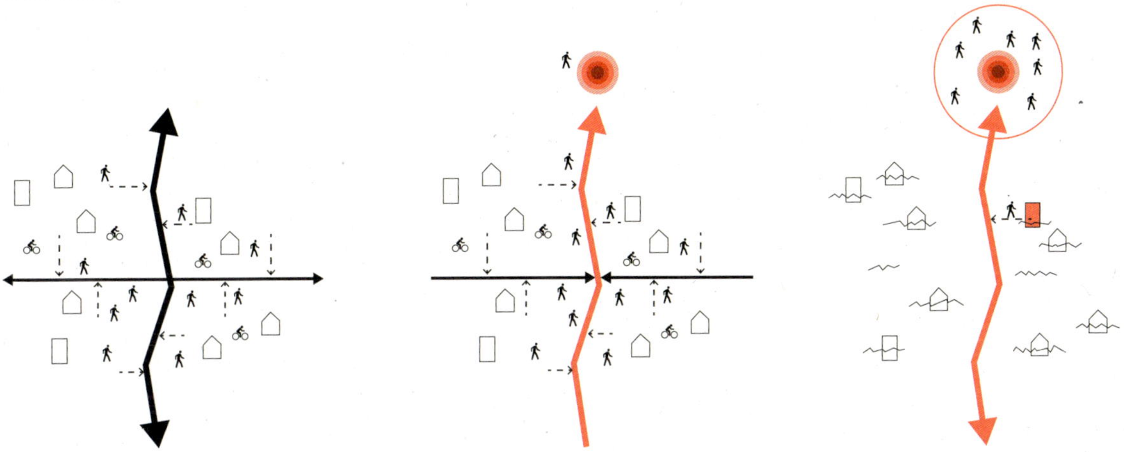

t = 0
future-proof mobility network in Dordrecht

t = 1
flood warning, evacuation: elevated route to safety, widely known before a dike breach

t = 2
safe evacuation after flooding to and from the Staart

The micro corridor, daily use and as operated during calamities
image: VenhoevenCS, IABR–Atelier Dordrecht

ADAPTIVE ESCAPE ROUTE WITH SDGS AS A CATALYST

SMALL
bicycle pumps
drinking fountains
landmarks
mini-library
trees
outdoor sports

MEDIUM
birding/vantage point
artist in residence
art
Eikenhof (existing)
WiFi spots
hortus
market
toy library
thrift store
minitheater De Melkbus

LARGE
parcel collection points
hub
repairshop/workshop
spaces
Eikenhof (existing)
KDV Brewery
shelter
open air theater

EXTRA LARGE
escape route
media library
hubs
eco bridge

allow the quick and safe transfer from slow traffic to other forms of mobility, and vice versa. And besides, the corridor is also the shortest route to greenery and water, a recreational cycling and walking route that allows residents to easily and quickly reach the Biesbosch via the Staart.
Raised above, yet deeply embedded in the fabric of the city, the corridor is both an enrichment of the city's living environment and a safe escape route in times of flooding.[47]

The micro corridor: adaptive escape route with SDGs as catalysts for design
image: VenhoevenCS, IABR–Atelier Dordrecht

[47] Research report VenhoevenCS

Artist's impression of the micro corridor, location intersection Noorderdijk
image: VenhoevenCS, IABR–Atelier Dordrecht

3. TIDAL PARK

The Wantij plays an important part in the IABR–Atelier's plans for the Staart. Currently, this tidal river has little to offer residents: its contribution to their quality of life is limited, its nature is not being developed and it is hardly directly accessible, although there is 30 km of embankment between the Staart and the Sliedrecht part of national park the Biesbosch. This existing landscape structure can be used as a basis for a future live-work area and tidal nature development – for a tidal park that forms a buffer between the embankment and the river and thus not only ensures more water safety, but also more biodiversity and more space for recreation. Only when the Wantij and the Biesbosch are made more accessible both visually and physically will people be able to directly and actively experience the Staart's sublime position in relation to water and greenery.

West 8's urban designers and landscape architects investigated how the reintroduction of tidal nature and new nature developments including new willow thickets along the banks of the Wantij would provide added value for not only the urbanity, accessibility, and appeal of Dordrecht, but also the biodiversity in this part of the city.

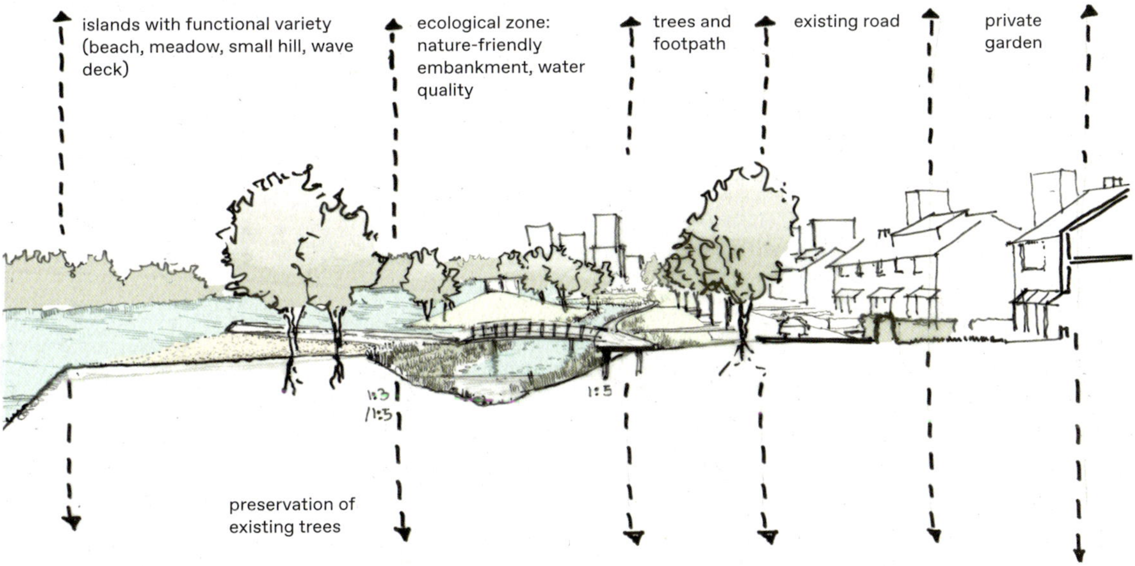

Two new, wooden bridges are to provide additional evacuation routes to the Staart and also link up with a new cycling and walking route, the 'Dordttrack,' which connects the city center with the Biesbosch via the Staart. This recreational route will be partially elevated to create more room for the river, increase biodiversity, and make it possible for residents of the Staart to repose in this tidal nature area. Along the Dordttrack, existing icons such as sawmill Nachtegaal will be revived and new icons added, such as pavilion De Staart, which will have a wave deck and a beach along the Wantij.

Concept cross section Wantij Tidal Park
image: West 8, IABR–Atelier Dordrecht

Sawmill Nachtegaal and pavilion De Staart with wave deck and city beach along Wantij
image: West 8, IABR–Atelier Dordrecht

The use of the willow cutting robot designed by West 8 results in an innovative cultural landscape in which several islands can be developed into new willow thickets. This landscape of increased biodiversity can simultaneously serve as an extra buffer in case the tide is high. The new willow thickets bear a (modest) wicker harvest, but above all serve as part of the recreational natural landscape and as stepping stones in the direction of the Biesbosch.

Dordttrack: attractive cycle route along the Wantij
image: West 8, IABR–Atelier Dordrecht

In this more accessible Biesbosch, to conclude, the Dordttrack can be connected to existing routes that currently encircle the nature reserve. This will create a 'Wantij lap' which will ingrain in its users that there is a route that, when the need arises, allows them to quickly flee, along now familiar paths, to safer areas outside Dordrecht.

4. SUSTAINABLE PROTOTYPE BUILDING

A fourth research question concerned the combination of living and working. What building type is required to facilitate the best possible mix of start-ups, light maritime industry, dwelling, and recreation and optimally fit the intended sustainable area development, ‘capture’ the desired urban activity in a new and sustainable prototype building with low rents and flexible spaces, and serve as a temporary shelter in case of flooding? And all this while there are people living and working in the building, and experiencing the urban dynamics right from the start?
The location chosen for such a building, the city yard in the Stadswerven district, offers realistic opportunities for a good mix of functions and financing.

EGM architects, a Dordrecht-based office with a lot of expertise in large-scale sustainable building, collaborated, under guidance of Roemer Pierik, with the economists of Dordrecht and builders experienced in maximum standardization. EGM came up with a highly flexible building design for a ‘vertical mini-village’ composed of linkable modules, each of the same size, that would accommodate various resident requirements and functions: from small apartments to schools.

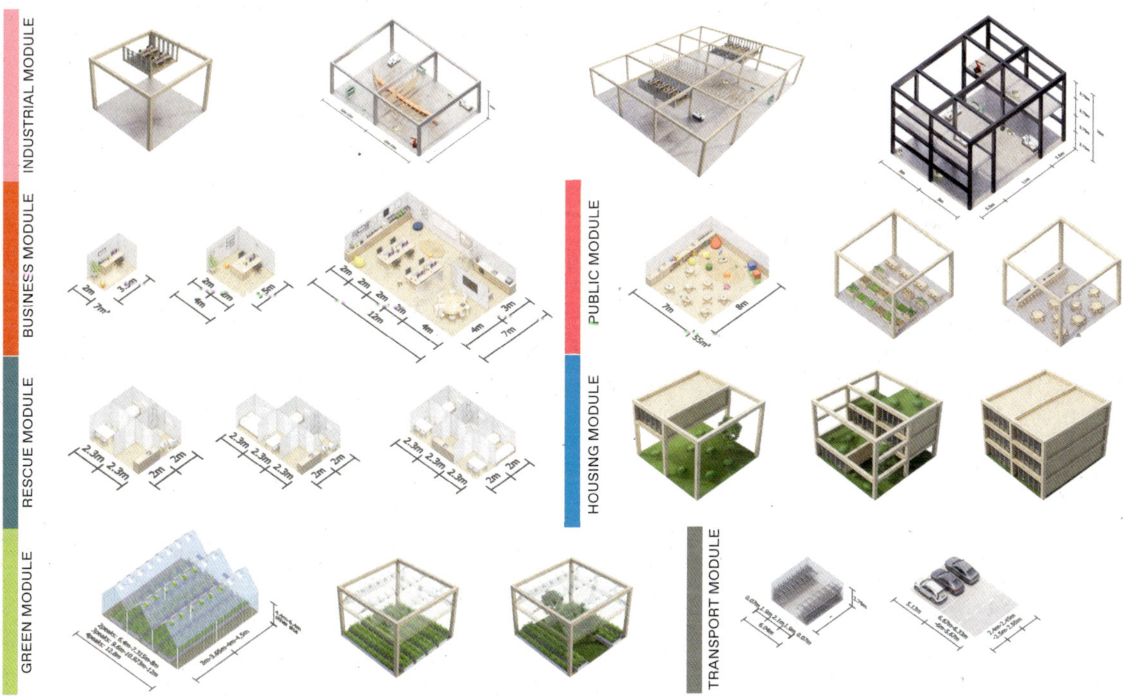

Concept modules for a vertical mini-village
image: EGM architects, IABR–Atelier Dordrecht

The design incorporated the Sustainable Development Goals into the program of requirements as cohesively as possible by combining the focus on affordable and diverse live-work options with vertically distributed main functions including working, living, communal spaces, meeting places and other collective facilities, as well as food and energy production. Community building and self-support capacity were identified as key objectives, also because of the need to accommodate evacuees in times of calamities.

The building's design should allow it to switch quickly from daily use to emergency shelter use. Flexibility and ease of quick access to all floors are crucial. If a flood strikes, it would be able to accommodate evacuees from Dordrecht; its base, square, and roof then provide temporary shelter to some 5,000 people. In extreme circumstances, the building can be both self-supporting and produce energy for its immediate environment for a week.[48]

[48] Research report EGM architects

24-HOUR CIRCULAR USE – SELF-SUPPORTING

images: EGM architects, IABR–Atelier Dordrecht

5. DE GROTE RUG

De Grote Rug, a large reservoir owned by water company Evides, is an emergency basin located on the Staart that is hindered in its operation by its size. It is in need of deepening and halving to reduce blue-green algae and maintenance costs. If this were to happen, De Grote Rug, which is located on the Wantij, near the railroad, would be a potentially interesting location for living on the water. Would it be possible, and if so how, to build a floating city here that would be self-supporting as well as, if necessary, make a suitable shelter?

Faced with this question, urban designer and former government advisor for infrastructure and the city Rients Dijkstra set to work with his office PosadMaxwan. The research by design into a new water city, partly floating, partly directly on the waterfront, aimed to explore a form of urbanization that may well turn out to be the most climate-adaptive one in the Netherlands in the future.
Existing water cities, as PosadMaxwan concluded on the basis of its own research, are often characterized by a uniform public space and low density; they tend to be monofunctional and accessible only to residents. De Grote Rug can distinguish itself by a mixed urban environment with high density and the presence of public functions and open-to-air space. The reservoir can accommodate some 2,500 dwellings, plus work spaces and associated facilities, thus contributing significantly to the solving of Dordrecht's housing challenge. Dordrecht aspires to transition its way into a CO_2-neutral, circular, green, and climate-adaptive future and this requires a different design of the urban environment.

The city's ambitions were included in the design on the basis of the Sustainable Development Goals that focus on sustainability in its full breadth: from social, to ecological, to energetic, to economic sustainability. With these goals in mind, and in the belief that an urban environment is only truly sustainable if people enjoy being there, PosadMaxwan formulated five principles for design in De Grote Rug that prioritize the quality of urban life: integrate residential quality and surrounding aquatic nature, create a

healthy and inclusive community, guarantee climate resilience, adopt a nature-inclusive approach, and commit to knowledge development and education.
To optimally integrate the starting points in the urban design, Posad-Maxwan developed a new urban grid in which every dwelling has outdoor space and maximum contact with the water. A pier structure provides space for rectangular buildings consisting of demountable modules that allow different varieties of both houses and outdoor spaces. This creates a diverse palette of housing types, water-land transitions, aquatic nature, and public spaces. It also makes the district easily accessible: walking, shared mobility, and public transportation are the primary forms of transportation in what primary is to be a city for pedestrians.

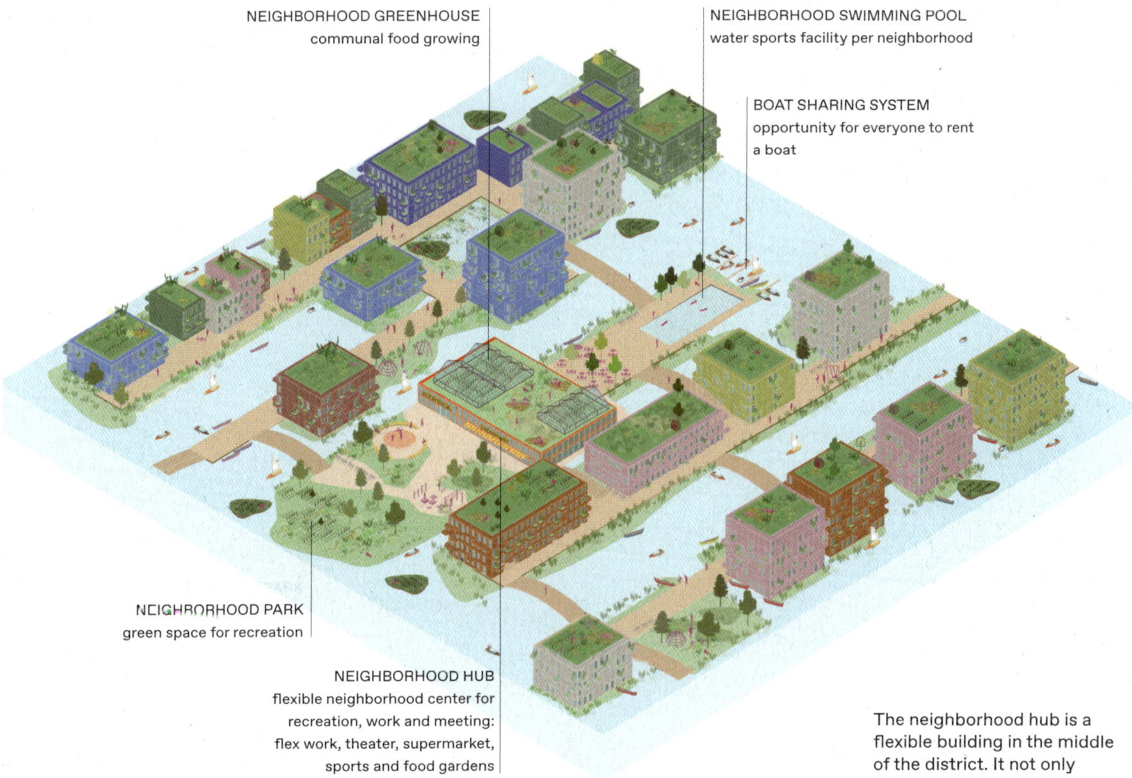

The neighborhood hub is a flexible building in the middle of the district. It not only contains flexible work spaces, a café, and a lending library for all kinds of amenities, but can also be temporarily trans-formed into a sports or cultural venue. The connected green-house and community garden allow for joint cultivation of plants and vegetables. This flexible combination of functions makes the hub the ultimate meeting place for all kinds of neighborhood residents.

images: PosadMaxwan, IABR–Atelier Dordrecht

The creation of a new district comes with opportunities to establish new forms of social cohesion. The collaborating, meeting, and accommodating of various population and income groups are important starting points. Combining different housing types in the residential blocks creates room for diversity at the building level as well: from young people to families and senior citizens.
The floating city consists of three neighborhoods, each with central neighborhood hubs that combine facilities, work spaces, and meeting places. Joint management is the starting point for, among other things, the maintenance of the public space, the availability of shared mobility, and the programming of the neighborhood hubs. The energy supply is managed by the residents as well, and all income is to be invested back into the district.

The application of the five starting points has led to a design of a water city full of nature, with room for (interaction among) various population groups, and powered by renewable energy. The floating city is not only always one step ahead of catastrophic water rise (it moves with the tides of the Wantij and follows the water level in case of flooding; the district therefore remains functional and safe regardless of the water level) but, with an estimated total relief capacity of almost 14,000 evacuees, is also very well suited to serve as a shelter.[49]

[49] Research report PosadMaxwan

Artist's impression of De Grote Rug
image: PosadMaxwan, IABR–Atelier Dordrecht

The Sustainable Development Goals and the Map of Opportunities for the Staart

Adriaan Geuze and West 8 used the results of the five studies to create the next in-depth, integrated systems analysis to provide a clear picture of the possible future sustainable development of the Staart and the goals that an ambitious city such as Dordrecht *could* want to achieve in the area.[50]

[50] Research report West 8

Map of Opportunities for the Staart
THE HIGH GROUND
photo: Aad Hoogendoorn

Developing his systems analysis, Geuze paid extra attention to those Sustainable Development Goals on which, although they are currently not being very intensively pursued in the Netherlands, urban design and landscape can have a lot of impact, for example when sustainable energy and nature management become equal partners in new area developments on both land and water. The research process that took place in collaboration with the partners Rijkswaterstaat, Delft University of Technology, and INTERREG North Sea Region[51] also included an assessment. Dordrecht's Structural Vision 2040 was taken as the zero point. The SDGs used as criteria in the assessment were chosen with the help of an expert group that included representatives of the Staart. The Map of Opportunities of the IABR–Atelier proved a significant improvement over the structural vision (85 percent versus 71 percent of the maximum score), but the test also made it clear that social aspects required more attention. In the Dutch context, it was particularly striking how much more could be gained if spatial policy paid explicit attention to the SDGs 2 (zero hunger), 10 (reduced inequalities) and 16 (peace, justice, and strong institutions). 'Ensure women's full and effective participation,' for example: while West 8 had initially (reflexively) designed playgrounds that were primarily attractive to boys, it turned out that the Staart actually needed more playgrounds for girls, to encourage them to play outside more often.

[51] Under the banner of the EU INTERREG NSR program, C5a, the Cluster for Cloud to Coast Climate Change Adaptation project, is developing an integrated approach to climate adaptation through flood risk management. The Staart in Dordrecht is one of seven case studies in six countries whose interrelatedness should ensure that C5a leads to an approach that is both evidence-based and practicable.

This means the SDGs also guided the development of the program of requirements. As part of the integrated design and planning process, they contributed substantially to the systems analysis and the Map of Opportunities for the Staart, which Geuze subsequently worked out in more detail and which would eventually be displayed at the biennale, as part of the exhibition THE HIGH GROUND.[52]

[52] Also see page 299 ff.

For this exhibition, the Map of Opportunities was also translated into a large overview model that showed all of the urban design explorations and highlighted the results of the five substudies. This model would form the heart of the exhibition and then continue to function as a publicly accessible visualization of the city's future around which all parties involved in the further area development of the Staart could exchange ideas and plans in the years to come.

Ready for the Staart . . . Go!

By then it was clear to all stakeholders that on the Staart, Dordrecht would be able to have its cake and eat it too: increase water safety while building housing and stimulating employment, optimizing connections in the city and with the region, realizing a more sustainable energy supply, and improving the quality of life and recreational opportunities for all residents. The Staart is an extremely interesting area to develop, not only as a flood refuge area, but also *in itself.*

The results of the IABR–Atelier study were received enthusiastically by both the Safety Region and the Dordrecht Municipal Executive. Soon, 'Ready for the Staart . . . go!' became a rallying cry.

The city adapted the existing Environmental Vision. From that moment on, the Staart, which had been divided into four different areas, was conceived as a single area for which a separate integrated vision must be developed, building on, among other things, the research results of the IABR–Atelier. To be able to better map out the long term, the Staart became the subject of further research in the context of two interdisciplinary research programs, Rethink the Delta (conducted by Deltares together with Delft University of Technology and Erasmus University, among others) and Red & Blue, in which research institutions, governments, and private parties are jointly mapping the risk assessments of and solutions to the consequences of the climate crisis.

What Can Be Done, Must Be Done

But how are all of these proposals supposed to come to fruition? After all, the biennale is not a means to merely present a beckoning perspective, this was not enough for the IABR, nor for Dordrecht. DOWN TO EARTH was supposed to be the launching pad for a real working agenda. Because what *can* be done, *must* be done.

To ensure that everyone, and especially those directly involved, could become familiar with the results, this to optimize the plans' chances of realization, the complete output of the IABR–Atelier was not presented in

Ready for the Staart!
Opening of the exhibition THE HIGH GROUND
photo: Aad Hoogendoorn

Rotterdam, but on the Staart itself – in the Biesboschhal, in the summer of 2021. This also made it possible for the DOWN TO EARTH exhibition THE HIGH GROUND to become part of the great Saint Elizabeth's Flood commemoration in Dordrecht.
The curator, George Brugmans, built the exhibition around the large overview model of the Staart, which he placed on a raised stage, its floor covered by a huge aerial photo of Dordrecht and its surroundings. Presentations of the five substudies and the Map of Opportunities were positioned around the stage. The overview model allowed visitors to zoom in on the smallest details and literally walk around on the Staart and discuss the plans with other visitors, while at the same time it made it impossible to lose sight of the regional water challenge – one look at the floor sufficed, it was easy to imagine getting one's feet wet.
The exhibition was thus primarily an invitation to discuss how to start work on the Staart, and with whom. And this exchange process began immediately on 2 July 2021, when THE HIGH GROUND opened with a closed meeting due to the pandemic called 'Klaar voor de Staart' (Ready for the Staart), especially for administrators and commissioners. [53]

However, the involvement and enthusiasm of the residents of the Staart itself are the most important prerequisites for successful realization. THE HIGH GROUND, the final exhibition of DOWN TO EARTH, took place in the summer of 2021, at a time when the pandemic still prevailed, but pressure was already subsiding. This is why it was possible to organize regular small gatherings in the spacious Biesboschhal, in which the plans presented during the exhibition were held up to the light of possible realization in all sorts of different settings – from workshops with specialists, to numerous guided tours with residents of the Staart.

[53] During 'Ready for the Staart,' Dordrecht councilors Piet Sleeking and Marco Stam, South Holland provincial executive Jeannette Baljeu, Delta Commissioner Peter Glas and representatives of Rijkswaterstaat, Staatsbosbeheer, Water Boards, Delft University of Technology and the business community, among others, welcomed the plans for the Staart. In conclusion, Special Envoy for International Water Affairs Henk Ovink remarked that 99 times out of 100, area development leads to additional climate challenges, and that 'this should be reduced to 1 out of 100 times.' According to Ovink, the results and proposals of the IABR–Atelier show that this is possible, and how it would create added social value.

The city decided to leave the exhibition in the Biesboschhal until well into 2022 and that is why the dialogue between the city and residents and other stakeholders could continue long after the biennale.

And also later on, the large model will remain publicly accessible at another, central location in the city. Together with the province of South Holland, Dordrecht can thus continue to involve residents, organizations, and entrepreneurs, step by step and in productive dialogue, in the realization of the plans for the improvement of their own residential and living environment on the Staart.

Residents of the Staart in conversation with representatives of the City of Dordrecht
THE HIGH GROUND
© City of Dordrecht

CREDITS

The IABR–Atelier Dordrecht (2019–2021) was a collaboration of the IABR and the City of Dordrecht.

STEERING COMMITTEE
George Brugmans, president IABR
Henk Kranendonk, director of Urban Development, City of Dordrecht

LEAD DESIGNER
Adriaan Geuze, founding director West 8

RESEARCH BY DESIGN
EGM architects
Roemer Pierik, Zita Balajti, Pieter Korstanje, Ádám Petróczki, Heidi Sairanen, Iris de Baat, Edwin van de Velde, Wanja van Zoest

PosadMaxwan
Rients Dijkstra, Gijs de Haan, Ada Jaskowiec, Emma de Haan, Cateau Albers, Lisa Gerards, Gianluca Berardi, Laura Thomas

Studio Donna van Milligen Bielke
Donna van Milligen Bielke, Ard de Vries

VenhoevenCS architecture+urbanism
Ton Venhoeven, Martijn Tjassens Keiser, Eliza Mante, Nicolò Santini, Shuxin Chi

West 8
Adriaan Geuze, Marco van der Pluym, Aditya Athreya Rao

Eindhoven University of Technology, Faculty of Architecture, Chair Architectural Design and Engineering
students: Melvin Driessen, Kyra Heijblom, Srilekha Iyyappan, Maartje de Kleijn, Carolina Menegon Nossig, Emma Schoonhoven, Karolina Szczepara, Annabel Tielemans
lecturers: Irene Curulli, Tom Veeger

PROJECT TEAM DORDRECHT
Ellen Kelder, Berry Gersonius, Edwin van Son, Rik Heinen

PRODUCTION AND PLANNING IABR
Johanna Fuhler, Vivian Ammerlaan

WE THANK THE FOLLOWING PEOPLE FOR THEIR CRITICAL REFLECTION AND/OR THEIR CONTRIBUTION
Han Bakker, Bas Kolen, Duco Hoogland, Marcel Knapen, Anouk Ros, Cor Schipper, Esmée te Velde, Stanford Wilson, Niek de Wit

The IABR–Ateliers were initiated and produced under the direction of George Brugmans from 2008 to 2021, both at home and abroad. The IABR produced a number of IABR–Ateliers in the Netherlands, including the IABR–Atelier Rotterdam, as lead partner of the Dutch National Government in the framework of the Action Agendas for Spatial Design, the ARO 2013–2016 of the Ministry of Infrastructure and the Environment and the ARO 2017–2020 of the Ministry of the Interior and Kingdom Relations.

DOWN TO EARTH

THE HIGH GROUND

CURATOR
George Brugmans

3 July – 14 August 2021
Biesboschhal, Dordrecht

THE HIGH GROUND
IABR—DOWN TO EARTH

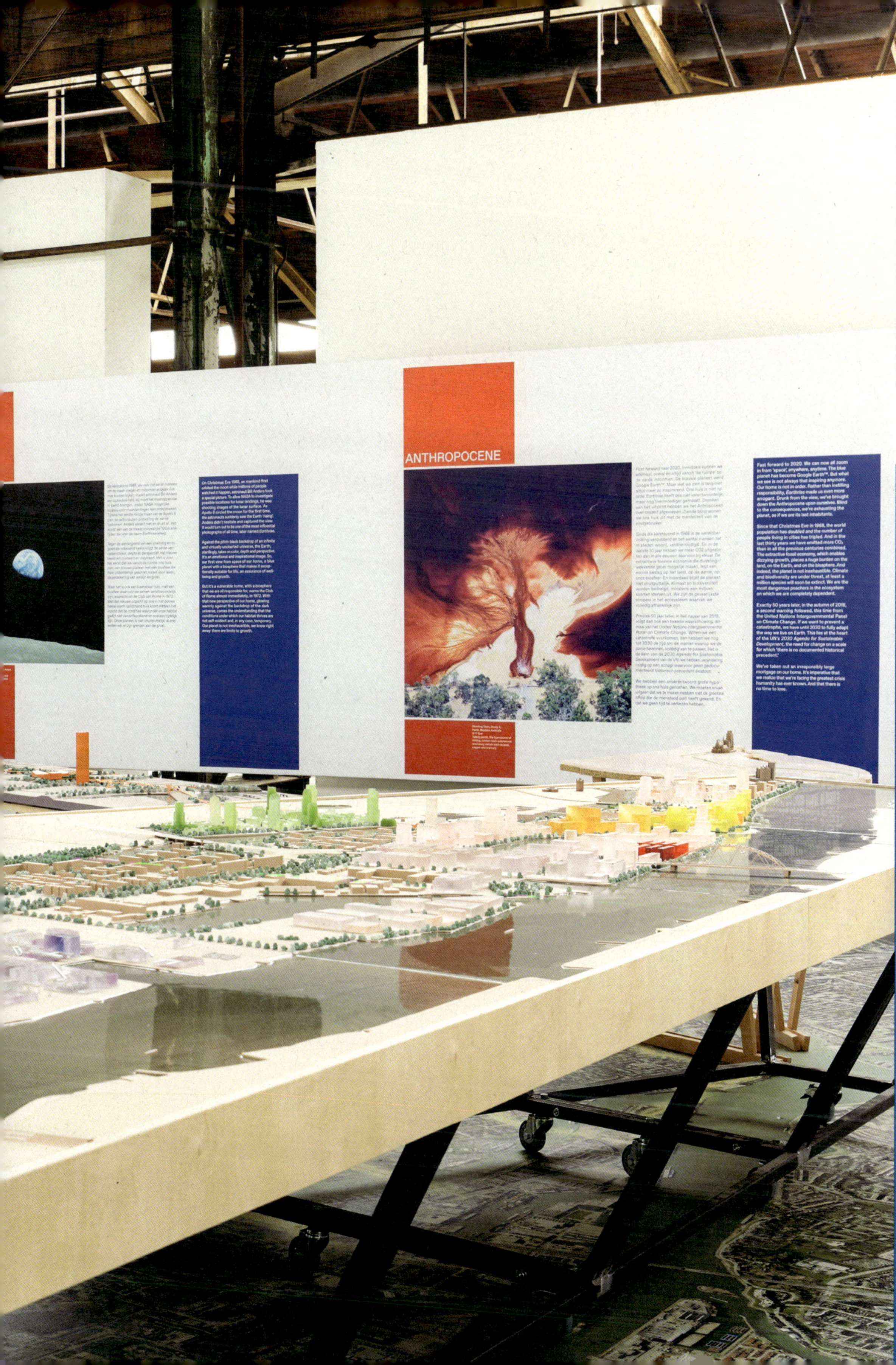
On Christmas Eve 1968, as mankind first orbited the moon while millions of people watched it happen, astronaut Bill Anders took a special picture. To allow NASA to investigate possible locations for lunar landings, he was shooting images of the lunar surface. As Apollo 8 circled the moon for the first time, the astronauts suddenly saw the Earth 'rising'. Anders didn't hesitate and captured the view. It would turn out to be one of the most influential photographs of all time, later named Earthrise.
Against the pitch-black backdrop of an infinite and virtually uncharted universe, the Earth, startlingly, takes on color, depth and perspective. It's an emotional and inspirational image. So, our first view from space of our home, a blue planet with a biosphere that makes it exceptionally suitable for life, an assurance of well-being and growth.
But it's a vulnerable home, with a biosphere that we are all responsible for, warns the Club of Rome almost immediately, in 1972. With that new perspective of our home, glowing warmly against the backdrop of the dark universe, comes the understanding that the conditions under which our habitat thrives are not self-evident and, in any case, temporary. Our planet is not inexhaustible, we know right away: there are limits to growth.
ANTHROPOCENE
Fast forward to 2020. We can now all zoom in from 'space', anywhere, anytime. The blue planet has become Google Earth™. But what we see is not always that inspiring anymore. Our home is not in order. Rather than instilling responsibility, Earthrise made us even more arrogant. Drunk from the view, we've brought down the Anthropocene upon ourselves. Blind to the consequences, we're exhausting the planet, as if we are its last inhabitants.
Since that Christmas Eve in 1968, the world population has doubled and the number of people living in cities has tripled. And in the last thirty years we have emitted more CO2 than in all the previous centuries combined. The extractive fossil economy, which enables dizzying growth, places a huge burden on the land, on the Earth, and on the biosphere. And indeed, the planet is not inexhaustible. Climate and biodiversity are under threat, at least a million species will soon be extinct. We are the most dangerous poachers in the ecosystem on which we are completely dependent.
Exactly 50 years later, in the autumn of 2018, a second warning followed, this time from the United Nations Intergovernmental Panel on Climate Change. If we want to prevent a catastrophe, we have until 2030 to fully adapt the way we live on Earth. This lies at the heart of the UN's 2030 Agenda for Sustainable Development, the need for change on a scale for which 'there is no documented historical precedent.'
We've taken out an irresponsibly large mortgage on our home. It's imperative that we realize that we're facing the greatest crisis humanity has ever known. And that there is no time to lose.

THE HIGH GROUND

CURATOR INTRODUCTION

In 2021 it was 600 years ago that Dordrecht was struck by what was perhaps the greatest flood disaster in the history of the Low Countries: the Saint Elizabeth's Flood. It made the city into an island, which to this day is very vulnerable to flooding. So water safety is clearly of the highest possible priority.

Water Safety as Leverage

Over a period of two years, the IABR–Atelier Dordrecht has investigated how the *future need* for self-sufficiency in the event of a major flood can be deployed in the search for an answer to the *current challenge* of sustainable urban development: How can water safety be used as leverage?

The results of the Atelier's research make clear that the Staart – now an isolated area with many problems and few prospects – can play an unexpectedly important role in realizing the Dordrecht water safety agenda. If water safety is wielded as leverage to accomplish sustainable and inclusive urban development, opportunities suddenly arise. Indeed, this approach requires that there be always flexible space on the Staart, to make it possible to quickly realize the extra square meters needed for peak absorption in the event of a disaster. By making room in the design process for the accommodation of evacuees and other emergency facilities, a city can be created where people not only live and work, but where there is also plenty of room for recreation, education and other public facilities, both through a different approach at the building level and in the outdoor areas. The leverage approach also requires that the Staart is always easily and quickly accessible. This calls for new, good connections in and with the city, and between the city and the region. It also facilitates access to greenery and water. The Wantij can be laid out as a Tidal Park: beneficial for nature, for recreation, and for the quality of life on the Staart. And living on the water, in and with space for nature, becomes a serious option.

Dordrecht has the opportunity to hit many pins with one ball: increase water safety and *at the same time* build housing and stimulate employment, optimize connections in the city and with the region, and improve the quality of life and recreational opportunities for all of its inhabitants. Thanks to the *water-safety-as-leverage* approach, a map of opportunities for the Staart reads like an unmistakable invitation to seriously and actually contribute to the *Growth Agenda Drechtsteden 2030* and the sustainability ambitions of Dordrecht.

←
THE HIGH GROUND
photo: Aad Hoogendoorn

THE FUTURE CAN START RIGHT NOW

Anyone who wants to understand the Staart, must see the island through the lens of its industrial history, which, to this day, results in high CO_2 emissions and serious noise and soil pollution. It's partly because of this that living and working are strictly separated. The existing residential neighborhoods are monotonous and introverted. Collective facilities and anchor points for a (climate) inclusive society are lacking.

However, the Map of Opportunities created by Adriaan Geuze, lead designer of IABR–Atelier Dordrecht, shows that the unique location of the Staart, on relatively high ground and surrounded by water, situated right next to the Biesbosch, also offers myriad possibilities. The area can start functioning as a new, sustainable living environment and as a refuge in the event of (water) emergencies.

The *water-safety-as-leverage* approach calls for a focus on the outdoor space, on prioritizing blue-green components, and good connections – on creating a flexible, sustainable, socially inclusive, and climate-adaptive framework for the development of the Staart.

First and foremost, the Staart needs to be lifted out of its isolation. Over and along the *getijdenwater*, the southern bank of the Wantij, new connections will provide slow traffic and pedestrians with direct access to and from the inner city, and open up the area's crown jewel, the Biesbosch. The Wantij Tidal Park and the Dordttrack are the backbone of this development. They provide accessible, nature-friendly banks that can function as an evacuation route in the event of a catastrophe. New urban meeting places will be created along the waterfront, directly linked to various neighborhoods: pavilion De Staart, sawmill Nachtegaal and an urban beach. The water banks will also be improved so that the unique biodiversity of the Biesbosch has a chance to flourish.
The Staart will then be transformed into a mixed and vital live-work area in various urban densities and with a twenty-first-century spectrum of subcultures, work locations, building types, and forms of dwelling; it is cooperative, collective, and individual, down to earth and amphibious. Renewable energy, such as solar and wind energy, is combined with aquathermal energy from the Wantij. Circularity is a condition. The future can start right now.

Map of Opportunities for the Staart

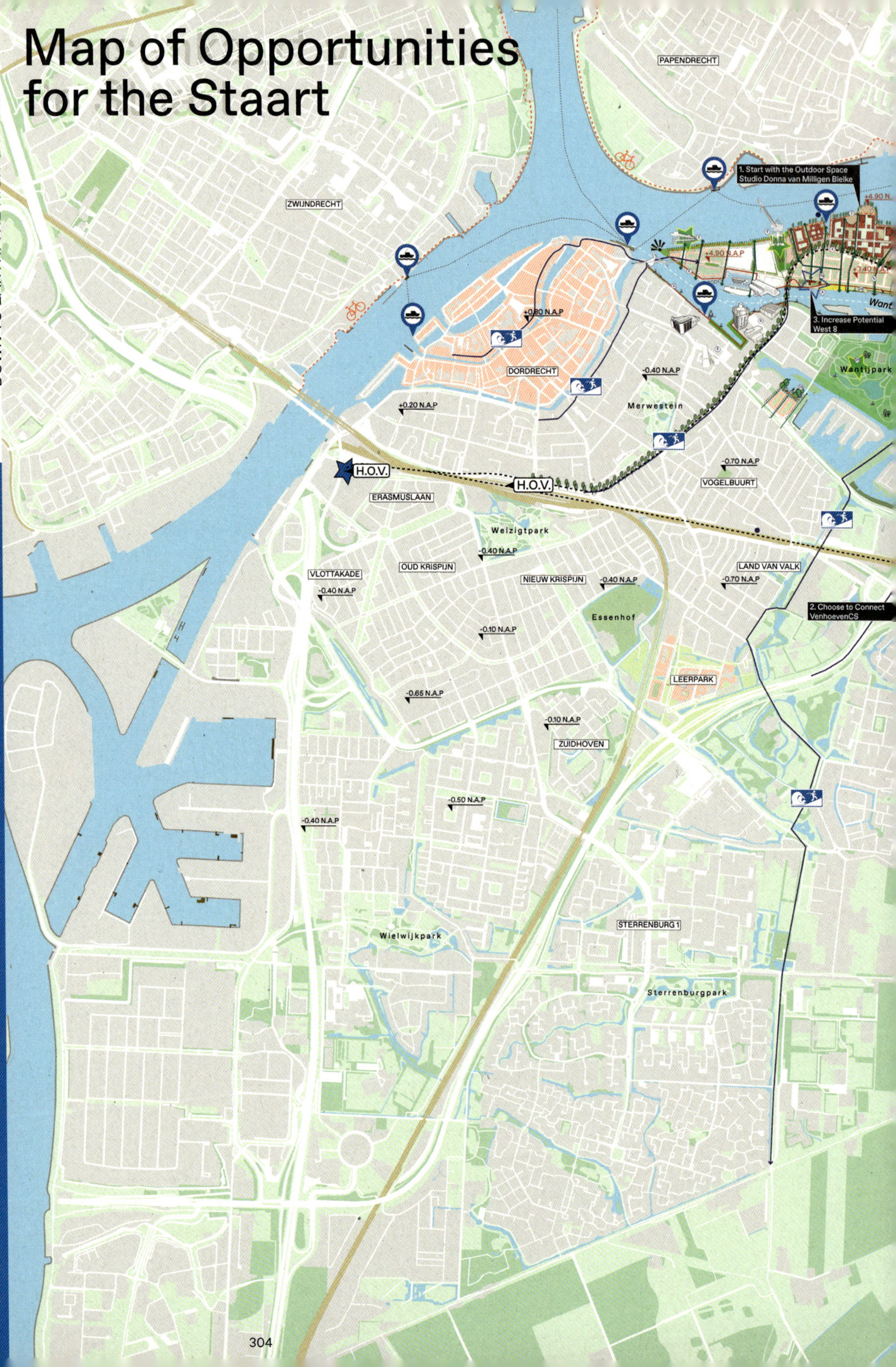

Flexibility
Wantij
SLIEDRECHT
H.O.V.
+4.90 N.A.P
+3.50 N.A.P
PARK BIESBOSCH
+26.20 N.A.P
+32.50 N.A.P
5. Live on the Water
PosadMaxwan
3. Dordttrack
West 8
0.00 N.A.P
IROKO
flushing of swimming lake
helophytes willow filter
AMAZONE
-0.10 N.A.P
PALISSANDER
-0.70 N.A.P
-0.60 N.A.P
widening of watercourse and connecting Biesbosch centres
connecting city's polders
-0.30 N.A.P
DUBBELDAM
facilitate long, recreational routes
-0.60 N.A.P below Amsterdam Ordnance Datum (N.A.P.), the Staart
+3.40 N.A.P above Amsterdam Ordnance Datum (N.A.P.), Dordrecht
tidal nature
national ecological network
connecting green zones
connect Wantij and neighborhood
proposed additional water structure
proposal for a bridge
continuous recreational route along the Merwede
Dordttrack
evacuation route
existing ferry connection
proposal for a ferry connection
iconic buildings
H.O.V. high-quality public transportation, and innovative passenger transport over water
ferry stop
Westergoot marina
park
willows
wet/marshy banks
increase biodiversity
lookout point
healthy in nature
campsite
Biesbosch center
active sports in nature
transferium (P+R)
evacuation station as second function
specials in the Wantijpark
landmarks

SLIEDRECHT
PARK BIESBOSCH
flushing of swimming lake
helophytes willow filter
Beneden-Merwede beach route
Shortcut
Biesboschroute
widening of watercourse and connecting Biesbosch centres
connecting city's polders
Nieuwe-Merwederoute
facilitate long, recreational routes
PARK BIESBOSCH

NEDER-HARDINXVELD
BOVEN-HARDIVNXVELD
PARK BIESBOSCH
Spotters area
Spotters area
TSE BIESBOSCH
WERKENDAM
-0.60 N.A.P
below Amsterdam Ordnance Datum (N.A.P.), the Staart
+3.40 N.A.P
above Amsterdam Ordnance Datum (N.A.P.), Dordrecht
tidal nature
national ecological network
connecting green zones
connect Wantij and neighborhood
proposed additional water structure
proposal for a bridge
continuous recreational route along the Merwede
Dordttrack
evacuation route
existing ferry connection
proposal for a ferry connection
iconic buildings
H.O.V.
high-quality public transportation, and innovative passenger transport over water
ferry stop
Westelgoot marina
park
willows
wet/marshy banks
increase biodiversity
lookout point
healthy in nature
campsite
Biesbosch center
active sports in nature
transferium (P+R)
evacuation station as second function
specials in the Wantijpark
landmarks

THE STAART AS MOTOR

The model of the Staart, scale 1:1000, demonstrates how the Map of Opportunities, based on West 8's systems analysis, and the five different design studies land in the area.

Placing this model on an aerial photograph of the whole of Dordrecht and its immediate surroundings clearly showed that the proposed interventions in and around the Staart, at different scales and always in cohesion, will cause a new dynamic, from the city center to the Biesbosch. With the Staart as the driving force, a distinctly conceivable three-dimensional future image emerges of what Dordrecht *can* realize if water safety is wielded as a lever.

Overview model of the Staart
THE HIGH GROUND
photo: Aad Hoogendoorn

←
THE HIGH GROUND
photo: Aad Hoogendoorn

WHAT NEEDS TO BE DONE AND WHAT CAN BE WON

Five Studies

After the IABR–Atelier Dordrecht conducted a systems analysis and mapped the opportunities for leveraging water safety on the Staart, it commissioned five research by design studies. While water safety was the premise, the integral, sustainable, and socially inclusive urban development of the area was always the main objective. The design offices were also asked to incorporate all of the United Nations' Sustainable Development Goals in the design process from the beginning.

Studio Donna van Milligen Bielke, which researches urbanity and the use of the city, suggested a different approach to outdoor space that keeps the existing character of Dordrecht intact. The infrastructure experts of VenhoevenCS designed an easily identifiable and climate-adaptive escape route that functions in everyday use as a new connection between the inner city, the Staart, and the Biesbosch. The urban designers and landscape architects of West 8 argued for new green structures and a Dordttrack to connect existing developments on the Staart and the Wantij-Merwede and to stimulate biodiversity. A new type of building by EGM, expert in large-scale sustainable construction, sought the optimally flexible mix of different forms of collective living and working. And PosadMaxwan, an urban design office with a future agenda, responded to the threat of flooding by conceiving an innovative form of living on water.

Each study was presented by means of a video animation and a (series of) scale model(s), in which the relationship between the *desired* everyday use and the *necessary* use in times of flooding, between what needs be done and what can be won, was made clear.

1. Start with the Outdoor Space

STUDIO DONNA VAN MILLIGEN BIELKE (DVMB)

Wielding water safety as a lever and putting the Sustainable Development Goals at the heart of the program of requirements means that designing a multifunctional, high-density city has to start with designing the outdoor space.

That conclusion arose from the research by design carried out by Studio Donna van Milligen Bielke and Ard de Vries Architecten into what type of urbanization such an approach could yield for the Staart. The development of the outdoor space has to be leading in this case precisely because it must have a double function. On a daily basis it will be used as public space, with all the specific qualities required for that purpose. But in the event of flooding that same space has to transform quickly and efficiently into an effective infrastructure for evacuation.

[54] video *Start with the Outdoor Space*

MODEL
Studio Donna van Milligen Bielke
with Ard de Vries Architecten

→
Every city has its own unique character. The urban fabric determines the atmosphere and success of a city, and public space plays a crucial role in this. In Dordrecht, the public space has a dual function: in daily use as a pleasant place to stay, in the event of a disaster as infrastructure for evacuation.
photo: Aad Hoogendoorn

Dordrecht Waterproof

EINDHOVEN UNIVERSITY OF TECHNOLOGY

Today's students belong to the generation that has to find solutions to the major climate problems. Taking their cue from the IABR–Atelier Dordrecht, master students of architecture from Eindhoven University of Technology therefore delved into the water challenges that Dordrecht is facing. They took the research of DVMB, the study *Start with the Outdoor Space*, as their point of departure but pursued their own architectural elaboration. Rising water levels and potential flooding threaten the lives of the residents and the future development of the city. To build an effective response, the students explored new and alternative ways to address the problems in a truly resilient manner. After analysis and research, they created three master plans that could be used to prepare the Staart for future flooding. In addition, each student chose a specific location to integrate the world of living and working in a hybrid building complex that provides security against rising water.

MASTER STUDIO: DORDRECHT WATERPROOF
Eindhoven University of Technology, Faculty of Architecture, Urbanism and Building Sciences, Chair of Architectural Design and Engineering

photo: Aad Hoogendoorn

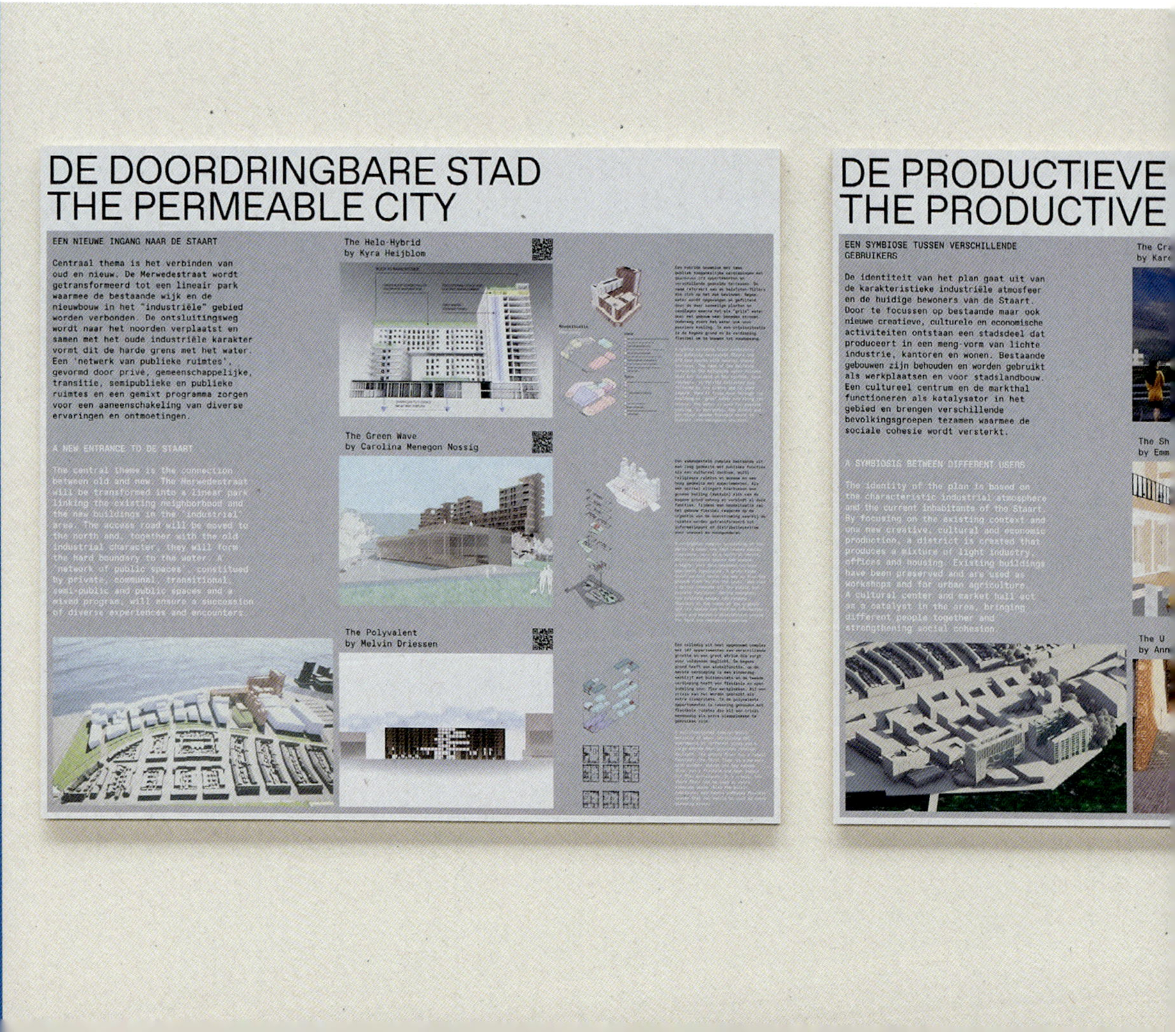

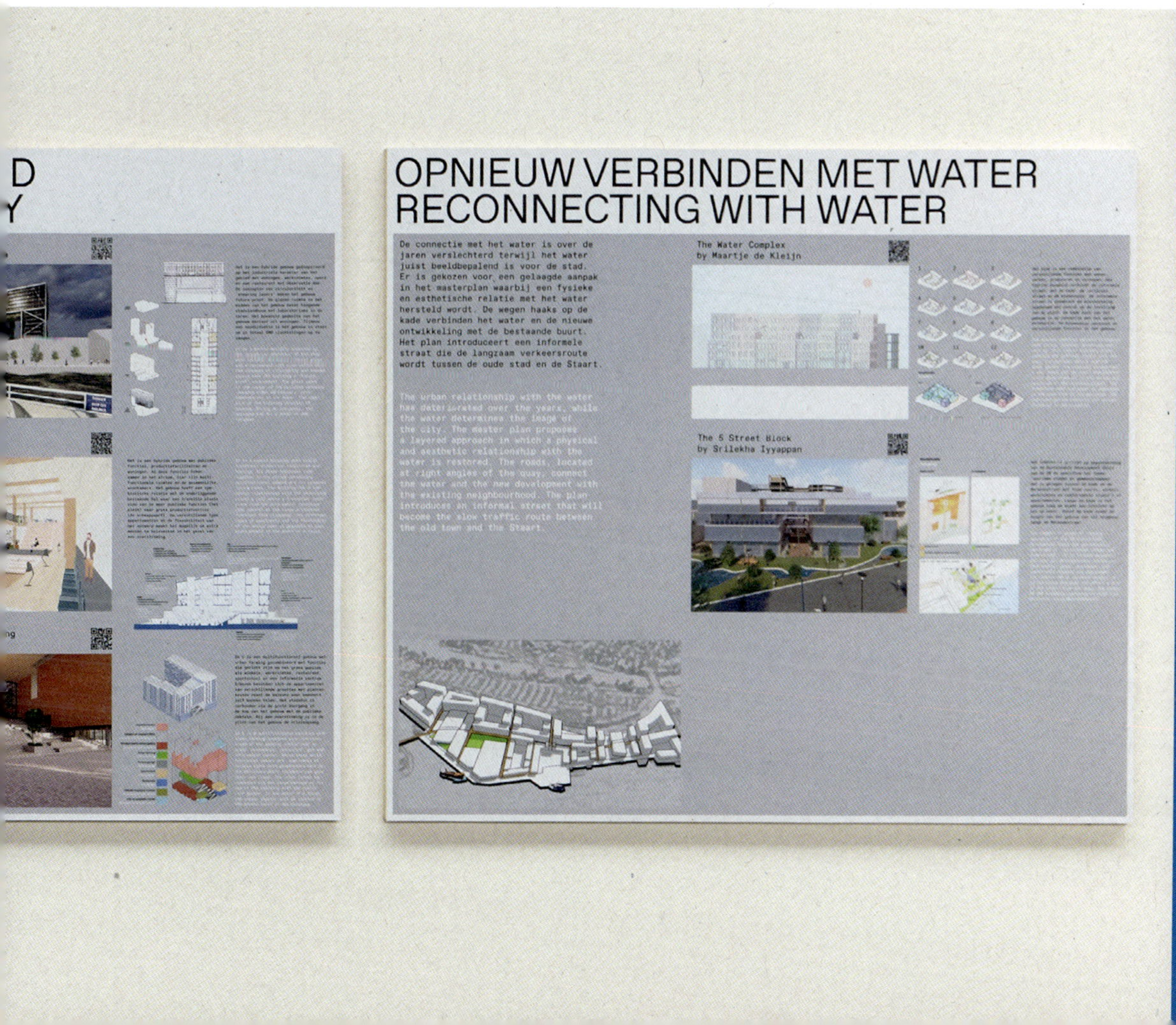
OPNIEUW VERBINDEN MET WATER
RECONNECTING WITH WATER
De connectie met het water is over de jaren verslechterd terwijl het water juist beeldbepalend is voor de stad. Er is gekozen voor een gelaagde aanpak in het masterplan waarbij een fysieke en esthetische relatie met het water hersteld wordt. De wegen haaks op de kade verbinden het water en de nieuwe ontwikkeling met de bestaande buurt. Het plan introduceert een informele straat die de langzaam verkeersroute wordt tussen de oude stad en de Staart.
The urban relationship with the water has deteriorated over the years, while the water determines the image of the city. The master plan proposes a layered approach in which a physical and aesthetic relationship with the water is restored. The roads, located at right angles of the quay, connect the water and the new development with the existing neighbourhood. The plan introduces an informal street that will become the slow traffic route between the old town and the Staart.
The Water Complex
by Maartje de Kleijn
The 5 Street Block
by Srilekha Iyyappan

2. Choose to Connect

VENHOEVENCS ARCHITECTURE+URBANISM

The *water-safety-as-leverage* approach emphasizes the need for good connections because, in case of emergency, evacuees must always be able to access the Staart quickly, albeit not by car. The IABR–Atelier therefore proposes the construction of three new bridges across the Wantij. This would improve accessibility to the Staart for slow traffic and lift the area out of its current isolation.

Design office VenhoevenCS's research focused on what this means for the mobility system. They recommend the establishment of a new, very recognizable route to better connect the Staart with the rest of Dordrecht. In case of a disaster, it can function as a safe and familiar escape route for everyone. New facilities along the route, such as a theater or a mobility hub, can function as a first refuge hub for evacuees in the event of a disaster, whereas they serve as connecting elements in the everyday urban fabric. Integrating the route into the new Stadspark XL creates a scenic connection with the Dordtse Biesbosch. The slender construction, built with sustainable materials, creates an attractive alternative to car traffic with new, direct connections that remove existing barriers in the city. In this way, slow traffic in Dordrecht becomes fast, and facilities in neighborhoods linked to the route become more accessible.

[55] video *Choose to Connect*

MODELS
Studio KU+

The raised climate-adaptive escape route forms a special cycling and walking route through the treetops of Stadspark XL, provides safety after a flood, bridges barriers in the city and connects the Staart across the Wantij to the city.
photo: Aad Hoogendoorn

→
photos: Studio KU+

3. Increase Potential

WEST 8

From the perspective of water safety, fast connections are not only needed in the urban area of Dordrecht itself.
Design office West 8 therefore proposed a new recreational (cycling) route, the Dordttrack, that will run from the center of Dordrecht across the Staart to the city of Gorinchem, connecting various locations in the region.
Thanks to this increase in scale, neighborhood centers acquire an urban importance as well. For example, a community center could be transformed into a pavilion with a beach that can be visited from anywhere in the region. Biodiversity too can be given more priority. Sloping banks make the water more accessible and expand the recreational possibilities: the Wantij becomes the ultimate playground.
Small-scale recreational areas can be given a second function thanks to the *water-safety-as-leverage* approach. This not only increases their appeal and potential for everyday use, but during an evacuation they can be used as crucial central distribution hubs that many people will already know how to find relatively easily.

[56] video *Increase Potential*

MODELS
West 8

←
Choose to Connect
THE HIGH GROUND
photo: Aad Hoogendoorn

Sawmill Nachtegaal: a meeting place for residents of and visitors to the Staart that also organizes activities for youths and training programs and provides space for the care of senior citizens.

District Pavilion: the existing community center has been expanded into pavilion De Staart, with iconic outdoor spaces such as a wave deck and a city beach, which allow direct contact with the water.

Griendrobot: an autonomous, electric, waterborne agricultural machine that cuts willows with a gripper suspended from a bridge and then unloads the willow twigs onto electric boats.

photos: Aad Hoogendoorn

4. Build for Flexibility

EGM ARCHITECTS

The IABR–Atelier made an analysis at the level of the city and of the district, but also conducted research at the building level. To turn the Staart into a high-density urban area with numerous additional functions, that is also able to serve as a temporary refuge in the event of an emergency, requires a flexible building type.

EGM architects proposed a multifunctional and energy-neutral building that can be produced economically and quickly. This sustainable building is attractive to different types of residents. It is composed of different modules, a standard unit can be divided, combined, and expanded in different ways, to facilitate different living needs. The multifunctional base is ideal for start-up companies, as rents can remain low. Above the base, space has been reserved that can be filled with public functions, also for people from the neighborhood who don't live or work in the building, while a large number of evacuees can be accommodated here in times of flooding. Inside are a market square and meeting places, among other things, and the green roof offers space for urban farming. The result is a rich and diverse live-work complex that facilitates cooperation and community, also in times of catastrophe.

57 video *Build for Flexibility*

MODEL
Made by Mistake

The prototype of the new live-work building: on the first floor the startups, on the second floor the public space that can be programmed with a community program, above it flexible housing and on the roof, space for urban farming. photos: Aad Hoogendoorn

5. Live on the Water

POSADMAXWAN

Because of climate change and urbanization, we are facing new spatial challenges in urban environments: there's a shortage of housing, our lifestyles contribute to excessive CO_2 emissions, and the risk of flooding is on the rise in waterfront cities.
With the design for a floating city in the former De Grote Rug reservoir, design office PosadMaxwan investigated how development on the water can contribute to sustainable urbanization and at the same time create a unique living environment. Whereas current water districts are often inaccessible, low-density residential enclaves, Water City De Grote Rug distinguishes itself by a mix of functions, attractive public spaces, and buildings of up to six stories high constructed sustainably of wood and floating on dismountable polystyrene modules. Energy is generated by water and wind, and rainwater is collected for use in the homes. Transportation is by foot over a dense network of piers and by means of a public, electric shared-boat system. Space for cars is unneeded, so that high density can be combined with green, biodiverse outdoor space. Centrally located in each neighborhood is a hub where amenities, vegetable gardens, and workplaces are shared, so that a sustainable, inclusive community can emerge on the water.

58 video *Live on the Water*

DRAWING
Merel Corduwener

Living on the water in the floating city De Grote Rug: surrounded by nature, accessible via self-propelled shared boats, and powered by energy from sun and water.

→
THE HIGH GROUND
photo: Aad Hoogendoorn

THE HIGH GROUND

LEVERS FOR
CHANGE

STRONG GIRLS

CREDITS
THE HIGH GROUND

CURATOR
George Brugmans

MODEL THE STAART
West 8
Adriaan Geuze, Marco van der Pluym,
Harry van Oorschot, Aditya Rao
Made by Mistake
Lukas Kropp, Dick Sman, Lia Zondag,
Brandon Zuijderwijk

please note, the credits for the research by design by the IABR–Atelier Dordrecht can be found on page 297

CURATOR ASSISTANTS
Alexandra Sonnemans, Noortje Weenink

GRAPHIC DESIGN
ARK
Roosje Klap, Nóra Békés, Nina van Tuikwerd

PRODUCTION AND PLANNING
Johanna Fuhler, Maartje Berendsen

PROGRAM AND GUIDED TOURS
Ellen Kelder, Berry Gersonius

SITE MANAGEMENT
Wouter Sieuwerts, Rosalie de Paepe

COPY-EDITING AND TRANSLATIONS
InOtherWords translation & editing
D'laine Camp, Gerda ten Cate, Maria van Tol

CONSTRUCTION
Bart Cuppens Tentoonstellingsbouw

PRINTING
Rocka Art & Sign
IVA Groep

←
THE HIGH GROUND
photo: Aad Hoogendoorn

WHERE CAN WE LAND?

SPACESHIP EARTH
George Brugmans
1: The Embarkment

They took all the trees put 'em in a tree museum
And they charged the people a dollar and a half just to see 'em
Don't it always seem to go
That you don't know what you've got till it's gone
They paved paradise and put up a parking lot
Ooh, bop-bop-bop-bop, ooh, bop-bop-bop-bop!

Joni Mitchell

[01]
In an unguarded moment, as they walked across the gangplank and embarked, burning with a longing for gold and silver, the first of us slipped from the Holocene into the Anthropocene – the *segundos* as the Spaniards called them, the second sons who, yearning for their share, along with their cronies, *padres* and domestiques, set out to conquer the new world. There, treasures awaited them. There – they just knew it – were seven cities made of pure gold. All aboard!

[02]
The Earth had been conveniently flat and motionless for a very long time. Also, man had been drawing courage from the stable and human-friendly Holocene climate with its harmonious seasonal cycle. After all, if you look up at the stars, the sun and the moon revolving around you in regularity for long enough, at some point you'll have dust in your eyes and the hubris to say: I am here, I am pivotal, and what exists around me, exists for me, now, and again tomorrow, *that is why it exists*. Thus, man conjured up a self, on a planet that was there for the taking, forever available, its pinnacle the harmony of heaven, awaiting, always a promise. Man settled.

This is how it may have happened. From living with the seasons to farming, from farming to liturgy and culture. This is how the great story of us may have emerged, of humans as protagonists marked by a deep-rooted belief in an available Earth and a better tomorrow. A promise, all.

So when the discoveries of Tycho, Brahe, Kepler, Copernicus, Galileo, and Newton began to follow in rapid succession and the evidence piled up that it was actually the Earth that revolved around the sun, we did not give up, but got moving. Once we understood that the Earth was round, we drew a new world map, a *globe*, and embarked for elsewhere. So it was over there, across the water, where the rich pickings were! Elsewhere was where the promised land was! All aboard!

[03]
This is how it may have happened. Man, with his *self* and his ritualized belief in the future – a *liturgy of longing* honed over thousands of years, ingrained, a *meme* that, along with knifes, bibles, rats, and germs, stole up the gangplank with him. It was a *longing machine* that boarded ship to the new world, a fortune hunter with, in his pack, a zero percent mortgage on the future.[1]

[04]
If this is how it happened, then what we now call 'globalization' was initially nothing but, in the words of philosopher Peter Sloterdijk, the 'Atlanticization of seafaring,' a dynamic driven by the conviction that happiness can be found on the other side of the water.[2] And so the seeds of the Anthropocene – the age of human life as a geological force – were sown: with the embarkation for a planet-wide pursuit of happiness elsewhere.[3]

[1] 'We are programmed to perceive identity in ourselves, when in truth there is only change. We are hardwired for the illusion of self.' John Gray, *Straw Dogs: Thoughts on Humans and Other Animals* (London: Granta, 2003), p 76.
'A meme is an idea, behavior, or style that spreads by means of imitation from person to person in a culture and often carries symbolic meaning representing a particular phenomenon or theme. A meme acts as a unit for carrying cultural ideas, symbols, or practices, that can be transmitted from one mind to another through writing, speech, gestures, rituals, or other imitable phenomena with a mimicked theme. Supporters of the concept regard memes as cultural analogues to genes in that they self-replicate, mutate, and respond to selective pressures.' Wikipedia (accessed 13 September 2022).
Evolutionary biologist Richard Dawkins introduced the term 'meme' in his now classic book *The Selfish Gene* (Oxford: Oxford University Press, 1976) to be able to speculate about the way culture is transmitted by analogy with genes and mimesis. He imagined a mind virus-like model of society in which cultural information is inherited and reproduced, sometimes with small mutations, just like genetic information. What that might mean is fascinatingly detailed in Neal Stephenson's novel *Snow Crash* (New York: Bantam Books, 1992).
Also see Susan Blackmore, *The Meme Machine* (Oxford: Oxford University Press, 1999).

[2] Sloterdijk writes: 'from its nautical, mercantile, and colonial beginnings, globalization has represented the inclusion of the entire Earth in the psychodynamics of the pursuit of happiness.' As a result: 'the conviction that great fortunes are to be found on the other shore,' took hold of people. They only accepted the 'extreme risks of seafaring . . , because distant worlds [were] imagined as immense treasure troves, from which the successful entrepreneur returns to the sea, laden with riches.' Following Columbus, 'modernity as a whole is based on a psycho-political fact: the pursuit of happiness become planetary.' Peter Sloterdijk, 'The Ocean Experiment: From Nautical Globalization to a General Ecology' in: Peter Sloterdijk, *What Happened in the Twentieth Century?* (Cambridge: Polity Press, 2018), p 36-37.

[3] Although I am using the word Anthropocene, which was popularized by Dutch chemist Paul Crutzen, I am aware that there are alternatives. Sloterdijk, for one, writes: 'When Crutzen speaks of an "Anthropocene," this is a gesture of Dutch courtesy – or avoidance of conflict. In fact, talk of a "Eurocene" or a technocene initiated by Europeans would be more fitting.' Peter Sloterdijk, 'The Anthropocene: A Stage in the Process on the Margins of the Earth's History?' in: Sloterdijk, *What Happened in the Twentieth Century?*, p 3.
For an alphabetical inventory of alternatives, from Aerocene to White Supremacy Scene, see: Clémence Hallé and Anne-Sophie Milon, 'The Infinity of the Anthropocene: A (Hi)story with a Thousand Names,' in: Bruno Latour and Peter Weibel, *Critical Zones: The Science and Politics of Landing on Earth* (Karlsruhe: ZKM, 2020), p 44-45.
Philosopher Timothy Morton rejects the alternative Capitalo-

[05]

And this is also how, simultaneously, man's addiction to extractive capitalism started: as a continuation of religion by other means.[4] Everything may no longer have revolved around *us-on-Earth* anymore but on Earth everything still revolved around us – Earth was there for man, as was all it had to offer, as were all the treasures it hid inside. And a creature that has opportunities can only see reality as an arena for the realization of opportunities: all aboard!

scene, a suggestion by Latour and others: 'Capital and capitalism are symptoms of the problem, not its direct causes.' Morton believes the Anthropocene is an interlude, a loop inside a much larger loop, the Bacterioscene. See: Timothy Morton, *Dark Ecology: For a Logic of Future Coexistence* (New York: Columbia University Press, 2016), p 23, 70. Those who consider this far-fetched may see, among others: Lynn Margulis, *The Symbiotic Planet: A New Look at Evolution* (London: Weidenfeld and Nicholson, 1998), in which humans are put in their paleontologically proper place as the most advanced in a long line of development of technological devices once designed by bacteria, that is, as survival machines for genetic information that stem from the time when bacteria took over the Earth, over 3.5 billion years ago.
When asked when exactly the Anthropocene begins, scientists give different answers depending on their *metier*. A cultural historian myself, I favor the view that the Anthropocene first announced itself when masses of people left for the New World in the last decades of the sixteenth and early seventeenth centuries and, *as a result*, were in a position to knock on the door of social history – even though we did not hear until centuries later. 'At that time, a global drop in surface air temperatures occurred – part of the "Little Ice Age" – which natural forces can't explain. Quite likely, European expansion in the Americas played a role. With perhaps 90 percent of the indigenous population eliminated by the effects of conquest and infectious disease, forests reclaimed regions in which terraced agriculture and irrigation had been practiced for centuries. In Mesoamerica, Amazonia and the Andes, some 50 million hectares of cultivated land may have reverted to wilderness. Carbon uptake from vegetation increased on a scale sufficient to change the Earth System and bring about a human-driven phase of global cooling.' See: David Graeber and David Wengrow, *The Dawn of Everything: A New History of Humanity* (London: Allen Lane, 2021), p 258.
On the Little Ice Age, when Europe was an 'icy empire' – harvests failed, birds fell frozen from the sky, the rich got richer and the poor poorer, the cost of living rose rapidly and inflation became a persistent problem – see: Philipp Blom, *Nature's Mutiny: How the Little Ice Age of the Long Seventeenth Century Transformed the West and Shaped the Present* (New York: Liveright Publishing Corp., 2019).
Donna Haraway and Anna Lowenhaupt Tsing also believe that the origins of the Anthropocene date back to the Little Ice Age that was the result of the expansionism of European fortune hunters, however, they do not opt for Eurocene, but suggest Plantationocene as an alternative, a direct reference to the violent colonization of the Americas that would never have succeeded without the ruthless application of the plantation model and the exhaustion of people, animals, nature and the biosphere that was organized by the state and entrepreneurs and justified by the church and moral philosophy. See: Addie Hopes and Laura Peddy (eds.), *Reflections on the Plantationocene: A Conversation with Donna Haraway and Anna Tsing* (Madison: University of Wisconsin-Madison, 2019). Their suggestion refers to the fact that the so-called end of colonialism did not end inequality. On the contrary, there is still a growing gap between the territories *on which*, and the territories *from which* we live – and that gap is growing faster rather than slower.
Politically charged or not, what all of these suggestions have in common is that they underline that the Anthropocene is, in Morton's words, 'the first fully anti-anthropocentric concept' (See: Morton, *Dark Ecology*, p 24). Humankind is no longer the crown of creation.
Those, however, who are compelled to follow the lead of the geological burden of proof – pre-eminently the members of the interdisciplinary *Anthropocene Working Group* of the *International Commission on Stratigraphy* established in 2009 which is due to give a decision in the course of 2023 – are likely to include the Anthropocene in the geological stratification, but probably (the working group is keeping up the suspense) identify its beginning as coincident with the start, in the late 1940s, of what we call the Great Acceleration. I am grateful to Dirk Sijmons for insight into the working group's interim considerations. Also see: Raymond Zhong, 'For Planet Earth, This Might Be the Start of a New Age,' *The New York Times*, 17 December 2022: 'The working group's members on Saturday completed the first in a series of internal votes on details including when exactly they believe the Anthropocene began. Once these votes are finished, which could be by spring, the panel will submit its final proposal to three other committees of geologists whose votes will either make the Anthropocene official or reject it.'
On the Great Acceleration, see further, page 340 ff.

[4] 'Capitalism as the continuation of religion by other means. From Immaculate Conception to Invisible Hand, the miracle play updated, but the original arrangement remained much the same. Whether paradise is "up there" or "down here", whether the promise regards life after death or of a better future for the next generation, what we cannot have today, we will still have tomorrow. From credo to credit; it is always possible to renew the mortgage on the future. The earth is there for man, and not the other way around. This is a deeply embedded article of faith'. George Brugmans, 'Imagination and Will', in: George Brugmans and Jolanda van Dinteren (eds.), *The Missing Link* (Rotterdam: IABR, 2018), p 15.
Also see: Gray, *Straw Dogs*, p XIII: 'The idea of progress is a secular version of the Christian belief in providence. That is why among the ancient pagans it was unknown.'

Cerro Rico, the 'Rich Mountain' in Potosí, Bolivia, the motor of the Spanish empire that converted raw material into kinetic energy, accounted for about 60 percent of all silver extracted from the ground in the second half of the sixteenth century. To be 'worth a Potosí' meant to be rich. To the Indians however, Potosí was 'the mouth to hell': over the three centuries the mine was operating, an estimated 8 million Indians died of mercury poisoning – 70 percent of all miners. Engraving by Theodor de Bry, from: Girolamo Benzoni, *Historia Americae Sive Novi Orbis* (Peru, 1596) courtesy of John Carter Brown Library

[06]
Let there be no mistake: all of this was predominantly a European delusion, this belief in a better world, if necessary at the expense of this one. It was European man who ventured into a global experiment in entrepreneurial fury for which the Earth had to be available at all times. 24/7.

[07]
Promises, especially those made to ourselves, are uniquely human tools with which to order the future, observed philosopher Hannah Arendt. In this light, all of those discoveries of half a millennium ago set in motion not only the Earth, but also man himself, or at least European man. He set off into the future. Our spinning and whirling around the globe, this all-encompassing, colossal, all-consuming scramble for earthly happiness by fortune hunters determined to bend the elsewhere to their will, the ordering of the future with the expectation of ever-higher quotes and ever-bigger rewards, had begun. And proved unstoppable.
Whereas all the while, we were making more and more discoveries that could have induced a little more modesty. Our sun turned out to be just one among countless stars, born 4.5 billion years ago from an imploding

cloud of gas and elements, destined to swell into a dying, red giant star in just under 5 billion years – the trajectory all stars take. The Earth itself, a byproduct of that implosion, is one of countless planets; ablaze on the inside, cold on the outside and provisionally covered in unstoppably shifting tectonic plates. Like a rudderless spaceship, it whizzes, revolves, spins, and whirls through an ever-expanding universe, perchance to be swallowed by a black hole or crashed into by another rock at any moment. It is surrounded by a thin rarefied shell, the biosphere, an unstable, highly *critical zone* in which life is possible but survival not a given.
This is where we now find ourselves: not in a better world, but doomed to try to survive in the thin translucid outer shell of a boulder with an expiration date, with no guarantee of a good outcome. Knowing that human life, set in motion globally by longing, has now become a geological force. Though unaware, we appear to have been fumbling with the controls. And despite the fact that we can now see that in all likelihood things will not end well, what can we still do about it? Welcome to the Anthropocene.

[08]

Just when more and more lights on the dashboard are flashing red, we wake up to the fact that we are the planetary pilots of Spaceship Earth. On the bridge there is neither an operating manual, nor a flight plan.

[09]

Those who leave hearth and home and embark soon realize that to successfully brave the elements, one is quite dependent on the proper functioning of all the equipment on board. No treasure fleet without properly functioning technology. If that fails, everything comes to a grinding halt and the elements take over.
Consequently technology, the set of techniques, skills, methods, and processes used in pursuit of a goal, boomed. Technology was the fundamental precondition for the enterprise of fortune hunters whose aim it was to conquer the world by conquering nature. It was not allowed to fail, it was a law onto itself and therefore was given all the space it needed.
The global expansion of longing materialized in what geologist Peter

Haff termed the technosphere.[5] There can be scarcely any misunderstanding about its current omnipresence in terms of volume. In 2016, the University of Leicester calculated that the entire technosphere, that is, the total of the human footprint on Earth 'in pursuit of a goal,' weighs some 30 trillion tons, 'representing a mass of more than 50 kilos for every square meter of the Earth's surface.'[6]

Geologists working on stratigraphy, a discipline that aims to date and describe earth layers, increasingly see the built environment as part of the most recent rock layer. Caracas, 2007
© George Brugmans

[5] Haff described the technosphere as: 'The set of large-scale networked technologies that underlie and make possible rapid extraction from the Earth of large quantities of free energy and subsequent power generation, long-distance, nearly instantaneous communication, rapid long-distance energy and mass transport, the existence of modern governmental and other bureaucracies, high-intensity industrial and manufacturing operations including regional, continental and global distribution of food and other goods, and myriad additional "artificial" or "non-natural" processes without which modern civilization and its present 7×10^9 human constituents could not exist.' Quoted in: Dipesh Chakrabarty, *The Climate of History in a Planetary Age* (Chicago: The University of Chicago Press, 2021), p 5. Also see: Peter Haff, 'Technology as a Geological Phenomenon: Implications for Human Well-Being,' in: C.N. Waters et al. (eds.), *A Stratigraphical Basis for the Anthropocene* (London: Geological Society, Special Publications, 2014).

[6] Quoted in: Chakrabarty, *The Climate of History*, p 6. Also see: Jan Zalasiewicz, 'The Anthropocene Square Meter,' in: Latour and Weibel, *Critical Zones*, p 36-43. In an article in *The Anthropocene Review* of November 2016 Zalasiewicz et al. point out that the technosphere can also be described as a system that has its own dynamic and individual energy flows or, one could say, a metabolism. We keep it going and it keeps us going. Also see above, page 20 ff.

As a worldwide explosion of infrastructure, this enterprise was also a resounding commercial success, particularly for property developers, cement stampers and asphalt layers, chemical and fossil refinery directors, miners and steel manufacturers, and of course their financiers, bankers and shareholders, their lobbyists and political agents – bully boys who were by no means idling away their time:

> *They took all the trees put 'em in a tree museum*
> *And they charged the people a dollar and a half just to see 'em*
> *Don't it always seem to go*
> *That you don't know what you've got till it's gone*
> *They paved paradise and put up a parking lot*
> *Ooh, bop-bop-bop-bop, ooh, bop-bop-bop-bop!* [7]

What we failed to notice at the time – *you don't know what you've got till it's gone* – but gradually found out is that, as we were carrying out this unconditional planetary experiment, we were also globalizing its side effects.[8] Globalization does not equal global warming, but what inextricably links the two are modern capitalism and technology, both global phenomena. Imperialism and the technological system do not wish to accept the limits of the possible. So we order the future, not only with promises, but also by categorical wishful thinking. Rather than reason, it is the psychodynamics of longing that is central to the ethics of the capitalist world.[9]

[10]

The technosphere is facilitated by a process that took off when industrial revolutionaries started using fossil fuel for their shopping carts, which were incessantly equipped with the latest gadgets and for which the imperialists soon began arranging worldwide logistics and distribution. This whirlwind caused a lot of damage. However, it is a misunderstanding to regard all of the side effects, which gradually made us feel increasingly uncomfortable – such as colonialism and slavery, the exploitation, oppression, and extermination of the weak and of other life forms, and

[7] Joni Mitchell, 'Big Yellow Taxi,' on: *Ladies of the Canyon* (1970).

[8] 'First and foremost, the modus vivendi of human beings also now becomes experimental. Such human beings devote their whole existence, by land and by sea, to spotting new realities, new opportunities for profit, and new procedures for controlling nature. ... . It has become increasingly apparent that every experiment *per se* is continually accompanied by a systematic neglect of constraining conditions.' See: Sloterdijk, *What Happened in the Twentieth Century?*, p 38-39.

[9] It was Max Weber who pointed out earlier that capitalism is not unethical. On the contrary, it is nothing but the result, or even the realization, of the Protestant ethics of the bourgeois – which, all things considered, is in danger of being slowly crushed, a victim of its own moral philosophy, in the twenty-first century.

the Earth's overexploitation and global warming – *as collateral damage*, as ethically undesirable but unexpected byproducts for which, however destructive at times, no one can really be held accountable. By dissociating 'culture' from 'nature,' 'me' from 'that,' that is, by *otherizing*, fortune hunters could unleash the violence inside themselves without having to worry too much about its consequences. Earth must be available, nature – and this often included women and Indigenous peoples – was there to be exploited, by force if necessary, and there was no sanction against this, in fact it was encouraged.

In this context, architect Eyal Weizman notes that, 'seen from the point of colonial history . . . climate change is no longer the collateral of history that we have made it out to be.' Since the end of the eighteenth century, human-induced changes along the ever-expanding – as a result, for example, of deforestation, the introduction of non-native species, irrigation, and cultivation – borders of colonized territories have indeed been the subject of discussion among colonists, administrators, and *hommes des lettres*. But, Weizman continues, 'once climate change was articulated as a possible result of human action, it also began to be considered as a potentially beneficial form of control over nature and men, indeed, as a possible tool in the arsenal of colonization.' The acclimatization of new, often unfavorable and unfamiliar habitats could make the terrain more agreeable and, above all, more productive for Europeans – of course, the opposite never came up. The concept of climate change had already spent a lifetime in the armory of colonization before it was whitewashed into 'an adverse, collateral, or unintentional side effect of industrialization.'[10]

[11]

The longing human, *homo desiderans*, created a monster that proved impossible to tame. This culminated in a twentieth century in which the world population grew from 1.5 to 6 billion people, the global economy increased 15-fold, the use of energy increased by a factor 14 and that of water by a factor nine, and the irrigated land area increased five-fold – *Ooh, bop-bop-bop-bop*! Especially after the Second World War, the accelerator was floored worldwide; this was the beginning of what was later called *The Great Acceleration*, and for good reason.[11]

[10] Eyal Weizman, *Forensic Architecture: Violence at the Threshold of Detectability* (New York: Zone Books, 2018), p 254-255.

[11] See: J.R. McNeill and Peter Engelke, *The Great Acceleration: An Environmental History of the Anthropocene since 1945* (Cambridge, MA: Harvard University Press, 2014).

←
The first decades after the Second World War were marked by an unprecedented, exponential growth of the world economy: the beginning of what also the French called La grande accéleration.
Couples, Paris, 1952
photo: Robert Frank
© 2023, Christie's Images, London/Scala, Florence

→
It was long thought that there was no precious metal in Brazil until gold was found in Minas Gerais. Founded in 1698, Vila Rica de Ouro Prêto, the 'rich city of black gold' quickly became the cradle of an unprecedentedly destructive and still ongoing process: under the rule of Jair Bolsonaro, numerous new illegal gold mines proliferated.
Gold mine in the Serra Pelada, Brazil, 1986 (detail)
© Sebastião Salgado
courtesy of nbpictures

What is generally missing from secular variations on the miraculous feeding of the multitudes that eulogize petroparadise are, again, the side effects. But doubts and even uneasiness about these side effects did slowly begin to haunt our dreams of the future.[12] Especially from the 1960s, when the Club of Rome warned that there were limits to growth and futurist and entrepreneur-inventor Richard Buckminster Fuller proclaimed that Spaceship Earth was lacking an operating manual.[13] We snoozed a little longer, we were not done dreaming: we had yet to festively hail the Internet. But now, at the dawn of the third millennium, we are being jerked awake, out of this global intoxication of kinetic entrepreneurialism and fossil expressionism. The Earth lies quite exhausted, ravaged by what Schopenhauer already scoffingly called the ephemeral fungus on the surface of the planet 150 years ago: the human race that, scraping and scratching and digging and drilling and sucking and burping and pulling and pushing and whacking and cracking and killing and looting

[12] In this context, political philosopher John Gray points to a different but related growth spurt: 'What makes the twentieth century special is not the fact that it is littered with massacres. It is the scale of its killings and the fact that they were premeditated for the sake of vast projects of world improvement. . . . Progress and mass murder run in tandem. . . . As the hope for a better world has grown, so has mass murder.' See: Gray, *Straw Dogs*, p 96.

[13] 'Now there is one outstandingly important fact regarding Spaceship Earth, and that is that no instruction book came with it. I think it's very significant that there is no instruction book for successfully operating our ship. In view of the infinite attention to other details displayed by our ship, it must be taken as deliberate and purposeful that an instruction book was omitted. . . . So we were forced, because of a lack of an instruction book, to use our intellect.' See: Richard Buckminster Fuller, *Operating Manual for Spaceship Earth* (Zurich: Lars Müller Publishers, 2008/2017 [1969]), p 60-61. On the role and influence of Buckminster Fuller, see below, part 2, page 351 ff.
See also Sloterdijk, *What Happened in the Twentieth Century?*, p 40-41.

and building, had thought that the plenty would never end but that, as it turned out, had actually been putting its own survival at stake. And even now, not everyone is done digging and drilling.[14]

[12]

Just when more and more lights on the dashboard are flashing red, we wake up to the fact that we are the planetary pilots of Spaceship Earth. On the bridge there is neither an operating manual, nor a flight plan. It is getting hotter and hotter. No chimney, no ventilation, no windows, no emergency exit. Anxiety sets in, maybe we ought to turn things down a notch? Consultations. Conferences. How to go about it? Together doesn't work. Because the barbarians are not at the gate, they are on board. They recognize that it will benefit them greatly to now burn as much as possible as quickly as possible. There is still a lot of money to be made from disasters! Fanatically, they seize power on the ship, their massive wealth taking the rest of us hostage.

[13]

The side effects of the planetary gold rush are poisoning both the biosphere on which we depend for our survival and the social sphere on which we depend for our coexistence. It is getting hotter and hotter, and the disparities are becoming more glaring, also because the adverse effects of the climate crisis are affecting the poor and poor countries in particular, not to mention hundreds of thousands of other life forms that are innocent of the disaster that is unfolding in slow motion.[15]
We are living in an age of mass extinction, as philosopher Timothy Morton summarizes.[16] It seems the endgame has begun, but we have no instruction book. Technology is part of the problem rather than the solution. We increasingly question the postponement of decisions in the blind hope that technical innovation will provide solutions, but we cannot seem to agree on an alternative systematic policy of landing on Earth, either. Nor, for that matter, is our political system set up to do that: *on the*

[14] For the history of violence, scraping, digging and pillaging, see among others: Eduardo Galeano, *Open Veins of Latin America: Five Centuries of the Pillage of a Continent* (New York: Monthly Review Press, 1973) and Caroline Elkins, *Legacy of Violence: A History of the British Empire* (New York: Alfred A. Knopf, 2022).

[15] Take the catastrophic floods in Pakistan in the summer of 2022. The country houses some 2.6 percent of the world's population and contributes less than 1 percent to global CO_2 emissions, but is now paying a huge price for its effects. Note that Americans, together about 4 percent of the world's population, account for 13 percent of CO_2 emissions.

[16] 'What is global warming anyway? The correct answer is that it is mass extinction. Maybe it would make it more obvious if we stopped calling it "global warming" (and definitely stopped calling it "climate

contrary. Another side effect of the planetary experiment was that the political thinking that had developed since the seventeenth century and that was based on the idea that the right of each individual to personal freedom and private property must be absolutely guaranteed, simply could not but drift into difficulties, because it never reckoned with the total number of human beings. No one had thought of that, the discipline did not have a Malthus and this has major implications today, as historian Dipesh Chakrabarty notes. 'This indifference to total numbers of humans translated into an indifference to the biosphere, the reigning assumption being that the globe was always resourced enough to support in perpetuity the human-political project no matter how demanding humans became of the earth.' We have now reached the point at which what should be safeguarded by our political and legal institutions is actually threatened by them. 'Late capitalism, in this sense, destroys the human-political project the world over. In such circumstances, there is surely the danger . . . of a rebarbarization of the world.' [17]

This rebarbarization – the arrival of the barbarians who are not at the gate, but are already inside, among us, perhaps even *within us* – has emerged, often under the guise of neoliberalism, as a genuine threat to democracy. From Trump and his gang storming the Capitol in Washington, DC on 6 January 2021, to Britain's partying prime minister mocking his own Covid-19 rules, to the farmer protests in the Netherlands: the pirates who could not care less about the internal rules that have been drawn up for our societies since the Enlightenment, will not budge from the front pages. They dominate the now hysterical public debate. Longing as a contaminant.

change", which is really weak) and started calling it "mass extinction", which is the net effect . . . Uncannily we begin to realize that we are somewhere. Not nowhere. And we may find ourselves living in an age of mass extinction.' See: Timothy Morton, *Being Ecological* (London: Penguin Random House, 2018), pp 44, 67.

[17] Chakrabarty, *The Climate of History in a Planetary Age*, p 90-91.

US Capitol attack
Washington, DC, 6 January 2021
© Ashley Gilbertson
courtesy of ANP, VII Photo
Redux

[14]

Meanwhile, what we now call the 1 percent can go about their business unimpeded. Late capitalism has given birth to an accumulation of private resources that no reasonable argument can defend. Warranting the right of each individual to personal freedom and private property has been largely privatized, as have the proceeds of the resulting planetary pillaging, which are unimaginably large. In the past 50 years alone, for example, the taxpayer-subsidized oil and gas industry made $2.8 billion in pure profit per day – *every* day.[18] Most of the money ends up in just a few pockets, but a not-inconsiderable amount has been and is being successfully used to cast doubt on facts, discredit scientists, buy into politics, and sabotage climate politics. A highly profitable dark money-funded lobby has emerged that benefits much more than the oil and gas industry alone.[19] What the rest of us got in return is a practice of *failure by design*, all too often secured, sometimes even arranged by our own political and legal institutions. We are witnessing a money storm that continues to gain momentum, fed by the privatization of profits and the transfer of losses

[18] 'The oil and gas industry has delivered $2.8bn a day in pure profit for the last 50 years, a new analysis has revealed. The vast total captured by petrostates and fossil fuel companies since 1970 is $52tn, providing the power to "buy every politician, every system" and delay action on the climate crisis, says Prof Aviel Verbruggen, the author of the analysis. The huge profits were inflated by cartels of countries artificially restricting supply. The analysis, based on World Bank data, assesses the "rent" secured by global oil and gas sales, which is the economic term for the unearned profit produced after the total cost of production has been deducted,' wrote *The Guardian* on 21 July 2022.
On 3 August that same newspaper added: 'These record profits are salt in the wound when we've seen that fossil fuel companies have successfully lobbied G20 governments for $151bn within Covid-19 recovery packages on top of their profit. They also spend nearly $200m a year lobbying to delay, control or block policies to tackle climate change.'
Thanks to this lobbying, the oil and gas industry also structurally receives lots of taxpayer subsidies: 'Globally, fossil fuel subsidies were $5.9 trillion in 2020 or about 6.8 percent of GDP, and are expected to rise to 7.4 percent of GDP in 2025.' See: Ian W.H. Parry, Simon Black and Nate Vernon, 'Still Not Getting Energy Right: A Global and Country Update of Fossil Fuel Subsidies,' *IMF Working Papers*, 24 September 2021.

[19] See, among others: Jane Mayer, *Dark Money: The Hidden History of the Billionaires Behind the Rise of the Radical Right* (New York: Doubleday, 2016) and Christopher Leonard, *Kochland: The Secret History of Koch Industries and Corporate Power in America* (New York: Simon & Schuster, 2019).

to society. We read about this financial superstorm in our newspapers every day and with growing anger, and not just because we were led to believe that it would put the house in order on our behalf, if not make us all richer – that long-punctured balloon of *trickle-down economics*. We do have to realize, and especially in the context of the climate crisis, that there is a lot of money to be made from disasters, that a crisis is an excellent *business model* and that, in neoliberal circles, this is an argument for postponing government measures that are a restraint to free enterprise. The argument that *repairing* is more expensive than *preparing* therefore makes no impression whatsoever: taking precautionary action does not win a politician the elections and reduces the entrepreneur's profits.[20] All in all, this is an all-destroying financial storm, in the face of which the vast majority of people is virtually powerless – and that's the way it is meant to be.[21]

[20] Those who think this is far-fetched might read Naomi Klein, *The Battle for Paradise: Puerto Rico Takes On the Disaster Capitalists* (Chicago: Haymarket Books, 2018), an account of the way the forces of shock politics and disaster capitalism undermined the country's radical vision of 'just recovery' for a profit on the ruins of Hurricane Maria. Social psychologist Harald Welzer also writes about markets of violence: 'They sow violence and reap the harvest.' He refers to the protracted wars in Africa, for example in Darfur, where 'it is evident that phenomena such as rapid desertification may become new sources of violent conflict, to be channeled and exploited in many ways by groups with an interest.' Harald Welzer, *Climate Wars: What People Will Be Killed For in the 21st Century* (Cambridge, MA: Polity Press, 2012), p 102-104.

[21] A random selection of newspaper stories published in the week I wrote these paragraphs. On 30 June 2022, the rightwing-dominated US Supreme Court ruled in West Virginia v. EPA that the Environmental Protection Agency may not use its authority to regulate CO_2 emissions in the face of climate change, and that the US government cannot, therefore, use its existing legal powers to unlink the country's energy production from coal – the government may not use the most important, democratically created environmental law in the country, the Clean Air Act.
On 6 July 2022, a majority of the European Parliament agreed to green-label gas and nuclear power while two days later the British government secured, through an auction, 'a record 11 gigawatts of new renewable energy capacity that will generate electricity four times more cheaply than current gas prices.' In Brussels, too, lobbyists are winning by and large.
Also on 6 July 2022, the management of Shell once again got a lot of media attention in the Netherlands, this time to communicate that the company is going to use (a lot of) green wind energy in the port of Rotterdam to produce (a little) hydrogen that it is going to use for greening the production of fossil fuels like diesel and gasoline. This is greenwashing pure and simple: clean wind energy is used to run environmentally polluting refineries that, by the way, are the property of a company that is going to drill for natural gas in the vulnerable Wadden Sea, a UNESCO World Heritage Site. And on 8 July 2022, *de Volkskrant* reported that the Port of Rotterdam itself is still barely trying to stop the transit of Russian oil – 'a partial boycott of Russian oil agreed to by the EU only comes into effect at the end of this year, so there are no legal obligations banning trade in Russian oil (products) now' – unlike other countries that had already voluntarily reduced their imports. Incidentally, in view of the climate crisis and the sacrifices it demands of us, I think it is not a bad idea to let go of the Dutch mainport policy that has successfully put Schiphol Airport and the Port of Rotterdam on the global fossil fuel map. After all, when all is said and done, the port is primarily thriving as a transit point for the addiction industry, a logistical chute for oil, gas, drugs, and all sorts of cheap stuff made in Southeast Asia, while its impact on the environment is very substantial and its added value for the regional economy limited, also compared to nearby ports like Antwerp and Hamburg.
On 30 June 2022, under the headline: 'Why Are We Feeding Crops to Our Cars When People Are Starving?' George Monbiot wrote in *The Guardian*: 'As the investigative group Transport & Environment shows, the land used to grow the biofuels consumed in Europe covers 14m hectares (35m acres): an area larger than Greece. Of the soy oil consumed in the European Union, 32% is eaten by cars and trucks. They devour 50% of all the palm oil used in the EU and 58% of the rapeseed oil. Altogether, 18% of the world's vegetable oil is turned into biodiesel, and 10% of the world's grains are transformed into ethanol, to mix with petrol. . . . If biofuel production ceased worldwide, according to one estimate, the saved crops could feed 1.9 billion human beings. The only consistent and reliable outcome of this technology is hunger.'
The only plausible answer to the question of what actually keeps all this destructive corporate greed in full swing, while the world is on fire, is money – an exorbitant lot of money, *dark money*. The political economist William Davies famously called neoliberalism 'the disenchantment of politics by economics.'

[15]
Democracy versus plutocracy, are they the white and black pieces in the endgame? Unquestionably, capitalism is an economic system aimed at unbridled growth and profit rather than the sensible fulfillment of human needs. The fact that we are now facing a climate crisis and mass extinction is not only due to erroneous political decisions, made deliberately or otherwise, but also follows directly from what capitalism fundamentally is: the ever more efficient organization of what began as a planetary quest for happiness, but turned into a ruthless raid of barbarians who inhabit the Earth as end users. To enforce fair climate policies we need a radical break with this system. Taking a strong countermovement to the streets, schools, and universities, and into politics and workplaces is absolutely necessary: we have to rebel, protest-glue, file lawsuits, and commit obstruction whenever and wherever we can.[22]
Individually, too, we have to do everything we can. So should we sell that second home in Southern Europe, skip the weekend to, again, Barcelona, and cancel yet another holiday by air to Thailand or ski trip with the family in Switzerland? Discontinue the traditional annual trip to Venice and other international art fairs? These seem like marginal issues that will bear putting off for a while. But as Timothy Morton notes, 'several thousand years from now, nothing about you as an individual will matter. But what you did will have huge consequences. This is the paradox of the ecological age. And it is why action to change global warming must be massive and collective.'[23]
Still, whatever we do, it is not enough. Has the war already begun?

[16]
Together with the all-inclusive travel package for the fortune hunter and the brilliant technological discovery production that was its precondition as well as consequence, the helm of Spaceship Earth has been pushed into our hands. Whether we like it or not, we are all pilots now. But we have no operating manual. And this much is clear: heat pumps and electric cars are not going to save us, and neither are global climate agreements. *Ooh, cop-cop-cop-cop!*

[22] The effectiveness of which has been commented on by, for example, Roy Scranton: 'No matter how many people take to the streets in massive marches, they cannot put their hands on the real flows of power because they do not help to produce it. They only consume.' See: Roy Scranton, *Learning to Die in the Anthropocene: Reflections on the End of a Civilization* (San Francisco: City Light Books, 2015), p 60.

[23] Morton, *Being Ecological*, p 35.
Some problems, by the way, come with their own solutions: the more people go skiing, the less snow there will be; the more people travel to Venice, the faster the city will be flooded.

And this is why we have to realize that although many people continue to ignore it, we are already in what can be seen as the first skirmishes of a war. 'Dramatizing somewhat extravagantly,' as the recently deceased philosopher Bruno Latour wrote, 'let us call it a conflict between modern humans who believe they are alone in the Holocene . . . and the terrestrials who know they are in the Anthropocene and who seek to cohabit with other terrestrials.' [24] This matter of survival, of how to inhabit the Earth together with other life forms, sows deep divisions, everywhere and in each of us. This is why Latour asks the question: *Where can we land?*

→
Where can we land?
São Paulo, 2010
© George Brugmans

[24] Bruno Latour, *Down to Earth: Politics in the New Climatic Regime* (Cambridge: Polity Press, 2018), p 90.

HOTEL JARAGUÁ

2: World Game Over

I'm pitting a world-around, bloodless, constructive, design transformation revolution against a world-around destructive bloody revolution . . . planners, architects, and engineers take the initiative. Go to work.

Richard Buckminster Fuller

[17]

Just when more and more lights on the dashboard are flashing red, we wake up to the fact that we are the planetary pilots of Spaceship Earth. On the bridge there is neither an operating manual, nor a flight plan. It is getting hotter and hotter. No chimney, no ventilation, no windows, no emergency exit. Anxiety sets in, maybe we ought to turn things down a notch? Consultations. Conferences. How to go about it? Together doesn't work. Because the barbarians are not at the gate, they are on board. They recognize that it will benefit them greatly to now burn as much as possible as quickly as possible. There is still a lot of money to be made from disasters! Fanatically, they seize power on the ship, their massive wealth taking the rest of us hostage. And so the temperature continues to rise. Apocalyptic heat waves. More and more people die, here, there, everywhere. Flooding. No escape. Ice caps melting, whole sections of glaciers breaking off. Insects on the decline. Land drying out. Yet another superstorm warning. Atmospheric rivers, waves of water crashing down from the skies. Where did the North Pole go? It was there a moment ago! No more bird song; no more butterfly wings.

[18]

To learn to dwell on Earth in a new way, to bring us back to Earth, that is now *the* challenge politics faces. Bruno Latour asks: Where can we land? It is a question that I, as chief curator of DOWN TO EARTH – an architecture biennale organized by a cultural research institute that is taking the 2030 climate deadline that the global community has set for itself absolutely seriously – wanted to read as follows: What can and should imaginers and designers do, now that the endgame has begun?[25]

[25] Bruno Latour formulates the question of where we can land in his book *Où atterrir?* (Paris: La Découverte, 2017), a key source of inspiration for DOWN TO EARTH. The book was released in the Netherlands under the title *Waar kunnen we landen?* – literally, where can we land? Its English title is *Down to Earth*.

[19]
The predicament of where to land is not new as such. Since Christmas Eve 1968, when astronaut Bill Anders photographed the Earth rising from behind the moon from Apollo 8, we have been able to make the astronaut's perspective our own and imagine the return to Earth. And in the same period, in the late 1960s, when the Apollos circled the moon and finally landed there, we also began to realize that our planet was not doing well. This was when Richard Buckminster Fuller proposed that the Earth itself should also be understood as a spaceship. Someone had to write an instruction book for Spaceship Earth, which seemed to be in trouble but lacked a manual, and for that purpose he appealed to designers. In *Operating Manual for Spaceship Earth*, which he published in 1969, he made no bones about it: 'I'm pitting a world-around, bloodless, constructive, design transformation revolution against a world-around destructive bloody revolution.' He propagated a 'grand strategy of *problem-solving comprehensive anticipatory design science*' and thought 'planners, architects, and engineers' uniquely able 'to do the largest scale comprehensive thinking of which we are capable . . . Take the initiative. Go to work.'[26]

[20]
In the 1960s and 1970s, the charismatic Buckminster Fuller was revered by both the counterculture and the establishment as a contemporary Leonardo da Vinci, and his appeal resonated widely. But was it reasonable for such a challenge – to pretty much save the world on behalf of all mankind – to be passed on to designers, no matter how adept they are at finding solutions and linking multiple disciplines?
Indeed, the *Whole Earth Catalog*, published irregularly between 1968 and 1972 and inspired in part by the optimism and ideas of Buckminster Fuller, and the 1972 Club of Rome report, which was still fairly optimistic, or at least not alarmist, had both made it perfectly clear that there was a lot of work to be done. Obviously, an operating manual or escape plan was not going to materialize overnight. And in the following decades, the years in which the Great Acceleration took hold and found its ideological reflection in neoliberalism, this did not happen, either: on the contrary, the ship drifted further and further off course.

[26] Buckminster Fuller, *Operating Manual*, p 9, 10, 66-67, 138.

Back cover of *The Last Supplement to The Whole Earth Catalog*, March 1971 courtesy of Department of Special Collections, Stanford University Libraries

Overall, Buckminster Fuller's call for designers to go to work has not led to the dream result. While there are designers who want to think big, comprehensively, and multidisciplinarily, a world in which the rest of us are jointly embracing the 'world-around, bloodless, constructive, design transformation revolution' has not materialized. Not an architect himself, he asked too much of architects' design potential.[27] Even though as if by reflex, many designers see an opportunity in every problem to this day, perhaps on the best possible grounds, for we must indeed find that operating manual (this realization undoubtedly constituted Buckminster Fuller's eureka moment), we cannot deny the facts: there is a wide gap between the possible world represented by design and the real world in which all designs must land. Surely designers can develop alternative strategies, or help develop these – but do they have the space to do it in?

[27] '"Bucky Fuller was no architect, and he kept pretending he was," complained Philip Johnson, who was immune to Fuller's charisma. Yet it was precisely among architects that Fuller acquired an active following. He taught at architecture schools, his work was published in architecture magazines and he was close to Charles Eames and Frank Lloyd Wright. It was Wright who slyly put Fuller in his place: "I am an architect interested in science. Buckminster is a scientist interested in architecture".' See: Witold Rybczynski, 'Buckminster Fuller, Role Model and Cautionary Tale,' *The New York Times*, 2 August 2022.
Also see: Alec Nevala-Lee, *Inventor of the Future: The Visionary Life of Buckminster Fuller* (New York: Dey Street Books, 2022).
It is striking in any case that it is often non-architects who have high expectations of architects or tempt architects to have high expectations of themselves. And I confess I, too, have been guilty of this, with both conviction and good intentions.

[21]

Author Jorge Luis Borges, who was proficient in doing just that, designing other possible worlds, observes that many may be skilled in 'diverse disciplines, but few capable of imagination – fewer still capable of subordinating imagination to a rigorous and systematic plan.'[28]

His fellow writer, semiotician Umberto Eco, who assumes that Borges has read more than all the books in existence because he has also reviewed imaginary books, calls many of Borges's stories 'perfect examples of that art of inference which Peirce called abduction, and which is nothing else but *conjecture*.' We should not underestimate the art of conjecture. Knowledge acquirers and designers, so landscape architect Dirk Sijmons agrees, find each other in abduction. The method produces plenty of valuable hypotheses, which however need testing later in the process. Eco also underlines this: 'When the detective, or the scientist . . . make an Abduction, they must bet that the solution they find (the Possible World of their hypothetical imagination) corresponds to the Real World.'[29]

In addition to the *framework* of a rigorous and systematic plan, and in conjunction with it, the *space* to actually be able to guess, interpret, imagine, test, and try is crucially important to designers. In the spatial discipline that is architecture, this requires – and this is not obvious – *free space*, or *test sites*, areas in which, for a certain period of time, one can experiment in space and with space – a process of learning by area developing; thinking about the way to do things while one is doing them, in a space that is mentally and physically free.[30] But after half a millennium of fortune hunting on and around the territory, how much space is left for free space?

[28] Jorge Luis Borges, 'Tlön, Uqbar, Orbis Tertius', in: Jorge Luis Borges, *Collected Fictions* (New York: Viking, 1998), p 72.

[29] Umberto Eco, 'The Interesting and Borges', in: Bart Verschaffel and Mark Vermink (eds.), *About the Interesting* (Antwerp: Antwerpen 93, 1993), p 64, 66.
Also see: Dirk Sijmons, 'When Research by Design Takes Politics on a Sabbatical Detour,' in: George Brugmans, Jolanda van Dinteren and Maarten Hajer (eds.), *The Next Economy* (Rotterdam: IABR, 2016), p 133: 'In the 1960s, the by-design method was connected to "abduction," a third way of acquiring knowledge introduced by logician Charles Peirce. Besides induction and deduction, Peirce posits abduction as a not strictly logical form of reasoning that can be used to deduce the best, or a sufficient, explanation for a given problem "which might be the case." It yields hypotheses that can be tested later in the process.'

[30] Naturally, this approach was part of the methodological armory of the IABR–Ateliers. The first IABR–Ateliers were initially called Test Sites. The three Test Sites São Paulo, Istanbul and Rotterdam were at the heart of MAKING CITY, the 5th IABR. Later, the IABR also set up Test Site M4H+. See above, pages 26, 144 ff. and 246 ff., among others.
For a complete overview of all IABR–Ateliers in the period 2008–2021, see:

[22]

To put it like Heidegger: 'Dasein is nicht im Raum vorhanden, sondern es räumt sich ein.' First there is only space, then everything that comes into being settles, it *makes space*, and not once and for all, but over and over again. If we have to (learn to) inhabit the Earth in a new way to be able to land, the point is not so much that we have to redistribute the space, but rather that we have to make sure that every 'being,' everyone and anything alive, can *settle in* again and again and again, and in a sustainable way. This is about finding – designing, guessing, imagining, testing – a new and ecologically viable, maximally adaptive balance among people, other life forms, and nature, among people, nature, and prosperity, between *being* and *space*. About finding and maintaining a just, necessarily unruly yet resilient balance among the economic, ecological, and social interests of all terrestrials, and those of the Earth. In the spatial domain all this comes together in a challenge-oriented way and designers can make a difference here. Give them a lever and they can start *making space*. This can happen.

But although the stakes are by now quite high, designers who explore and try alternative strategies get little response, and thus have little leeway to begin with. After all, no matter how much strength of design and imagination they use to show us *what we can want* by the solutions they design, these have to be able to land. But they rarely do.[31]

[23]

Perhaps in today's political and economic climate a rigorous and systematic plan in which the imagination is both rigorously and systematically contextualized and allowed to take wing should ultimately not be a design plan, but rather a war plan, if it is to succeed. For because the report of the Club of Rome and all the warnings that followed have been neglected for too long, because we are caught up in the endgame, space, the spatial, has now been swallowed up by a worldwide, fierce battle for the system itself. After all, pillaging and barbarism *make space* too – and rather a lot of it. Friedrich Hayek, an early proclaimer of the neoliberal faith cult, came out squarely against protecting nature. He advocated depleting the soil com-

[31] That it *can* be done was the conviction that drove the IABR–Ateliers. That it is nevertheless not always done is the conclusion we have to draw from 15 years of international experience with those very Ateliers. Also see above, *How Can We Land?*, page 18-329. This important issue – why do integrated, sustainability-oriented design plans run aground far more often than not in practice? – was the central theme of THE MISSING LINK, the 8th IABR, in 2018. See: Brugmans and Van Dinteren, *The Missing Link*. Also see below: Dirk Sijmons, 'The System's Ceiling,' p 360 ff.

pletely; after all, you could always just start over elsewhere. The point was to invest profits in other sectors as quickly as possible – only elsewhere, having torn itself away from the plundered Earth, could the free market really spread its wings.[32] Politicians such as Bolsonaro, Trump, and Putin have advocated the deliberate application of this depletion strategy, and resisting it can cost you your life. What it takes to form a countermovement, then, is quite a bit more than just design and imagination. Other, non-extractive uses of the Earth, alternative approaches to *making space*, require a political transformation that may not come about without bloodshed.

First World Game Seminar, led by Richard Buckminster Fuller and Edwin Schlossberg, New York, July 1969 courtesy of The Estate of R. Buckminster Fuller

For now, it is clear, the endgame is not just a game, and for globe-tinkerers such as Buckminster Fuller it's *world game over!* The battle must be fought not (only) behind the drawing board or in classrooms, but first and foremost in the political realm, in society, in space, on the *killing fields* of late capitalism.

[32] Speaking of *Test Sites*: it looks like the neoliberals are the ones who get to experiment to their heart's content, sometimes with whole countries at stake, which happened after Brexit in the United Kingdom: Hayek and Thatcher made their comeback just at the moment when nothing at all was allowed to go wrong anymore on the road to 2030. The provisional highlight has been Liz Truss's ultra-short regime in late summer 2022. 'The ecological destruction Liz Truss plans to unleash on this country is not collateral damage. It is not a byproduct of her economic programme. It's a mark of true faith, a sign that she is following her ideology to the letter. For fundamental to this doctrine – neoliberalism – is the belief that everything on Earth can and should be turned into something else. . . . We should see Truss's government as an experiment: what happens when neoliberal ultras, schooled by the dark-money thinktanks, get everything they want? Result: the economy falls off a cliff, while the fabric of the nation is ripped apart.' George Monbiot, 'Environmental Destruction Is Part of Liz Truss's Plan,' *The Guardian*, 30 September 2022. And one week later, in the same newspaper: 'This is naked conservatism that believes in itself with such fervour it thinks facts should make way for fantasies . . . [Truss is] determined to jump of the cliff, insistent that all the talk of gravity is so much stuffy scientific "orthodoxy". The refusal to bow to empirical evidence, to reality, is Truss conservatism's defining feature.' Jonathan Freedland, 'Fair Play to Truss: Stripped of Competence or Compassion, Her Extremism Is Refreshingly Clear,' *The Guardian*, 8 October 2022. Incidentally, another two weeks later, on 20 October, it turned out that sometimes gravity does work after all. The panic she caused – *Truss Crashes Markets!* – triggered counterforces. After 44 days Truss fell; this was an alternative variant of trickling down in high gear. But promptly another neoliberal ultra popped up to take over. The once so successful pirates' nest United Kingdom is in its final days, a *test site* for *failure by design*: we certainly can't land there!

[24]

So have designers really run up against the limits of their discipline? How should they proceed in times of climate crisis? What part can design still play in the political realm and on today's battlefield?

I am leaving the bridge now, to see what the mood is like on board, given the current turbulence – it's getting a bit frightening after all. I want to let the designers themselves have their say before I come back to report on the turmoil.[33] So first, two messages from the front.

[33] See page 394 ff.

←
Blast #0608
from: *Blast Series, 1995-1998*
photo: Naoya Hatakeyama, 1995

THE SYSTEM'S CEILING
Dirk Sijmons

Designers rarely realize that, almost routinely and under the guise of technology, they perform acts of magic every day. And that this magic sometimes literally has ancient roots.
Take, first of all, the map. Every map is primarily a cultural monument: the product of patient exploration, triangulation and, later, aerial photos, which today have of course been replaced by satellite images and geodesic point clouds. At the same time, maps are miracles that allow you to travel without setting foot outside the door. You can use them – without a word of explanation – to transfer topographical knowledge to other people. Bent over a map, you can plot a strategy together. Sometimes maps communicate secret knowledge and – as was the case in the days of the Dutch East India Company – are kept in lead safes, because the mapped knowledge of foreign coasts must never fall into the hands of the competition.
Plan drawings are even more miraculous, if that's possible. The plan drawing is an instrument that allows us to see into a future – *a* future and not *the* future, because it isn't predicative but, using free will and imagination, reveals what future we *can* want as we are designing. Thanks to the plan drawing, space and time behave like tamed tigers that will jump through burning hoops to please clients.
The third form of routine magic is the model, the *maquette*, which oozes the irresistible appeal of the miniature. Every architect knows that after a presentation, clients, speakers, and local residents will mostly crowd around the model. This fascination with the miniature has everything to do with the illusion of overview and control over the desired object, and at the same time serves to exorcise it.

These three forms of magic go as far back as Stone Age cave paintings, at least. That is to say, we can read those earliest artistic expressions as the earliest plan drawings. They demonstrate the hunting of herds of bison, the stalking of giant deer, and the trapping of mammoths during their seasonal migration. Three ingredients of these earliest plan drawings have survived to this day: their topographical reference, where is the herd; their 'instructive' nature, how are we going to go about it; and their 'predictive' element, the strange sensation that comes with conceptualization, once you've drawn the animals themselves, you're already halfway to accomplishing your goal. Against the backdrop of the cave paintings, the model was undoubtedly represented by the dancing shamans, dressed as animals, whose spells ritually secured the success of the hunt. Architecture's three main means of persuasion predate even the primitive hut.

Much, much later, in the middle of the nineteenth century, a fourth medium joined this magical trio: the cross section. Having been in use in architecture for quite some time, the cross section only entered the large-scale stage of the landscape with the emergence of geology as a science. Pioneers such as William Smith and Charles Lyell construed the strata of Earth's history in colored cross sections. These were considered blasphemous drawings, as they depicted an Earth that was much older than the 5,500 years that you find when you add up the subsequent genealogies described by the Bible book Genesis. The cross section is the best possible tool to explain what something is like or what it should be like. A good one gives insight into the way something works. Steam locomotives, oil rigs, moon rockets, but also bacteria and cells, and other complicated structures: (online) encyclopedias often explain them by means of illuminating cross sections.

These four means of explication and evocation are worth their weight in gold when making, and communicating about, designs, but they have also been used to great effect in research by design. For two decades, the IABR has been proving that architects, urban designers, and landscape architects have become better and better at this. Maps now even glow in the dark – remember the diapositive maps of FABRICations. and Field Operations created for IABR–Atelier Rotterdam, which unlocked the new topography of the urban metabolism of Rotterdam and the Rijnmond region.[33] Rendering techniques now give plan drawings a hyperrealistic

[33] See page 20 ff.

→
Grotte Chauvet-Pont-d'Arc (Ardèche)
Panneaux des Rhinocéros et des Lions, Salle du Fond
© J. Clottes/MC

style, especially when they are also in motion, like the floor projection of IABR–Atelier 2050: An Energetic Odyssey. But even low-tech still turns out to be able to make a big impact, as evidenced by the indeed magical, tapestry-like woven plan drawing made for the water strategies of Brabant, which AWB, Floris Alkemade, and LOLA created for IABR–Atelier Brabantstad. The tapestry continues to adorn the reception hall of the Provincial Government Building in 's-Hertogenbosch. And at the second biennale, THE FLOOD (2005), the model was the protagonist of an exhibition about beautiful water cities and miniature waterworks including a huge model of Rotterdam Water City 2035 that has meant so much to the city. Ever since, 3D printing technology has been increasing the magical eloquence of models by the breathtaking precision it made possible, as evidenced, for example, by the models created for IABR–Atelier Dordrecht.[34] Finally, we are getting better at drawing all kinds of time-space phenomena in the cross sections. DOWN TO EARTH included a beautiful example, Drought in the Delta, a system cross section in which the Dutch water problems were made intelligible from the perspective of drought. This cross section took a victory lap through the delta, visiting all types of landscapes and at the same time showing what we could do to address the issue.[35]

Varying Returns

Scanning the returns of the IABR–Ateliers' impressive production of research by design over the years, a number of things stand out. Without the pretense of in-depth evaluation, they have on occasion succeeded in putting new problems on the political agenda. They have also succeeded in getting environmental problems addressed because of their spatial implications. And, conversely, Ateliers have succeeded in showing that spatial means still matter when we want to solve social problems. Downright liberating is the fact that research by design has been able to address problems that will never get a paid commission. With varying degrees of success, apparently insoluble policy problems have been taken on – as George Brugmans, who conceived and directed the Ateliers, termed it – a *sabbatical detour* through the cultural domain to identify solutions together with the actors using imagination and design. Individual sectors subsequently avidly picked the low-hanging fruit from

[34] See DOWN TO EARTH: THE HIGH GROUND, page 299-329.

[35] See DOWN TO EARTH: DROUGHT IN THE DELTA, page 167-237, especially page 170-201.

among the results of the research by design. What failed, however, was the attempt to convince policymakers to pick up on the strong cohesion at the scale of the landscape – at which the cross section Drought in the Delta, for example, is aimed – and to use this as leverage as they work on major transitions.
In other words, the agenda has been set and directions for solutions have been identified, but they are too easily ignored by policymakers, bar a few exceptions.[36] Leafing through the IABR catalogs, you get the feeling that, at this scale level, we've been trying to make more or less the same point again and again. Ateliers act on the dire urgency of the global environmental problems by formulating and drawing solutions, but it seems the message does not come across: we face a splendid *surplace*, a standstill that cannot be overcome by good plans, beautiful drawings, or evocative models. Will long-term design for the large scale forever remain a skill in search of an application?[37]

Is the magic gone? Certainly not. But you could argue that although at times there's been a lot of designing going on in our country, there has also been too little actual research. Labelling everything 'research by design' may sometimes have made this label too non-committal. Is it possible that there is a degree of overproduction? Especially now that governments and commercial parties have also discovered the medium, there seems to be an arms race going on in which competitors are deploying a motley collection of research-by-design projects. We're looking at a jumble of commercial propositions, design competitions, cultural initiatives, and academic spatial research. In Harry Potter terms: we're looking at a wizarding contest in which too many wizards are competing, their combined spells and incantations creating a whole lot of fireworks, flashing, and crackling, before sadly extinguishing. It's not that the magic is gone, it's just that multi-planning agencies all getting in each other's way doesn't work. Add to this the superimposed orgware of plan-reviewing

[36] As far as the Netherlands is concerned, exceptions I would like to mention are the IABR–Ateliers Planet Texel (2013-2014), 2050: An Energetic Odyssey (2016), and Dordrecht (2019-2021).

[37] 'Forever' may be a bit of an exaggeration, but nearly 40 years is still a long time. See: Dirk Sijmons, 'Regional Planning as a Strategy,' *Landscape and Urban Planning* 18 (1986), p 265-273; Eric Luiten and Dirk Sijmons, 'Regionale planvorming: een vaardigheid op zoek naar een toepassing,' in: Harry Harsema (ed.), *Jaarboek stedenbouw en landschapsarchitectuur 1997-1999* (Bussum: Thoth Publishers, 2000); Dirk Sijmons, 'De regio als belofte,' in: Maarten Hajer, Dirk Sijmons, Fred Feddes (eds.), *Een plan dat werkt: Ontwerp en politiek in de regionale planvorming* (Rotterdam: NAi Uitgevers, 2006); Dirk Sijmons, 'When Research by Design takes Politics on a Sabbatical Detour,' in: George Brugmans, Jolanda van Dinteren, Maarten Hajer (eds.), *The Next Economy* (Rotterdam: IABR, 2016).

agencies in the Netherlands, demanding legions of environmental impact statements and spatial quality tests, and it's quite conceivable that all of this magic can only actually produce a disenchanting result.

Mind the Gap

In 2018 the IABR focused on the problem of the diminishing return on investment of research by design. It was diagnosed as a gap between a growing collection of ambitious long-term political goals on the one hand, and an impressive number of initiatives, including spatial plans, on the other. The 2018 biennale was aptly named THE MISSING LINK.[38]

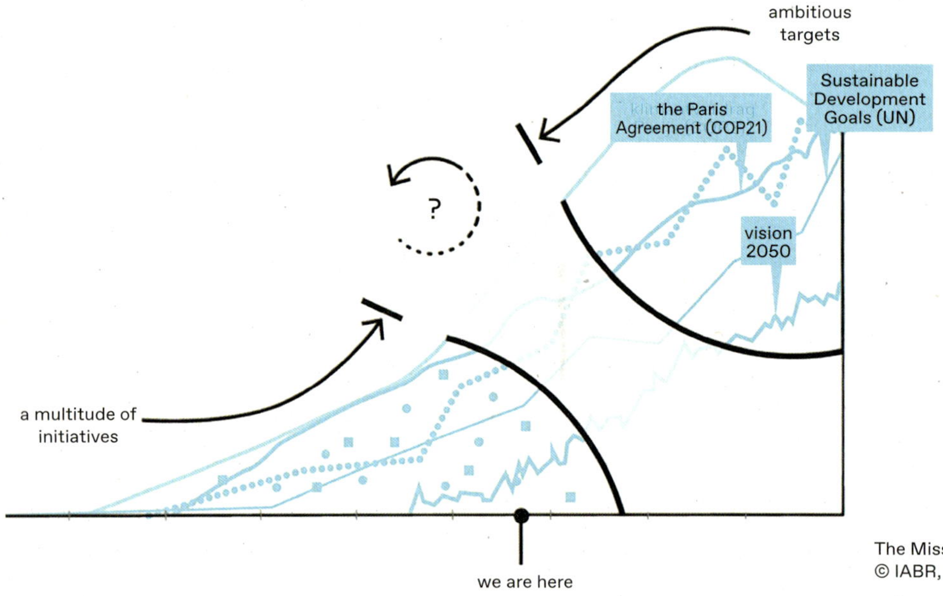

The Missing Link
© IABR, 2017

The argument was that the *gap* could only be bridged by the design community escaping from 'the observational,' 'the diagnostic,' and 'the

[38] Floris Alkemade, Leo Van Broeck, Joachim Declerck (curators), and George Brugmans (president): *IABR–2018+2020–THE MISSING LINK: Curator Statement and Research Agenda IABR* (Rotterdam: IABR, 2017).

conceptual,' and exchanging these attitudes for 'the practical': by rolling up their sleeves and using 'practices' to make the connection between the multitude of initiatives and the ambitious political goals. This observation was apt and did not fall on deaf ears, but it was somewhat apolitical. Of course, on the designer side of the gap, there are those who are satisfied with a nice plan. 'A great many ideas want to remain comets,' as Elias Canetti wrote.[39] But in fact most designers carry out research to be able to force a breakthrough in public or political debate. The tenacity of the gap is largely caused by the fact that many bombastic goals have been formulated by politicians and CEOs who secretly hope that the gap doesn't really need to be bridged, or only once their term in office is over. But even this 'grudging collaboration' fails to explain the phenomenon of diminishing returns. I suspect that the disappointing continued effect of inventions from the spatial laboratory has a lot to do with what I would like to call 'the System's Ceiling' against which we hit our heads. Rather than a ceiling, insidiously and deliberately constructed by The System, this ceiling is the result of several long lines sprouting from the neoliberal *zeitgeist* and that have been interwoven into a tough and unruly whole.

The Neoliberalization of Spatial Planning

The first long line traces the gradual dismantling and decentralization of environmental design. Since people like Ad Geelhoed started calling environmental design 'a stagnating arrangement in our economy' in the 1990s, erosion has been rapid. Like in other areas of government policy, without much political discussion the Rhineland capitalism management model was gradually abandoned in favor of an Anglo-Saxon style of planning.[40] The carrot of a new Environmental and Planning Act was held out to us, an Act that – completely in line with the new paradigm – is to be mainly about streamlining the granting of permits in response to requests from citizens, initiators, and businesses, but that is much less clear and directive in terms of what the withdrawing government itself can and

[39] Elias Canetti, *Notes from Hampstead: The Writer's Notes: 1954-1971* (New York: Farrar, Straus and Giroux, 1998), p 152.

[40] Which, in the Netherlands, was erroneously oversimplified to mean 'more freedom for citizens and organizations,' while freedom Anglo-Saxon-style is embedded in a system of firm prohibitions that cannot be tampered with. The latter component was conveniently set aside so that we ended up in what may well be called the worst of both worlds.
At the time, from 1990 until 1997, Ad Geelhoed was the secretary-general of the Dutch Ministry of Economic Affairs.

ought to want. To this we add – as the System's Ceiling's second component – the obvious tendency not to take the long term into account. At the beginning of this century, 'vision' was dismissed as 'out of date.' People with vision were immediately referred to the optician, to be fitted with corrective glasses that would help them become shortsighted. This ideology, which was packaged as 'new realism,' seemed to be supported scientifically by insights from complexity theory, where it became increasingly clear that non-linear, complex systems, such as our society, are often fundamentally unpredictable. Ergo: looking ahead beyond the planning board of a concrete project or the quarterly figures of a publicly traded company could be dismissed as presumptuous and fanciful. Ultimately, neoliberal economic policies made market thinking increasingly dominant. Market thinking has permeated the whole of society, right down to its very foundations. It is a way of thinking in which everything has a price, but nothing has a value. It determines all policies and actions, from Youth Care to the Zuidas, Amsterdam's rapidly developing business district. Everything has to be based on a profitable business case. The largest grain size of spatial policy has therefore become the project, and it is and remains difficult to include values other than monetary ones in projects. There have been many attempts to re-broaden the scope. 'Market imperfections' had to be corrected by using point systems for 'circularity' or 'nature-inclusive building' in tenders, or by connecting them in parallel in environmental impact assessments. Looking through neoliberal glasses the climate problem is sometimes characterized as 'the biggest market imperfection of all.' [41] However, real costs, including all externalities, are never actually factored in, but rather the buck is passed: on to society and the environment.

The neoliberalization of spatial planning led – surprise, surprise – to a neoliberal environmental order. This is perhaps best illustrated by the Dutch landscape. This landscape is the expression, the spatial expression, of an agriculture that pairs unprecedentedly high productivity, in both animal and vegetable protein, with an equally sky-high use of additives. Through strong lobbying – the sector will defend its interests to the death – agriculture has succeeded in passing on most environmental problems,

[41] Sir Nicholas Stern: 'Climate change is a result of the greatest market failure the world has seen. We risk damages on a scale larger than the two world wars of the last century.' In: 'Stern: Climate change a "market failure",' *The Guardian*, 29 November 2007. See also: Nicholas Stern, *The Economics of Climate Change: The Stern Review* (London: Government of the UK, 2006).

such as the decline in biodiversity, nitrogen, and water abstraction, to nature and the rest of society. Its earning power is high, the price of land correspondingly so.
Land can generate even higher returns when it is used for business parks. As we put our faith on the lazy and outdated earnings model of the Netherlands as a distribution hub, our landscape has also become the favorite landing spot of distribution centers (excellent accessibility) and data centers (close to green energy production). However, these not only reflect our own national online shopping behavior, but also distribute packages and data across the rest of Europe. All of this has been accelerated by municipalities that have been forced to become more entrepreneurial and – increasingly bled by government cuts in the municipal funds – more dependent on the income made by their land development departments. This one-sided cumulative economic pressure on the land market has resulted in an agricultural land price that, at an average of € 70,000/ha, is among the highest in the world.[42] To give you an idea: it is about twice as high as in Germany and almost ten times the average price per hectare in France.[43] This money has to be earned one way or another, which cold-showers all kinds of initiatives to – for increasingly urgent environmental reasons – expand the land use.

How Can We Lose When We're So Sincere?

Another scan, but now of the characteristics of the type of solutions put forward by research by design for the transition paths, and several things stand out.
Problems identified at the scale of the delta or landscape are met with solutions at the same scale.
Elegant research-by-design solutions usually require quite a lot of space, because they make use of natural processes. The bonus is that in doing so they also address the erosion of biodiversity. At stake here are problems that have built up over many decades, sometimes centuries, and require a correspondingly long time to solve. Perspectives developed are therefore mostly long term.

[42] Kadaster and Wageningen Economic Research, *Kwartaalbericht agrarische grondmarkt, 2021 - 4e kwartaal*, 26 January 2022.

[43] Huib Silvis and Martien Voskuilen, *Agrarische grondprijzen in de EU in 2016* (Wageningen: Wageningen Economic Research, 2016).

Spatial management is weakened: it is of course possible to break up a 'big' problem to solve it with a number of small projects, but then you have to be able to manage those projects. In cases in which this form of management is necessary but lacking, it is either invented separately or included in the design.[44] You can be critical of this, but in my view it mainly demonstrates the need for new forms of collectivity and a desire to revitalize spatial planning.

A thread connecting much research by design is the integrated approach: problems are not approached in isolation, but often linked to other social issues. This is not strange, after all: the various 'transitions' come together in the spatial domain. It is typical of designers to try to kill several birds with one stone.

Lastly, solutions often result in (the addition of) high-quality public space, such as the emergence of brownfield parks during the refurbishment of disused industrial sites.[45]

Detail from Charles Schulz's *Peanuts*, April 6, 1963. from: *The Complete Peanuts 1963–1964* Vol. 7 (Fantagraphics, 2007) © Peanuts Worldwide, LLC.

These are all, in short, great social benefits. But still, as Charlie Brown sighs when his non-starter baseball team has lost, yet again: 'How can we lose when we're so sincere?'

[44] In my comparative study on research by design initiatives for the agricultural transition, I came across suggestions such as value commissions, marks, new commons, area funds, prosumer democracy, and new deals between society and agriculture. See: Dirk Sijmons and Ingeborg Thoral, 'Wat niet kan is nog nooit gebeurd,' accompanying essay in EO Wijers #11, *Verrukkelijk Landschap* (Wageningen: Blauwdruk, 2020).

[45] René van der Velden, *Transformation in Composition: Ecdysis of Landscape Architecture through the Brownfield Park Project (1975-2015)*, dissertation Delft University of Technology (Delft: Faculty of Architecture and the Built Environment, 2018).

Charlie seems to be putting into words our amazement as to why these obvious benefits are not understood and fail to materialize. The reason might be that the space that 'our' integrated solutions require is expensive compared with competing technical options that claim to have the same effect. Acknowledging blame: 'our' attitude towards economic stumbling blocks, such as the abovementioned land price and the financing costs, is rather unfocused. Pens often cheerfully draw around them, as if they don't matter. It's also fair to say that the time 'our' solutions will take is outside the usual timeframes of financial depreciation. Another competitive disadvantage: all too often, the sought-after integration proves too difficult for the siloed orgware of the government. Finally, the scale at which 'our' solutions are formulated no longer matches the scale at which policies are developed. In short: 'our' solutions are very sensitive to the neoliberal agent with which the System's Ceiling is impregnated. No matter how good and sincere we are, we fail to break through.

Let me give an example. The images of flooding in southern Limburg in the Netherlands, Wallonia in Belgium, and the German states of North Rhine-Westphalia and Rhineland-Palatinate in 2021 are etched in our memories. They combined erratic rainstorms, too much precipitation in the 'wrong' season, and a remarkably stationary low-pressure area that poured rain for days.[46] Limburg could not get the water out. The Meuse Projects (the Grensmaas and the recently completed Ooijen-Wansum project)[47] and downstream the 'Room for the River' program[48] did help to transport the bulk of the water to the North Sea via the rivers without problems, but had less to offer the hilly area itself. Things went wrong along streams and in the upper reaches. The Ruhr, a tributary of the Meuse, reached an unprecedented water level; normally calm South Limburg streams like the Geul, Gulp, and Caumerbeek changed into roaring torrents. Once the water had subsided, the call for measures grew louder. Actually, there is no antidote to these kinds of increasingly frequent extremes, but there are ways to soften the blow. We need to sing a completely different tune in the hills than we do in the lower reaches of the rivers.

[46] It is estimated that such extreme precipitation may occur once every six years under the influence of climate change. See Abdullah Kahraman et al., 'Quasi-Stationary Intense Rainstorms Spread across Europe under Climate Change,' *Geophysical Research Letters* 48/13 (2021).

[47] Floris Alkemade and Peter-Paul Witsen, *Stuurmanskunst, Gouden Piramide 2020: Rijksprijs voor inspirerend opdrachtgeverschap* (The Hague: Atelier Rijksbouwmeester, 2021), p 44-53.

[48] Dirk Sijmons et al., *Room for the River: Safe and Attractive Landscapes* (Wageningen: Uitgeverij Blauwdruk, 2017).

If we were to use the type of structural, elegant spatial solutions described above, then you could think of changes in land use, rewetting the plateaus, strategically afforesting the slopes, bringing back landscape elements such as grafts and hedges, and removing drains in the low-lying parts near the stream. These are appropriate tools for stripping the drainage of its most dangerous peaks.
A technical (partial) solution has already been suggested by an engineering firm. This is the construction of a water tunnel, a kind of bypass for the water, under the stricken town of Valkenburg, which will move the problems downstream, but ensure that Valkenburg's now affected restaurants, tourist stores, and hotels keep their feet dry.[49]
More integrated and structural solutions are challenging, as they would require reversing several water interventions that were made for agriculture in the past. The (relative) water safety would come with bonuses such as a greatly increased biodiversity and a more attractive landscape, and thus a more interesting tourist product. The technical 'solution' takes up less space – land use will not have to change – but it intensifies the problems downstream. Pop question to readers: Which solution will local politicians choose?

Regression or Action?

Should we, after all these lessons in humility, decide to abandon all of this unrealistic daydreaming about integrated and structural designs and throw ourselves, with a little more engineering ethos, into technically and economically feasible solutions? In my opinion, that would be a terrible mistake. The (eco)modernist premise that there is an engineering solution to every individual problem is an *idée fixe*. Such solutions are often based on the very school of thought that caused the problems in the first place. They are solutions with strong side effects, which in turn must be addressed by other technical means, ad infinitum. To upscale the Limburg dilemma to a global level: the acidity of the oceans must not be combated by lime and iron ions, but by stopping the discharge of acidifying substances and by restricting overfishing. The climate crisis must not be

[49] Witteveen + Bos, *Tunnel kan overstromingsoverlast Valkenburg beperken*, witteveenbos.com (9 September 2021).

→
Planetary Boundaries. adapted from: Steffen et al., 'Planetary Boundaries: Guiding Human Development on a Changing Planet', *Science* (2015). © Owen McGaffney

PLANETARY BOUNDARIES

A safe operating space for humanity

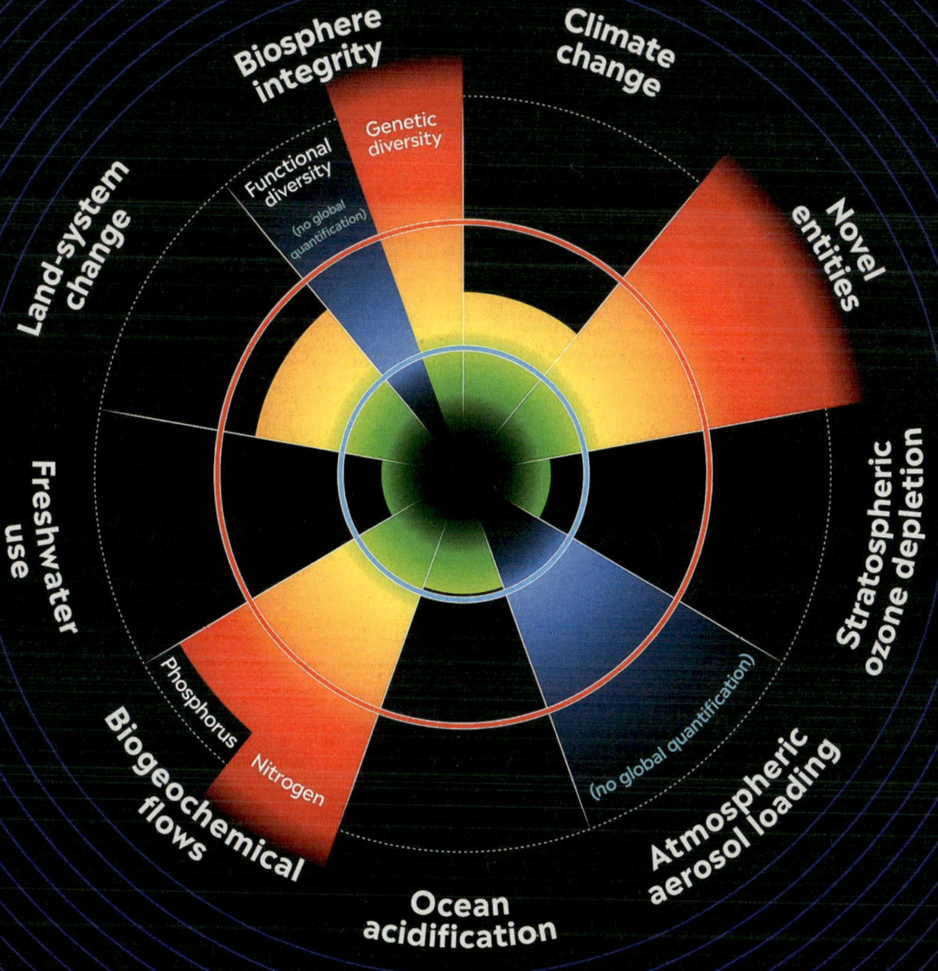

- **Beyond zone of uncertainty** (high risk)
- **In zone of uncertainty** (increasing risk)
- **Below boundary** (safe)
- **Boundary not yet quantified**

THE SYSTEM'S CEILING

defused by introducing sulfur particles into the atmosphere, but by stopping the emission of greenhouse gases. Land use change and soil degradation must not be solved by a new green revolution, but by agro-ecological insights. The biodiversity crisis must not be solved by believing in novel ecosystems or de-extinction programs. And the reduction of sediment discharge from all major rivers must not be achieved by compensating the effects with hard coastal defenses, but rather by removing unnecessary dams – which also hinder fish migration – and by giving rivers more space. And, finally, the lack of natural resources must be combated, first and foremost, by a lower turnover rate of our economy, and not by blind faith in the modern fairy tale of the circular economy. The dilemma surfaces all over the world and accompanies all major environmental problems. A glance at the planetary dashboard that comprises nine critical limits makes it clear which warning lights are flashing, and in which cases we have already far exceeded those limits. The most alarming cases of limits exceeded are directly or indirectly related to space usage. Three indicators that are deep in the red concern the bio-geochemical cycles of nitrate and phosphate (that is, for fertilizer and agriculture), land-use changes (urbanization and especially agricultural development), and, through the cumulative effects of the two, dramatically declining biodiversity.[50]

I believe we must put our trust in an integrated approach: that using soft spatial means and natural processes is the right way to connect these spatial problems and 'repair' the damage already done. Not to become anti-technological, but in the full awareness that technology, in addition to being a blessing, can also be our downfall. Rather than regressively embrace modernism, the design community should be in full action mode to enforce healing solutions. This struggle, this rowing against the current, requires an action-oriented attitude. We cannot arrogantly stand by, cherishing our hypothetical professional neutrality.

So what *can* designers do, other than continue to make good plans? What can we do at home, close to home, and further afield, to ensure that we will not at some point find ourselves too far away from home?

[50] Johan Rockström et al., 'Planetary Boundaries: Exploring the Safe Operating Space for Humanity,' *Ecology and Society* 14/2 (2009), article 32.
For the planetary dashboard see previous page, 373.

At Home

Although every little bit helps, I am not going to talk about eating less meat, using fewer dairy products, and buying fewer palm oil-based products. Perhaps the best thing you can do personally, as a designer, is to develop a reflective form of professional practice – if you don't already. This also means introspection: When can I, in my professional practice, be part of the solution and when am I part of the problem? What would my project look like if all life on the planet was my client, instead of some councilor? As it becomes clear that the familiar (eco) modernist solutions are no longer solving the problems and globalism is reaching its planetary limits, should I perhaps adjust my worldview? And what ways are there to escape the modernism of which designers were long the heralds?[51]

Close to Home

Close to home is where the political action is. After all, landscape architecture is an inherently political profession.[52] We can argue – through our professional organizations or otherwise – for a much bolder form of spatial planning. Indeed, for the kind of spatial planning that is 'outdated,' but that our times emphatically require. In short, we can help break the System's Ceiling. Do away with all of that national, provincial, and municipal planning stuff, do away with cowardly waiting for 'public support' that, just like Godot, is never going to come. Show that design can overcome the largely aesthetic objections to the only working vaccine against pandemic climate change that we know of: sustainable electricity and heat production. Also: for the agricultural transition to work, we urgently need to take collective rezoning plans back into use. The land development machine is rusting in the barn, while at the request of the provinces the Land Development Act has become an integral part of the new Environmental and Planning Act.[53] So there still is a way to negotiate with each other in an orderly fashion. At this time, the agricultural

[51] Every year, itineraries and exit visas are provided during the Citizens of the Anthropocene course I teach at the Independent School for the City in Rotterdam.

[52] On the political nature of landscape architecture, see: Sara Zewde et al., in: B. Cannon Ivers et al., *250 Things a Landscape Architect Should Know* (Basel: Birkhauser, 2021).

[53] Sijmons and Thoral, 'Wat niet kan is nog nooit gebeurd.'

transition may well be the challenge that is most important, most comprehensive, and closest to our profession – and also one in which our country plays a crucial role.[55] Let's get to it!

Away from Home

The System's Ceiling is firmly attached to the concrete structure of the capitalist economy itself. It's a hard nut to crack. As both Fredric Jameson and Slavoj Žižek noted earlier: most people can imagine the end of the world more easily than the end of capitalism.[55] This is why transformation-oriented economists do not wait for this system to succumb to its own contradictions, but devise reforms that can combat or at least mitigate its consequences and inequalities. Our profession can latch on to several initiatives, which I touch on below, in order of increasing radicality.

Broadening the economy to include other than financial imponderable elements. No more GNP![56] In the slipstream of this movement it could be arranged that the social benefits that farming can provide (biodiversity, water retention, carbon storage, landscape maintenance, care), would actually become income components for the farmers (rather than allowances for expenses!).

Providing capitalism with a mission. Mariana Mazzucato calls for the formulation of 'Moonshot Projects.'[57] These are projects in which – just like in the race to the moon unleashed by US President John F. Kennedy – a substantial part of the economy is aimed at a single goal. In our domain, you might think of a World Park Project, in which an ecological mega corridor connects the biodiversity hotspots on different continents. Three continuous, restored landscapes with hiking trails as central nervous systems, from Patagonia to Alaska, from Namibia to Türkiye, and from Australia to Morocco.[58] And this would also involve attempts to persuade the

[54] We have to realize that the agriculture/food system has a far-reaching impact on six of the nine planetary boundaries visualized in the Johan Rockström *Dashboard* embraced by the UN (see note 50 and the image on page 373). These are, in order of planetary urgency: freshwater use (still below the critical limit, share of agricultural use significant); climate change (in the uncertain zone, agriculture is directly responsible for 14 percent of global emissions and indirectly for another 18 percent through land-use change); biogeochemical flows (nitrate and phosphate, two components of fertilizers: planetary limit far exceeded, high risk, share of agriculture in the Netherlands some 43 percent, globally very high); integrity of the biosphere (genetic biodiversity: in the red zone, planetary limit exceeded, high risk, share of agriculture very high also through nitrate and mining).

[55] Mark Fisher attributes this observation to both Jameson and Žižek, in: Mark Fisher, *Capitalist Realism: Is There No Alternative?* (London: Zero Books, 2009).

[56] Rutger Hoekstra, *Replacing GDP by 2030: Towards a Common Language for the Wellbeing and Sustainability Community* (Cambridge: Cambridge University Press, 2019).

[57] Mariana Mazzucato, *Mission Economy: A Moonshot Guide to Changing Capitalism* (London: Allen Lane, 2021).

[58] Richard J. Weller et al., *The World Park Project* (Philadelphia: Weitzman School of Design PENN, 2021).

world's richest people to trade in their space toys for this project, and to divert their billion-dollar investments to preserve the biodiverse Earth. *Down to Earth*, indeed. But let us not forget *Down to Holland* either, and first orderly finish the Ecological Infrastructure – aka Nature Network Netherlands – in our own country!

A similar initiative comes from philosopher Roman Krznaric, who wants to improve investment decision making by giving seven consecutive future generations a voice. This will help us to become good ancestors and to think in terms of cathedral projects, which are built by successive generations.[59] In our domain, that should be quite possible. The Pleistocene Park initiative of father and son Simov comes to mind.[60] In Siberia, these ecologists are experimenting with restoring the mammoth steppe system that was the dominant biome in the Pleistocene. They are doing this by replacing the existing unproductive coniferous forest ecosystems with highly productive grasslands through the use of massive grazing. Not out of a nostalgic longing for primeval nature, but to counteract the thawing of the permafrost.[61] And back to the Netherlands: Why not roll up our sleeves in support of our own rewilding initiatives? That could yield projects as interesting as our recent meddling with the moraines of industrial glaciers.

Too Far Away from Home

A 2022 report of the Intergovernmental Panel on Climate Change (IPCC) dealt with climate change-instigated impacts, adaptations, and vulnerabilities.[62] It addressed climate change in relation to other disruptions to planetary systems taking into account, more particularly, biodiversity loss, the excessive use of natural resources, and the ability of human societies and ecosystems to adapt. To the observant reader, it's clear that the globalization of our economy is reaching its planetary limits.

59 Roman Krznaric, *The Good Ancestor: A Radical Prescription for Long-Term Thinking* (New York: The Experiment, 2020).

60 Eli Kintish, 'Born to Rewild: A Father and Son's Quixiotic Quest to Bring Back a Lost Ecosystem – and Save the Planet,' *Science* 350/6265 (2015), p 1148-1151.

61 The Simovs' philosophy is based on paleontological evidence that Arctic grasslands at the time had as rich a herbivore fauna as the African savannahs of today. The new grasslands provide a wealth of protein for the grazers and store more CO_2 than coniferous forests. The land is white again in winter and reflects sunlight better than coniferous forests, to which snow does not stick as well. Large numbers of herbivores punch holes in the snowfield in winter, allowing heat stored in summer to escape. Their 300-km² Pleistocene Park proves effective: the permafrost remains frozen.

62 Hans-Otto Pörtner et al., 'Summary for Policymakers,' *Climate Change 2022: Impacts, Adaptation, and Vulnerability*. Contribution of Working Group II to the Sixth Assessment Report of the Intergovernmental Panel on Climate Change (Cambridge: Cambridge University Press, 2022).

The IPCC thus entered the realm of wicked problems. The picture painted and the short timeline for necessary action were alarming, to say the least. 'Any further delay in coordinated global action in the areas of adaptation and mitigation will miss the now rapidly diminishing opportunity to turn the tide and ensure a livable and sustainable future for all' – from a scenario labeled 'very high confidence.'

Because of that other war the world faced in February 2022, the IPCC's urgent recommendations met with a near-total silence in terms of press and public attention. Some 1,000 young scientists from 25 countries subsequently took to the streets under the motto 'Scientist Rebellion,' a motto they 'borrowed' from their peers. An unusual sight: the whitecoats took to the streets and in places were even removed with a great show of (police) force.

Scientists deal with facts, with matters of fact. As designers, we're more concerned with the domain in which engagement plays a leading part: with matters of concern. In the IPCC report, these overlap. As a design community, we can take over the baton from the scientists and play a part in the political discussion of how to tackle the issues: 'Designer Rebellion.' It is to be hoped that the above plea has made clear that what type of solutions we choose can make quite a difference. There are solutions that make bad things worse (the IPCC report even introduces a new category: 'maladaptations,' or solutions that are more harmful than helpful). The measures agreed in the context of the COP, the annual climate conference of the United Nations, are already too little too late; it could be disastrous if the interventions that will soon be taken in a panic – think of geoengineering – also turn out to be counterproductive. We *have* to succeed in breaking the System's Ceiling, to ensure that the supporting structure of the planetary processes on which all ecosystems and human societies are grafted is not irreversibly weakened. Because if we let it get that far, we will likely find ourselves too far from home and unable to find our way back.

Dirk Sijmons
May 2022

DESIGNING IN TIMES OF CLIMATE CRISIS Rotterdam Academy of Architecture and Urban Design

The Rotterdam Academy of Architecture and Urban Design (RAvB) is transitioning from an institution that trains designers to work in practice to one that trains designers to change practice. It is important for the RAvB to permanently and clearly voice its new position in the ecosystems in which it operates – the city of Rotterdam, the design sector and the cultural institutions that put social issues on the agenda. This is why the decision to enter into a partnership with the IABR was easy to make. By connecting the research capacity of design education to the free space of culture, the two institutions can now explore ways to relate to the climate crisis and transitions we need to make, together.

NOW! DESIGNING IN TIMES OF CLIMATE CRISIS

As part of the collaboration, over 120 students from the RAvB together with 30 students from the Royal Academy of Art (KABK) in The Hague, guided by DOWN TO EARTH curator team member Thijs van Spaandonk, curated the exhibition: NOW! DESIGNING IN TIMES OF CLIMATE CRISIS. Central to this exhibition were nearly 400 posters; lying in a grid, they almost filled the entire space of the Keilezaal in Rotterdam. Each in its own way, the posters provided the answer of tomorrow's designers to the question posed by chief curator George Brugmans, referring to French philosopher Bruno Latour: *Where can we land?*

During a three-day workshop in February 2021, 12 students from the KABK and RAvB worked with Thijs van Spaandonk to assemble the material from the two institutions and translate it into a narrative and spatial concept. photo: RAvB

ALONG FOUR THEMATIC LINES

This poster field covered four themes to which designing has to relate: the *extremes*, the *other*, the *commons*, and the *departure*.

THE EXTREMES

The climate crisis is leading to more extreme weather conditions. What can we expect, and what adjustments to our living environment do we need to make, now and in the future? Also, how do we deal with this? Should we perhaps make sure that we actually experience these extremes more expressly in our living environment, to increase our awareness of the crisis?

THE OTHER

We are all part of a single biosphere; there is no getting away from it. Our actions have consequences for other people as well as all other lifeforms. Our activities (or lack thereof) in Rotterdam affect the prospects for actions of all lifeforms across the planet.

THE COMMONS

The climate crisis is a consequence of the extractive way we have been treating the Earth for the purpose of relentless economic growth. We are

→

Life as a Verb
The Soil of our Environment

IMPACT

becoming increasingly aware that we need a different value model, based on reciprocity and connection to place and community. So what does urban development based on the idea of the commons look like?

THE DEPARTURE

We need to let go of certain raw materials and fuels, and, therefore, certain routines. Letting go hurts. But letting go also involves reflecting on and appreciating elements of the past (recognizing that some may well add value again in the future).

INITIATIVE AND CREDITS

The exhibition was an initiative by Thijs van Spaandonk (RAvB), Roosje Klap and Marthe Prins (KABK), and George Brugmans (IABR).

CONCEPT, CURATION, DESIGN AND REALIZATION
KABK
Ieva Gailiušaitė, Petra Erős
RAvB
Amal Habti , Samil Kahraman, Tom Koetsenruijter, Lotte de Koning, Angéla Kortleven, Sven Schouten, Petula de Smit, Nancy Smolka, Thijs van Spaandonk, Anneke Wisse, Milou van Zomeren

GRAPHIC DESIGN
Petra Erős

REFLECTION

That the exhibition in the Keilezaal was never open to visitors due to Covid-19 measures – which is why the 400 posters were presented via Instagram – was an additional reason for further, public reflection on the academies' question of how designing, designs, and designers can and ought to deal with the climate crisis. This took place in the spring of 2022 in the form of, among other things, conversations that three students had with Mark Minkjan and Thijs van Spaandonk, researcher and head of the master's program in urban design at the RAvB, respectively. Below is the abstract.

WHO IS ACTUALLY THE STUDENT HERE?

The Rotterdam Academy of Architecture starts reflection on the question: *Where can we land?* from, among other things, the design practice for which it trains students who simultaneously work in it.[63] During their training, our students are continuously invited and encouraged to use their design tools to support an activist position. But what are the opportunities for design activism responses to the climate crisis in the field? How can the urge to change things, which students develop through their research by design at the Academy, result in a changed practice? To formulate answers to these questions, we talked to three Academy students, Amal Habti, Milou van Zomeren, and Daan de Jong. First, we discussed our awareness of the practice in which we work. Next, we diagnosed the manifestations of destructive policy and building culture in order to pinpoint underlying causes. Finally, we addressed the role of the Academy in relation to an alternative practice and the position of the designer with respect to the climate crisis.

DOWN TO EARTH was the result of research by design into the question of where to land, for which the IABR chose to deploy two levers: the energy transition and the water challenge. It was clear that an integrated approach to these two was required. Water and energy (and therefore the energy transition) are inextricably linked to, and even a prerequisite for, virtually all aspects of our daily lives, our economy, our culture and our environmental planning. They are levers design practice must use to achieve systemic improvement.

Unfortunately, we have had to acknowledge that urban design and architecture do not generally appear to operate from a desire for systemic improvement. Yes, projects are becoming more sustainable due to stricter legal rules and regulations. Clients also want to distinguish themselves by sustainable projects. Tenders can therefore score points by including a 'sustainability statement.' However, these statements only concern technical solutions that meet the client's program of requirements. Sustainability

[63] All students at the Rotterdam Academy of Architecture combine studying with working in practice. The knowledge, skills and perspectives that they develop at the Academy, can immediately be used in practice. And vice versa, they can use the skills acquired in the professional field in their studies.

has become an item to be checkmarked. If it comes up to the building standards, then the client is happy. Promising more than what the client asks for will not achieve anything. Even barely adequate solutions require that cuts are made to stay within budget. Amal Habti, architecture student: 'In many cases, construction budgets do not realistically reflect ambition levels.'

Inside or Outside the Frameworks

More problematic in light of the question: *Where can we land?* is that in the field, thinking about sustainability never transcends the level of the project itself. The building, plot, or project area determine the boundaries of action as well as thinking. The question of where the raw materials, labor and energy needed to complete the project come from is rarely raised. Architecture student Milou van Zomeren: 'From your actions on a specific plot result duties of care with respect to other places, which are currently not being fulfilled.' Projects and practices hardly ever seek to relate to places outside the project sites, even though they do affect these places. Examples are mines for the extraction of metals, sea beds for the extraction of sand and pebbles, and quarries for the extraction of (natural) stone. And if we also include the waste flows caused by our projects in this approach, counting greenhouse gas emissions, their impact in other places is even greater.

Efforts to improve sustainability mostly take place inside existing frameworks, by making that which already exists just a little bit better, while everyone increasingly realizes that this is in denial of the emergency situation in which we find ourselves. We need to work on an alternative practice, one that can break through current frameworks and preconditions. So why can we still not do this successfully?

External Pressure

Part of the problem can be considered external, such as the conditions, the production chain, the ecosystem, and the context in which the practice of architecture and urban design has to operate and on which it largely depends. Most architecture and urban design practices are entirely dependent on the construction industry and the real estate market. Except in places where government regulation has a somewhat moderating effect, architecture and urban design primarily serve two purposes: to create sales for as many building products as possible and to increase property value. Both of these are problematic in terms of sustainability. It is precisely the extraction and processing of raw materials for construction purposes that have the greatest impact on the health of the biosphere. And in an environmental planning system in which property value is dominant, biosphere health value will always lose out. Also, both the construction industry and the real estate market have but one goal and that is growth. 'And it is this doctrine of growth that has brought us to the verge of disaster,' concludes urban design student Daan de Jong.

Most projects that are realized within these parameters are only partially sustainable. Or even worse, it is suggested that they are sustainable, a sales trick with the aim of building even more: greenwashing. Examples include concrete buildings with a few trees on top, or a sustainable building right next to a highway, or even worse, in a city like Dubai.

Internal Pressure

Daan de Jong: 'We have to realize that we do not *have* to reduce ourselves to servants of the construction industry.' We have to find alternatives. But this takes us to another part of the problem, and that is that a sizeable number of architectural and urban design practices is actually quite happy to operate within the parameters of the construction industry and the real estate market. Indeed, the core business of many such offices is to meet the preconditions of the market as best it can. And quite a few elements of this core business actually get in the way of change.

First, there is the focus on winning tenders and competitions. Individual profit and prestige take precedence over collective achievement, despite the fact that it has been demonstrated that every European tender is, on balance, a loss for the sector.
Also, for those who want to obtain commissions directly it is too important to maintain good contacts with developers to critically scrutinize their actions. Its unilateral dependence on the client ('plenty more pebbles on the beach') makes the sector very vulnerable.
In addition, there exists an unhealthy corporate culture which – founded on the romanticization of making overtime and the alleged elusiveness of

creative processes – we ourselves perpetuate. We often think this fight to the finish is simply part of the job. All because the next project will surely be our dream project.
Amal Habti: 'Time, reflection, learning, and contemplation are aspects of different kinds of growth, welfare and wellbeing, which design culture now hardly appreciates.'

Architects are often seen as *the* solvers of all kinds of problems, 'this while the problem-solving capacity of designers is not infinite, although their proposals often suggest otherwise,' says Daan de Jong. We need major policy and cultural changes to be able to realize the UN's Sustainable Development Goals – designers cannot realize these by themselves. And given the current systems, designers are unfortunately part of the problem due to their destructive urge to build whatever the cost. Even prevailing sustainability ambitions are accompanied by 'a stubborn belief in the ingenuity of designers and a future in which everything will get better, but we forget that this perpetuates our thinking in terms of growth,' says De Jong.

Another problem in the sector is the outright focus on the built result. The work of an architect or urban designer is not truly appreciated unless it is a construction. If it is not, it is considered not (sufficiently) realizable. 'While the most sustainable building is the building that you don't have to build,' says Milou van Zomeren. 'Not building' is an active refusal to hide behind the parameters of the industry and market, and the privilege of not having to speak out. 'Not building' can also be read as an umbrella term for all the research, organization, and knowledge sharing that do not involve destructive construction, but rather offer valuable vistas and can be a lever for accelerating meaningful cultural change, especially in a field that so directly impacts the environment of many.

Towards an Alternative Practice

We will have to develop an alternative practice that can contribute to an alternative reality. Because of its training model, the Rotterdam Academy – and essentially all other Academies of Architecture in the Netherlands – can play an important part in the quest for such an alternative practice. After all, students and most lecturers are only active at the Academy for part of the week. The rest of the time, they work in architecture practices, either as employees or as employers and business owners. This puts the members of the Academy community in a unique position, because they can put the insights they gain at the Academy directly into practice and, vice versa, also ensure that reflection on practice inside the Academy is both possible and realistic.

It is a position we are happy to proactively fill. In recent years, we have been transitioning from an institution that *trains designers to work in practice* to one that *trains designers to change practice*. This means, specifically, that a smaller part of the curriculum than before is now devoted to exercises that target the execution of the profession. We are using the time that became available for exercises aimed at (re)positioning ourselves as designers in relation to the climate crisis and other collective challenges.

We do this, first, by collectively creating awareness of the fact that 'business as usual' is primarily a race to the bottom, not an attractive perspective. We are inviting lecturers and guest speakers, often from outside our immediate field, to make us face the facts through engaging in broader reflection, expanding our design vocabulary, and helping to outline alternatives. Also, design offices that develop alternative practices are asked to mentor students or otherwise enrich our program. Think of offices that are uncompromisingly but successfully experimenting with the use of materials that have no negative impact on the environment, or of peers who have found a way to operate independently and activistically.

In design education and in the theoretical exercises, new insights are visualized and translated into new spatial proposals. Daan de Jong: 'The beauty of imagination is that you can make visible what seems invisible and give it a voice. Whether it concerns the representation of future generations or that of non-human entities, making them part of our imagination allows us to relate to them empathically, which is necessary to understand and change our role as humans.'

We also explicitly look for new tools and products to present and represent spatial proposals, because the traditional products of spatial design are inadequate. Series of cross sections, floor plans, and renderings on a presentation wall may be appropriate for peer meetings called to assess a project in terms of mastery of craftsmanship, but they are totally inappropriate for conveying new perspectives and convincing stakeholders outside the profession. We have noticed a lack of tools and routines, especially for talking to citizens, as if we have forgotten to involve them; as if we have forgotten to value the stories, communities and everyday uses of the living environment.

Ambassadors and Activists

The lessons that students and faculty develop together in the safe haven that is the Academy do not stay inside its walls. We not only invite guests to attend presentations, lectures, and talks to share the lessons, but we also bring the results of the collective learning process to various venues and platforms in the city, including the IABR.
However, the most important tool for the sharing of these collective lessons are the students and lecturers themselves. We are like ambassadors, translating insights about an alternative future into a new practice, which will be able to formulate answers to the question: *Where can we land?* And the contours of this new practice are increasingly clear. It works inside the boundaries of the biosphere, is biobased, circular, inclusive, and based on collective ownership.

More and more people are taking up the role of ambassador; new practices that focus on tomorrow's challenges are being established by (former) students and lecturers. Students actively participate in the operations of the offices at which they work, to help these take their departure of all efforts that do not contribute to a sustainable future. But more importantly, students increasingly realize that our profession is not apolitical, that political activism does not distract from craftsmanship, but rather contributes to its social anchoring. More and more often our students pick up the pen, microphone, or protest board, to make their voices heard. And more and more often, it is painfully clear that these young professionals have a much more pointed idea of how to relate to the future than the establishment does. So, who is actually the student here?

Thijs van Spaandonk together with Mark Minkjan
June 2022

SPACESHIP EARTH

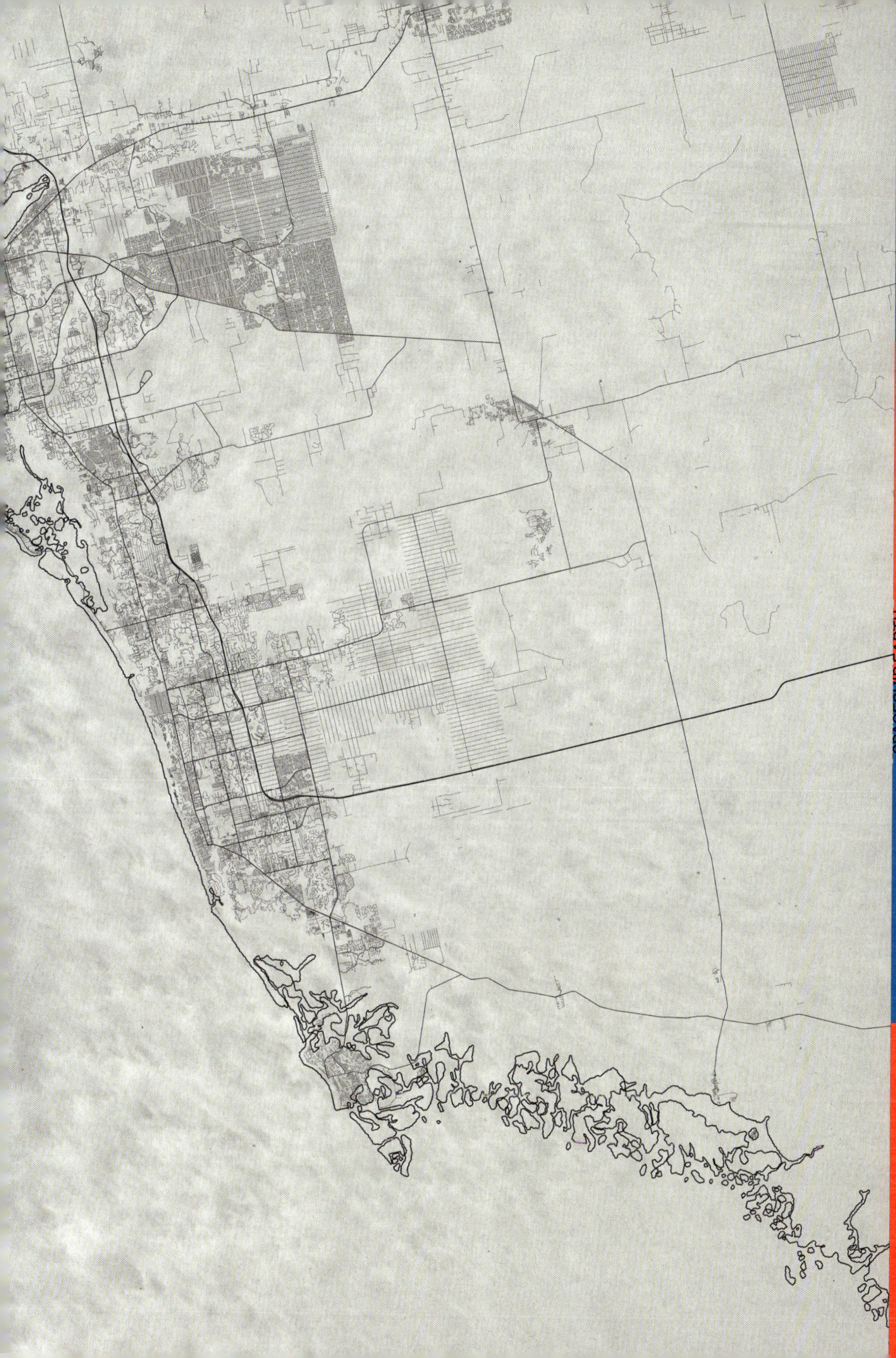

SPACESHIP EARTH George Brugmans

3: Turbulence

Disturbance is a change in environmental conditions that causes a pronounced change in an ecosystem . . . Disturbance is ordinary . . . Whether a disturbance is bearable or unbearable is a question worked out through what follows it: the reformation of assemblages. Disturbance opens the terrain for transformative encounters, making new assemblages possible . . . Assemblages are open-ended gatherings. They allow us to ask about communal effects without assuming them. They show us potential histories in the making.

Anna Lowenhaupt Tsing

[25]
At the academies of architecture, like the one in Rotterdam, at which staff and students work together on a transition 'from *training for practice* to *training to change practice*,' young designers, fraught with a sense of urgency, act as the empowered ambassadors of a new approach. But the invisible barrier – the system's ceiling – that they, like their older colleagues, come up against is, according to Dirk Sijmons, 'firmly attached to the concrete structure of capitalist economy itself.' Changing one's own practice is one thing, but changing the capitalist economy in which this practice has to land, changing the system itself, is quite another. 'A tough nut to crack,' concludes Sijmons.[64]
Let's take a look at the situation as it is, at whether it's possible to clear the way for this new change-oriented design practice, and whether we can perhaps expect help from other quarters. Are designers in a position to crack Sijmons' nut? Where and how and with whom should they crack it? What helps and who doesn't? What position should they take? And is there space to do this in? If not in the market, then where? In the free

[64] See above, pages 380, 389 ff. and 376.

←
Staring into Ian's Eye
28 September 2022, hurricane Ian barrels across the Gulf of Mexico toward the west coast of Florida.
courtesy of NASA

space of culture? But how free is that, or can it possibly be, at this point? In it, how much of a difference can one still make? And what is culture in times of neoliberalism, surveillance capitalism and algorithms? How much power does imagination even have left? And, on the other hand, how much imagination can we bear? *Can* we really, do we really *want* to imagine where we can land? And on what exactly?

[26]
In times of turbulence, for Peter Sloterdijk in any case, it is 'evident to us that not design, but meteorology has come to power.'[65] And indeed, the predictions of so-called visionary architects such as Rem Koolhaas proved unreliable, they came up with tempting scenarios, but for even more of the same. While meteorologists manage to somewhat adequately forecast what the future has in store for us, and not just in terms of weather predictions for the coming week.[66] When, together with other climate scientists, they visit the now rapidly warming Greenland, for example, or inform us of the fate of the Antarctic glacier Thwaites – the Doomsday Glacier now in its death throes – they have hundreds of thousands of followers for good reason. There's a great need for such clarification.
But what meteorologists cannot do is face the threat and build us a landing strip. All the while, Spaceship Earth is leaking and squeaking and creaking and burning, and the question of where and how we can land has become a matter of life and death. Even on what exactly we are going to have to land is in question. Because whatever we do next, we have to face the fact that when we are going to land, if we manage to land at all, it will be in the Critical Zone of a planet that is no longer what it once was.

[27]
In 2014, earth scientist Ugo Bardi wrote a report on the planet's mineral exhaustion for the Club of Rome. His forebodings are worth repeating here in their entirety: 'It is the end of a cycle that, in geological terms, was extremely short but that for us seemed to be the way things were to be forever and ever. It wasn't so; it was only the brief cycle of the period we call Anthropocene, where humans thought themselves masters of a

[65] Peter Sloterdijk, 'The Anthropocene - A Stage in the Process on the Margins of the Earth's History?' in: Sloterdijk, *What Happened in the Twentieth Century*? (Cambridge, MA: Polity Press, 2018), p 15.

[66] It is not much of an exaggeration to say that meteorologists now help predict inflation as well: when they announce falling temperatures, the daily price of natural gas on the spot market rises immediately.

whole planet. But the planet was plundered to the limit, and what we will be left with are only the ashes of a gigantic fire. We are leaving to our descendants a heavy legacy in terms of radioactive waste, heavy metals dispersed all over the planet, and greenhouse gases – mainly CO_2 – accumulated in the atmosphere and absorbed in the oceans. The Earth will never be the same; it is being transformed into a new and different planet.' [67]

This, therefore, is what we need to realize: that this burning, polluted and plundered Earth has been transformed into a new and different planet.

[28]

Rather than shy away from even more quotations – we do not want to have the last word, but neither do we want to have the first – it is necessary that we deliberately stand on the shoulders of those who have stated things plainly before us.[68] Music historian and theorist Gary Tomlinson made the following, disturbing observation: 'Across millions of years of biocultural evolution . . . certain systems remained *outside* the feedback cycles of hominin niche construction. Astronomical dynamics, tectonic

[67] Ugo Bardi, *Extracted: How the Quest for Mineral Wealth Is Plundering the Planet – A Report to the Club of Rome* (White River Junction: Chelsea Green Publishing, 2014), p 241-242. We can also see that Earth has become a different planet if we take a closer look at Earthrise, the photo of the astronaut Bill Anders from 1968. It looks dated. In it, the Earth is a whiter planet than it is now, because since then large parts of the ice caps have melted at the poles.

[68] Walter Benjamin supposedly once said he would write a book consisting entirely of quotations, to avoid any hint of subjectivity.

shifts, volcanism, climate cycles, and other such forces were in essence untouched by human culture and behavior (or if touched, touched in a vanishingly small degree). In the language of systems theory, all these forces were in effect *feed-forward* elements: external controls that "set" the feedback cycles from without, affecting the elements within them but remaining unaffected by the feedback themselves . . . The Anthropocene . . . registers a systemic rearrangement in which systems *that had always acted as feed-forward elements from outside human niche construction have been converted into feedback elements within it.*' [69]

Why is this alarming? Because Tomlinson exposes the kind of problem we are dealing with: a *wicked problem*. We can diagnose it, but we cannot make it go away. In the Anthropocene, we are part of the problem, but not part of the solution – this too is what we have to realize, that we're fumbling with the controls and only making it worse.

[29]

Just when more and more lights on the dashboard are flashing red, we wake up to the fact that we are the planetary pilots of Spaceship Earth. On the bridge there is neither an operating manual, nor a flight plan. It is getting hotter and hotter. No chimney, no ventilation, no windows, no emergency exit. Anxiety sets in, maybe we ought to turn things down a notch? Consultations. Conferences. How to go about it? Together doesn't work. Because the barbarians are not at the gate, they are on board. They recognize that it will benefit them greatly to now burn as much as possible as quickly as possible. There is still a lot of money to be made from disasters! Fanatically, they seize power on the ship, their massive wealth taking the rest of us hostage. And so the temperature continues to rise. Apocalyptic heat waves. More and more people die, here, there, everywhere. Flooding. No escape. Ice caps melting, whole sections of glaciers breaking off. Insects on the decline. Land drying out. Yet another superstorm warning. Atmospheric rivers, waves of water crashing down from the skies. Where did the North Pole go? It was there a moment ago! No more bird song; no more butterfly wings. Millions on the run. Heading for war. Spaceship Earth is leaking and squeaking and creaking and burning. The turbulence is frightful.

[69] Gary Tomlinson, 'Two Deep-Historical Models of Climate Crisis,' *South Atlantic Quarterly* 116/1 (January 2017); quoted in Dipesh Chakrabarty, *The Climate of History in a Planetary Age* (Chicago: The University of Chicago Press, 2021), p 140.

No lifeboats. No safety belts but VR goggles. Is hope naive, lethal? No emergency exits! Jump overboard? There is no overboard. There is panic.

[30]
The current course of events may well lead to failure, and social collapse on a global scale may be inevitable. Those who manage to survive wars, massacres, and shortages of energy, food, and water, the complete implosion of civilization as we know it, will have to live in totally different circumstances. And the only thing left is to prepare for this as best we can.

[31]
The question of where we can land is not about coordinates or terrain conditions, landing cannot be yet another agrilogistical venture, or a military operation. Nor are we interested in ocean views and five-star reviews: never again will we be on vacation. This is a mass disembarkation, after a turbulent return flight to unknown terrain, the outcome of which is uncertain and which requires a great deal of us. As human beings, or as humankind, we have to surrender our passports. We have to land as terrestrials among other terrestrials, and not on the globe, or back to nature, but in the Critical Zone of 'a new and different' planet. This makes disembarkation a revolutionary undertaking. With a crucial cultural component, because returning across the gangway requires *hacking* the *meme*: we need a completely new narrative, new plans, new design, a new myth as a lever for urgent change on a new planet – a new politics.[70]

[32]
Our disembarkation will hardly be festive. For this is, all things considered, what 8 billion fortune hunters get out of 500 years of kinetic expressionism: the sneaking suspicion that the only practically attainable life is an extremely austere life for all, and that, in retrospect, our somewhat ill-considered planetary experiment ultimately forces us into formidable planetary moderation. That the landing strip, if we manage to find it at all,

[70] 'Redirecting attention from "nature" toward the Terrestrial might put an end to the disconnect that has frozen political positions since the appearance of the climate threat and has imperiled the linking of the so-called social struggles with those we call ecological. . . . Saying "We are earthbound, we are terrestrials amid terrestrials," *does not lead to the same politics as* saying "We are humans in nature".' See: Bruno Latour, *Down to Earth: Politics in the New Climate Regime* (Cambridge: Polity Press, 2018), p 82 and 86.

will not have a celebratory welcoming committee, cheerful music, and well-deserved medals waiting for us – that the mission has failed. That we need to start a cultural revolution that forces us to look at where we are, at each other, rather than ahead; to what's here rather than to the El Dorados across the water. That we need to stop living *here* by squeezing life dry *there*; to stop wanting things *now* that mortgage *tomorrow*. That we need radical change, which amounts to *re-civilizing the entire search for human happiness*, as Sloterdijk puts it. We have to try to reconnect longing with the reality from which capitalism has dissociated us. And yes, this is a tough nut to crack, when the end of the world is easier to imagine than the end of capitalism.[71]

[33]
So, here's another question: Do we actually even want to land? Wouldn't we rather take our individual longings to the holodeck than our common fears to the cockpit? It's easy to imagine that while the 1 percent – with its mod cons, under the leadership of Elon Musk – embark to move to Mars, to new El Dorados, the 99 percent would rather sign up for Mark Zuckerberg's metaverse. They would just as soon go where the wind blows the ship. Assuming they notice at all, wearing VR goggles.[72]

[34]
In Wim Wenders's film *Until the End of the World* (1991), which plays around the turn of the millennium against the backdrop of a world-threatening catastrophe, a scientist develops a device that translates the brain's electrochemical activity into digital images. His son and a girlfriend agree to act as guinea pigs and now they can follow their own dreams on small monitors. They soon become mesmerized by

[71] Peter Sloterdijk,'The Ocean Experiment: From Nautical Globalization to a General Ecology' in: Sloterdijk, *What Happened in the Twentieth Century?*, p 42.
Also see above, Sijmons, 'The System's Ceiling,' page 376.
Also see: Gilles Deleuze and Félix Guattari, *Anti-Oedipus, Capitalism and Schizophrenia* (Minneapolis: University of Minnesota Press, 1983), a 'wild' and now classic book published in 1973 that demonstrates how and with what consequences longing is central to our society. And speaking of hacking the meme, in his preface Michel Foucault describes *Anti-Oedipus* as an introduction to non-fascist living and the key issue as: 'How do we ferret out the fascism that is ingrained in our behavior?' p xiii.

[72] 'First introduced on Star Trek: The Next Generation in 1987, the . . . holodeck is a universal fantasy machine, open to individual programming: a vision of the computer as a kind of storytelling genie in the lamp.' See: Janet H. Murray, *Hamlet on the Holodeck: The Future of Narrative in Cyberspace* (Cambridge, MA: MIT Press, 1997), p 15. The first virtual reality headsets, such as the unreleased Sega VR and the Forte VFX1, were developed in the early 1990s.

the fantasies they secretly cherish, the images they would otherwise forget, the scenes they would otherwise repress. The images, richer and more captivating than real life around them, seduce. They become addicted, unable to bear being separated from their device. They are trapped in their screens, the keys to satisfying their longings ever so slightly out of reach. They do not interact with others anymore.

Mark Zuckerberg at the 2016 Mobile World Congress in Barcelona
source: Facebook

Wenders portrayed a dystopia, and of course we are longing machines, this in itself was not a new observation.[73] But 30 years later, most of us are clutching a screen virtually all day and are resigned, knowingly or unknowingly, to Big Tech earning billions from our dreams and experiences, the free resource of a commercial practice that has turned us into commodities. Entirely new branches have now grown on the tree of design. But surveillance capitalism comes at a price. This increasingly dominant variant of the late-capitalist system – data is the oil of the twenty-first century – appears to be designed for the explicit purpose of producing both spectacle and isolation, of trapping consumers as longing machines in their own longings and, consequently, of keeping them away from reality, or at least from the things they don't like about it – away, in other

[73] See, among others: Deleuze and Guattari, *Anti-Oedipus*, p 8 ff. and Guy Debord, *La Societé du spectacle* (Paris: Gallimard, 1967).

words, from the others and from what is different – and trapped in a possible world that needs to be self-sufficient.[74]

And that's how we get stuck, how we fail to reconnect the possible and the real world, if each individual merely wants to be a product of power, a longing machine programmed by ever smarter algorithms that, like in *Until the End of the World*, does not bother about the other anymore, preferring to cherish the illusion of its self on Instagram and TikTok, or seeing it uncritically confirmed on Twitter and Facebook. Meanwhile our conception of what is the real world is perverted by populists and their trolls, colonized by Big Tech and fragmented by search engines and social media, and finds itself mocked and vilified, in the dock, defenseless against all accusations. The facts without which our collective memory and common imagination collapse are under attack, and tribalism and rebarbarization are the logical outcome.[75]

It is truly catastrophic, laments writer Amitav Ghosh, that 'at exactly the time when it has become clear that global warming is in every sense a collective predicament, humanity finds itself in the thrall of a dominant culture in which the idea of the collective has been exiled from politics, economics, and literature alike.' Therefore to Ghosh, the climate crisis is actually a crisis of culture, of the imagination as well: 'To imagine other forms of existence is exactly the challenge that is posed by the climate crisis: for if there is one thing that global warming has made perfectly clear it is that to think about the world only as it is amounts to a formula for collective suicide. We need, rather, to envision what it might be.'[76]

[74] In the film *The Matrix* (1999) by Lana and Lilly Wachowski, the character Morpheus describes the matrix, a virtual reality in which people are imprisoned in what is effectively a battery cage for humans, as 'the world that has been pulled over your eyes to blind you from the truth.' It is no coincidence that, in *The Matrix Reloaded* (2003), Schopenhauer's *The World as Will and Representation* is on the bookshelf, the German philosopher's *magnum opus* in which he writes about Maya, the veil of illusions that has fallen over the eyes of mortals.
For a masterly introduction to and in-depth analysis of surveillance capitalism, see: Shoshana Zuboff, *The Age of Surveillance Capitalism: The Fight for a Human Future at the New Frontier of Power* (New York: Public Affairs, 2019). Zuboff begins her important book by explaining surveillance capitalism in eight definitions: 1. A new economic order that claims human experience as free raw material for hidden commercial practices of extraction, prediction, and sales; 2. A parasitic economic logic in which the production of goods and services is subordinated to a new global architecture of behavioral modification; 3. A rogue mutation of capitalism marked by concentrations of wealth, knowledge, and power unprecedented in human history; 4. The foundational framework of a surveillance economy; 5. As significant a threat to human nature in the twenty-first century as industrial capitalism was to the natural world in the nineteenth and twentieth; 6. The origin of a new instrumentarian power that asserts dominance over society and presents startling challenges to market democracy; 7. A movement that aims to impose a new collective order based on total certainty; 8. An expropriation of critical human rights that is best understood as a coup from above: an overthrow of the people's sovereignty.

[75] Also see above, page 343.

[76] Amitav Ghosh, *The Great Derangement: Climate Change and the Unthinkable* (Chicago: The University of Chicago Press, 2016) p 80, 128.
Also see: Naomi Klein, *On Fire: The Burning Case for a Green New Deal* (London: Allen Lane, 2019), p 120: 'Climate change is a collective problem demanding collective action on a scale that humanity has never actually accomplished. Yet it entered mainstream consciousness in the midst of an ideological war being waged on the very idea of the collective sphere.'

What can they be like, these 'other forms of existence'? What do we want them to be like? Where do we want to land? How do we go about it, about this collective envisioning of our collective disembarkation on a new planet?

[35]

It's time to talk about *culture*. Only the cultural domain can provide the free space I earlier termed a precondition for realizing, shaping, and empowering such a *Selbstaufklärung project*, such a collective envisioning of what we want.

In the following, some repetition and digression, I readily admit, is inevitable. As Laurence Sterne explained himself, 'I progress as I digress.'

[36]

We are living in times of radical uncertainty. Now that the interest rates on any mortgage on the future have become unaffordable, everything is in flux. Everything is now becoming, as anthropologist Anna Lowenhaupt Tsing calls it, precarious: 'Precarity *is* the condition of our time . . . We can't rely on the status quo; everything is in flux, including our ability to survive. Thinking through precarity changes social analysis. A precarious world is a world without teleology.' [77]

And it is a world with ecology. The end no longer justifies the means; it is our own currently precarious condition that will now have to guide our actions in the Critical Zone. This is the only way we can address the question of whether we want to continue to chug along on our leaking and squeaking spaceship or, half a millennium after embarkation, tie ourselves to the mast and go home, like lost planetary pilots faced with having to write a new future scenario, a new odyssey. What are we capable of, now that we are forced to show our hands? Can we give our collective memory, our collective imagination, our civilization for those who want to call it that, a total reset? Where and with whom are we actually here? How do we want to be here? Who do we want to be, here?

[37]

These are cultural-political issues. On automatic pilot, telling each other the same stories we have been telling each other for centuries, landing will not succeed – that much is now clear. If we want to put an end to this

[77] Anna Lowenhaupt Tsing, *The Mushroom at the End of the World: On the Possibility of Life in Capitalist Ruins* (Princeton: Princeton University Press, 2015), p 20. In this book, Tsing searches the ruins of capitalism for traces of what managed to resist capitalist logic.

fatal raid that we started half a millennium ago and that now threatens to make the territory, the Critical Zone, unlivable, then it is time for some thorough *Selbstaufklärung*, for a new narrative about where we came from and where we are headed. Indeed, this means that, with appropriate modesty, for there is little to suggest that we will easily master this, we are going to have to *re-civilize the search for happiness itself*.

[38]
So yes, let's talk about culture.
First, what do we actually mean when we say 'culture'? The concept of culture – this is common knowledge but worth repeating in this context – has roots in the Latin verb *colere* (*cultum*), meaning to cultivate, care for, cherish the land. So, it's an *earthly* word that conveys *action*: to culture. That is, I culture and you culture, and together we culture – the land, the globe, the Earth.
With his red flag 'I must put "culture" in quotation marks because the term is hopelessly agrilogistic,' it's Timothy Morton who puts us on the right track.[78] Indeed, what exactly is it that we do, when together we *culture*? If we argue from the root *colere*, Morton's caveat is immediately understandable. *Cultivating* the land begins with cutting down or burning everything that is already growing there – and therefore in the way. Next is a process of excavating, digging, and ploughing, because without this we cannot sow and plant. After all this destructive *cultivating*, it is time for the extractive *caring*. Nowadays, we cannot even do this without chemically capturing nitrogen from the air and using it on a large scale as synthetic fertilizer; without manipulating groundwater levels, building dams, and depleting underground lakes; and without the day-in-day-out spraying of water that, due to increasingly frequent droughts, has to be hauled in from elsewhere.
All human labor, Hannah Arendt writes, requires material, 'but this material itself is not simply given and there, like the fruits of field and trees which we may gather or leave alone without changing the household of nature . . . This element of violation and violence is present in all fabrication, and *homo faber*, the creator of the human artifice, has always been a destroyer of nature.'[79]

[78] Timothy Morton, *Dark Ecology: For a Logic of Future Coexistence* (New York: Columbia University Press, 2016), p 85.

[79] Hannah Arendt, *The Human Condition* (Chicago: University of Chicago Press, 1958), p 139.

And so we arrive at *cherishing*: here, nature forces itself on us in its other form, after having been *subjected*, it becomes the *subject*. In this light, to *culture* is to fabricate if not violate in order to subject – which is exactly what project developers do: *they took all the trees put 'em in a tree museum.*[80]

Back to Morton who, hardly surprising at this point, also has his reservations about the concept of nature. 'Nature' is an 'illusion created by an accidental collaboration between the Holocene and agrilogistics. . . . Carbon dioxide fluctuated in a harmonious-seeming cycle for twelve thousand years – until it didn't. We Mesopotamians took this coincidence to be a fact about our world and called it Nature. The smooth predictability allowed us to sustain the illusion.'

In this light, nature is a 12,000-year-old fabrication about something that, in terms of geological time scales, was nothing more than an extremely brief and for humankind fortunate coincidence. And for those who still want to talk about cherishing, I will let Morton finish the story himself. The Anthropocene does not mean the destruction of nature, he writes with wry amusement, 'the Anthropocene is Nature in its toxic nightmare form. Nature is the latent form of the Anthropocene waiting to emerge as catastrophe.' It serves us right, he implies, this makes sad fools of 'we Mesopotamians' and their *meme*.[81]

[39]

But does that mean, 12,000 years after this agrilogistical slip-up between the Euphrates and Tigris, that we've made no strides forward at all? Surely the Enlightenment finally put our culture on the path of progress?

This was the question on the agenda 100 years ago on the Magic Mountain in Davos, where, amid great interest, German philosophers Ernst Cassirer and Martin Heidegger held their now historic debate on culture.[82] For the former, a passionate advocate of Enlightenment ideals, culture was *transcendence turned into form*. Culture builds *man's spacious*

[80] Joni Mitchell, 'Big Yellow Taxi,' on: *Ladies of the Canyon* (1970). Also see page 338.

[81] Morton, *Dark Ecology*, p 58-59. We are all Mesopotamians, or so says Morton. Some 12,000 years ago, between the Euphrates and Tigris, we yielded to a type of (agri)logistics that eventually could not but lead to global warming. 'Logistics because it is a technical, planned, and perfectly logical approach to space. Logistics, because it proceeds without stepping back and rethinking the logic. A viral logistics, eventually requiring steam engines and industry to feed its proliferation.' p 42.

[82] For an account of this debate see, among others: Rüdiger Safranski, *Martin Heidegger: Between Good and Evil* (Cambridge, MA: Harvard University Press, 1998), p 186 ff. and Wolfram Eilenberger, *Time of the Magicians: The Great Decade of Philosophy, 1919-1929* (London: Allen Lane, 2020), in particular p 325 ff.

dwelling, which is more easily destroyed than preserved, for it is a *fragile protection against the barbarism* that, *as that which humankind is capable of*, is a constant threat. For Cassirer, 'to culture' meant to continuously re-build our home to protect us from our own instincts.
Heidegger counters that man wants to make things too easy for himself in these *dwellings of the spirit*. He warns against rigidity, against freedom that has *congealed into a cultural condition*, and is therefore lost. He wants to free this freedom from itself, and *to always again become liberation*. As a philosopher Heidegger wants to frighten, he wants to *nullify* and force man *back into that homelessness from which he then, always anew, embarks on his flight into culture*.

Protect or frighten? Build the spacious dwelling or be forced back into homelessness? Transcendence turned into form or perpetual embarkment on another flight, always anew? A century later, in a spaceship battered by violent turbulence, there is little opportunity for peaceful philosophizing among ourselves. Rather than on a high magic mountain, we find ourselves falling down into a deep air pocket, because the Earth's system has had its fill of us and started superstorming. We need to get the job done, quickly. We need to be willing to face that we are part of the problem, that we have been too accommodating to ourselves in this spacious home with its salon full of enlightenment specialists who *house-hold* with the mentality of the end user. That we are, by all accounts, exploiters, barbarians ourselves, and within the gates. It really is too late now for the *Baukultur's* spacious dwelling.[83] There's nothing we can do but face our homelessness, frightened and all, and free freedom from

[83] In March 2020, at the very time that the pandemic broke out, the concept of *Baukultur* was suddenly on the agenda of the Dutch cultural world. On 22 January 2018, perhaps on that same Swiss magic alp where Cassirer and Heidegger crossed swords in 1929, coincidentally or not, all European Ministers of Culture had signed 'The Davos Declaration: Towards a European Vision of High-Quality *Baukultur*.' It is a call to promote environmental quality. The term *Baukultur*, which the Dutch minister's advisers deliberately left untranslated, is defined in the Declaration as 'every human activity that changes the built environment. . . . *Baukultur* calls for contemporary creation and the existing buildings, infrastructure and public space, including, but not limited to, monuments of cultural heritage, to be understood as a single entity.' The term, the advisers further explained in 2020, stands for 'the knowledge and skills necessary to design the living environment in a way that enhances environmental quality.' It also covers 'regulations, procedures and user involvement, and encompasses all levels of scale, from buildings to cultural landscapes.' Council for Culture and Board of Government Advisors, *Verder met de Verklaring van Davos* (The Hague, 2020), p 2. This vision of a *Baukultur* finds its inspiration in the *Bauhaus* (the EU speaks of a *New European Bauhaus*) and concerns both the production of the built environment and the way we interact with it (regulations, procedures, use). To promote this all-encompassing *Baukultur* in the Netherlands, or so the design sector maintained, we needed nothing less than the 'Pact of Soesterberg' – which I, myself nevertheless cordially forbore to ceremonially co-sign. For given the precarious state we find ourselves in, which requires us to thoroughly reassess the Enlightenment project, considering the trail of destruction that belief in progress left in its wake, those who refrain from first engaging in a fundamental debate about our concept of culture, while bearing in mind that the *Bauhaus* co-sired modernism – that too a homogenizing, universalizing western imposition –, are in danger of signing up for something that has 'congealed into a cultural condition,' that is, for business as usual – the conveniently selective dynamics between forgetting and remembering – and, in this particular case, for provincial fossilization. I'd rather be homeless.

itself, from its self-sufficiency, and come to terms with freedom as a challenge. Because we have to land – the conditions in this air pocket are on the whole quite unpleasant and so far, there's no operational landing strip in sight. But how? [84]

[40]

All of this is indeed frightening, but that should not deter us – we must not remain rigid and end users. Let's put it this way: those who are not at least in a mild panic, or considering panicking, have not exhaustively reflected on the matter. And those who have not exhaustively reflected on the matter cannot really take meaningful action. And those who cannot take meaningful action have every reason to panic, because they have *de facto* given up all hope of resolution.[85]

Some degree of panic can also help us to free freedom from itself. Paranoia puts us on edge and is an excellent starting point for action. Not, of course, action for the sake of action, or from feelings of nullity, resentment, fear, or anger: after all, recklessness born of homelessness usually ends badly, as Heidegger, too, discovered.[86] But yes, activism that frees the rebel inside us who wants to actively take responsibility for a better, more just world, a livable planet – *whatever it takes*. And not because it was promised, but because it is likely to be taken away from us as a result of the congealed cultural condition of late capitalism, now that it has become increasingly difficult, if not impossible, to reconcile the *possible* and the *real* world.

Such activism, therefore, is a purposeful form of testing, in the sense of actively testing, on the go, what science dictates and what future generations will judge us by. And when all scientists warn us more and more forcefully and desperately about the disastrous consequences of irreversible climate change; when millions of schoolchildren, foreseeing the future more adequately than their parents, take to the streets around the

[84] 'This seems to be the situation we're stuck in. On the left and on the right, among diplomats, energy company executives, investors, scientists, anarchists, clergy, and activists, serious people are worried about global warming and feel the urgent need to do something about it. Across the spectrum, however, nobody seems to have the tools, clout, or conceptual framework we need to fix it, or even to come up with a good plan to protect ourselves from the greatest dangers.' Roy Scranton, *Learning to Die in the Anthropocene: Reflections on the End of a Civilization* (San Francisco: City Light Books, 2015), p 67.

[85] Bruno Latour sees it differently. He has given up hope, and he calls those who have not, with a borrowed term, *esperados*. 'The craziest of all are those who appear to believe that they can do something despite the odds, that it isn't too late, that the rules of collective action are surely going to work here again, that one has to be able to act rationally, with eyes wide open, even in the face of threats as serious as these, while respecting the framework of existing institutions. But the people in this group are probably bipolar, full of energy in the manic phase, before the letdown that gives them a terrible urge to jump out of the window – or to toss their adversaries out instead.' Bruno Latour, *Facing Gaia: Eight Lectures on the New Climate Regime*, (Cambridge: Polity Press, 2017), p 12.

[86] See below, page 415 ff.

world and beg us to take action; when Greta Thunberg cries out on behalf of an entire generation: Listen to science! then we really need to stop being sidetracked by the very forces that make the facts suspect because the free market profits from business as usual if not disaster. We have fought for it for centuries, people have died at the stake for it: it's only free science that can send us more or less reliable smoke signals from the real world. We should really insist that the contract we have entered into, as society, stands firm, that free science is an achievement that cannot be challenged. It's crucial for us to hold onto it now that nothing, in the current maelstrom of questioning, can be lasting or self-evident anymore, nothing is a given and everything is a challenge. Everything is precarious, says Anna Tsing.

[41]
Whether all of this turbulence is still tolerable for us humans ultimately depends on what we think will follow, on whether and where and how we think we will be able to land. Whether our whole endeavor still serves a purpose. And whether there's anything we can still hope for. This calls for communal *Selbstaufklärung projects*, or for what Tsing calls 'the reformation of assemblages,' which she describes as 'open-ended gatherings. They allow us to ask about communal effects without assuming them. They show us potential histories in the making.'[87]
In all kinds of combinations and open associations, under great time pressure and therefore partly instinctively – so guessing, exploring, feeling, versing, dancing, sketching, singing, articulating, imagining, designing as we go along – we have to look for alternative scenarios for an unknown future. Technology alone is not going to save us. Our creativity and imagination are crucial and partly determine our adaptability as we focus on ways to cope with change, to become resilient, to adapt at this late stage, and on what we can still do. And in a manner that does not lead to murder and mayhem, because this alone poses a colossal challenge for a democratic society without a collective memory and common vision of the future, divided by populists and colonized by Big Business, and increasingly plundered by politicians who are no longer willing to take their losses.[88]

[87] Tsing, *The Mushroom at the End of the World*, p 22-23.

[88] Unless the market forces them to.

How to do this, nobody knows, and that of course includes me. But given the parameters in which we find ourselves in this book, which are those, one might almost forget, of an architecture biennale – still a creative space, but currently constricted in an ever-tightening corset of neoliberal cultural policy, always gasping for breath because the cultural subsidy it receives is never quite enough, made part of the cultural sector, made suspect by politicians and fed to the cultural industry – I would like to present three proposals for taking rebellious steps nevertheless, to safeguard the truly free space that the creative space is and should remain, more than it is today. I propose stretching the *Jetztzeit* to an un-human scale, purposefully practicing schismogenesis, and casting overboard as quickly as possible, and along with all other superfluous dead weight, the concept of culture itself, in so far as it currently refers to the neoliberal *container* into which, for policy purposes, creativity and imagination must fit.

[42]
Observing that we have entered a new geological era inevitably confronts us with a new perspective on historical time. Paradoxically, in the Anthropocene *Jetztzeit* is no longer just a reflection of our awareness of human time, of human history, however far we manage to stretch it as such, but also and increasingly of biological and geological time scales.[89] If we want to internalize this *Jetztzeit*, to truly try to account not for the history of the world but for the history of the planet, and this is no mean task, we cannot do so without taking away the central role of mankind and integrating the modest timespan of our own human history into the *un-humanly* vast geological time scales in which there was life on Earth. Rather than before or after Christ, the GSSA, the *Global Standard Stratigraphic Age*, provides guidance in geochronology.[90]
Geologists, geochemists, paleontologists, and other natural scientists reconstructing the evolution of life on Earth in the geological past are now helping to lay the rigorous foundations for what is called Earth System

[89] I am using – this is nothing but a personal preference – the German *Jetztzeit* and not the English 'now-time' to designate the historical time in which we want to position human existence on Earth, the span of time of life on Earth to which we too belong, its past as well as its future.

[90] Whereas, when I began my history studies in the late 1960s, it was still inappropriate to ask questions about where the Greeks got their ideas – my professor of ancient history had identified with his beloved Athenians, the Persians were the enemy and students were not supposed to speak of things that had been going on further east – this is no longer the case today, for example thanks to the Long Now Foundation of Stewart Brand, Brian Eno, and others, and bestsellers by Jared Diamond, Yuval Noah Harari, David Graeber and David Wengrow, and others. Our sense of the 'now' of human history has been transformed considerably, from 3,000 or 4,000 to 20,000 or 30,000 years. But that is still no more than a blink of an eye compared with the time scale we have to internalize when we identify with life on Earth. In any case, the oldest fossil remains are about 3.7 billion years old.

Sciences.[91] Writers of Big History, a new discipline, start their story of life on Earth more than 3.5 billion years ago, when bacteria took over the planet.[92] And anthropologists like David Graeber and archaeologists like David Wengrow are rewriting the history of the human species on Earth and underlining that there always have been and always will be alternatives, and that we therefore do not have to simply reconcile ourselves to the prevailing version of the story about *homo sapiens* that we have used to deceive ourselves for millennia, with all the consequences that this entailed. We don't *have to be* Mesopotamians.

Historian Dipesh Chakrabarty also argues for such a new approach to history and for the different perspective this creates: 'The global is a humanocentric construction; the planet decenters the human.'[93] Once we get our heads around that, if we even can, perhaps it will become more conceivable that we can land as terrestrials among other terrestrials. At the very least, it will help us shed the feathers of anthropocentrism. Chakrabarty gives an example that is relevant in this context. The still most widely used definition of *sustainable development* is that of the World Commission on Environment and Development, known as the Brundtland Commission after its chairman. In 1983, in the report *Our Common Future*, this commission defined it as 'development that meets the needs of the present generation without compromising the ability of future generations to meet their own needs.' Who would object to our children and grandchildren still being able to reap the Earth's rewards? Yet here, in what appears to be a very attractive formulation, sustainability is linked one-on-one to human history, without much regard for the needs of other life forms, or even life itself. What we need now, if we are to reload notions such as sustainability and next generations, is a new, non-anthropocentric history, a 'potential history in the making' that creates a new and alternative cultural *frame* for our imagination, in which

[91] See, for an introduction to Earth System Sciences (ESS) and the journey of discovery that led to it, among others: Peter Westbroek, *De ontdekking van de aarde: Het grote verhaal van een kleine planeet* (Amsterdam: Balans, 2012). ESS, by the way, should not be confused with *geoengineering*, the large-scale manipulation of natural systems to combat climate change. Whereas ESS is looking for a new symbiotic worldview on the basis of which integrated and interdisciplinary solutions can be found, *geoengineering* is still a typically modernist, technological reflex arising from the need for control, and that, it is to be feared, is part of the problem rather than part of the solution. One might say, ESS is about wanting to understand, *geoengineering* is about wanting to intervene. For *geoengineering* see, among others: Clive Hamilton, *Earth Masters: The Dawn of the Age of Climate Engineering* (New Haven: Yale University Press, 2013).

[92] Also see: Chakrabarty, *The Climate of History in a Planetary Age*, p 117-118: 'The point that not humans but microbial and other small forms of life constitute both by weight and numbers the bulk of life on the planet and are central to the drama of life – from the production of soil to the integral workings of the human body, not to speak of the maintenance of the share of oxygen in the atmosphere – may have to be assigned, as the climate crisis unfolds, the status of a salutary fact that humans will need to keep in mind in thinking about planetary conditions that make our existence and flourishing possible.'
For the important role that microorganisms play in our laboratories as well as in our daily lives, also see: Bruno Latour, *The Pasteurization of France* (Cambridge, MA: Harvard University Press, 1993).

[93] Chakrabarty, *The Climate of History in a Planetary Age*, p 19.

timescales are stretched and become un-human, growth is not a given but a temporary condition at best, and previous and future generations are a much more inclusive and biodiverse notion.

Can designers leave anthropocentrism behind and connect to such new practices and paradigms? Earth System Sciences cannot just simply accommodate Earth System Design. The latter would also require many lessons in modesty, a process of adaptation that has to start deep in the recesses of education. But there is just no time left for the fight against bureaucracy and establishment that this would involve. If future designers like the Rotterdam students, who wonder how to design in times of climate crisis, choose not for *education for practice*, but for *education to change practice*, they will have to find their own way. Which is why they need to know that there is always an alternative.

[43]
During the Covid-19 pandemic the extent to which the catering and cultural sectors are in the same boat became clear, especially in the Netherlands. Both are economic sectors that were very much affected by the fact that people were confined to their homes.[94] The cultural sector had drank the Kool-Aid of neoliberalism so deeply that it had become virtually addicted to audience revenues. By focusing almost entirely on the consumer, practically every cultural institution had inevitably also become an entertainment company. When the pandemic broke out and box offices had to close, there was nothing to fall back on, so the sector soon began lobbying governments for support operations – just like any other hard-hit economic sector.[95]
But, and I had been asking myself this long before the pandemic happened, why would a cultural institution be part of the economic sector? Does it exist to promote that which exists, the kind of *freedom that has congealed into a*

[94] By 2020, the two sectors were actually hardly distinguishable anymore. The cultural sector had allowed neoliberal economizers to push it toward box office, catering, and retail, often to the extent that cultural institutions had become dependent, to the very core of their functioning, on what – somewhat perversely, because it sounds quite brave, 'paying one's own way,' but what it comes down to is having to pay out of one's own pocket for getting stripped – is called 'earned revenue': the proceeds from ticket sales, but increasingly also coffee, services, venues, and *merchandise*. I am not likely to forget how, in 2013, a year after he had tossed the successful national architecture culture policy out the window with one careless gesture, the then-Minister of Culture Halbe Zijlstra reopened the renovated Het Nieuwe Instituut in Rotterdam with a self-satisfied speech. He especially praised the museum's new grand café, he was sure it would attract a lot of customers. Indistinctly he added that, after coffee and some cake, perhaps some would even go to see an exhibition. An afterthought. *His* mission had been accomplished.

[95] Consequently, rather than those who had taken measures and did not need support, it was those who managed to unlock it or, conversely, were left out in the cold that made it into the media. Full disclosure: after the very drastic culture budget cuts of 2012, I had made the IABR completely independent of box office revenues. Not that it had no 'earned revenue,' on the contrary, it earned quite high revenues compared with other institutions, thanks to the funds the IABR generated from commissions it acquired to conduct research by design with and for urban, provincial, and national

cultural condition – 'I shop therefore I am'? [96] Culture doesn't have to offer entertainment to promote economic prosperity, or to be a lubricant for tourism. It didn't use to be, it shouldn't be now, and it can change. No matter what we are led to believe, *there is always an alternative*.

[44]
In the 1930s, anthropologist Gregory Bateson coined the notion schismogenesis to describe the human tendency to oppose the other. Whereas Bateson was referring to a psychological process in a group or society, David Graeber and David Wengrow apply the notion to a process that takes place among societies. This process may very well result in a *conscious* choice for an alternative course: 'Conscious cultural inversion.' If this is the case we see that cities or societies, 'end up joined within a common system of differences, even as they attempt to distinguish themselves from one another.' Athens and Sparta make a case in point, representing two types of urban society that, consciously and combatively, developed as each other's antitypes. [97]
A cultural institution can consciously opt for schismogenesis, consciously behave and develop antitypically, opt for barely workable relationships in a 'common system of differences,' but *de facto* act outside the system, possibly very tactically, that is, without showing up on the radar of system administrators, advice-givers, and process managers as an irritant.

Behaving *antitypically* implies: not acquiescing to what is asked of you, if this is not consistent with how you want to achieve what you want to achieve, because what you want to achieve is what must be achieved. And of course only you can decide what the latter is; the power over what a cultural institution does, and how it does it, need not and must not be relinquished.

governments. As this research could largely continue during the pandemic, the IABR proved highly resilient to Covid-19. With the solution-oriented comprehensive implementation of research and knowledge developed in the free creative space, the organization proved to have vaccinated itself well against cultural market failure. However, neither the media nor the subsidizers showed the slightest interest, probably because this form of success does not, or is not permitted to fit the currently hegemonic mindset. Indeed, the IABR behaved not typically or atypically, but antitypically. See below, [44].

[96] *I Shop Therefore I Am* (1987) is a famous and iconic work of art by Barbara Kruger that bit its own tail. Originally intended as social criticism, the message was soon found on consumer products such as t-shirts and shopping bags.

[97] David Graeber and David Wengrow, *The Dawn of Everything: A New History of Humanity* (London: Allen Lane, 2021), p 332, 56-58, 180.
Another example is the Dutch Partij voor de Dieren (Party for the Animals), which does and does not follow the standard behavior of a political party. The party deliberately behaves antitypically, as it represents, in the parliament of human beings, animals rather than human beings to achieve what it believes humans should want to achieve. In this light, the PvdD also uses the leverage principle: it uses animals and the need to protect them as a lever for change on the planet.

Let me suggest a few 'exercises' in cultural schismogenesis: not market expansion but mind expansion, not target group but coalition, not innovative but disruptive, not promotion but exchange, not efficient but evolving, not in-and-out but commitment, not knowing but searching, not asserting but probing, not convenient but wayward, not voguish but vital, not agreeable but upsetting, not free trade but free thought, not commodification but commoning, not transaction but access, not products but ideas, not social media but social gatherings, not frictionless but sticky, not lobbying but activism, not toward the center of power but away from it to the issues over which one wants or needs power, that is, not private assignments but public challenges, not profit but value, not globe but planet. This list is easy to improve and expand, and it certainly must be – and we will do so several times later in this text. But just like in, for example, the application of the United Nations' 17 Sustainable Development Goals, it is important to never forget that its strength lies in the crucial condition of complete coherence – no *cherry picking*, then, but *all or nothing*.[98] Its strength also depends on the degree of fearlessness with which we look for alternatives. True fearlessness that is, and in all respects, without hesitation. Life as a dance to the music of the 'what if?' requires shedding one's moral feathers while searching for new values. As Nietzsche, philosopher with a hammer, proclaimed: 'O my brothers! With whom lies the greatest danger to the whole human future? Is it not with the good and just?'[99] Former spy and writer John Le Carré, too, knew: 'Immoralism is a necessary precondition of new values.'[100] From a schismogenetic point of view, immoralism, the resolute undoing at the seams of conventions, can be an effective and even professional attitude to those who want to change a system that itself doesn't care very much about morality. So we can add to the list: don't consolidate but undo, don't conform but *hack*.[101]

[98] Cherry picking does not achieve much because it inevitably leads to the picking of low-hanging fruit. Only if all SDGs are pursued as rigorously as possible, simultaneously and coherently, can social transformation be realized. For example, working on the energy transition is one thing, but doing so in conjunction with a public agenda and programs that strive for greater social equality, more rights and opportunities for women, and good education, is another thing altogether: it links technological change to socio-civic change and questions given ownership relations. (For an example from practice, see above, page 30 ff.) In this case, too, an integrated approach, systems thinking including leveraging, is crucial. Also see the 1972 report of the Club of Rome, *The Limits to Growth*, and Donella H. Meadows (edited by Diana Wright), *Thinking in Systems: A Primer* (White River Junction: Chelsea Green Publishing, 2008).

[99] Friedrich Nietzsche, (edited by Adrian Del Caro and Robert Pippin), *Thus Spoke Zarathustra* (Cambridge: Cambridge University Press, 2006), p 170.

[100] I cannot remember in which of Le Carré's books I came across this statement. That is why I recommend reading all of his books; they are not only very well written as well as highly entertaining, but *en passant* offer an excellent insight into the inner world of the collapsing British Empire, the greatest and perhaps most violent colonial world power ever.

[101] Undo with resolve. Not an easy subject, one about which there is still much to be said and written. Those who resolutely rid themselves of their moral shackles are inevitably faced with an ethical vacuum, but at the same time, setting and having boundaries is as much a necessary condition for finding new values as immoralism. This is the cross that every rebel bears: having to live and think sincerely in in-between-time.
For a discussion about the need for the strategic acceptance of violence and property destruction in the fight against the fossil industry, also see: Andreas Malm, *How to Blow Up a Pipeline* (London: Verso Books, 2012).

[45]
Behaving antitypically is not easy, of course. You don't make a lot of friends. Also, most cultural institutions are entwined with the power on which they have made themselves dependent to the point that they have invited shareholders, lobbyists, and captains of fossil capitalism to sit on their own supervisory boards. This means that often the only option left is to take the fight to the boardroom table. Because the cultural sector does need to free itself from the kind of freedom that it currently has, from its congealed cultural condition, and *take up arms*. If an all-encompassing, profoundly transformation-oriented new practice of change is needed, then this practice itself, right down to its core, must be maximally adaptive, want to keep pushing the boundaries, want to become truly activist – also when it demands accepting homelessness and un-human-ness, and even if it implies being immoral and irritating.[102]

[46]
Last summer, the great French filmmaker Jean-Luc Godard, who never felt any need to please the public, died. Already in his early years, as a film critic for the influential *Cahiers du cinéma*, he opposed traditional French cinema and the conventions imposed by Hollywood, together with kindred spirits like Serge Daney.
Daney, later the legendary film critic of leading newspaper *Libération*, died as early as 1992, at a relatively young age. He had AIDS but also suffered from what felt to him like the loss of *cinéma*, the loss of morality behind the images. Cinema had lost out to publicity, to visual culture, to the hysteria of the visible. Publicity, Daney wrote, 'is only interested in the exemplary, in the empirical, in evidence.' He wanted images to be encounters that remind us that we are not alone in the world. Daney wanted to write about art, but the others wanted to read about culture. So he felt that the gap that separated him from the others had become too wide.[103]

102 Especially in this section, I speak from personal experience, both good and bad, and on the basis of my own antitypical interventions, both successful and unsuccessful exercises in stepping out of line, and I base these arguments and conclusions in part on this experience.

103 See: Chris Dercon, 'Am I Now Getting Sentimental?,' *Parkett* 33 (1992), p 155-158.

Still from the film *Weekend* (1967), a black comedy by Jean-Luc Godard in which a bourgeois couple, determined to claim an inheritance from a dying relative, travels through the French countryside, while the civilized world around them grinds to a halt and collapses. Godard's slow images of roads full of traffic jams and accidents make a sardonic comment on the Great Acceleration.

And yes, these others had indeed allowed matters to get quite out of hand. The neo-Marxist critic Fredric Jameson had warned as early as the 1980s that postmodernism represented the cultural logic of late capitalism. Encroaching, coercive mass culture was bringing us all under the influence of media culture – a process Jameson called hegemony. It is a form of hegemony in which media and capitalism play key parts in the colonization of the mental worlds and lifestyles of human beings.[104]
All in all, in the art world there was less and less interest in making publicity for and about something that has merit of its own, because it has been created, and more and more in *recreation*, in the manufacturing of what has publicity value. Makers, artists, and designers became subservient to the hysteria of what can distinguish itself in the marketplace. And so the arts evaporated and what lingers on is called the cultural industry.[105]

[104] See: Fredric Jameson, 'Postmodernism, or The Cultural Logic of Late Capitalism,' *New Left Review* I/146 (July/August 1984). Also see above, page 399 ff.

[105] I have been angry and sad about this for nearly 40 years, but I don't want to bother my readers with cross quotes from old publications. Take it from me, and I hope they can laugh about it now should they read this: I have always fought one-man battles with my publicity departments. And with cultural officials who, for example during consultations about the opening of a biennale, would, rather than about the content of the minister's speech, talk about ways to turn the latter into a fitting media moment. A hopeless struggle, and things only got worse. A provisional low point were the terms and conditions for funding of the City of Rotterdam that urged cultural institutions to segment (sic!) their audiences into categories such as 'urban omnivores,' 'suburban convenience seekers,' 'colorful fighters,' 'modal culture avoiders,' and 'elitist culture lovers.' This was not only unnecessarily stigmatizing, it was exactly what the hegemony Jameson had warned about ultimately leads to: infantilization. In general, the publicity departments, steadily growing against the tide of austerity, nevertheless went about their business of segmentation – but not at the IABR. Especially since the 2015 biennale, MAKING CITY, our 'target group' had been broad and large, international and inclusive: they were city dwellers cum city makers, and we did not target them but we reached out to them, and not so much with publicity as with projects.

So now we can add the following to our list of exercises in schismogenesis: not publicity but self-direction, not recreation but creation. And not culture but art.
But wait a minute, *art*? Art, which we haven't really talked about for such a long time? Can we still, or again?

[47]
Can we still, or again trust anything coming from Martin Heidegger? The fact is that he, in his yearning to free freedom from itself, very rashly walked straight from his Black Forest mountain cabin into the arms of the shock troops of global barbarism, which in the years to follow would cause many and very unpleasant varieties of enforced homelessness. Surely he should have learned *something* from his opponent on the Magic Mountain, Ernst Cassirer, a Jew who continued to zealously defend the moral idealism of the Enlightenment and the cause of liberal democracy at a time when the rise of fascism made it increasingly difficult for him to do so – until he fled Germany in 1933.
Heidegger's former student Hannah Arendt has suggested that his coquetry with his own 'nullity' made him susceptible to barbarism. Yet she reached out to him once again 25 years after the Second World War, and his mental legacy was very much present in her last major, unfinished work, *The Life of the Mind*.[106] Heidegger also greatly influenced the French existentialists. This had already begun in the 1930s, and it reaccelerated immediately after the war. He actively sought dialogue with their foreman, Jean-Paul Sartre, a hero of the postwar generation who wrote his own roads to freedom and, by his existentialist dictates, played a major part in what we now subsume under the banner of 'May 1968,' the month in which the imagination was briefly in power: *Sous les pavés, la plage!* Sartre's philosophy was easier to popularize than Heidegger's. Parisian existentialism *decreed* human beings to be free: 'Commit yourself, sweep mankind along with you, re-create yourself time and again, solely through your actions!' It was a philosophical dictate perfectly suited to a time in which *La grande accélération* was pushing out of the starting blocks.[107]

[106] Hannah Arendt, *The Life of the Mind* (New York: Harcourt Brace Jovanovich, 1978). Also see: Safranski, *Martin Heidegger*, p 427, 372.

[107] 'Sartre introduces striking formulations, which soon become known throughout Europe: "Existentialism defines man by his actions. It tells him that hope lies only in action, and that the only thing that allows man to live is action. Man commits himself to his life and thereby draws his image, beyond which there is nothing. We are alone without excuses. This is what I mean when I say that man is condemned to be free."' Safranski, *Martin Heidegger*, p 357. Also see Sartre's three-volume novel *Les chemins de la liberté*, which he published in the 1945-1949 period.

At last, or so it seemed, freedom was actually freeing itself from itself. But not much later and, all in all, remarkably rapidly, it was every man for themself. Self-realization became self-staging. With the edge taken off, made wholly fit for consumption and the ever accelerating society of the spectacle, this *amor sui*, this dictate to 're-create yourself', meant that contemporary man, condemned to freedom, got busier by the day. For some, being yourself has now become a day job, or even an obsession. Man, the self-exploiter.
Far more worrying is that those hyper-individual roads to freedom have all too often ended in what Arendt calls negative solidarity, a, in the words of the writer Pankaj Mishra, 'tremendous increase in mutual hatred and a somewhat universal irritability of everybody against everybody else . . . There is plainly much more longing than can be realized legitimately in the age of freedom and entrepreneurship.'[108] Between diversity ideologues and identity entrepreneurs on one side, and neoconservative retro-thinkers and radical *anti-wokers* on the other, a black hole has formed in which any nuance disappears without a trace, just as tolerance and consideration for one another. As Augustine observed, resentment is like taking poison yourself and hoping the other will die. The longing machine that 're-creates itself time and again' just to remain visible, to unceasingly *self-stage*, causes a lot of turbulence.

[48]

In the years after the war Heidegger published several percipient texts, among other things on the role of art in times dominated by technology. In *Der Ursprung des Kunstwerkes* (1950), in his idiosyncratic and often difficult language use, he defined art as *welteröffnend*: it un-conceals, it is the actuation of truth. Truth, he wrote, 'is the essence of the true. What do we have in mind when speaking of essence? Usually it is thought to be those features held in common by everything that is true.' This allows him to say that 'art is in its essence an origin: a distinctive way in which truth comes into being, that is, becomes historical.' If we make way for art and its creators, art becomes a forward leap, an 'un-concealment,'

[108] Pankaj Mishra, *The Age of Anger: A History of the Present* (New York: Farrar, Straus & Giroux, 2017), p 14, 340. Note that negative solidarity or ressentiment must not be confused with schismogenesis or antityping. In the first case, someone cannot have a certain something and therefore, others must not have it, either – a sentiment based on frustration and exclusion. The second presupposes what I want to call *symbiotic enmity*, in which mutual differences are more matched and mutual respect is not necessarily ruled out – one must understand the other very well in order to be able to antitype at all.

ather than an 'appendix . . . [that] can only be carried along as a routine ultural phenomenon.'[109]

do not pretend to understand Heidegger to the core. Undoubtedly, herefore, I am reading too much of my own thinking into his. But why ot? After all, if art is *un-concealment*, if this is how to reconcile the ossible and real world, then this is a concept of art that is surprisingly ertinent. I can get by with the assertion that 'Kunst ist welteröffnend.' It ollows that we are emphatically not talking about a return to autono-nous art, but about a forward leap; about art that wants to un-obscure, hat wants to be subversive, if not immoral, that wants to move on by ringing to light, however hard that may be in times of turbulence, when ost of us prefer to be reassured and entertained, in our own safe bub-les, and without paying any real attention to the other.

A new policy that makes ample and unconditional way for art and its creators, for the art of *un-concealment*, would finally set art free again from the ever-tightening corset of the current neoliberal cultural policy, according to which art must routinely enter into an obligatory alchemi-cal connection with spectacle because only that which can be marketed may become gold. This liberation would also allow new practices space to breathe – practices young designers currently find it very difficult, if not impossible, to develop in the economic space, whereas it would be much easier for them to do so in the creative space, if the latter no longer has the hysteria of marketing as its imposed objective, but when the bringing to light of real solutions to our real problems can be its un-concealed goal. Such a free space, such a fulcrum on which to place their levers, would certainly help designers break through the system's ceiling.

[49]

An inevitable final question is what we are actually talking about when we say 'design.' I wrote the following about this in 2016: 'In *A Cautious Prometheus?*, a speech he delivered in 2008, French theorist Bruno Latour, observed that "design as a concept implies humility that seems rather absent from the word 'construction' or 'building' . . . and that is

[109] Martin Heidegger, 'The Origin of the Work of Art', in: Martin Heidegger, *Basic Writings* (New York: Harper, 2008), p 175, 202-203.

completely lacking in the heroic promethean hubristic dream of action." He welcomes the "remedial" in design as "an antidote to hubris and the search of absolute certainty, absolute beginning, radical departure." It's from this position, this *remedial* perspective if you want, that I think we need to challenge the often still-prevailing notion of design. It should no longer be a quest for beginnings and departures, for grand gestures and blank slates, the architect's imagination roaming freely. To design would be to want to depart from a given or a problem, to look at the emergent, unplanned, unstoppable process that lies beneath it, and to turn it into something more vibrant, more viable, more usable or user friendly – and more resilient. To design would not be a process of heroic imagining but of explorative re-imagining. Re-imagining . . . is a pertinent exercise. And I think the idea of design may well be facing one of the most compelling paradigm shifts in history. Ongoing globalization and urbanization, climate change, technological and scientific advances and convergences, and so forth, are rapidly changing how we live and interact. The speed of change is growing exponentially. . . . We have to leave behind us the big wasteful aggressive systems we can now see for what they are, creation and construction predicated on eternal economic growth. While what tomorrow's cities urgently need are new feedback loops with deep implications for the relations between user and designer, and between user and user. We must move from wasteful to sustainable consumption, and from linear to circular production systems that are regenerative by intention and design. We must move from creating systems to mending our ways. And mend our ways is what we I think we have to do, and sooner rather than later. The future is now; it's the mess we have to make sense of.'[110]

[50]
I still hope, but with a great deal more impatience than when I wrote the above, that 'the idea of design may well be facing one of the most compelling paradigm shifts in history.' But I also have growing doubts – given the dictates of the current neoliberal cultural policy it was and is quite an ambition, a necessarily modest practice of *remedial design*, while we know *everything has to change*. In the 18 years I led the IABR, I could not fail to notice that not everything is possible, not everything is *allowed* to

[110] See: Brugmans, 'It's the Culture, Stupid!,' in: George Brugmans, Jolanda van Dinteren and Maarten Hajer (eds.), *The Next Economy* (Rotterdam: IABR, 2016), p 113-114.

succeed, no matter how good plans are. And by now, we're almost half-way to the deadline that the world community set itself six years ago, in Paris in 2016, to get Spaceship Earth on target – *prepare for landing, ETA 2030!*
However, in view of their position, expertise, and responsibility, designers now have to take action; Dirk Sijmons, too, advocates for a 'Designer Rebellion.'[111] To help promote this, we can expand our list of exercises one more time: not an operating manual but a book of clues, not design but redesign, not creating systems but mending our ways, not *hubris* but modesty, not grand gestures but everything must change, and not tomorrow but today, not construction but remedy, not bowing to clients but listening to users, not a beginning but a given, not linear but loopy, not extractive but regenerative, not aggressive but healing.

But while they're practicing – and they might well do so in the free space of an art that opens the world, that *brings to light* – the *Letzte Generation* of designers must realize that sooner or later they need to break down the doors that will not open. A new design practice, certainly, and it will be modest, regenerative and remedial. But at the same time it is antitypical, an implacable un-concealer, and the gun is on the drawing board, always within reach. Design as a weapon. Designers as hackers. The worn rules and old morals thrown overboard. Then it would be possible.

[51]
The designer as a detective. Eyal Weizman and his colleagues at Forensic Architecture use architecture as an 'optical device' to investigate and visualize connections among armed conflicts, human rights violations, and environmental and habitat destruction. In their hands architecture, in combination with forensic expertise, becomes a critical practice in which the *designer-as-a-detective* is forced to abduct, and to focus on the materiality of the built environment and its media representations, from social media to satellite imagery. The architect has to reason, infer, and guess like a *true detective*, starting *from* the spatial materializations of the 'scene of the crime.' This approach challenges architects, Weizman writes, 'to use their disciplinary tools to make claims publicly and politi-

[111] See above, page 378.

cally in the most antagonistic of forums.'[112]

Forensic Architecture works with activist groups, NGOs, Amnesty International, and the United Nations. Their visual analyses regularly provide crucial evidence for cases before international courts against parties, usually states, that prefer to withhold evidence, or stamp it *classified*. Sometimes these are cases in which architecture has literally been used against architects. 'Crimes were committed in the most basic gestures of architecture – lines drawn on paper. The violence performed on the drawing was later transferred to the ground,' concludes Weizman, following his research in Israeli-occupied areas of the West Bank.[113]

Politics considered as relationships in space. If, in the old practice, walls start out as lines on paper, in the new practice of design in times of climate crisis it has to be turned on its head: drawing has to topple walls. Because, 'what we see in disasters is not an exceptional state of society but simply a dimension that remains hidden in everyday life,' as social psychologist Harald Welzer noted in his study of climate wars.[114] And indeed, the climate crisis now leads to an accumulation of disasters that painfully exposes hidden inequality and injustice while causing temporary societal formations about which nothing is now known – the *butterfly defect* asserting itself.[115] Along with social psychologists, cultural scientists, and activists, *designers-as-detectives* can *un-conceal* the hidden dimensions of existence with their designs and help develop strategies by which social beings can secure their future existence.

Understood as an exercise in modesty, designers can choose an opposite, antitypical approach to help us land and live on a damaged planet: choosing to heal and remedy, and not by drawing lines, but by un-concealing the fault lines. They can find inspiration, for example, in Japanese aesthetics, in which traces of breaks and repairs contribute to the beauty of an object. Kintsugi is the art of repairing broken ceramics with gold or silver lacquer,

[112] Eyal Weizman, *Forensic Architecture: Violence at the Threshold of Detectability* (New York: Zone Books, 2018), p 11. Also see above, page 353. Umberto Eco: 'when the detective, or the scientist . . . make an Abduction, they must bet that the solution they find (the Possible World of their hypothetical imagination) corresponds to the Real World.'

[113] Weizman, *Forensic Architecture*, p 137.

[114] Harald Welzer, *Climate Wars: What People Will Be Killed For in the 21st Century* (Cambridge: Polity Press, 2012), p 26. Incidentally, we also witnessed this during the Covid-19 pandemic, which exposed problems – in logistics, in healthcare, in the cultural sector – that most were previously unable to perceive.

[115] For the *butterfly defect* see: Ian Goldin and Mike Mariathasan, *The Butterfly Defect: How Globalization Creates Systemic Risks, and What to Do about It* (Princeton: Princeton University Press, 2014).

of remedying fractures by un-concealing them. Kintsugi, the 'golden connection,' as guidance for the new design practice: use gold and silver, that is, all accumulated profits, in every sense of the word, everything that half a millennium of global fortune hunting and extractive entrepreneurial rage has taken from what now is a damaged planet, to help heal and remedy it.

[52]
Now back, one last time, to Anna Tsing, with whose words this chapter about turbulence begins, a quote that should be read not as a short operation manual, but as one of many helpful suggestions – clues in fact. And not only for today's planetary pilots of our vandalized and contaminated spaceship, but especially for the rebels who want to *actuate the truth* to be able to take over the helm.[116] *Designers-as-detectives-as-rebels* no longer need big gestures, they need modesty, they need an iterative process that might best be described as *picking up the pieces*, starting everywhere at once while figuring out *how* to do things *as* we do them. The planet should become one big Test Site, one big fulcrum to firmly stand on to work the levers. A forensic exercise in antitypical regeneration, flying in the mist without an operating manual, going forward step by step – the one guiding the other.

Disturbance, which we have called turbulence, is 'ordinary,' Tsing says, it is the order of the day, such is the human condition in the Anthropocene.[117] Things are going to get more and more intense, but they will be more bearable as soon as we can find a way to dare to hope that a landing in the Critical Zone can take place, in the *un-concealed*, with all the cards on the table, and with equal opportunities for all lifeforms. So new assemblages become possible in which we find our place, learn to *make space* in new histories of life that we must learn to write, stories that we have to exercise, futures that we have to re-design, the search for happiness that we have to re-civilize. These will be stories that started billions of years ago and in which we have to uncover our connections to the reality

[116] Rebels and not terrorists, let's reserve that last term for, in the words of author Joy Williams, 'the bankers and builders, the industrial engineers, purveyors of war and the market, it goes without saying, the exterminators and excavators, the breeders and consumers of every stripe, those locusts of clattering, clacking hunger.' Joy Williams, *Harrow* (London: Tuskar Rock Press, 2021), p 185.

[117] See: Tsing, *The Mushroom at the End of the World*, p 160, 22-23.

of what is in fact a new planet, this time with an eye for an un-human now, for each other, for all other terrestrials, for a common future that can no longer be mortgaged and in which not man, but life is central. Not man but life.

[53]
Designers who, today, say: I choose such resistance, I am subversive, I stretch the now into the un-human, I stand in solidarity with the survival of all that lives, with all beings that make space, again and again and again; as I imagine I set the truth in operation and no one can stop me anymore, I no longer adapt, I remedy, I look for truly free space – must rearrange all their notes and with the little grip they have, start from scratch again – listen, watch, read – to draw for the endgame.

←
We live on a damaged planet. More and more animal species are becoming extinct. The World Wildlife Fund's Living Planet Index indicates there are 70 percent fewer wild animals sharing the Earth with us than there were in 1970. Worldwide, animals have less and less space to live in due to a loss of natural habitat of at least 33 percent since 2001. This is also the case in the dwindling wetlands of Miankaleh, in Iran, which face ecological disaster.
The Bitter Death of Birds
© Mehdi Mohebi

Epilogue

I am not proposing to return to the Stone Age. My intent is not reactionary, nor even conservative, but simply subversive. It seems that the utopian imagination is trapped, like capitalism and industrialism and the human population, in a one-way future consisting only of growth. All I'm trying to do is figure out how to put a pig on the tracks.

Ursula Le Guin

[54]

Just when more and more lights on the dashboard are flashing red, we wake up to the fact that we are the planetary pilots of Spaceship Earth. On the bridge there is neither an operating manual, nor a flight plan. It is getting hotter and hotter. No chimney, no ventilation, no windows, no emergency exit. Anxiety sets in, maybe we ought to turn things down a notch? Consultations. Conferences. How to go about it? Together doesn't work. Because the barbarians are not at the gate, they are on board. They recognize that it will benefit them greatly to now burn as much as possible as quickly as possible. There is still a lot of money to be made from disasters! Fanatically, they seize power on the ship, their massive wealth taking the rest of us hostage. And so the temperature continues to rise. Apocalyptic heat waves. More and more people die, here, there, everywhere. Flooding. No escape. Ice caps melting, whole sections of glaciers breaking off. Insects on the decline. Land drying out. Yet another superstorm warning. Atmospheric rivers, waves of water crashing down from the skies. Where did the North Pole go? It was there a moment ago! No more bird song; no more butterfly wings. Millions on the run. Heading for war. Spaceship Earth is leaking and squeaking and creaking and burning. The turbulence is frightful. No lifeboats. No safety belts but VR goggles. Is hope naive, lethal? No emergency exits! Jump overboard? There is no overboard. There is panic. Blood on the wall. What to do? Head splitting. Last chance. To do what? Shout out the facts? Barbarians don't listen. Un-conceal the facts? Barbarians don't read. I entrench myself in the library. Silence. Listening. Voices. Reading. Gathering. Commoning. Clues.

[55]
Roaming the spaceship's huge library, a vast labyrinth of countless narrow corridors with shelves on either side up to an invisible ceiling, endless rows of shelves for books that have or have not yet been written, which is not instantly clear, most have fallen off due to the ship's jolting and rocking and are scattered all over the floor, in chaotic heaps, some open some closed, undented or damaged, no system to it, I realize, as a detective looking for clues, that a library is a forest of expectations, filled with notes, ideas and references, secrets and pointers, insights and perspectives, but also full of big bad wolves, temptations, detours, wrong turns, pitfalls, and full circles in which doubt easily breeds fear, and so I have no idea where to begin, which corner to turn, what to listen to, what to hold on to, until I, near despair, suddenly recall Borges's words and realize that those who envision their own book labyrinths will always know their way around them, know how to find those books that need to be heard, or written.

[56]
The ship is thrashing and thumping, ranting and raving. Only the emergency lights are on, but the light is getting weaker and weaker. Energy issues? Feeling my way around, I stumble over a heap of books. On the floor, right in front of me, not to be missed, stuck on the spine of a book, is a small Post-it. On it, in bold red letters, someone has written the word `PIG`, and below that, in pencil, barely legible: `thoughts, words, women, places - Ursula / pig (vs blood?) on the tracks - riff on what if not the segundos but the segundas? - degrowth!!` See [118]

[57]
Pig? Track? Shrink? Clue!
I pick up the book, scramble to my feet and carefully walk on. I listen. After more futile roaming – which voices should I listen to, what story is helpful? – I stumble upon three books that, strikingly designed as a trilogy, cry for attention. One is open, at a description of how, in the 1990s,

[118] Ursula K. Le Guin, 'A Non-Euclidean View of California as a Cold Place to Be', in: Ursula K. Le Guin, *Dancing at the Edge of the World: Thoughts on Words, Women, Places* (New York: Grove Press, 2006). For the quote with which the Epilogue begins, see p 85. In this essay, Le Guin takes a stand against those who promise the impossible: perpetual green economic growth that will not harm the environment. More generally, she believed that in terms of systemic change, green utopians were shortsighted in their focus, too shallow and unwilling to really push the imagination to its limits. So she wanted to put a 'pig on the tracks': revive the debate about what sustainable development really is, and firmly put *degrowth* on the agenda.

London's Tate Modern Gallery researched what caused the most damage to its paintings. A red felt-tip pen has drawn a circle around the sentence: 'The flashes of Japanese cameras, pawings by badly behaved children, the passage of time itself – all were exonerated; the most corrosive thing turned out to be the wind emitted from the anuses of the millions of visitors every year.' [119]

Scrawled in the margin, same pencil, same handwriting – I vaguely recognize it, is it my own? – are the words: `own fault / cultural industry - anthropocene / turbulence - bloop / homo inflatus / deflate!!! - elaborate! laughter allowed!!??`

Hordes of tourists, windy from the cheap breakfast buffet, are museums' greatest pest! Junk food. If only Schopenhauer had lived to see this. The ephemeral fungus on a city trip! The culture consumer too, is what he eats. Laughing allowed! Raging and crying, too. Damn growth! Degrow! Deflate! The tires of all SUVs! Drain those tourist streams! And blow up those pipelines!

Pig! Track! Shrink! Boom!

[58]

The damage the longing machines have done has truly unimaginable, unexpected, irreparable consequences. Things will never be all right again; we cannot go back to the Holocene, even if we clench our butt-cheeks forever. Merely asking the question of where we want to land causes emotional scenes. Too late! The future is the mess we have made of it. Or mayb . . . message from the cockpit:

[59]

`Hallucinant heavenly spectacle. Sunsets liquid projections that run amok. Grandiose explosions of burning colors. We're dancing on the edge, but of what? Millions of lights in the sky, but we can't tell the stars from the runaway satellites. A galaxy garbled. All harmony gone. No landing strip in sight. No music for airports. Just ch-ch-ch-ch-changes. We are bouncing about on the road to nowhere. To...`

[119] Agustín Fernández Mallo, *Nocilla Experience, Nocilla Project #2* (New York: Farrar, Straus & Giroux, 2016), p 83, part two of The Nocilla Trilogy.

[60]
Crackling and sputtering. The last of the planetary pilot chatter.
The ship is yawing and bouncing more and more violently. The dance on the edge, the dance of maybe, the dance of what if. Where are we? Near touchdown, finally?
Strangely, it has become quiet. There is a lot of quiet, a quiet I have not heard before. The sort of quiet we cannot talk about. I am listening.
It's getting warmer, too hot, much too hot. And darker and darker. I want to go outside, but there is no outside. I am on Earth, in the Critical Zone, at the endgame, it can't be helped.

[61]
What is truly harrowing is not only the damage we have done, but its irreversibility. That it is, what it is. That the past is now forever the story of missed opportunities and made blunders, and the future the mess we have made of it. And that is all it is. That's it. *The planet will never be the same again.* That is your big bad wolf, right there! The things I feel when I truly realize there is no way back, when I internalize what that means, how catastrophic that can be, are overwhelming.

[62]
I am listening.
In the distance, what appears to be all the way to the back, the faint glow of a tiny light weakly illuminates a large sign left against a wall.

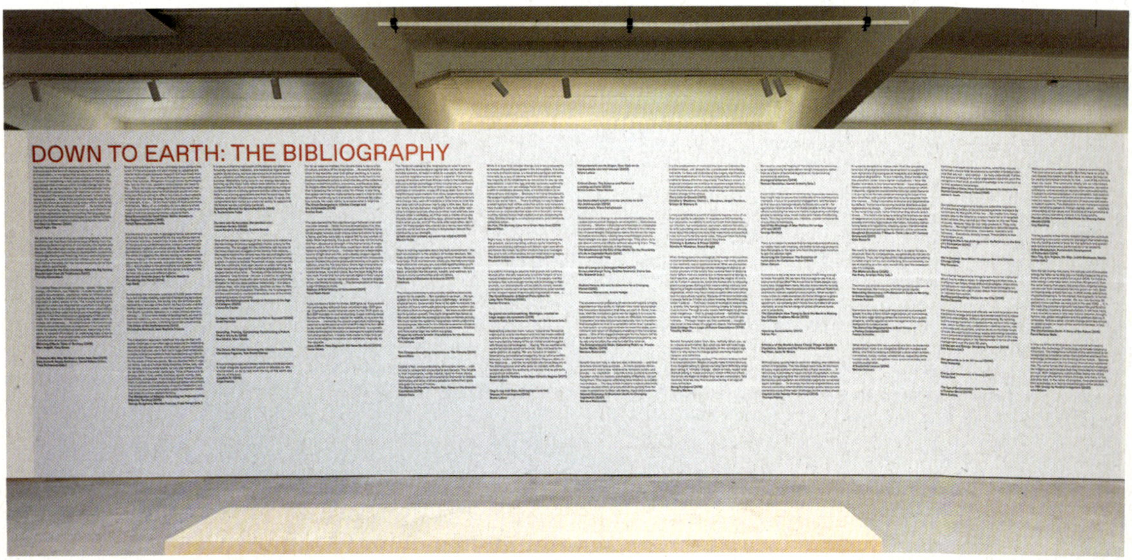

On the floor, a large heap of well-thumbed books. Voices. The closer I get, the more voices I hear. Chanting.
On a frayed piece of paper, scrawled, seemingly in haste, as if there was no time left to lose, a flow of words. I've underscored the first line: beware of falling books - smart ass, incontinence / note: modest, helpful - clues!! and below that [120]

[120] DOWN TO EARTH/RECLAIM THE COMMONS/THE BIBLIOGRAPHY dd.~~09/06 3-10 28-12~~ 29-01:
Yussef Agbo-Ola, *Architect as Shaman* (2021); Timothy Ahrensbach, *Compendium for the Civic Economy: What the Big Society Should Learn from 25 Trailblazers* (2017); Marc Angélil, Cary Siress, *Mirroring Effects: Tales of Territory* (2019); Hannah Arendt, *The Human Condition* (1958); Hannah Arendt, *The Life of the Mind* (1978); Arjun Appadurai, *Modernity at Large: Cultural Dimensions of Globalization* (1996); Kate Aronoff, Alyssa Battistoni, Daniel Aldana Cohen, Thea Riofrancos (eds.), *A Planet to Win: Why We Need a Green New Deal* (2019); Christine de Baan, Joachim Declerck, Veronique Patteeuw (eds.), *Visionary Power: Producing the Contemporary City* (2007); Abhijit Banerjee, Esther Duflo, *Good Economics for Hard Times: Better Answers to Our Biggest Problems* (2019); Ugo Bardi, *Extracted: How the Quest for Mineral Wealth Is Plundering the Planet* (2014); Philipp Blom, *Nature's Mutiny: How the Little Ice Age of the Long Seventeenth Century Transformed the West and Shaped the Present* (2019); Christophe Bonneuil, Jean-Baptiste Fressoz, *The Shock of the Anthropocene* (2013); George Brugmans, Jan Willem Petersen (eds.), *Making City* (2012); George Brugmans, Jolanda Strien (eds.), *Urban by Nature* (2014); George Brugmans, Marieke Francke, Freek Persyn (eds.), *The Metabolism of Albania: Activating the Potential of the Albanian Territory* (2016); George Brugmans, Jolanda van Dinteren, Maarten Hajer (eds.), *The Next Economy* (2016); George Brugmans, Jolanda van Dinteren (eds.), *The Missing Link* (2018); Richard Buckminster Fuller, *Operating Manual for Spaceship Earth* (1969); Laura Burgers, Eva Meijer, Evanne Nowak, *De stem van de Noordzee: Een pleidooi voor vloeibaar denken* (2020); Lieven De Cauter, *Ending the Anthropocene: Essays on Activism in the Age of Collapse* (2020); Dipesh Chakrabarty, *Climate of History in a Planetary Age* (2021); A. Chteraf, *Asides: On the Exigency of Marginalia* (2023); Mike Davis, *City of Quartz: Excavating the Future in Los Angeles* (1990); Gilles Deleuze, Félix Guattari, *Anti-Oedipus: Capitalism and Schizophrenia* (1983); Jared Diamond, *Collapse: How Societies Choose to Fail or Succeed* (2005); O.M.G. Evallen, *Digressional Records: The Detour as a Methodology* (2023); Christiana Figueres, Tom Rivett-Carnac, *The Future We Choose: Surviving the Climate Crisis* (2020); Pope Francis, *Laudato Si'* (2015); Eduardo Galeano, *Open Veins of Latin America: Five Centuries of the Pillage of a Continent* (1973); Helen Gordon, *Notes from Deep Time* (2021); Amitav Ghosh, *The Great Derangement: Climate Change and the Unthinkable* (2016); Amitav Ghosh, *The Nutmeg's Curse: Parables for a Planet in Crisis* (2021); David Graeber, *Debt: The First 5,000 Years* (2011); David Graeber, David Wengrow, *The Dawn of Everything: A New History of Humanity* (2021); John Gray, *Straw Dogs: Thoughts on Humans and Other Animals* (2002); Ursula K. Le Guin, *Dancing at the Edge of the World: Thoughts on Words, Women, Places* (2006); Clive Hamilton, *Earth Masters: The Dawn of the Age of Climate Engineering* (2013); Yuval Noah Harari, *Sapiens: A Brief History of Humankind* (2011); Martin Heidegger, *The Origin of the Work of Art* (2008); Jason Hickel, *Less is More: How Degrowth Will Save the World* (2020); Massih Hutak, *Jij hebt ons niet ontdekt, wij waren hier altijd al* (2020); Interboro, *The Arsenal of Exclusion & Inclusion* (2017); Tim Jackson, *Prosperity without Growth: Foundations for the Economy of Tomorrow* (2016); Naomi Klein, *This Changes Everything: Capitalism vs. The Climate* (2014); Naomi Klein, *The Battle for Paradise: Puerto Rico Takes on the Disaster Capitalists* (2018); Naomi Klein, *On Fire: The Burning Case for a Green New Deal* (2019); Andrew H. Knoll, *A Brief History of Earth* (2021); Elizabeth Kolbert, *The Sixth Extinction: An Unnatural History* (2014); Elizabeth Kolbert, *Under a White Sky: The Nature of the Future* (2021); Roman Krznaric, *The Good Ancestor: A Radical Prescription for Long-Term Thinking* (2020); Bruno Latour, *Down to Earth: Politics in the New Climatic Regime* (2017); Bruno Latour, *Facing Gaia: Eight Lectures on the New Climate Regime* (2017); Bruno Latour, *Het parlement van de dingen: Over Gaia en de representatie van niet-mensen* (2020); Bruno Latour, *The Pasteurization of France* (1993); Bruno Latour, *After Lockdown: A Metamorphosis* (2021); Bruno Latour, Peter Weibel (eds.), *Critical Zones: The Science and Politics of Landing on Earth* (2020); Harald Lesch, Klaus Kamphausen, *Die Menschheit schafft sich ab: Die Erde im Griff des Anthropozän* (2016); Andreas Malm, *Fossil Capital* (2016); Andreas Malm, *How to Blow Up a Pipeline* (2021); Francesco Manacorda, Ariella Yedgar, *Radical Nature: Art and Architecture for a Changing Planet* (2010); Robert B. Marks, *The Origins of the Modern World: A Global and Environmental Narrative from the Fifteenth to the Twenty-First Century* (2015); Jane Mayer, *Dark Money: The Hidden History of the Billionaires Behind the Rise of the Radical Right* (2016); Mariana Mazzucato, *The Entrepreneurial State: Debunking Public vs. Private Sector Myths* (2014); Mariana Mazzucato, *Mission Economy: A Moonshot Guide to Changing Capitalism* (2021); J.R. McNeill, Peter Engelke, *The Great Acceleration: An Environmental History of the Anthropocene since 1945* (2014); Donella H. Meadows, Dennis L. Meadows, Jørgen Randers, William W. Behrens, *The Limits to Growth* (1972); Donella H. Meadows, Diana Wright, *Thinking in Systems: A Primer* (2008); Pankaj Mishra, *The Age of Anger: A History of the Present* (2017); Timothy Morton, *Dark Ecology: For a Logic of Future Coexistence* (2016); Timothy Morton, *Being Ecological* (2018); Mohsen Mostafavi, Gareth Doherty (eds.), *Ecological Urbanism* (2016); George Monbiot, *Out of the Wreckage: A New Politics for an Age of Crisis* (2017); Elinor Ostrom, *Governing the Commons: The Evolution of Institutions for Collective Action* (1990); David Owen, *The Conundrum: How Trying to Save the World is Making Our Climate Problems Worse* (2012); Adrian Parr, *Hijacking Sustainability* (2012); Raj Patel, Jason W. Moore, *A History of the World in Seven Cheap Things: A Guide to Capitalism, Nature and the Future of the Planet* (2018); Thomas Piketty, *Capital in the Twenty-First Century* (2013); Kate Raworth, *Doughnut Economics: 7 Ways to Think Like a 21st Century Economist* (2017); Tim Rieniets, Jennifer Sigler, Kees Christiaanse (eds.), *Open City, Designing Coexistence* (2009); Ilka Ruby, Andreas Ruby (eds.), *The Materials Book* (2020); Cormac Russell, *Rekindling Democracy: A Professional's Guide to Working in Citizen Space* (2020); Fabian Scheidler, *The End of the Megamachine: A Brief History of a Failing Civilization* (2015); Michiel Schwarz, *A Sustainist Lexicon* (2016); James C. Scott, *Seeing Like a State: How Certain Schemes to Improve the Human Condition Have Failed* (1999); Roy Scranton, *Learning to Die in the Anthropocene: Reflections on the End of a Civilization* (2015); Roy Scranton, *We're Doomed. Now What? Essays on War and Climate Change* (2018); Richard Sennett, *Building and Dwelling: Ethics for the City* (2018); Dirk Sijmons (ed.), *Landscape and Energy: Designing Transition* (2014); Peter Sloterdijk, *What Happened in the Twentieth Century?* (2018); Vaclav Smil, *Energy and Civilization: A History* (2017); Marc Swilling, *The*

Age of Sustainability: Just Transitions in a Complex World (2019); Guy Standing, *Plunder of the Commons: A Manifesto for Sharing Public Wealth* (2019); Greta Thunberg (ed.), *The Climate Book* (2022); Nico Tilly, Eric Frijters, Olv Klijn, Judith Borsboom, Martin Looije (eds.), *Urban Metabolism: Sustainable Development of Rotterdam* (2014); Anna Lowenhaupt Tsing, *The Mushroom at the End of the World: On the Possibility of Life in Capitalist Ruins* (2015); Anna Lowenhaupt Tsing, Heather Swanson, Elaine Gan, Nils Bubandt (eds.), *Arts of Living on a Damaged Planet* (2017); David Wallace-Wells, *The Uninhabitable Earth: A Story of the Future* (2019); Julia Watson, *Lo-TEK: Design by Radical Indigenism* (2020); Eyal Weizman, *Forensic Architecture: Violence at the Threshold of Detectability* (2018); Harald Welzer, *Climate Wars: What People Will Be Killed For in the 21st Century* (2012); Peter Westbroek, *De ontdekking van de aarde: Het grote verhaal van een kleine planeet* (2012); Andrea Wulf, *The Invention of Nature: Alexander von Humboldt's New World* (2016); Slavoj Žižek, *Living in the End Times* (2010); Shoshana Zuboff, *The Age of Surveillance Capitalism: The Fight for a Human Future at the New Frontier of Power* (2019).

[63]
We are not who we think we are, not who we are when thinking. That's why we read . . .

[64]
. . . to understand that we need to modestly merge into an ecological chain of permanent change in which the human species has no specific priority. That about 3.5 billion years ago what was to become man was launched by bacteria as a survival machine for genetic information. Man, a longing machine with a built-in manufacturing fault, the illusion of self. A destructive machine with an expiration date, a glorious maybe, but short and violent accident of evolution. Meaningless, just as all of evolution is meaningless change. Just change, and that's it. And that is truly a tough nut to crack. That we, flukily, will leave conspicuous geological traces is no consolation. We're just a tough nut to crack:

[65]
`Full recall action all hominin types, repeat, full recall action...`

[66]
Disembarking after this spectacular adventure that has failed equally spectacularly, back across the gangplank, a *full recall action*, without much hope left, really, for a better future, without illusions and with empty pockets, unsteadily trooping into the Critical Zone of what is *in fact* another planet: quite possibly, then, this complete un-loading, un-burdening, un-longing and un-selving can offer a moment of solace. A brief moment. Next, we have work to do. There is no alternative. Pig! Track! Shrink! Boom! Go to work! With all the pain and sorrow and hope and strength we have.

[67]
No doubt preparing for the worst, with pain and sorrow and hope and strength, is the only way to possibly avoid the worst. We may snatch it from the jaws of defeat yet, now we're beat. Possibly maybe. Preparation as leverage precisely because it's too late.

With pain and sorrow – not because we pity ourselves, not out of *amor sui*, but because we grieve and we rage.
With hope – hope with our eyes wide open, hope not for a better tomorrow, not to lengthen the agony, but because hope is a risk we must run. Because for hope we must want to continue to take responsibility. Call it *amor mundi*.
And with strength. But remember the lessons we need to learn from human history: imagination, man flying into the sun, closer and closer, this *pas de deux* of contempt for death and death wish, this virtuoso dance on the edge, might just save us but just as easily lead to our final demise.

[68]
Earth couldn't care less about our demise. Or, if we want to see the Earth as our mother one last time, for her it would be one care less.

[69]
It's now up to each and every one of us. To continue to delay and drift, or to prepare for landing. Because whether we can still land or not, in the endgame the only reasonable question is how and where.

[70]
And this is therefore, all in all, what I, adamantly, have been doing: suggesting clues for designing for the endgame.

George Brugmans
in the course of 2022

APPENDIX

BIOGRAPHIES

GEORGE BRUGMANS chief curator DOWN TO EARTH

Historian George Brugmans (Utrecht University and University of Florida) obtained his degree in 1981. Specialized in the history of change, by that time, he had already decided to pursue a career in the arts to be able to continue his research in practice. He was, among other things, the director of an avant-garde theater in Utrecht; artistic director of theater, dance and music festivals in Utrecht, Rotterdam, Lisbon, Salzburg and Polverigi; curator of film programs and exhibitions in Ottawa, Porto, São Paulo, Istanbul and Rotterdam; producer and writer of operas, feature films and documentaries; maker of some 15 documentaries, and producer and editor-in-chief at national television station VPRO before – increasingly fascinated by exploding urbanization – he became general director of the IABR in 2004. He also led the IABR–Ateliers from 2008, chaired the international curatorial team of the 5th edition, MAKING CITY, in 2012, and became chief curator of DOWN TO EARTH in 2019, until he retired, now as president of the biennale foundation, in 2021.
Brugmans expressly chose to develop an IABR that prioritized the future of the city. Successive biennale editions increasingly reflected the climate crisis, and had a progressively activist orientation. He did not see the biennale as an end in itself, but rather as a tool for socio-civic change; as its director, he fought for the free space needed to enable research by design aimed at true transformation. He was always looking for real-world change and entered into strategic alliances with governments at home and abroad to set up test sites and ateliers that could contribute to finding solutions to major challenges that people could actually implement.
As chief curator of DOWN TO EARTH, the pandemic helped him bring this research trajectory to a provisional conclusion. Through the four most recent IABR–Ateliers; as co-curator of WHOSE ENERGY IS IT, ANYWAY? and RECLAIMING THE COMMONS; as curator of DROUGHT IN THE DELTA and of THE HIGH GROUND, and as author and editor of this book, Brugmans asked one last time if, and how, design can help us land on Earth.

ADRIAAN GEUZE lead designer IABR–Atelier Dordrecht

Adriaan Geuze graduated as an agricultural engineer from Wageningen University in 1987 and founded West 8 in that same year. This globally active office for urban design, landscape architecture and infrastructure stands for a multidisciplinary approach and specializes in complex, large-scale design challenges. It combines a classic civil engineering approach with a philosophical approach to practically and culturally anchor design in its context. West 8 has since overseen more than 1,000 projects around the world and won numerous international design competitions, including for Madrid RIO, Governors Island in New York, Toronto's new Central Waterfront, and Yongsan Park in Seoul. In 2022 Geuze was appointed professor of Landscape Architecture at Delft University of Technology and received the pre-eminent landscape architecture award, the Sir Geoffrey Jellicoe Award. In 2005, Adriaan Geuze curated THE FLOOD, the 2nd edition of the IABR, in which designers collaborated with engineers and other experts to put the water issue on the agenda. As lead designer of IABR–Atelier Dordrecht (2019-2021) he investigated how, in his hometown of Dordrecht, the need to stay ahead of the ever-present threat of catastrophic flooding can be harnessed to the current challenge of sustainable urban development: water safety used as a lever.

RIANNE MAKKINK AND JURGEN BEY members of curator team DOWN TO EARTH

The starting point for all of the work of designer/architect Rianne Makkink and designer Jurgen Bey is that urban design, architecture, and landscape architecture are inextricably linked to product design. The oeuvre of Studio Makkink & Bey – active since 2002 and based in the Merwe-Vierhavens area of Rotterdam – covers a wide range of disciplines, from interior, product and exhibition design to architecture, research, and applied art. Their design strategy of choice aims to embed the role and strategic position of the designer/architect in society as firmly as possible: in 2013, for example, Bey curated the 5th edition of the Utrecht Manifest, Biennale for Social Design. An important part of their strategy is to actively pass it on to future generations: Rianne Makkink lectures at Ghent University, the Design Academy Eindhoven, Kunstuniversität Linz, and Delft University of Technology; Jurgen Bey is the director of the Sandberg Institute of the Gerrit Rietveld Academie in Amsterdam. In 2012, they initiated the Waterschool, a school network exploring water as a building and product material as well as a social and political phenomenon. The Waterschool first took shape as an exhibition as part of IABR–2018–THE MISSING LINK, after which Makkink and Bey continued their research as co-curators of DOWN TO EARTH, culminating in WATERSCHOOL M4H+: project, program, interventions, research, public archive, and exhibition in their own studio in the Rotterdam city harbor.

EVA PFANNES lead designer IABR–Atelier Rotterdam III

Eva Pfannes studied Architecture and Design at University College London and the Staatliche Akademie der Bildenden Künste Stuttgart and worked at Maxwan, Zaha Hadid, and Studio Makkink & Bey, among others, before founding OOZE architects & urbanists in 2003 with Sylvain Hartenberg. Operating at different scale levels worldwide, including in Water as Leverage Asia, OOZE links research into the sociocultural behavior of users of the built environment with knowledge of natural, ecological processes and technical expertise. The office works with interdisciplinary teams, opts for nature-based solutions wherever possible and, using multi-system models and other methods, focuses mainly on participatory strategies for climate-proof cities.
As the lead designer of IABR–Atelier Rotterdam III, Eva Pfannes took over from Joachim Declerck in 2019. She investigated how the energy transition can be used as a lever for the socially inclusive and sustainable redevelopment of the Bospolder-Tussendijken district. The result, the Local Energy Action Plan (LEAP), was central to the DOWN TO EARTH-exhibitions: WHOSE ENERGY IS IT, ANYWAY? and RECLAIMING THE COMMONS.

DIRK SIJMONS landscape architect

Landscape architect Dirk Sijmons graduated from Delft University of Technology in 1997 and was one of the founders of H+N+S Landscape Architects. Sijmons has devoted himself to combining landscape planning with the design disciplines of architecture and urban design, successively as the first Government Advisor for the Landscape (2004-2008), as chair of the Room for the River quality team (2006-2012), and as a professor of Environmental Planning and Landscape Architecture at Delft University of Technology (2008-2015). Partly due to his efforts, landscape architecture has become an integrated part of spatial planning, according to the jury of the Maaskant Prize, which he received twice, in 2002 and, as one of the 'creators' of Room for the River, in 2018. At the World Design Summit in Montreal in 2017, he received the most important landscape architecture award, the Sir Geoffrey Jellicoe Award. Book publications include *=Landscape* (2002), *Landscape and Energy: Designing Transition* (2014), *Moved Movement* (2015), *Room for the River: Safe and Attractive Landscapes* (2017) and the book chapter 'In the Anthropocene, Site Matters in Four Ways' in: Andrea Kahn et al., *Site Matters* (2021).
In 2014, Dirk Sijmons curated URBAN BY NATURE, the 6th IABR, which studied urban metabolism, the metabolism of our urban landscapes, through the lens of landscape architecture, asserting that we can solve global ecological problems if we solve the problems of the city. He was also the lead designer of several IABR–Ateliers. In his contribution to the book DOWN TO EARTH, he analyzes the role and position of design in light of the major challenges.

THIJS VAN SPAANDONK member of curator team DOWN TO EARTH

Architect Thijs van Spaandonk, who graduated from Eindhoven University of Technology in 2008, worked at Studio Marco Vermeulen and VenhoevenCS architecture+urbanism, among others, before founding 'cooperation for research and design in the living environment' Bright with Gerjan Streng in 2014. He is especially curious about the cultural aspects and spatial impact of radical social transitions, designing at all scales of energy transition and exploring a socially rooted, circular district economy. Since 2018, Van Spaandonk has also been head of the master's program in Urban Design at the Rotterdam Academy of Architecture and Urban Design (RAvB), where his curriculum focuses on designing for Rotterdam's climate challenge and discussing the position of the designer.
As member of the DOWN TO EARTH curator team, Thijs van Spaandonk was co-curator of the exhibitions WHOSE ENERGY IS IT, ANYWAY? and RECLAIMING THE COMMONS. He also curated the guest exhibition NOW! DESIGNING IN TIMES OF CLIMATE CRISIS in which students of the RAvB and the Royal Academy of Art in The Hague explored the cultural aspects of the climate challenge and energy transition to question their own position as designers, a process he reports on with Mark Minkjan, architecture critic and research associate at the RAvB, in this book.

MARCO VERMEULEN lead designer IABR–Atelier Drought in the Delta

Architect and urban designer Marco Vermeulen graduated from Eindhoven University of Technology in 1999. That same year, he founded his first office, Urban Affairs, followed ten years later by Studio Marco Vermeulen (SMV). The common theme in SMV's research, which in a broad sense focuses on renewable energy, circular economy, climate adaptation, biobased economy, knowledge economy, food production, and logistics, is establishing relationships between program, location, and resources, so that new programmatic alliances and typologies emerge. In 2021, Vermeulen curated the 5th edition of the Landscape Triennale that took place in the Van Gogh National Park in Brabant.
Marco Vermeulen was lead designer of the IABR–Atelier Drought in the Delta (2018-2020) which, focusing on the problem of drought that, in the Netherlands, has been acute since the summer of 2018, explored what possibilities there are to use the water issue as a lever, i.e. to increase the water buffering capacity of the Dutch delta and the opportunities this creates for other major transition challenges such as in the domain of energy, food production, and urbanization. The result, conceived by Vermeulen as a giant time-based computer animation, was the centerpiece of the DOWN TO EARTH-exhibition DROUGHT IN THE DELTA.

CREDITS
DOWN TO EARTH

CHIEF CURATOR
George Brugmans

CURATOR TEAM
Thijs van Spaandonk (energy transition)
Rianne Makkink, Jurgen Bey (Waterschool)
Robbert de Vrieze (IABR@BoTu)

LEAD DESIGNERS
Adriaan Geuze, Eva Pfannes, Joachim Declerck, Marco Vermeulen

ASSISTANT TO THE CHIEF CURATOR
Alexandra Sonnemans

ASSISTANTS TO THE CURATORS
Noortje Weenink, Umut Türkmen

GRAPHIC DESIGN
ARK – Roosje Klap, Loes Claessens

PRODUCTION AND PLANNING
Melanie van Twuijver, Jolanda van Dinteren, Maartje Berendsen, Johanna Fuhler, Lisa Lambert

EVENTS
Yonca Özbilge

PUBLICITY AND MARKETING
Antoinette Veneman, Melanie van Twuijver, Dewi Baggerman

OFFICE MANAGER
Vivian Ammerlaan

MANAGING DIRECTOR
George Brugmans

MAIN PARTNERS
Ministry of the Interior and Kingdom Relations
Creative Industries Fund NL
City of Rotterdam
City of Dordrecht
Province of East Flanders

Government of the Netherlands

creative industries fund NL

City of Rotterdam

DORDRECHT

provincie Oost-Vlaanderen

MISSION

The IABR, the International Architecture Biennale Rotterdam, was founded in 2001 in the conviction that architecture, and especially urban design, is of great social importance. The IABR therefore focuses entirely on the future of the city, where, by 2050, almost 80 percent of the world's population will produce more than 90 percent of our wealth – and this will *have to* be done sustainably. We can therefore best help solve the global climate crisis in the city – where we live, work and play. Design plays a crucial role: well and sustainably designed socially inclusive, fully resilient cities are our gateway to the future.

The challenge is complex, urgent, and clear, it's now or never, and co-operating to the best of our abilities is essential. The IABR has therefore wholeheartedly endorsed the United Nations' *2030 Agenda for Sustainable Development* and all of its activities are steeped in the objective to contribute to the realization of the world community's social and climate goals to the best of its ability.

The IABR is both a culture and a knowledge institution. This combination enables it to optimally and resolutely use the power of imagination and design to foster real-world change. Since 2008, its two most important instruments are the IABR–Ateliers, in which research by design is done, and the biennale itself, the international cultural platform where the results are shown and contextualized, and the public debate takes place.

The biennale is not an aim, but a means. Every edition bridges the gap between imagination, research and action, between plans and ideas and societal conception and support. Purposefully using the free cultural space, linking research by design to public presentations in a continuous open and cultural work process aimed at the real-world implementation of results, makes the IABR unique in the world.

QR CODES

The following overview includes all website addresses to which the QR codes in this book refer. The web archive also includes a complete overview of all links, at https://iabr.nl/archive.

HOW CAN WE LAND?

[1] p 20, *IPCC Special Report on Global Warming of 1.5 °C*: https://iabr.nl/archive/01/

[2] p 20, information about IABR–2014–Atelier Rotterdam: https://iabr.nl/archive/02/

[3] p 21, *Urban Metabolism*: https://iabr.nl/archive/03/

[4] p 23, *The Metabolism of Albania*: https://iabr.nl/archive/04/

[5] p 24, *An Energetic Odyssey* (video): https://iabr.nl/archive/05/

[6] p 24, *The Nordic City: Energy Transition as a Driver for Spatial and Economic Development:* https://iabr.nl/archive/06/

[7] p 25, *The Nordic City: The Energy Transition and the Economic Opportunities It Offers* (video): https://iabr.nl/archive/07/

[8] p 26, *The Productive City: Development Perspectives for a Regional Manufacturing Economy:* https://iabr.nl/archive/08/

[9] p 27, *Wat heb je nodig? Circulaire gebiedsontwikkeling in M4H* (only available in Dutch): https://iabr.nl/archive/09/

[10] p 27, *Lexicon Energie & Architectuur* (only available in Dutch): https://iabr.nl/archive/10/

[11] p 34, *Energiewijk Bospolder-Tussendijken* (only available in Dutch): https://iabr.nl/archive/11/

[12] p 35, *(On)bekende netwerken* (only available in Dutch): https://iabr.nl/archive/12/

[14] p 36, *Ontwerpend onderzoek Dakparkschool en binnengebied* (only available in Dutch): https://iabr.nl/archive/14/

[17] p 147, *Closing the Water Cycle* (video): https://iabr.nl/archive/17/

[18] p 150, *Istanbul at the Crossroads*: https://iabr.nl/archive/18/

[22] p 154, *Reweaving the Urban Carpet:* https://iabr.nl/archive/22/

[23] p 154, *The Mosaic Metropolis of Brabant* (video): https://iabr.nl/archive/23/

[24] p 155, *Memorandum of Understanding*: https://iabr.nl/archive/24/

[30] p 164, *Drought in the Delta* (video) and *Drought in the Delta* (zoom box): https://iabr.nl/archive/30/

[32] p 247, *The Productive City: Development Perspectives for a Regional Manufacturing Economy* (see also QR-code 8, p 26): https://iabr.nl/archive/08/

[33] p 247, *Wat heb je nodig? Circulaire gebiedsontwikkeling in M4H* (only available in Dutch; see also QR-code 9, p 27): https://iabr.nl/archive/09/

[35] p 251, *IABR–DOWN TO EARTH—WATERSCHOOL M4H+: #0 Introduction*: https://iabr.nl/archive/35/

[36] p 257, *IABR–DOWN TO EARTH—WATERSCHOOL M4H+: #1 Garden of Delight:* https://iabr.nl/archive/36/

[37] p 260, *WATERSCHOOL M4H+* (web application): https://iabr.nl/archive/37/

[38] p 263, *IABR–DOWN TO EARTH—WATERSCHOOL M4H+: #2 Fungi*: https://iabr.nl/archive/38/

[39] p 265, *IABR–DOWN TO EARTH—WATERSCHOOL M4H+: #3 Seaweed*: https://iabr.nl/archive/39/

[40] p 267, *IABR–DOWN TO EARTH—WATERSCHOOL M4H+: #4 Insects*: https://iabr.nl/archive/40/

[41] p 269, *IABR–DOWN TO EARTH—WATERSCHOOL M4H+: #5 Wood*: https://iabr.nl/archive/41/

[42] p 271, *IABR–DOWN TO EARTH—WATERSCHOOL M4H+: #6 Duckweed*: https://iabr.nl/archive/42/

[46] p 281, research report Studio Donna van Milligen Bielke (only available in Dutch): https://iabr.nl/archive/46/

[47] p 284, research report VenhoevenCS (only available in Dutch): https://iabr.nl/archive/47/

[48] p 289, research report EGM architects (only available in Dutch): https://iabr.nl/archive/48/

[49] p 292, research report PosadMaxwan (only available in Dutch): https://iabr.nl/archive/49/

[50] p 293, research report West 8 (only available in Dutch): https://iabr.nl/archive/50/

[54] p 312, *Start with the Outdoor Space* (video): https://iabr.nl/archive/54/

[55] p 316, *Choose to Connect* (video): https://iabr.nl/archive/55/

[56] p 320, *Increase Potential* (video): https://iabr.nl/archive/56/

[57] p 322, *Build for Flexibility* (video): https://iabr.nl/archive/57/

[58] p 324, *Live on the Water* (video): https://iabr.nl/archive/58/

WHERE CAN WE LAND?

[30] p 353, complete overview IABR–Ateliers 2008-2021: https://iabr.nl/archive/B30/

COLOPHON

COMPOSITION AND TEXTS
George Brugmans

WITH TEXT CONTRIBUTIONS BY
Dirk Sijmons, Rotterdam Academy of Architecture and Urban Design (Thijs van Spaandonk et al.)

GRAPHIC DESIGN
ARK
Loes Claessens, Roosje Klap

EDITORS
George Brugmans (senior editor)
Noortje Weenink, Alexandra Sonnemans

PRODUCTION
IABR / ARK / XToGo
Noortje Weenink (production manager)
Maaike Menheere (image acquisition)

TRANSLATION AND TEXT EDITING
InOtherWords translation & editing
D'Laine Camp, Gerda ten Cate, Maria van Tol

WEB ARCHIVE DEVELOPMENT
Maurits de Bruijn

LITHOGRAPHY AND PRINTING
Zwaan Lenoir

PAPER
Cyclus Silk

LETTERTYPE
Favorit, Dinamo

PUBLISHERS
Saskia van Stein, IABR
Marcel Witvoet, nai010 publishers, Rotterdam

DISTRIBUTION AND SALES
nai010 publishers is an internationally orientated publisher specialized in developing, producing and distributing books in the fields of architecture, urbanism, art and design.
www.nai010.com

ISBN / EAN
978-94-6208-801-6

NUR 648
BISAC ARC000000, ARC001000
THEMA AM

also available as Dutch edition:
978-94-6208-802-3

APPENDIX